SOUTH ASIA'S PATH TO RESILIENT GROWTH

Editors
RANIL SALGADO
RAHUL ANAND

Cataloging-in-Publication Data
IMF Library

Names: Salgado, Ranil, editor. | Anand, Rahul, editor. | International Monetary
    Fund, publisher.
Title: South Asia's path to resilient growth / Ranil Salgado Rahul Anand Editors.
Description: Washington, DC : International Monetary Fund, 2023. | Jan. 2023. |
    Includes bibliographical references.
Identifiers: 978-1-51358-721-9 (paper)
        979-8-40022-533-8 (ePub)
        979-8-40022-530-7 (PDF)
Subjects: Economic development—South Asia.
Classification: LCC HC430.6.S6 2023

Recommended citation: Salgado, Ranil, and Rahul Anand, editors. 2023. *South
Asia's Path to Resilient Growth*. Washington, DC: International Monetary Fund.

ISBNs: 978-1-51358-721-9 (paper)
        979-8-40022-533-8 (ePub)
        979-8-40022-530-7 (PDF)

Please send orders to:

International Monetary Fund, Publication Services
PO Box 92780, Washington, DC 20090, USA
Tel: (202) 623-7430 Fax: (202) 623-7201
E-mail: publications@imf.org
Internet: www.elibrary.imf.org
www.bookstore.imf.org

Contents

Foreword

Over the past two decades, extreme poverty has declined from 500 million to fewer than 250 million people in Bangladesh, Bhutan, India, Maldives, Nepal, and Sri Lanka—a remarkable success story for the region and the world. Per capita income during this time has doubled, helping to deliver improved health care, education, and infrastructure, as well as better access to financial services, the Internet, and mobile technology to millions of South Asians. However, the COVID-19 pandemic and the economic repercussions of Russia's war in Ukraine have slowed down the fight against extreme poverty and—together with the effects of climate change—impeded growth and poverty reduction in the region.

South Asia's Path to Resilient Growth tackles these headwinds, first setting the stage by reviewing South Asia's experience during the pandemic, its economic impact, and the postpandemic recovery marked by both challenges, such as persistent output losses from the pandemic, and important downside risks and setbacks, including the adverse impact from Russia's war in Ukraine. Several chapters of the book then take a longer-term perspective and draw lessons from South Asia's own development experience over the past decades to chart a path forward.

The key, overarching question is how can South Asia return to the growth rates of the past two decades, achieve resilient and climate-friendly growth without a renewed buildup of macroeconomic vulnerabilities, and resume the momentum of poverty reduction? The chapter authors address these questions by discussing how policies can make growth more resilient, covering a wide range of topics including the expenditure needs to meet the Sustainable Development Goals; improving equity through labor market and social protection reforms, and gender policies; the benefits of digitalization; and policies to mitigate and adapt to climate change. The authors also explore how trade liberalization and the resulting diversification have helped South Asia narrow the income gap to other regions and highlights the large potential for gains from reforms, including better integration into global value chains. Finally, several authors discuss the role of macrofinancial management through improved quality of infrastructure investment, sound monetary policy frameworks, and financial development.

South Asia's Path to Resilient Growth reflects a collaborative effort between IMF staff and academics and policymakers from the region and integrates lessons from the IMF staff's close engagement with the South Asian authorities through regular annual consultations (Article IV discussions) and technical collaboration. It has been made possible by generous financial support from the Korean authorities to advance peer learning in the region. Since its inception in 2017, the South Asia Regional Technical Assistance and Training Center in Delhi, India, supported by the South Asian member countries and development partners, has facilitated these peer-learning activities and contributed significantly to capacity development in the South Asia region.

I look forward to continuing and further deepening our cooperation in the region through policy dialogue, capacity development, and research. I hope you enjoy reading this book's discussion on the fast-growing and dynamic South Asia region, home to one-fifth of the world's population.

Kristalina Georgieva
Managing Director
International Monetary Fund

Abbreviations

ADB	Asian Development Bank
ADBI	Asian Development Bank Institute
AEs	advanced economies
AFTA	ASEAN Free Trade Agreement
ANM	auxiliary nurse midwife
APD	Asia and Pacific Department
APDMOD	Asia and Pacific Department Model
APTA	Asia-Pacific Trade Agreement
ASEAN	Association of Southeast Asian Nations
ASEAN+3	ASEAN countries plus China, Japan, and Korea
ASEAN-5	Indonesia, Malaysia, Philippines, Singapore, and Thailand
ASEAN-6	Indonesia, Malaysia, Philippines, Singapore, Thailand, and Vietnam
BIMSTEC	Bay of Bengal Initiative for Multi-Sectoral Technical and Economic Cooperation
BRCS	Brazil, Russia, China, and South Africa
BRI	Belt and Road Initiative
BRICS	Brazil, Russia, India, China, and South Africa
BRR	Building Regulation for Resilience
CADP	Comprehensive Asia Development Plan
CAT	Climate Action Tracker
Cat DDO	Catastrophe Deferred Drawdown Option
CCS	carbon capture and storage
CEIC	Census and Economic Information Center
CEPEA	Comprehensive Economic Partnership for East Asia
CGE	computable general equilibrium
CIT	corporate income tax
CMIS	Customs Administration Management Information System
CPI	consumer price index
EM	emerging market
EM-Asia	emerging market economies in Asia
EM-DAT	Emergency Events Database
EMDEs	emerging market and developing economies
EPL	employment protection legislation
ERIA	Economic Research Institute for ASEAN and East Asia
EU	European Union

FAD	Fiscal Affairs Department
FDI	foreign direct investment
FIT	flexible inflation targeting
FLFP	female labor force participation
FSGM	Flexible System of Global Models
FTA	free trade agreement
GMM	generalized method of moments
GVC	global value chain
HFC	housing finance company
HS	Harmonized System
IADB	Inter-American Development Bank
iBAS++	Integrated Budget and Accounting System
ICT	information and communications technology
ID	identification
IDE	Institute of Developing Economies
IFRC	International Federation of Red Cross and Red Crescent Societies
ILO	International Labour Organization
IPI	industrial production index
JAM	Jan Dhan-Aadhaar-Mobile
LFPR	labor force participation rate
LFS	labor force survey
LHV	lady health visitor
LIC	low-income country
LIDC	low-income developing country
MFN	most favored nation
MIC	middle-income country
MGNREGA	Mahatma Gandhi National Rural Employment Guarantee Act
MSME	micro-, small-, and medium-sized enterprise
MSP	minimum support price
NBFC	nonbank financial company
NBFI	nonbank financial institution
NDC	nationally determined contribution
NITI	National Institute for Transforming India
NPL	nonperforming loan
NRB	Nepal Rastra Bank
NTB	nontariff barrier
NTM	nontariff measure
OECD	Organisation for Economic Co-Operation and Development

OLS	ordinary least squares
OMO	open market operation
PIMA	Public Investment Management Assessment
PIT	personal income tax
PPP	public–private partnership
PSB	public sector bank
PVB	private sector bank
RAI	Rural Access Index
RBI	Reserve Bank of India
RCEP	Regional Comprehensive Economic Partnership
RM	registered midwife
RMA	Royal Monetary Authority
RN	registered nurse
ROA	return on assets
SAARC	South Asian Association for Regional Cooperation
SAFTA	South Asia Free Trade Area
SAP	student-age population
SDG	Sustainable Development Goal
SEZ	special economic zone
SLR	statutory liquidity ratio
SOE	state-owned enterprise
STR	student–teacher ratio
TFP	total factor productivity
TFPR	total factor productivity revenue
TMIS	Tax Management Information System
TOT	Toll-Operate-Transfer
TSA	Treasury single account
UN	United Nations
UNCTAD	United Nations Conference on Trade and Development
UNESCO	United Nations Educational, Scientific, and Cultural Organization
UNICEF	United Nations International Children's Emergency Fund
USAID	US Agency for International Development
VAT	value-added tax
WASH	water, sanitation, and hygiene
WEO	World Economic Outlook
WHO	World Health Organization
WTO	World Trade Organization

Acknowledgments

We thank Changyong Rhee, who set the vision for this book when he was Director of the IMF's Asia and Pacific Department (APD); Krishna Srinivasan, his successor; and Anne-Marie Gulde-Wolfe, APD Deputy Director, for their support in completing the project. The book seeks to discuss and identify how South Asia can build on its development success in the aftermath of the COVID-19 pandemic and the war in Ukraine to achieve its developmental potential. It has been a collective effort over several years that has benefited from contributions by authors and comments by interlocutors from both inside and outside of the IMF, including policymakers and academics from the region. It has received generous financial support from the Korean government to advance peer learning in the Asian and Pacific region.

We are grateful for support from many others, especially Manuela Goretti and Daisaku Kihara, who helped lead work on "Is South Asia Ready to Take Off? A Sustainable and Inclusive Growth Agenda," an IMF departmental paper published in November 2019 covering the initial phase of this project, along with discussants of the preliminary work at a workshop in New Delhi in February 2020. In addition to the chapter authors, we also thank Vaishali Ashtakala and Nimarjit Singh for excellent research assistance and Seble Abebe and Gulrukh Gamwalla-Khadivi for superb administrative assistance during the project.

We are also grateful for the excellent work of Rumit Pancholi of the IMF's Communications Department in overseeing book production and Six Red Marbles for editing and layout.

Ranil Salgado
Rahul Anand
Editors

Contributors

EDITORS

Ranil Salgado is Assistant Director of the IMF's Asia and Pacific Department and is the IMF's Mission Chief to Japan. He previously served as Mission Chief to India, the Marshall Islands, Myanmar, and Nepal, as well as Chief of the Regional Studies Division and IMF Resident Representative in Singapore. He has worked at the IMF for about 26 years, including in the Western Hemisphere Department; the Research Department; and the Strategy, Policy, and Review Department. He previously worked for a strategy management consulting firm and as a teaching and research assistant at The University of Pennsylvania, The Johns Hopkins University, and the Federal Reserve Board of Governors. He received an MA and PhD in economics from The University of Pennsylvania, a master's degree in biochemistry from Cambridge University, and a bachelor's degree in chemistry from Harvard University.

Rahul Anand is Division Chief in the IMF's Asia and Pacific Department and the IMF's Mission Chief to Bangladesh. He previously worked in the IMF's Institute for Capacity Development and the African Department. He has a broad range of experience of working in the Asia and Pacific region and in the Eastern and Southern Africa region, participating in many IMF missions and coauthoring a book on drivers of inflation in India and South Asia. In addition to working on surveillance and program cases in Asia and Africa, he has been closely involved in the IMF's capacity development work, including leading missions on modernizing monetary policy frameworks in Asia and Africa. His research spans a range of areas, including general equilibrium modeling to studying monetary policy issues in emerging market and developing countries, macro-critical structural reforms, subsidy reforms, and growth-enhancing structural transformation. Before joining the IMF in 2010, he held various senior positions in India as a member of the Indian Administrative Service—designing, implementing, and monitoring government economic programs and policies. He earned a PhD in applied economics from Cornell University and an MA in public administration from Harvard University.

AUTHORS

Ruchir Agarwal is an economist who has worked on a range of policy issues in advanced economies, emerging markets, and frontier economies. He is a research fellow at the Harvard Kennedy School and the cofounder of the Global Talent Lab. He was previously Head of the IMF's Global Health and Pandemic Response Task Force. He is currently on sabbatical from the IMF. He received a PhD in economics from Harvard University.

Faisal Ahmed is Mission Chief for Bhutan and Senior Desk for India at the IMF. From 2015 to 2019, Mr. Ahmed served as Chief Economist and Senior Advisor to the Governor at the Bangladesh (Central) Bank. Mr. Ahmed has worked on a broad range of advanced, emerging market, and developing economies and has served as the IMF Resident Representative in Cambodia from 2011 to 2015. He has previously worked as an actuary for a global reinsurance company and as an economist at the US Federal Reserve Bank. Mr. Ahmed has also taught at the University of Minnesota and the Royal School of Administration in Cambodia. Mr. Ahmed completed graduate studies in economics and finance at the University of Minnesota and Princeton University.

Gerard J. Almekinders is Deputy Division Chief in the Macrofinancial Surveillance and Review Division of the IMF's Monetary and Capital Markets Department where he was a member of the team who undertook the 2022 Financial Sector Stability Assessment for Germany. He has also worked in the IMF's Strategy, Policy, and Review Department and the Asia and Pacific Department, including as a mission chief for Lao P.D.R., Mongolia, and Nepal, and Deputy Mission Chief for India and Singapore. He earned a PhD in economics from Tilburg University in The Netherlands.

Vybhavi Balasundharam is an economist in the Fiscal Affairs Department of the IMF. Her research interests include productivity, firm dynamics, structural reforms, fiscal policies, and fiscal risks. Some of her recent analytical work focuses on climate change issues. She earned a PhD in economics from the University of Michigan.

Olivier Bizimana is a senior economist in the IMF's Middle East and Central Asia Department. Before joining the IMF in 2015, he was a senior economist in the Global Economics Team at Morgan Stanley in London. He was previously responsible for economic research for the euro area at Crédit Agricole Group in Paris. He has also taught postgraduate courses in macroeconomics at Paris-Dauphine University for five years. His research interests include international finance, monetary policy, macro-financial issues, and business-cycle fluctuations. He earned a PhD and an MPhil in economics from Paris Dauphine University and an MSc in economics and statistics from the École Nationale de la Statistique et de l'Administration Économique (ENSAE) in Paris.

Patrick Blagrave serves as the Macroeconomics Advisor at the IMF's Caribbean Regional Technical Assistance Center, where he develops capacity among member-country government and central-bank staff in macroeconomic analysis and forecasting. He has worked as an economist and senior economist at the IMF and before that at the Bank of Canada. In his capacity at the IMF, he regularly contributed to the *World Economic Outlook,* collaborated to develop several global macroeconomic models for use in policy analysis and forecasting, and published numerous working papers and academic journal articles on a variety of topics, including economic modeling, business-cycle analysis, cross-country spillovers, and inflation dynamics. He also guided analysis on real, monetary, and fiscal issues as a member of the IMF's India and Nepal country teams. He earned a BA in economics from Mount Allison University and an MA in economics from Queen's University, both in Canada.

Eugenio Cerutti is Advisor and Senior Reviewer in the IMF's Strategy, Policy, and Review Department. He also served as Assistant to the Director in the IMF's Research Department from 2014 to 2019, in the Macro-Financial Division of the Research Department, as well as on the IMF teams of a number of countries including Maldives (Mission Chief), Indonesia (Deputy Mission Chief), and Philippines (Deputy Mission Chief), as well as Barbados, Bolivia, Lithuania, Sweden, Turkey, and Venezuela. His research interests are in the international macroeconomics, with a particular focus on capital flows, financial regulation, and macro-financial linkages. He earned a PhD in economics from The Johns Hopkins University and a BA in economics from the National University of Córdoba in Argentina.

Pragyan Deb is an economist in the Australia and New Zealand Division of the IMF Asia and Pacific Department. He previously was part of the team working on the IMF's financing arrangement with Mongolia and Myanmar and has done surveillance work on a varied set of countries, including China, Estonia, Finland, Latvia, and Saudi Arabia. In addition, he has worked on a variety of analytical topics such as the effect of the COVID-19 pandemic, macro-financial spillovers and policy frameworks to address external shocks, analysis of financial stability risks, and emerging market issues; and has contributed to analytical chapters of the IMF's *Global Financial Stability Report and Regional Economic Outlook* reports. Before joining the IMF, he worked on macroprudential policy and banking regulation at the Bank of England. He earned a PhD in finance from the London School of Economics.

Mercedes García-Escribano is Division Chief of the Inclusive Growth and Structural Policies Division in Institute for Capacity Development of the IMF. She has worked on emerging economies and advanced economies in the fields of macroeconomics and fiscal policy analysis and has provided technical advice on topics related to public expenditures. She has led some of the most-read IMF work on inequality—namely, the October 2017 *Fiscal Monitor* on tackling inequality—and on costing the Sustainable Development Goals. She has published on a range of topics in fiscal, financial, and labor market issues. She earned a PhD in economics from University of Chicago.

Chetan Ghate is Director of the Institute of Economic Growth in New Delhi. Since 2003, he has also been Professor of Economics in the Economics and Planning Unit at the Indian Statistical Institute in Delhi. He received a PhD in economics from Claremont Graduate University in California in 1999, an MA in economics from the Delhi School of Economics, and a BA in economics from

Colorado College. His research focuses on the fields of macroeconomics, monetary economics, economic growth and development, and the Indian macroeconomy. In 2014, he was awarded the Mahalanobis Memorial Gold Medal given to the best research economist in India under the age of 45. Chetan has held several visiting faculty positions in India and elsewhere and has been closely involved with the Reserve Bank of India in an advisory capacity. He was a member of the Reserve Bank of India's first Monetary Policy Committee until October 2020. From 2012 to 2013, he was the Reserve Bank of India Chair Professor in Macroeconomics at the Indian Council for Research on International Economic Relations in New Delhi. From February 2013 to September 2016, he was a member of the Technical Advisory Committee for monetary policy at the Reserve Bank of India. In September 2013, he served as a member of the Expert Committee to Revise and Strengthen the Monetary Policy Framework. Mr. Ghate chairs the academic advisory board of the Reserve Bank of India Academy and serves on the editorial board of the RBI Occasional Paper Series. Mr. Ghate is also a member of the advisory committee of the National Accounts System (ACNAS) at the Ministry of Statistics and Program Implementation. He is also an external affiliate of the Centre for Research in Macroeconomics and Macro-Finance at Swansea University in Wales in the United Kingdom. He is a member of the Macro Finance Society.

Ragnar Gudmundsson is the IMF's Resident Representative in the Philippines. He was previously the IMF's Resident Representative in Bangladesh, Kenya, and the West Bank and Gaza, and was also a senior economist in the Asia and Pacific Department and the African Department. Before joining the IMF, he held various positions at the Central Bank of Iceland, UNESCO's Analysis and Forecasting Office, and UNDP's Human Development Report. Ragnar was educated at the London School of Economics, Columbia University, and the Institut d'Etudes Politiques de Paris. He earned a PhD in economics.

Klaus-Peter Hellwig is a senior economist on the Sri Lanka desk of the IMF's Asia and Pacific Department. Since joining IMF staff in 2014, he has worked on IMF program and surveillance countries in Central and East Africa, the Caribbean, the Caucasus, and South Asia and has contributed to a range of publications and policy papers. He earned a diploma in economics from the University of Bonn, an MSc from the Barcelona Graduate School of Economics, and a PhD in economics from New York University.

Andrew Hodge is a senior economist in the IMF's Western Hemisphere Department, working on the United States. He previously served in the IMF's Asia and Pacific Department and the Fiscal Affairs Department with a focus on emerging market economies and low-income countries. His current areas of research are optimal fiscal and monetary policy as well as nonbank financial institutions. Before joining the IMF, he served as economist at the Reserve Bank of Australia. Andrew earned a PhD from the London School of Economics.

Laura Jaramillo is Advisor and Mission Chief for Somalia in the IMF's Middle East and Central Asia Department. Since joining the IMF in 2002, she has worked on surveillance, programs, and technical assistance for a range of countries in Africa, Asia, Europe, and Latin America. Her research interests include fiscal policy, productivity, and growth. Ms. Jaramillo previously worked at the Ministry of Finance of Colombia. Ms. Jaramillo was also a Fulbright Scholar and completed graduate studies at Princeton University.

Bazlul Haque Khondker is an economist and a professor in economics, Dhaka University in Bangladesh. He has extensive works and publications in social protection. His work focuses on areas of social protection, including developing social protection strategies and preparing social protection policies following the life cycle approach and gender; developing results-based monitoring and evaluation system for social protection implementation; analyzing the fiscal consequences of introducing or expanding the social protection system using customized investment model; estimating poverty and inequality effects of social protection schemes using micro-simulation model; assessing the implication of changing demographic transition on social protection system; and assessing the macroeconomic implications of introducing or expanding the social protection schemes on an economy using macroeconomic model or framework. He has supported social protection reforms in more than 10 countries in Africa and Asia. He was directly involved in the preparation of social protection systems for Bangladesh, Lesotho, Samoa, and Saint Lucia. He has authored 42 papers and reports on various aspects of social protection. He has also obtained an MSc in quantitative developing economics and a PhD in economics from Warwick University in the UK.

Emmanouil Kitsios is an economist in the IMF's Asia and Pacific Department. He previously worked in the IMF's Fiscal Affairs Department, Research Department and African Department. His research interests include fiscal, financial, and external sector issues. He earned a PhD in economics from the University of Cambridge.

Weicheng Lian is an economist in the IMF's Western Hemisphere Department. He previously worked in the IMF's Research Department and the European Department. He contributed to the *World Economic Outlook* and has extensive country surveillance experiences. He has published articles in the *IMF Economic Review*. He earned a PhD in economics from Princeton University.

Fei Liu is a senior economist in the Middle East and Central Asia Department of the IMF. Previously, she was an economist in the IMF's Strategy, Policy, and Review Department and also has held positions in the Secretary's Department and the Research Department. She has worked on a diverse set of countries, including Kuwait, Oman, Sierra Leone, Sri Lanka, and Tonga. Ms. Liu has also conducted analytical work on a wide range of topics including exchange rates, structural reforms and growth, housing market, and economic policies. Her work has been published in academic journals and trade journals. Ms. Liu earned a BA in economics from Peking University in China and an MS and PhD in economics from the University of Indiana–Bloomington.

Tewodaj Mogues joined the IMF in 2018 and is a senior economist in the Expenditure Policy Division in the Fiscal Affairs Department of the IMF, where she conducts analysis and provides technical advice on topics related to expenditure, with a focus on the Sustainable Development Goals, public investment, spending efficiency, and food security. She worked for 13 years in the Development Strategy and Governance Division at the International Food Policy Research Institute, where, as a Senior Research Fellow, she led a Consultative Group for International Agricultural Researchcluster on public investments and institutions, and led the International Food Policy Research Institute's country programmes for Mozambique and Nigeria. Her fields of expertise include food security and agricultural economics, expenditure analysis, development economics, political economy, and decentralization. Ms. Mogues also serves as coeditor of the *European Journal of Development Research*; has authored more than 40 peer-reviewed academic publications, including four books/monographs, more than 10 book chapters, and numerous journal articles; refereed for 25 journals; and served on various research evaluation committees, including for the National Science Foundation. She received a bachelor's degree in economics from Kalamazoo College and a PhD in agricultural and development economics from the University of Wisconsin–Madison.

Mariano Moszoro is a senior economist in the IMF's Fiscal Affairs Department. His work experience and research focus on public finance, political economy, and infrastructure development. During 2005–06, he was Deputy Minister of Finance of Poland and Chairman of the state development bank BGK. He earned a PhD and *habilitation* (French HDR/US tenure equivalent) in economics from SGH Warsaw School of Economics and interned as a postdoctoral fellow at the University of California Berkeley-Haas under Nobel Laureate Oliver E. Williamson. He has published in top academic journals and has held academic positions at the University of California Berkeley, Harvard University, and George Mason University.

Racha Moussa is an economist in the Open Economy Division in the Research Department of the IMF. She previously held positions in the Debt Policy Division in the Strategy, Policy, and Review Department and in the Asia and Pacific Department, where she worked on Bangladesh, Bhutan, East Timor, India, and Maldives. She earned a PhD from the University of North Carolina at Chapel Hill and a BA from the American University of Beirut. Before joining the IMF, she was an assistant professor at Middlebury College in Vermont.

Sanghamitra Warrier Mukherjee is a PhD candidate in the Department of Economics at the University of Oxford. Sanghamitra's research interests include development economics, labor economics, and household finance. Her current work focuses on firms and households in low- and middle-income countries. Using empirical methods grounded in economic theory, she studies the drivers of firm productivity. She also works on the role of digitalization in the overall growth strategy. Ms. Mukherjee has previously worked for three years in the finance department at Goldman Sachs. She has also worked with a range of policy and research organisations including the IMF, World Wildlife Fund, Center for Effective Global Action, Government of Colombia, SaveAct in South Africa, and with think tanks in India. She also earned a Master of Public Policy from the University of California–Berkeley, a Master of Arts in economics from the Delhi School of Economics, University of Delhi, and a bachelor's degree in economics from Miranda House at the University of Delhi. Ms. Mukherjee contributed to this book while working at the IMF.

Sumiko Ogawa is Assistant to the Director in the IMF's Monetary and Capital Markets Department. Since joining the IMF in 2009, she has worked on countries in Latin America and the Caribbean in the Western Hemisphere Department and on financial sector issues including as Deputy Mission Chief for the Financial Sector Assessment Program for Thailand. She previously worked at the IMF's Regional Office in Tokyo and in the private sector. She earned an MA in international relations from the University of Tokyo.

Shanaka Jayanath (Jay) Peiris is currently the IMF's Asia and Pacific Department's Division Chief of Regional Studies in charge of the Asia and Pacific Department's *Regional Economic Outlook* report. Before that, he was Mission Chief for Myanmar and Deputy Division Chief covering the ASEAN's macrofinancial surveillance. He was previously IMF's Resident Representative in the Philippines and Mission Chief to Tonga and has extensive surveillance and program experience in Africa and Asia.

Piyaporn Sodsriwiboon is Deputy Division Chief in the ASEAN II Division of the IMF's Asia and Pacific Department. She was previously a lead desk economist on the IMF's India and Japan teams and has worked on several advanced and emerging market economies in Europe including Cyprus, Portugal, and Spain. Her research spans macro-financial linkages, labor market issues, digitalization, and climate change. She earned a PhD in economics from the University of California at Los Angeles.

Mauricio Soto is Deputy Division Chief in the Expenditure Policy Division of the IMF's Fiscal Affairs Department. He focuses on a range of critical public finance issues, including social spending, government compensation and employment, and Sustainable Development Goals. He has worked on fiscal policy issues in more than 20 countries in surveillance, lending, and capacity development activities. At the IMF, he has previously worked in the Front Office of the Communications Department. Before joining the IMF, he was a researcher on social insurance issues at the Center for Retirement Research at Boston College and The Urban Institute.

Katsiaryna Svirydzenka is Deputy Division Chief in the South Asia 1 Division and the IMF Mission Chief for Bhutan. Her past assignments include Mission Chief for Tuvalu, advisor to the previous Asia and Pacific Department director Mr. Rhee, economist in the Asia and Pacific Department's Regional Studies division and in the Emerging Markets division of the Strategy, Policy, and Review Department. Since joining the IMF in 2010, she contributed to the work of multiple IMF country teams, including India, Malaysia, Mongolia, Russia, Serbia, Solomon Islands, and others. Her research interests include financial cycles, network analysis and systemic risk, financial spillovers, financial development, firm-level productivity, and zombie firms. She earned a PhD in economics from the Graduate Institute of International and Development Studies (Geneva, Switzerland), an MA in international economics and international relations from The Johns Hopkins School of Advanced International Studies (Bologna, Italy, and Washington, DC), and a BA in economics from the American University in Bulgaria.

Saji Thomas is a senior economist in the IMF's Western Hemisphere Department's Caribbean II Division. Since joining the IMF in 2004, he has worked on several countries in sub-Saharan Africa, the Caribbean, the Middle East, and South Asia. Before joining the IMF, he worked in the World Bank's Research Department. His main areas of research are sovereign debt restructuring, taxation of natural resources, and fiscal rules. He earned a PhD in economics from the University of Minnesota.

Jarkko Turunen is Deputy Division Chief in the South Asia 1 Division and Mission Chief to Nepal in the IMF's Asia and Pacific Department. In addition to country work, his area of expertise covers fragile states, governance, and cross-cutting financial sector issues in Asia. Mr. Turunen was previously Deputy Mission Chief for India and Mission Chief to Solomon Islands and Cambodia and has worked on the United States (with a focus on monetary policy) and the Caribbean (also as Mission Chief to The Bahamas). He has also worked in the Strategy, Policy, and Review Department on Belarus and Egypt and on various IMF policy issues, including conditionality in IMF programs, international trade and competitiveness, and jobs and growth. Before joining the IMF, he was Principal Economist at the European Central Bank and visiting scholar in the Economics Department at the Massachusetts Institute of Technology. He earned a PhD in economics from the European University Institute in Florence, Italy. His main research interests are macroeconomics, monetary policy, development economics, and labor economics, and has work published in the *Journal of the European Economic Association, Journal of Economic Perspectives, IMF Economic Review, Journal of Economic Dynamics and Control, Empirical Economics,* and *Economics Letters.*

Ganeshan Wignaraja is Professorial Fellow in Economics and Trade at Gateway House: Indian Council of Global Affairs in Mumbai and Senior Research Associate at ODI Global in London. He is a member of the Central Bank of Sri Lanka's Stakeholder Engagement Committee on monetary policy and financial stability and has a visiting appointment at the National University in Singapore. He previously held senior roles in the United Kingdom and Asia, including as Executive Director of Sri Lanka's Foreign Ministry's think tank, Director of Research at the ADB Institute, Advisor to the Chief Economist of the Asian Development Bank, Chief Project Officer at the Commonwealth Secretariat, Global Head of Trade and Competitiveness at Maxwell Stamp PLC, and Visiting Scholar at the IMF. Mr. Wignaraja earned a DPhil in economics from Oxford University and has published extensively on international trade, regional integration, economic development, and macroeconomics. His books include *Pan-Asian Integration: Linking East Asia and South Asia* and *Connecting Asia: Infrastructure for Integrating South Asia and Southeast Asia*.

Naihan Yang is a machine learning specialist at the Ant Group. Before joining the Ant Group, he worked in the Asia and Pacific Department of the IMF. His research interests include macroeconomics, risk control, and financial inclusion. He has participated in several research projects with colleagues in the Asia and Pacific Department, focusing on how fiscal and monetary policy facilitate economy recovery from COVID-19. He earned a master's degree from Georgetown University and bachelor's degree from Renmin University of China. Mr. Yang contributed to this book while working at the IMF.

Jiae Yoo is an economist in the IMF's Fiscal Affairs Department. She previously worked in the Asia and Pacific Department on Nepal and Singapore as well as on the issues related to infrastructure development in South Asia and digital economy. Her current research interest includes fiscal policy, financial stability, and development. She earned a PhD in economics from The Johns Hopkins University.

Biying Zhu is an extended term consultant in the Macroeconomics, Trade, and Investment division of the World Bank. She focuses on the macroeconomics of Nepal, Sri Lanka, and Pakistan. From 2019 to 2022, she worked as a research assistant in the Asia and Pacific Department of the IMF, where she covered countries including Bangladesh, Japan, Maldives, and Sri Lanka. She earned a master's degree in applied economics from The George Washington University. Ms. Zhu contributed to this book while working at the IMF.

CHAPTER 1

Introduction: From Postpandemic Recovery to Inclusive Growth and Sustainable Development in South Asia

Klaus-Peter Hellwig

The marked decline in extreme poverty around the world can be counted among humanity's great achievements since the beginning of the 21st century. According to World Bank estimates, the number of people in the world living with less than US$1.90 per day fell from 1.7 billion in 2000 to around 700 million in 2017. A sizable part of this remarkable success story occurred in the South Asian countries of Bangladesh, Bhutan, India, Maldives, Nepal, and Sri Lanka, where the number fell from 500 million to fewer than 250 million people. Per capita incomes more than doubled in real terms, and the region's share of global GDP grew from less than 5 percent in 2000 to more than 8 percent in 2019. Continued growth at this pace would put the goal of eradicating extreme poverty by 2030 within reach, and it would continue to transform people's daily lives in ways that cannot be captured by GDP numbers. Many South Asians today receive better health care and education than their parents' generation did and have access to expanded and more reliable power grids, financial services, and transportation infrastructure. Mobile phones and broadband Internet are now ubiquitous, connecting people to the world and allowing them to participate in the global exchange of ideas.

However, the global COVID-19 pandemic and the economic repercussions of the Russian invasion of Ukraine have dealt a double blow to the fight against poverty. As with elsewhere in the world, South Asian countries have experienced not just the devastating health effects of COVID-19. As GDP growth has slowed, South Asian countries have also seen an increase in the number of poor households and a decline in per capita incomes. The World Bank estimates that the number of people living with less than $1.90 per day in South Asia increased by 58 million in 2020, accounting for more than half of the global increase in poverty (Mahler and others 2021). The pandemic has also exposed and sometimes exacerbated preexisting vulnerabilities that will pose headwinds to growth if left unaddressed. Also, the effect of the war in Ukraine and related sanctions as well as global spillovers from the exit from the pandemic are having pervasive effects on the region, posing more challenges. In addition, the effects of climate change are increasingly visible in the region and, if left unaddressed, will leave their mark on economic growth and the pace of poverty reduction.

Overcoming these economic challenges to achieve the Sustainable Development Goals (SDGs) in South Asia is the central theme of this book. In the first part, the book discusses policies to make growth inclusive and sustainable, covering a wide range of topics including (1) the expenditure needs to meet the SDGs, (2) improving equity through labor market reforms, social protection reforms, and gender policies, (3) digitalization, and (4) mitigating and adapting to climate change. The middle part explores how trade liberalization and the resulting diversification have helped South Asia narrow the income gap to other regions and highlights the large potential for further income gains from a renewed reform momentum and a better integration into Asian and global value chains. The third part focuses on the role of macro-financial management through improved quality of infrastructure investment, sound monetary policy frameworks, and financial development. Throughout the book, by drawing lessons from South Asia's own history as well as from cross-country comparisons with peers, the analysis shows that finding the right policy design is crucial for the region's rapid growth trajectory. Poverty reduction cannot be taken for granted but is the result of policy choices. Finding the right policies matters not only for the pace of growth but also for ensuring that growth is sustainable, inclusive, and benefits all.

To set the scene, this first chapter starts by looking back at the first two years of the pandemic and takes stock of its effect on South Asia. The chapter then widens the lens to place the current juncture into the broader context of the subcontinent's growth trajectory since the middle of the 20th century—a period of remarkable transformation but also one of stubbornly persistent economic inequalities. Previewing some of the book's main findings, this chapter then discusses the role of policies and the remaining challenges to overcome in shaping South Asia's economic trajectory in the postpandemic era.

COVID-19 IN SOUTH ASIA

Like many other regions of the world, South Asia was hit hard by COVID-19 (see Figure 1.1). The region was particularly affected by the highly contagious delta variant that emerged in the second quarter of 2021 at a time when vaccination efforts in the region were still at an early stage and hampered by global supply shortages. In early 2022, the omicron variant led to a renewed surge in case numbers, this time also affecting Bhutan, which had previously been spared by major outbreaks. As of the middle of 2022, 47 million cases and approximately 584,000 deaths of COVID-19 were confirmed, around 9 percent of global confirmed deaths. But the humanitarian toll is likely even higher, as health systems were overstretched, limiting access to preventive care and treatment for other medical conditions. Moreover, several studies suggest an undercounting of COVID-19 cases and fatalities (see Anand, Sandefur, and Subramanian 2021). Excess mortality figures reported by the World Health Organization show cumulative deaths through the end of 2021 ranging between 3.3 and 6.8 million in South Asia.

Figure 1.1. COVID-19's Health Effects and Vaccinations in South Asia

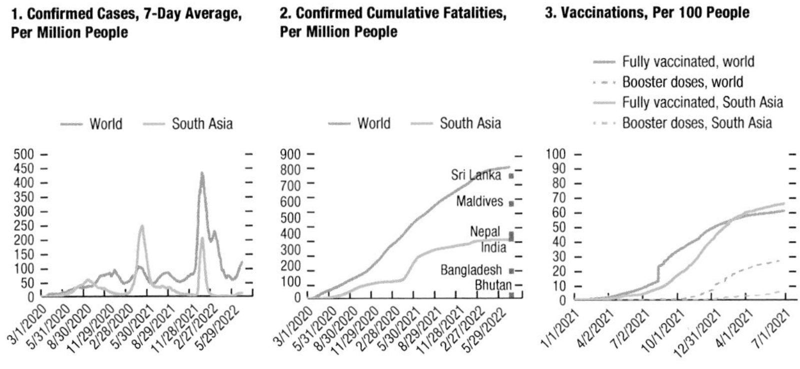

1. Confirmed Cases, 7-Day Average, Per Million People
2. Confirmed Cumulative Fatalities, Per Million People
3. Vaccinations, Per 100 People

Sources: Johns Hopkins University/Our World in Data; and IMF staff calculations.

Vaccination efforts played a key role in bringing the delta variant under control and keeping the death toll from omicron low despite very high case numbers.[1] Bhutan, having fully vaccinated its adult population by July 2021 and administered booster doses to 70 percent of the population by the middle of 2022, has had one of the lowest death tolls in the world. India, by being one of the leading manufacturers of vaccines in the world and the key supplier of vaccines to COVAX, which provides vaccines to low- and middle-income countries, made a crucial contribution to the global economic recovery.[2] Since the middle of 2022, vaccination rates in all South Asian countries have been above the global average (Figure 1.1, panel 1). However, in terms of administered booster doses, the region is still lagging.

Economic Effects of COVID-19

The economic fallout from the pandemic in South Asia was severe, particularly in the early stages when the most restrictive lockdowns were in place (Figures 1.2 and 1.3). In India, by far the region's largest economy, real GDP in the second quarter of 2020 fell by 23.8 percent relative to the same period in 2019. In tourism-dependent Maldives, the drop was by more than 50 percent. In Bangladesh and Bhutan, production indices point to a similar pattern. In addition to being large, the economic effect of COVID-19 has also been persistent. In all South Asian countries except Bangladesh, annual real GDP per capita in 2021 remained below the 2019 level. Contact-intensive service sectors were

---

[1] Watson et al (2022) estimate that vaccinations averted around 3.55 million deaths (as of December 2021) in Bangladesh, Bhutan, India, Maldives, Nepal, and Sri Lanka.

[2] According to India's Ministry of External Affairs, as of November 1, 2023, India has exported around 272 million doses, including around 39 million doses to other South Asian countries (Government of India 2022).

Figure 1.2. COVID-19's Effect on Mobility in South Asia

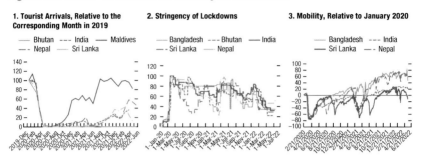

Sources: Haver Analytics; Royal Monetary Authority of Bhutan; and IMF staff calculations (panel 1); Our World in Data; Oxford Coronavirus Government Response Tracker; and IMF staff calculations (panel 2); and Google COVID-19 Community Mobility Reports; and IMF staff calculations (panel 3).
Note: The figure shows seven-day moving average mobility, calculated as the simple average of four mobility indices: workplaces, transit stations, retail and recreation, and grocery and pharmacy.

Figure 1.3. COVID-19's Effect on Economic Activity in South Asia

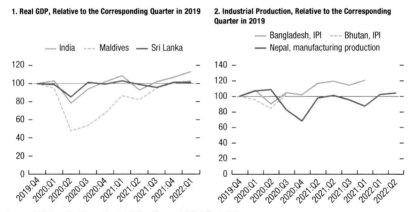

Sources: CEIC; Haver Analytics; national statistics offices; and IMF staff calculations.
Note: IPI = industrial production index; Q = quarter.

especially hard hit, particularly tourism where activity is still far below prepandemic levels.

The economic effects would have been even more severe without policies to support the economy. Governments increased spending, not just on the health sectors but also on programs to support vulnerable households, including through cash transfers, food rations, and subsidized utility bills. Demand was also stimulated through infrastructure investment. On the revenue side, relief was provided through extended tax filing and payment deadlines and tax exemptions. Fiscal stimulus was accompanied by monetary easing through reduced policy rates and, in some instances, central bank lending to the government. In the financial sector, wide-ranging loan moratoria and low-interest loans provided liquidity support to borrowers, whereas macroprudential measures helped preserve financial stability

(Hodge and Moussa 2021). Studying a large sample of firms in India, Górnicka, Ogawa, and Xu (2021) showed that policy measures have been instrumental in improving liquidity conditions of corporate balance sheets.

Chapters 3 and 4 of this book discuss that low-income households have suffered disproportionately from the pandemic. Workers in South Asia's large informal sector, which relies highly on physical operations and has few employment protections, were hit hard. For example, survey data for Sri Lanka indicate that the decline in sales was much steeper for micro-size enterprises than for other small- and medium-size enterprises and that smaller firms were more likely to close operations and lay off workers (IMF 2022b). Informal workers also had few savings and no access to finance to buffer the shock of a job loss. At the same time, government transfers to support households were lower than in many other emerging market and developing economies.

Chapter 5 discusses how the pandemic also appears to have aggravated existing gender inequities. Deshpande (2020) found that during India's early lockdowns, women were 20 percent more likely to lose their jobs than men were. Survey evidence from Bangladesh and Maldives suggests that women were more likely to reduce their work hours than men were.

A Recovery with Challenges and Setbacks

With the COVID-19 crisis of 2020–21 in the rearview mirror, there are many signs that, although the pandemic is far from over, it has become more manageable. A large share of the population has been vaccinated and medical therapeutics and care have improved, slowing the spread and making infections less harmful. Hence, the gruesome trade-offs of the first year of the pandemic, between saving lives and saving livelihoods, have become less pressing. IMF staff project India's economy to grow at 6.8 percent in 2022–23, which is the fastest pace among major advanced and emerging market economies.

Even so, the scars of the pandemic are likely to be felt in the region for many years to come. In the near term, COVID-19 will remain a large uncertainty factor, as new variants are likely to emerge, and the long-term effectiveness of vaccines is still unknown. The global economy continues to be affected by the pandemic, as supply chains, although improving, are still not operating smoothly. In addition to the lingering uncertainty about its trajectory, the pandemic has also exacerbated preexisting challenges and vulnerabilities that could create headwinds along the recovery path.

Balance sheets of the public and private sector, which in some cases had already been under stress before the pandemic, deteriorated throughout the region. A case in point is public debt. Government intervention helped prevent a worse health crisis and protected the economy. However, the drop in tax revenues and higher spending led to widening deficits, resulting in a rapid buildup of public debt in 2020–21 from already-high levels in some countries (Figure 1.4). Governments also took on additional risks to support state-owned enterprises or make loans to support firms struggling during the pandemic.

Figure 1.4. General Government Debt
(Percent of GDP)

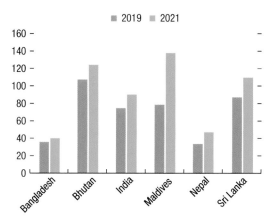

Source: IMF's World Economic Outlook database.

Corporate balance sheets have suffered similarly. In India, for example, non-financial corporate debt increased by about 17 percent of GDP from 2019 to 2021 (see IMF 2022a).[3] Firms that borrowed to expand capacity before the pandemic or those that borrowed to stay afloat during the pandemic, sometimes through government programs, could face difficulties repaying their loans. Moreover, the long-term viability of some firms may have been affected by the pandemic, and policies going forward will need to support resolution of non-viable firms so that limited resources are not kept from more dynamic firms. This debt overhang could also make it more difficult to finance new investments, contributing the overall decline in investments observed in the wake of the pandemic (IMF 2022a).

The pandemic has also held back investment in human capital. On average, South Asia's students have experienced far longer school closures than their peers have in other parts of Asia and other continents (Figure 1.5). As we will see in the following, South Asia's literacy rates still lag those of peer countries, making the region less competitive in skill-intensive manufacturing. Learning loss from school closures during the pandemic is likely to exacerbate these challenges with effects that could be felt for decades.

In this still-difficult economic environment, the fallout of Russia's war in Ukraine has dealt another heavy setback to the recovery. Higher global food prices have hit South Asian countries particularly hard, given the high share of food in household consumption (Figure 1.6, panel 1), leading to higher inflation and eroding the real incomes of vulnerable households. Although in some cases (such as in India, Nepal, and Sri Lanka) policy measures have been deployed to curb

---

[3] More recently, corporate sector balance sheets in India have somewhat improved, as confirmed by the declining leverage of listed firms and falling delinquency rates across sectors and borrower types.

Figure 1.5. School Closures as a Result of COVID-19
(Average number of days)

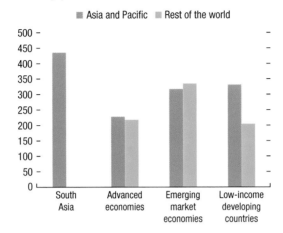

Sources: UNESCO; and IMF staff calculations.
Note: Analysis excludes Pacific Island countries.

Figure 1.6. The Role of Food and Fuel in South Asia

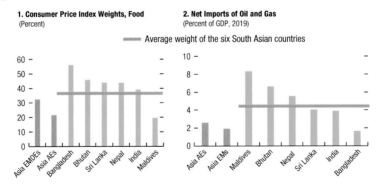

Sources: CEIC; IMF country authorities; and IMF staff estimates.
Note: AEs = advancd economies; EMDEs = emerging market and developing economies.

Sources: IMF Country Desk Survey; and IMF staff estimates.
Note: AEs = advancd economies; EMs = emerging markets.

the effect of inflation, the rise in food and energy prices will likely erode real incomes and push more households below the poverty line. The broadening of headline inflation to core inflation is turning these effects into macro-fiscal challenges as in some cases fiscal measures are untargeted and permanent while fiscal space is shrinking.

Considering the region's dependence on oil and gas imports (Figure 1.6, panel 2), the higher global fuel prices have put pressure on external current account balances. Moreover, Maldives and Sri Lanka have lost considerable earnings from

Figure 1.7. IMF Staff's Real GDP Projections in *World Economic Outlook* Reports (2015 = 100)

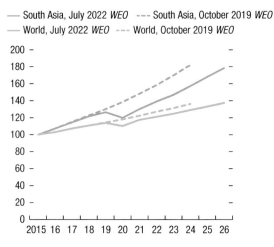

Source: IMF's World Economic Outlook database.
Note: *WEO = World Economic Outlook.*

Russian and Ukrainian tourists. These external sector shocks are compounded by a tightening of global financial conditions, as central banks in advanced economies fight inflation by raising interest rates. During the Taper Tantrum of 2013, India was vulnerable to such tightening episodes. Today, sizable reserves and smaller external imbalances suggest improved resilience. Nonetheless, the renewed large outflows in 2022 are a reminder that continued vigilance is needed.

Given the nature and severity of the recession induced by the pandemic and compounded by multiple shocks including Russia's war in Ukraine, output losses are likely to persist. While India is back on a healthy GDP growth plan in 2022–23, downside risks have become more likely to materialize in some countries—particularly in Sri Lanka, which is experiencing a severe balance of payments and sovereign debt crisis. IMF staff projections indicate that real GDP in South Asia and in the world is expected to remain below its prepandemic trends over the medium term (Figure 1.7).

DEVELOPMENT AND INEQUALITY IN SOUTH ASIA: A LONG-TERM VIEW

How can South Asia return to the growth rates of the past two decades and resume the momentum of poverty reduction in the postpandemic era, and how can this be achieved in an equitable and climate-friendly way and without a renewed buildup of macroeconomic vulnerabilities? To understand the engines of long-term growth and inequality and to identify policies that could help South Asia achieve its development potential, several chapters of this book take a long-term perspective and draw lessons from South Asia's development experience over the past decades.

Figure 1.8. Selected Development Indicators

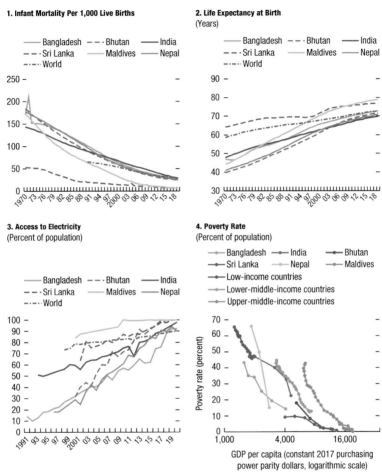

Sources: World Bank's World Development Indicators; and IMF staff calculations.

Hence, this section attempts to provide some context by revisiting the region's economic history and comparing its trajectory with that of other Asian economies. In doing so, we come across many themes previously discussed by other authors, notably Goretti and others (2019) and Lamba and Subramanian (2020).

Over the past five decades, South Asia outpaced global changes along a wide range of development indicators (Figure 1.8). In 1970, infant mortality exceeded the global average in all South Asian countries except Sri Lanka. By 2019, the infant mortality rate was below the global average throughout the region. A child born in Bhutan in 1970 could expect to live 40 years, 19 years shorter than the global average. This gap in life expectancy at birth between Bhutan and the rest of the world had shrunk to less than one year in 2019. South Asians do not just live longer than their parents and grandparents, they are also less likely to be poor and more likely to have access to public infrastructure such as electricity. Panel 4

Figure 1.9. GDP Per Capita in South Asia and Asian Peers
(Constant US dollars, logarithmic scale)

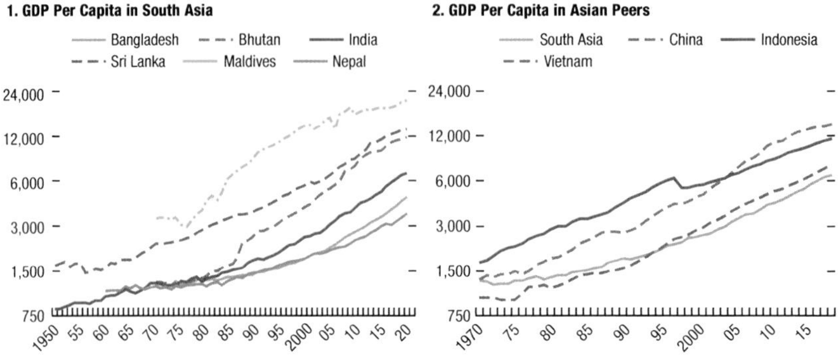

Sources: Penn Word Tables; and IMF staff calculations.

of Figure 1.8 suggests that poverty rates declined even faster than implied by the pace of economic growth.

These improvements in human development would not have been possible without economic growth. Indeed, as can be seen from Figure 1.9, South Asia can look back on a growth performance that was remarkable. After India gained its independence in 1947 and Sri Lanka in 1948, real GDP per capita in both grew more than sevenfold. Bangladesh's real GDP per capita more than tripled in the five decades since its independence in 1971. At the same time, growth in the region lagged that of other Asian economies over the past 50 years—except for Bhutan and Maldives, small countries that rapidly transformed as tourism and hydropower expanded.

Figure 1.9 further highlights that South Asia has always been an economically diverse region, and that the growth experience was distinctly heterogeneous across countries within the region. In 1950, shortly after gaining independence, Sri Lanka's GDP per capita was nearly twice that of India. During the 1970s, income levels within the region diverged further, with Maldives and Sri Lanka benefiting from some liberalization, while Bangladesh and India remained stagnant. With reforms in India beginning in the 1980s and in Bangladesh in the 1990s, growth began to pick up, turning into a boom in the 2000s and 2010s.[4] This coincidence of growth spurts and liberalizing reforms suggests that trade openness has been an important part of Asia's growth story. Growth accelerations in Maldives and Sri Lanka in the late 1970s, in Bhutan in the 1980s, and in Bangladesh and India in the 1990s and 2000s coincided with substantial increases in exports of goods and services (Figure 1.10).

However, the ratio of exports to GDP in South Asia has remained below the levels observed in China, Indonesia, or Vietnam, where GDP growth was driven

[4] See Rodrik and Subramanian (2005) for a discussion of Indian reforms in the 1980s and 1990s.

Figure 1.10. Exports of Goods and Services in South Asia and Asian Peers
(Percent of GDP)

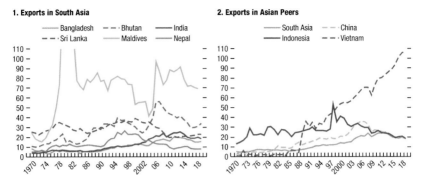

Sources: World Bank's World Development Indicators; and IMF staff calculations.

Figure 1.11. Manufacturing Exports in South Asia and Asian Peers
(Percent of GDP)

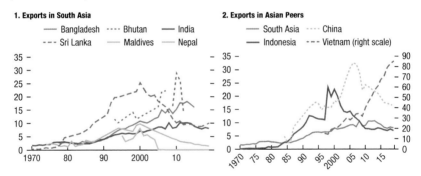

Sources: World Bank's World Development Indicators; IMF's World Economic Outlook database; and IMF staff calculations.

by spectacular export growth. Moreover, in Nepal and Sri Lanka, export growth slowed down dramatically over the past 20 years. In Sri Lanka, exports dropped from 36 percent of GDP in 1995–99 to 22 percent in 2015–19. In Nepal, the drop was from 24 to 8.4 percent. Reinvigorating South Asia's trade through diversification, investment, and integration with other parts of Asia is the topic of Chapters 8 through 10.

This rise and fall of exports in Asia cannot be understood without looking at the manufacturing sector (Figure 1.11). In most Asian countries, the export-led growth was driven by manufacturing exports—as was the more recent decline in exports in Nepal and Sri Lanka. In Maldives, manufacturing exports also fell dramatically in the early 2000s. An important factor of South Asian manufacturing export dynamics may have been the changes in trade policy in advanced economies. The quota system, which had protected South Asian apparel exports to the United States and the European Union, was gradually phased out in

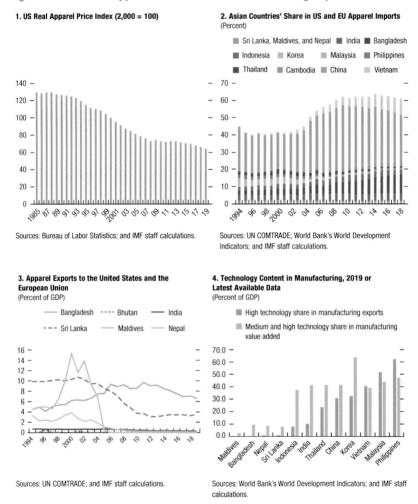

Figure 1.12. Role of Apparel in South Asian Manufacturing Exports

1. US Real Apparel Price Index (2,000 = 100)

Sources: Bureau of Labor Statistics; and IMF staff calculations.

2. Asian Countries' Share in US and EU Apparel Imports
(Percent)

◼ Sri Lanka, Maldives, and Nepal ◼ India ◼ Bangladesh
◼ Indonesia ◼ Korea ◼ Malaysia ◼ Philippines
◼ Thailand ◼ Cambodia ◼ China ◼ Vietnam

Sources: UN COMTRADE; World Bank's World Development Indicators; and IMF staff calculations.

3. Apparel Exports to the United States and the European Union
(Percent of GDP)

─── Bangladesh ···· Bhutan ─── India
─ ─ ─ Sri Lanka ─── Maldives ─── Nepal

Sources: UN COMTRADE; and IMF staff calculations.

4. Technology Content in Manufacturing, 2019 or Latest Available Data
(Percent of GDP)

◼ High technology share in manufacturing exports
◼ Medium and high technology share in manufacturing value added

Sources: World Bank's World Development Indicators; and IMF staff calculations.

1994–2005, leaving South Asia more exposed to competition from countries with lower unit labor costs. This competition intensified dramatically as the United States and the European Union reduced trade barriers for other Asian economies such as Cambodia, China, and Vietnam. Hence, for those countries which had previously benefited from quota protections and preferential market access in the United States and the European Union, trade liberalization resulted in negative terms of trade shock. Figure 1.12 shows that, relative to other consumption goods, US prices of apparel dropped by 25 percent from 2000 to 2010.

While Asia's overall share in advanced economy apparel imports increased as a result of trade liberalization in the early 2000s, market shares declined drastically for Maldives, Nepal, and Sri Lanka (Figure 1.12). Bangladesh was the only South

Asian country that expanded its market share in apparel, competing successfully with Cambodia, China, and Vietnam. Unlike other Asian countries with previously significant apparel exports such as Korea, Malaysia, the Philippines, or Thailand, most South Asian apparel exporters found it difficult to diversify into other, more skill-intensive, manufacturing industries. Among South Asian countries, only India has significant high-technology manufacturing exports (Figure 1.12).

Growth and Inequality

Has growth in South Asia been inclusive? This question matters for several reasons. First, meeting the SDGs means improving the lives of the poorest. Hence, if growth benefits only a few without reaching poor households, then it will be difficult to meet the SDGs. Second, if growth-enhancing reforms lead to an increase in inequality, these reforms are less likely to be politically sustainable. Experience from other countries has shown that reforms are less likely to succeed if some regions or groups are left out. A large body of literature highlights that inequality can hold back growth if those born in poverty lack access to the means necessary to fulfill their potential.[5]

A first look at the data in Figure 1.13 shows that the evolution of household inequality has varied across the region. In Bangladesh, India, and Sri Lanka, inequality measured by the Gini coefficient increased, whereas in Bhutan, Maldives, and Nepal inequality declined, albeit from high initial levels. Gini coefficients are comparable to those of other Asian emerging market economies. Chapter 4 of this book takes a closer look at household inequality and argues that inequality across households is at a level where it poses headwinds to development.

Figure 1.13. Household Income Inequality
(Gini index, percent)

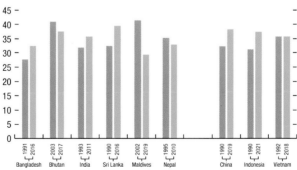

Source: World Bank's World Development Indicators.

---

[5] See, for example, Cerra, Lama, and Loayza (2021) for a recent survey of the literature on growth, inequality, and poverty reduction, including additional transmission channels.

Figure 1.14. Regional Inequality and Convergence: Estimates from Nighttime Light Intensity

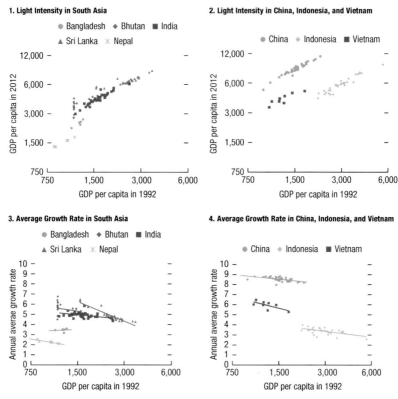

Sources: Lessman and Seidel 2017; and IMF staff calculations.

Assessing regional inequality trends is more difficult because statistical information on incomes at the subnational level is limited for many countries. However, regional GDP per capita can be estimated from the intensity of nighttime lights in satellite images.[6] Figure 1.14 plots these estimates for regions of South Asian countries, comparing income levels in 2012 against 1992. The estimates suggest that within each country except Bangladesh, per capita incomes of the poorest regions grew the fastest, so that income levels converged within countries. However, the figure also shows that there remained substantial regional inequality in 2012, despite this convergence. For example, India's poorest state had only half the per capita income of the richest state, a degree of inequality across regions comparable with that in China and Indonesia. In the rest of South Asia, the gap between richest and poorest regions was smaller.

---

[6] See, for example, Henderson, Storeygard, and Weil (2012). For an application to South Asia, see Beyer and others (2018).

Figure 1.15. Nighttime Light Intensity, by District, 2014–19

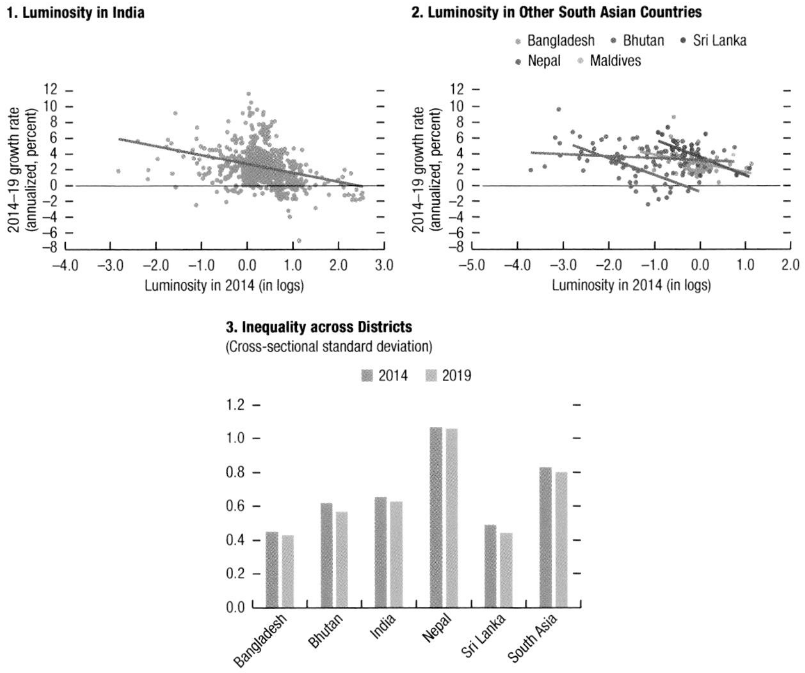

1. Luminosity in India

2. Luminosity in Other South Asian Countries

● Bangladesh   ● Bhutan   ● Sri Lanka
● Nepal   ● Maldives

3. Inequality across Districts
(Cross-sectional standard deviation)

■ 2014   ■ 2019

Sources: World Bank staff; and IMF staff calculations.

Regional inequality was the smallest in Bangladesh. In a comparison of growth rates, Figure 1.14 illustrates that the degree of convergence in the 1990s and 2000s was relatively highest in Sri Lanka, as can be seen from the slope of the relationship between initial income levels and growth rates. For India, convergence was relatively weak.

Using district-level estimates constructed by World Bank researchers from a different satellite data set for the more recent period of 2014–19, we can compare the evolution of nighttime light intensity in South Asia at a more granular level.[7] Figure 1.15 shows that convergence effects became stronger in the years preceding the pandemic, as districts with low light intensity in 2014 tended to have higher growth rates than districts with higher light intensity. This convergence was most pronounced in Bhutan and Sri Lanka, whereas Nepal, the country with the largest inequality across districts, showed only relatively weak convergence.[8] The figure also shows that convergence is only a part of the story, as growth rates were

---

[7] The author thanks Robert Beyer for sharing the district-level estimates.

[8] These findings come with the caveat that, for some regions, luminosity may be a weaker proxy for per capita incomes than in other regions. For example, in the mountainous regions of Bhutan and Nepal, the growth in tourism may not have seen a commensurate increase in luminosity.

Figure 1.16. Labor Market Indicators, by Gender

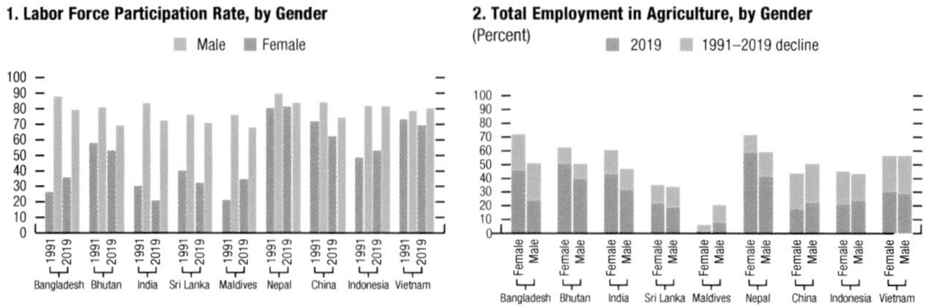

Sources: World Bank's World Development Indicators; and IMF staff calculations.

heterogeneous, causing some regions with similar luminosity in 2014 to diverge over the subsequent years. As a result, the overall inequality in luminosity declined only marginally from 2014 to 2019 (Figure 1.15, panel 3).

A particularly important aspect of inclusiveness is gender equity, a topic discussed in Chapter 5. In South Asia, gender disparities are particularly prevalent in the labor market. Figure 1.16 highlights that, except for Nepal, female labor force participation in South Asia is much lower than in China or Vietnam, whereas male labor force participation rates are comparable. There is also a considerable gap in occupations that is less prevalent in other parts of Asia. Women are much more likely to work in agricultural occupations which, as we will see in the following, have much lower productivity than jobs in the service or industrial sectors.

POLICIES FOR THE POSTPANDEMIC ERA

The historical experience of South Asia and the contrast with other regions hold several lessons for policy makers in the wake of the pandemic. First, there is strong evidence that sustained growth is essential for poverty reduction (see Dollar, Kleineberg, and Kraay 2016). Second, the experience of past growth accelerations that came in the wake of reforms suggest that South Asian countries have benefited immensely from economic reforms. Third, reforms in South Asia were typically less profound than in other parts of Asia, and the reform momentum in the region has slowed in recent years. Trade barriers remain high, and governments exercise a large degree of control over economic activity, including through regulation, directed lending by state-owned banks, and production in state-owned enterprises. Incumbent firms have few incentives to innovate and diversify to become competitive in new export markets, and those who do innovate find it difficult to compete for resources to expand their businesses. As a result, the region's economies have difficulties to absorb a growing labor force, pushing many young workers to migrate elsewhere instead of starting new businesses at home. Hence, to unlock South Asia's full potential, reforms to make the region more dynamic and open are needed.

Fostering Structural Transformation

One important way in which liberalization has unlocked growth in South Asia in the past is by making it easier for economies to shift resources to more productive activities. As Lewis (1954) pointed out, economies grow not just by becoming more productive in each sector but also by shifting labor from less productive to more productive sectors, particularly from smallholder agriculture to manufacturing and services. These forces of structural change are more easily at work in an environment where land, labor, and capital can be easily reallocated between sectors without excessive state control. Figure 1.17 illustrates the mechanics of structural change in South Asia. In all countries, labor productivity in agriculture, measured as value added per worker, has been lower than in the industrial and service sectors. In all countries, the employment share in agriculture has declined over time, as workers moved to more productive activities in the manufacturing and service sectors.

Figure 1.18 quantifies the contributions of structural change and sectoral productivity growth to the long-term change in labor productivity in the region, using the decomposition of McMillan and Rodrik (2011). The contribution of structural change was particularly large in Bangladesh, caused by the large productivity gap between agriculture and other sectors and by the rapid decline in agricultural employment. In India and Sri Lanka, by contrast, structural change

Figure 1.17. Structural Change and Sectoral Productivity Dynamics

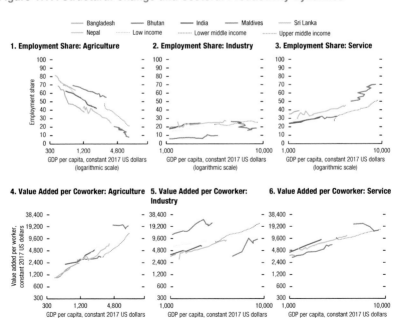

Sources: World Bank's World Development Indicators; and IMF staff calculations.

Figure 1.18. Decomposition of Long-Term Labor Productivity Growth Rates
(Percentage points)

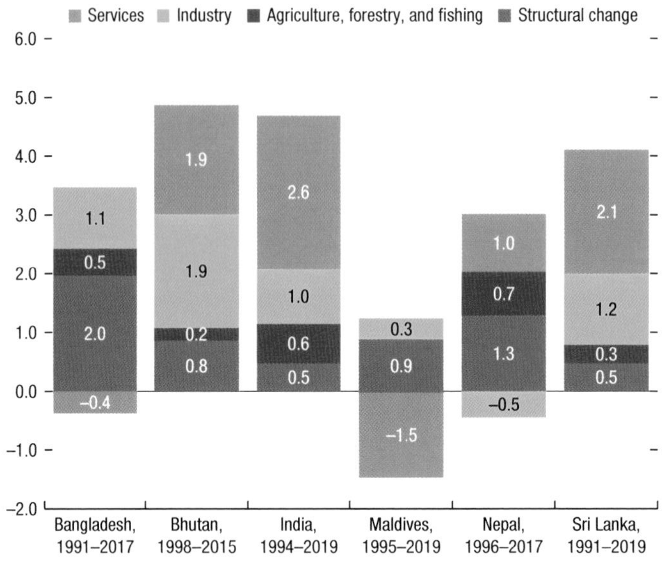

Sources: World Bank's World Development Indicators; and IMF staff calculations.

has been less important because most productivity gains occurred within sectors. The speed at which agricultural employment has declined has also been heterogeneous across countries. Whereas agricultural employment shares in Bangladesh, Maldives, and Sri Lanka are low for their level of development, they remain relatively high in Bhutan and Nepal. Given the relatively high absolute agricultural employment shares and the persistent productivity gaps between agriculture and other sectors, the potential for further gains from structural changes are large almost everywhere.

Policy reforms should aim to facilitate the realization of these gains. Labor market reforms, including those discussed in Chapter 3 of this book, would enable the large young rural population to get a foothold in the manufacturing and service sectors instead of seeking work abroad. Cutting excessive bureaucracy to make it easier to start a formal business in productive sectors would also contribute to job creation. Fewer restrictions on owning and selling land would make it easier for less productive farmers to sell their land to start a business. As we have previously seen, agricultural employment shares are especially high for women, so that reforms to foster structural change should include tackling institutional gender disparities.

Investing in Capital

In addition to structural change, public and private investment have been an important driver of growth in South Asia over the past 30 years, as can be seen

Figure 1.19. Public and Private Investment as Drivers of Growth

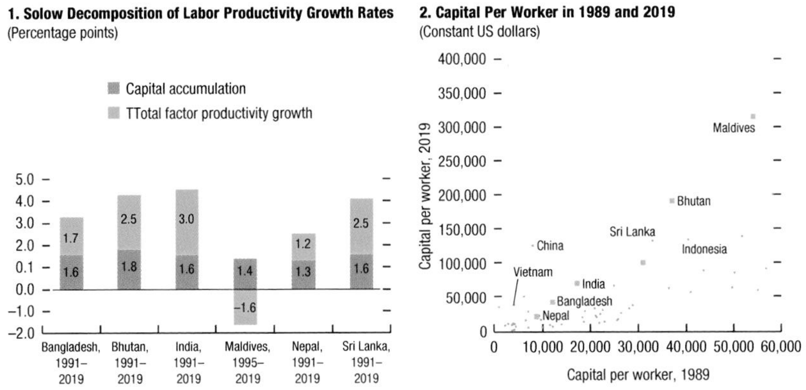

1. Solow Decomposition of Labor Productivity Growth Rates
(Percentage points)

2. Capital Per Worker in 1989 and 2019
(Constant US dollars)

Sources: World Bank's World Development Indicators, Penn World Tables; and IMF staff calculations.
Note: Estimates are based on Solow decomposition with capital and labor elasticities of output of 0.33 percent and 0.67 percent, respectively.

from panel 1 in Figure 1.19. Panel 2 in Figure 1.19 shows that capital per worker in South Asian economies increased faster than in countries that had a similar capital intensity in 1989—with a few notable exceptions, including China and Vietnam. Going forward, the importance of capital accumulation as an engine of growth is likely to decline over time, unless domestic savings rates increase.[9] Greater financial inclusion, a topic of Chapter 13, would help mobilize savings.

The gains from capital accumulation crucially depend on whether the additional capital is used productively. For public investment, this can be achieved through rigorous project appraisal and selection procedures and through a transparent procurement process (Chapter 11). In the case of private investment, an efficient and stable financial sector is critical for ensuring that savings are channeled toward financing the most productive activities. In South Asia, where public sector banks play a dominant role, institutional reforms are needed to improve the allocation of credit (see Chapter 13).[10]

Investing in People and Ideas

It is noteworthy that, although value-added per worker in agriculture and services has evolved broadly in line with peers, productivity in the industrial sector is below the average of other countries at the same stage of development (see Figure 1.17), despite the relatively rapid capital accumulation.[11] This is consistent

---

[9] As famously demonstrated by Solow (1956), the growth rate of the capital stock tends to decline when countries become more developed, since a greater share of investment will be needed to replace depreciating existing capital.

[10] See also Schipke and others (2022) for a recent in-depth discussion of India's financial sector.

[11] A notable exception to this pattern is Bhutan, where productivity in the industrial sector benefited from growth of the capital-intensive hydropower sector, while agricultural productivity lagged.

Figure 1.20. Literacy Rates
(Percent)

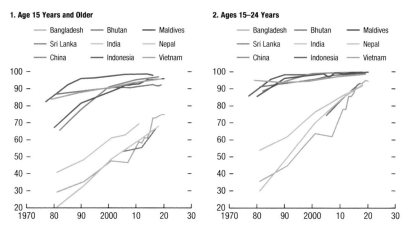

Sources: World Bank's World Development Indicators; and IMF staff calculations.

with our earlier observation that manufacturing activities in South Asia have a relatively low technology content. A comparison of the sources of growth in Figures 1.17 and 1.18 (panel 1) reveals that, for Bangladesh and Nepal, total factor productivity growth is mostly explained by structural change and less by technological improvements.

Given that the growth payoffs from capital accumulation and structural change will eventually decline over time, South Asian countries need to boost alternative growth engines. Perhaps the largest investment gaps are in South Asia's people. Basic skills are needed for workers to switch from agriculture to other sectors. Literacy rates have shown drastic improvements, especially in Bangladesh and Nepal. Overall, except for Maldives, the levels remain far below those observed in faster growing peers such as China, Indonesia, or Vietnam (Figure 1.20). Bhutan had the same literacy rate as Nepal in 2017, despite having more than twice the level of GDP per capita. Sri Lanka, which once prided itself for having one of the highest literacy rates in Asia, has long been surpassed by other Asian countries as literacy rates have stagnated. The higher literacy rates among the young are an indication that over time the gaps in literacy will close. In India, however, the increase in youth literacy rates has been slower than elsewhere.

Investments in the health sector need to be stepped up, too. Notwithstanding the large improvements in health outcomes highlighted in Figure 1.8, there is still a large gap across countries in the region. To meet the SDGs and close these gaps, a big push is required. Moreover, a sound health infrastructure is a key element in managing pandemics. Chapter 2 of this book estimates that the overall spending needs in education, health, and infrastructure (water and sanitation, electricity, and roads) required to meet the SDGs are around 6 percent of GDP in India and 11 percent of GDP in the rest of South Asia.

Figure 1.21. Patent Applications per 1,000,000 Persons

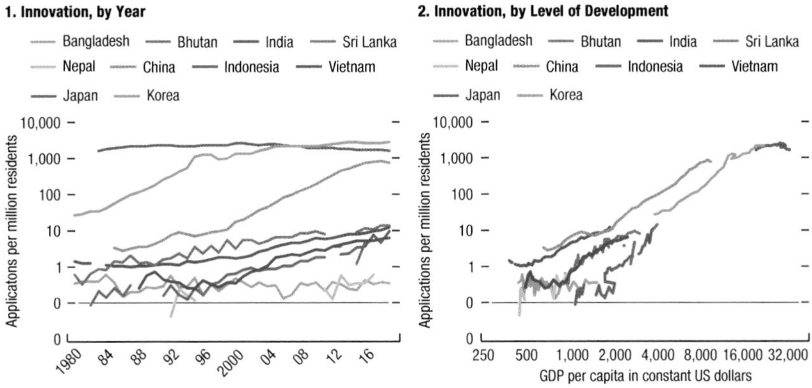

1. Innovation, by Year

Bangladesh — Bhutan — India — Sri Lanka
Nepal — China — Indonesia — Vietnam
Japan — Korea

2. Innovation, by Level of Development

Bangladesh — Bhutan — India — Sri Lanka
Nepal — China — Indonesia — Vietnam
Japan — Korea

Sources: World Bank's World Development Indicators; and IMF staff calculations.

South Asia also needs to invest more in ideas. The experience of China and Korea has shown that innovation can become an engine of growth for countries that have reached middle-income status and where the labor costs are no longer a comparative advantage. Figure 1.21 documents how Korea has become more innovative over time, surpassing Japan in the number of worldwide patent applications per capita. China has seen a remarkable increase in patent applications which accelerated in the early 2000s. In absolute numbers, South Asia lags far behind China in terms of patent applications per capita. However, relative to its GDP per capita, India is on a similar trajectory as China. The rest of South Asia, however, lags along both measures.

Managing the Demographic Transition

South Asia's growing population holds a vast potential for sustained economic growth in the decades to come. According to the United Nations, the region's working-age population in 2050 will be 19 percent larger than in 2020. Making the most of this demographic opportunity requires ambitious reforms. As discussed previously, investment in education needs to be fast-tracked, so that the growing number of young people entering the labor market have the necessary skills. Also, labor market reforms should be an urgent priority so that young workers can more easily be absorbed into productive sectors. Chapter 3 reports that youth unemployment rates in South Asia are relatively high compared with those in other developing and emerging economies. Labor force participation needs to improve as well. As we have seen in Figure 1.16, female labor force participation rates in the region are extremely low and have declined in recent decades in Bhutan, India, and Sri Lanka. Removing formal constraints to female employment should be complemented with increased flexibility and policies to

Figure 1.22. Population Projections

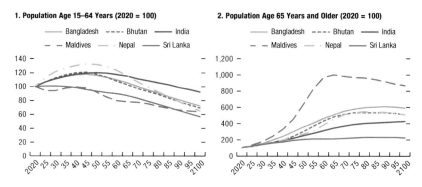

Sources: World Bank's World Development Indicators; and IMF staff calculations.

facilitate access to childcare.[12] These reforms are particularly urgent in Maldives and Sri Lanka, where the working-age population is already at its peak and bound to begin its decline.

Although the increase in the size of the labor force associated with the demographic transition is temporary, the increase in the size of the elderly adult population will be much longer lasting. The region's population age 65 years and older is projected to nearly double by 2040 and more than quadruple by 2075 (Figure 1.22). In many countries, population aging has led to increased private savings and hence to more investment and improved external positions. Facilitating this process requires policies that promote greater access to finance and policies that ensure that private savings are channeled into productive investments. However, population aging also means that public spending on pensions and social transfers to address old-age poverty are likely to increase over time. Fiscal policy planning should take these implicit liabilities into account.

Fostering Trade Integration

Ample evidence suggests that trade liberalization has benefited the region.[13] Yet, liberalization in South Asia is less advanced than in the rest of Asia. High tariffs and nontariff barriers protect domestic producers, giving them few incentives to innovate or to search for new export opportunities abroad (see Figure 1.23). Meanwhile, as we have seen previously, competition in South Asia's traditional

---

[12] Khera (2018) found that gender policies in India are most effective if they are combined with greater flexibility in the formal sector.

[13] For example, when studying wages in different industries in India, Mishra and Kumar (2005) found a strong positive effect of tariff reductions on sectoral productivity and wages, which led to a reduction in overall wage inequality in the 1990s.

Figure 1.23. Tariff Rates and Nontariff Barriers

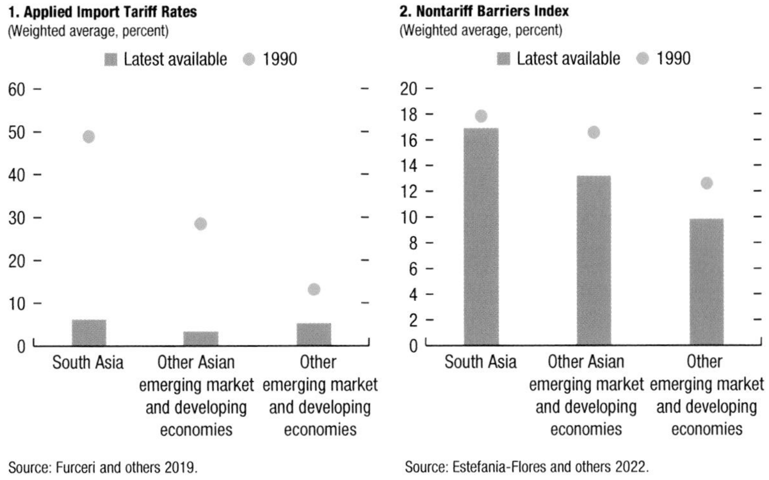

1. Applied Import Tariff Rates
(Weighted average, percent)

■ Latest available   ● 1990

2. Nontariff Barriers Index
(Weighted average, percent)

■ Latest available   ● 1990

Source: Furceri and others 2019.

Source: Estefania-Flores and others 2022.

export destinations has intensified. As a result, exports of South Asian countries accounted for less than 2.5 percent of global cross-border trade in 2017–19.

The link between trade and growth is explored in more depth in the middle section of this book. Chapter 8 documents how the region's gradual opening has brought a diversification into new exports and an increase in economic complexity. The chapter then identifies policies that could help diversify the region's economies further. Key findings include that, to become more diversified, South Asia needs to invest in infrastructure, education, and research and development, facilitate bank credit to productive companies, and become more open to trade.

Chapter 9 documents that South Asia's integration into global value chains lags that of other regions and that trade links within South Asia remain underdeveloped. The authors find that the region's still-relatively-high tariffs and nontariff trade barriers are responsible for the low degree of trade openness and, using the example of India, quantify the growth effects from further liberalization. Chapter 10 takes a closer look at fostering trade ties between South Asia and East Asia. It argues that South Asian economies can reap economic welfare gains from closer integration with East Asia. Policy priorities include gradually reducing trade barriers accompanied by adjustment assistance, investing in special economic zones to promote exports and industrial clustering, pursuing comprehensive free trade agreements and reinvesting in BIMSTEC as a regional organization.

Addressing Inequality

Although the policies discussed so far (for example, investment in education and financial inclusion) would help reduce poverty, greater trade openness may give rise to inequality, as exporting sectors may benefit more than sectors facing higher import competition. The link between inequality and growth-enhancing policies is complex and can change over time. For example, Kuznets (1955) famously observed that structural transformation initially tends to lead to higher inequality, as only some workers move to better opportunities in the manufacturing or service sectors. In later stages, structural transformation reduces inequality, as the number of lower-income agricultural workers declines.

Redistribution mechanisms are needed to ensure that the gains from reforms are more evenly spread. Chapter 4 of this book explores policies to reduce inequality from relatively high levels, through better functioning insurance and redistribution mechanisms. In most South Asian countries, the levels of government spending on social protection are relatively low, and transfer schemes suffer from large inclusion and exclusion errors. Hence, reforms should aim to enhance the generosity and coverage of social transfer schemes while improving mechanisms for households to graduate once their income is sufficiently high. Moreover, social protection systems should consider that the nature of risks changes over the life cycle.

Leveraging Digitalization

Digitalization offers many new opportunities to promote inclusive growth. Information and communication technology services are a significant source of export revenues for most countries in the region. However, digitalization can also support the domestic economy. In some cases, digital solutions have helped overcome access gaps in the traditional infrastructure. For example, in Bangladesh, where access to commercial banks has lagged, digital alternatives have become a popular substitute with mobile money transactions of more than 20 percent of GDP in 2020. In India, the introduction of Adhaar, the biometric digital identification system, in 2011 greatly facilitated access to bank accounts (Khera 2022). The subsequent take-off of financial inclusion under the government's Pradhan Mantri Jan Dhan Yojana program in 2014 also benefitted from digitalization, through both the reliance on Adhaar identification numbers and the availability of digital technology for low-cost service delivery. After the program was introduced, the share of the population with a bank account increased from 53 to 70 percent (Khera 2022).

The potential gains from digitalization have increased over the past few years, as South Asia has seen a rapid increase in Internet access across the population, a development that accelerated further during the pandemic (Figure 1.24). In India and Maldives, where online banking transaction volumes reached 14.5 and 85.5 percent of GDP in 2019, respectively, the number of online banking transactions more than doubled in 2020, according to the IMF's Financial Access Survey.

Chapter 5 of this book makes the case that digitalization can be an important tool to close gender gaps in the region. As we have seen previously, women are disproportionately affected by a lack of access to finance, so that digitalization can contribute to closing existing gender gaps. At the same time, gender gaps in South Asia are also prevalent in the extent of digitalization.

The benefits of digitalization go beyond the financial sector. According to the McKinsey Global Institute (2019), core digital sectors accounted for 7 percent of

Figure 1.24. Fixed and Mobile Internet Subscriptions Per Capita

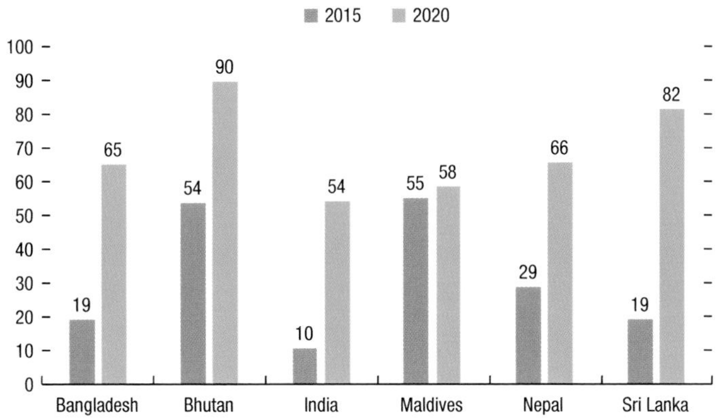

Source: International Telecommunication Union.

India's GDP and are projected to grow significantly faster than the rest of the economy. In 2020, India's e-commerce sales alone grew by close to 40 percent (see Dabla-Norris and others 2021). Digitalization can also make public administrations more efficient while reducing the risk of corruption (Chapter 6). Customs administrations in most countries in the region now use electronic systems to facilitate customs clearance. Some countries have introduced electronic business registrations (Bangladesh) and online building permit applications (India and Nepal). Evidence from India and Indonesia shows that e-procurement can improve the quality of infrastructure investment (see Lewis-Faupel and others 2016). Electronic taxpayer registrations and e-filing can facilitate the work of tax administrations while reducing the administrative burden on taxpayers (see Dabla-Norris and others 2021). E-filing platforms for at least some tax types now exist in Bhutan, India, Maldives, and Sri Lanka. Also, e-filing is mandatory for all corporate income taxpayers in Bhutan, India, and Sri Lanka and for large businesses in Maldives. Digitalization often reduces the scope for discretion and fraud. In India, the adoption of an electronic platform for managing a social assistance program resulted in a decline of 17 percent in spending with no corresponding decline in benefits (IMF 2019).

Preserving Macroeconomic Stability

The recent volatility in oil and food prices have underscored the need to be vigilant against risks to macroeconomic and financial stability. Responding to shocks has become more challenging, given that the pandemic has weakened South Asia's public and private sector balance sheets. Climate change will not just pose headwinds to growth. It will also increasingly become an additional economic risk factor throughout the region with rising sea levels affecting coastlines in Bangladesh, India, Maldives, and Sri Lanka. Changing weather patterns and shrinking glaciers will affect hydropower production in Bhutan, Nepal, and Sri Lanka. Climate change will also disproportionately affect the region's agricultural sector that will continue to employ a large share of the population. Chapter 7 of this book documents South Asia's exposure to climate risks and discusses the mitigation and adaptation policies undertaken by countries in the region.

Considering these heightened vulnerabilities, the role of macro-financial management—the topic of the third part of this book—is more important than ever. Given signs of fiscal dominance in several countries, a credible strategy for fiscal consolidation will be needed to keep inflation expectations anchored. Chapter 11 discusses how the region's large infrastructure needs can be met despite limited fiscal space. It shows that both the quality and quantity of public investment need to increase and, through a simulation exercise, explores the growth impact of various alternative financing strategies. Chapter 12 takes stock of the region's monetary policy frameworks and discusses policies to enhance their effectiveness.

CONCLUSIONS

South Asia's future holds the promise of continued poverty reduction and rapid economic development that would make the region a powerhouse of the global economy. Unlocking the region's potential, however, requires bold reforms. History has shown that all South Asian countries have benefited from reform episodes, and this chapter has explored ways to build on these earlier successes to unleash a renewed dynamism. The remainder of this book explores the design of reforms in much more detail, making the case for private sector led growth accompanied by strong policy frameworks to keep the region on a stable path and address inequalities, so that prosperity is shared, and no one is left behind.

REFERENCES

Anand, Abhishek, Justin Sandefur, and Arvind Subramanian. 2021. "Three New Estimates of India's All-Cause Excess Mortality during the COVID-19 Pandemic." CGD Working Paper 589, Center for Global Development, Washington, DC.

Beyer, Robert, Esha Chhabra, Virgilio Galdo, and Martin Rama. 2018. "Measuring Districts' Monthly Economic Activity from Outer Space." World Bank Policy Research Working Paper 8523, World Bank, Washington, DC.

Cerra, Valerie, Ruy Lama, and Norman Loayza. 2021. "Links between Growth, Inequality, and Poverty: A Survey." IMF Working Paper 2021/68, International Monetary Fund, Washington, DC.

Dabla-Norris, Era, Ruud A. de Mooij, Andrew Hodge, Jan Loeprick, Dinar Prihardini, Alpa Shah, Sebastian Beer, Sonja Davidovic, Arbind M. Modi, and Fan Qi. 2021. "Digitalization and Taxation in Asia." IMF Departmental Paper 21/017, International Monetary Fund, Washington, DC.

Deshpande, Ashwini. 2020. "The COVID-19 Pandemic and Lockdown: First Effects on Gender Gaps in Employment and Domestic Work in India." Discussion Paper 30, Department of Economics, Ashoka University, Sonepat, India.

Dollar, David, Tatjana Kleineberg, and Aart Kraay. 2016. "Growth Still Is Good for the Poor." *European Economic Review* 81 (January): 68–85.

Estefania-Flores, Julia, Davide Furceri, Swarnali A. Hannan, Jonathan David Ostry, and Andrew K. Rose. 2022. "A Measurement of Aggregate Trade Restrictions and Their Economic Effects." CEPR Discussion Paper 16919, Center for Economic and Policy Research, Washington, DC.

Furceri, Davide, Swarnali A. Hannan, Jonathan David Ostry, and Andrew K. Rose. 2019. "Macroeconomic Consequences of Tariffs." IMF Working Paper 19/009, International Monetary Fund, Washington, DC.

Goretti, Manuela, Daisaku Kihara, Ranil M. Salgado, and Anne Marie Gulde. 2019. "Is South Asia Ready for Take Off? A Sustainable and Inclusive Growth Agenda." IMF Departmental Paper 2019/016, International Monetary Fund, Washington, DC.

Górnicka, Lucyna, Sumiko Ogawa, and TengTeng Xu. 2021. "Corporate Sector Resilience in India in the Wake of the COVID-19 Shock." IMF Working Paper 21/278, International Monetary Fund, Washington, DC.

Government of India. 2022. "Vaccine Supply." Ministry of Finance, Government of India. https://www.mea.gov.in/vaccine-supply.htm.

Henderson, J. Vernon, Adam Storeygard, and David N. Weil. 2012. "Measuring Economic Growth from Outer Space." *American Economic Review* 102 (2): 994–1028.

Hodge, Andrew, and Racha Moussa. 2021. "Financial Sector Policies in South Asia during the COVID-19 Pandemic." In *Policy Advice to Asia in the COVID-19 Era*, edited by Chang Yong Rhee and Katsiaryna Svirydzenka. IMF Departmental Paper 21/04, International Monetary Fund, Washington, DC.

International Monetary Fund (IMF). 2019. "Curbing Corruption." Fiscal Monitor, April 2019.

International Monetary Fund (IMF). 2022a. *Regional Economic Outlook for Asia and Pacific.* Washington, DC: IMF.

International Monetary Fund (IMF). 2022b. "Sri Lanka: Selected Issues." IMF Country Report 2018/176, Washington, DC.

Khera, Purva. 2018. "Closing Gender Gaps in India: Does Increasing Womens' Access to Finance Help?" IMF Working Paper 18/212, International Monetary Fund, Washington, DC.

Khera, Purva. 2022. "Digital Financial Services and Financial Inclusion." In *India's Financial System: Building the Foundation for Strong and Sustainable Growth*, edited by Alfred Schipke, Anne-Marie Gulde-Wolf, Nada Choueiri, and Jarkko Turunen.

Kuznets, Simon. 1955. "Economic Growth and Income Inequality." *American Economic Review* 45 (1): 1–28.

Lamba, Rohit, and Arvind Subramanian. 2020. "Dynamism with Incommensurate Development: The Distinctive Indian Model." *Journal of Economic Perspectives* 34 (1): 3–30.

Lessmann, Christian, and Andre Seidel. 2017. "Regional Inequality, Convergence, and Its Determinants—A View from Outer Space." *European Economic Review* 92: 110–132.

Lewis, W. Arthur. 1954. "Economic Development with Unlimited Supplies of Labour." *The Manchester School* 22 (2): 139–91.

Lewis-Faupel, Sean, Yusuf Neggers, Benjamin A. Olken, and Rohini Pande. 2016. "Can Electronic Procurement Improve Infrastructure Provision? Evidence from Public Works in India and Indonesia." *American Economic Journal: Economic Policy* 8 (3): 258–83.

Mahler, Daniel Gerszon, Nishant Yonzan, Christoph Lakner, R. Andres Castaneda Aguilar, and Haoyu Wu. 2021. "Updated Estimates of the Impact of COVID-19 on Global Poverty: Turning the Corner on the Pandemic in 2021?" World Bank Blogs. https://blogs.worldbank.org/opendata/updated-estimates-impact-covid-19-global-poverty-turning-corner-pandemic-2021.

McKinsey Global Institute. 2019. "Digital India: Technology to Transform a Connected Nation." McKinsey Global Institute.

McMillan, Margaret, and Dani Rodrik, 2011. "Globalization, Structural Change and Productivity Growth." NBER Working Paper 17143, National Bureau of Economic Research, Cambridge, MA.

Mishra, Prachi, and Utsav Kumar. 2005. "Trade Liberalization and Wage Inequality: Evidence from India." IMF Working Paper 05/20, International Monetary Fund, Washington, DC.

Rodrik, Dani, and Arvind Subramanian. 2005. "From 'Hindu Growth' to Productivity Surge: The Mystery of the Indian Growth Transition." IMF Working Paper 04/77, International Monetary Fund, Washington, DC.

Schipke, Alfred, Anne-Marie Gulde-Wolf, Nada Choueiri, and Jarkko Turunen. (Forthcoming). *India's Financial System: Building the Foundation for Strong and Sustainable Growth.* Washington, DC: International Monetary Fund.

Solow, Robert M. 1956. "A Contribution to the Theory of Economic Growth." *Quarterly Journal of Economics* 70 (1): 65–94.

Watson, Oliver J., Gregory Barnsley, Jaspreet Toor, Alexandra B. Hogan, Peter Winskill, and Azra C. Ghani. 2022. "Global Impact of the First Year of COVID-19 Vaccination: A Mathematical Modelling Study." *Lancet Infectious Diseases* 22 (9): 1293–302.

CHAPTER 2

The Spending Challenge of Achieving the SDGs in South Asia: Lessons from India

Mercedes García-Escribano, Tewodaj Mogues, Mariano Moszoro, and Mauricio Soto

South Asia has experienced significant progress in improving human and physical capital over the past few decades. Within the region, India has become a global economic powerhouse with enormous development potential ahead. To foster human and economic development, India has shown a strong commitment to the Sustainable Development Goals Agenda. This chapter focuses on the medium-term development challenges that South Asia, and in particular India, faces to ensure substantial progress along the Sustainable Development Goals by 2030. We estimate the additional spending needed in critical areas of human capital (health and education) and physical capital (water and sanitation, electricity, and roads). We document progress on these five sectors for India relative to other South Asian countries and discuss implications for policy and reform.

The authors express their sincere appreciation for the close cooperation and support given by officials and staff of the various organizations met on December 4–17, 2019, in Delhi, India, when this work was initiated. These include Indian government agencies: NITI Aayog (National Institute for Transforming India), the Department of Expenditure at Ministry of Finance, the Department of Drinking Water and Sanitation at Ministry of Jal Shakti, the Ministry of Statistics and Programme Implementation, the Ministry of Human Resource Development, the Ministry of Health and Family Welfare, the Ministry of Road Transport and Highways, the Ministry of Power, and the Ministry of Housing and Urban Affairs. The team is especially grateful to NITI Aayog staff members Sanyukta Samaddar and Alen John and the staff of the SDG Division. The team also benefited from meetings with Renata Lok-Dessallien (United Nations) Henk Bekedam (World Health Organization), Sabyasachi Mitra (Asian Development Bank), Jorge Coarasa (Human Development, World Bank), and staff of development partners. The authors are also thankful for comments and suggestions from participants during the IMF Asia and Pacific Department's South Asia seminar in January 2020, an event "Regional Forum on Fostering Growth in South Asia" in Delhi in February 2020, and an IMF Fiscal Affairs Department seminar in August 2021.

INTRODUCTION

South Asia has experienced significant progress in improving human development over the past few decades. With sustained income growth and strong policy
efforts, the region, which accounts for one-fifth of the world's population, has
contributed to more than 200 million people exiting poverty in the course of the
last three decades (Goretti and others 2019). Nonetheless, some South Asian
countries' human capital index is lower than what their GDP per capita would
predict. And South Asia, on average, still lags East Asia and the Pacific as well as
Latin America and the Caribbean in access to key infrastructure such as electricity, water, sanitation, and telecommunication (Jha and Arao 2018).

Within the region, India has become a global economic powerhouse with
enormous development potential ahead. Unlocking this potential requires investments in human and physical capital. In this regard, India has made astonishing
progress along several dimensions. Hundreds of millions have lifted themselves
out of poverty over the past decades. Education enrollment is now nearly universal for primary school. Infant mortality rates have been halved since 2000. Access
to water and sanitation, electricity, and roads has greatly improved. Nonetheless,
to further capitalize on economic growth, India should continue to close gaps in
human and physical capital—gaps that have recently widened as a result of the
pandemic. Indeed, after years of steady progress, during the COVID-19 pandemic health and education systems have been disrupted, poverty has increased, and
the prevalence of undernourishment has risen (Food and Agriculture Organization
2021; UN 2021). However, South Asia is projected to have the strongest
improvement in poverty reduction of any region in 2021, with only a minor
deterioration relative to prepandemic projections (Mahler and others 2021).

To foster human and economic development, India has shown a strong commitment to the Sustainable Development Goals (SDG) Agenda. The government
has aligned its development priorities with the SDG framework. India recently
underwent two Voluntary National Reviews (Government of India, NITI Aayog
2017, 2020), and carried out a third round of stocktaking of progress in meeting
the SDGs (Government of India, NITI Aayog 2021) providing SDG metrics,
including at the state level. Numerous national flagship programs that seek to
connect villages to roads, launch initiatives to provide universal health coverage
and sanitation, and aim at other ambitious development objectives are intimately
linked to the SDGs. States and union territories are taking proactive steps to
implement the goals, underpinned by national and regional consultations,
although more can be done to reduce wide subnational disparities (Government
of India, NITI Aayog 2021).[1]

This chapter focuses on the medium-term development challenges that South
Asia, and in particular India, faces, namely, the additional spending—public and

---

[1] For example, based on government calculations, states and Union territories range in their SDG
index from 52 to 75.

private—needed to ensure substantial progress along the SDGs by 2030. The focus of the chapter is on critical areas of human capital (health and education) and physical capital (water and sanitation, electricity, and roads), following the methodology developed by Gaspar and others (2019).[2] We find that an additional 6.2 percent of GDP per year will have to be spent in India in these five areas to achieve a high SDG performance in 2030, and preliminary desk estimates for the other South Asian countries combined point to an additional spending need of 11.3 percent of GDP in the year 2030.

The next section of the chapter documents progress on these five sectors for India relative to South Asian countries and other large emerging markets. Section 3 reports the estimate of the additional spending that would be required to make substantial progress toward the SDGs in India. The data collection and validation, carried out in New Delhi in 2019, and the analysis presented in this chapter use 2019 as the base year for the analysis—thus, the available data does not enable accounting for the potential effects of COVID-19. Section 4 briefly discusses comparable additional spending estimates for the region, and Section 5 concludes and reflects on the potential implications of the pandemic for the SDGs in South Asia.

BACKGROUND AND CONTEXT

Health

All countries in South Asia have seen a steady improvement in health outcomes over the past 50 years. Sri Lanka and Maldives outperform other South Asian countries as well as the world's average in health outcomes, with Sri Lanka having the lowest under-1-year-old infant mortality in South Asia since the early 1970s (Figure 2.1), and Maldives catching up with Sri Lanka in recent years. Other countries—in particular, Pakistan since the 1990s, and Afghanistan—lag peers and, albeit exhibiting continued improvement, have infant mortality levels that double the current world average.

India has also made noteworthy strides in health outcomes. Infant mortality stands at around 30 deaths per 1,000 live births, similar to the world average, compared with about 140 deaths per 1,000 live births in the early 1970s. Mortality rates of children under 5 years old dropped from 95 to 37 deaths per 1,000 live births in 2000–18, and 2018 infant mortality is also less than half the rate of 25 years ago. Significant progress has also been made in maternal mortality, which declined by 77 percent from 1990 to 2016 (Government of India, Ministry of Health and Family Welfare 2018).

---

[2] Similar studies have been carried for Benin and Rwanda (Prady and Sy 2019), Nigeria (Soto, Moszoro, and Pico 2020), and Pakistan (Brollo and Hanedar 2021); however, this is the first in-depth costing exercise presented along with its regional comparators.

Figure 2.1. Evolution of the Infant Mortality Rate in South Asia
(Per 1,000 live births)

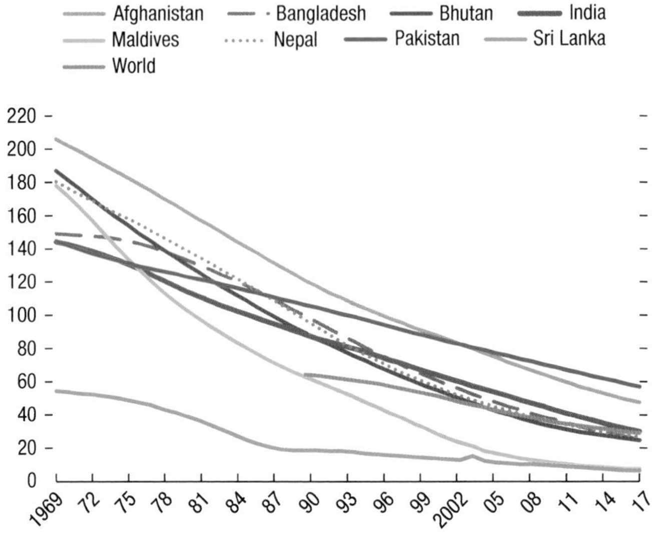

Source: World Bank 2020.
Note: The rate refers to the mortality of children under 1 year of age. "World" is the simple average across all countries in the world for which the index is available.

Yet, most countries in the South Asia region have a long way to go toward the health SDG. To assess this, we examine performance in terms of an index published in the annual Sustainable Development Report (for example, Sachs and others 2019) for each of the 17 goals, where index values of 0 and 100 indicate worst- and best-possible performance, respectively. We also assess India's health outcomes against those in emerging markets and in particular against other BRICS (Brazil, Russia, India, China, and South Africa) countries, deemed emerging economic powerhouses. As panel 1 in Figure 2.2 shows, only Maldives and Sri Lanka have an SDG3 index above the world average and above the median of emerging market economies.[3] In India, and despite past progress, health outcomes measured with the SDG3 index (or other indicators displayed in panel 2 in Figure 2.2) are below the median of emerging economies and still behind the country's own targets. For example, current under-five mortality, at 37 per 1,000 live births, is more than three times as large as the country's goal to have a mortality rate of 11 by 2030.

---

[3] The SDG3 index comprises 14 health variables relating, for example, to mortality rates, life expectancy, incidences of diseases, access to vaccines and other health services, and so on.

Figure 2.2. Health Outcomes in South Asia and India

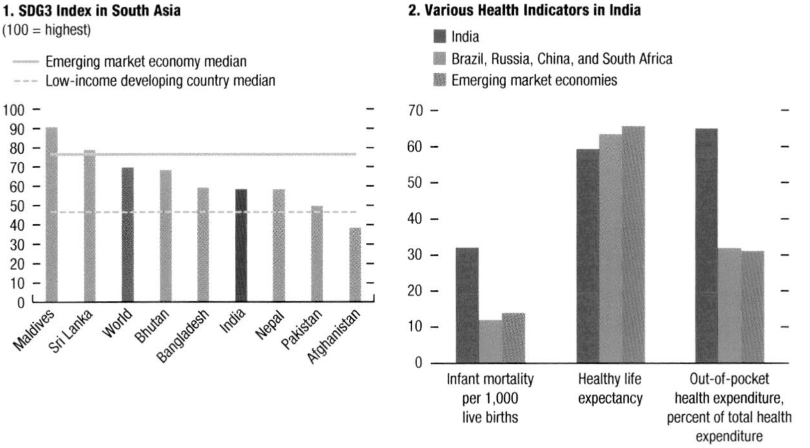

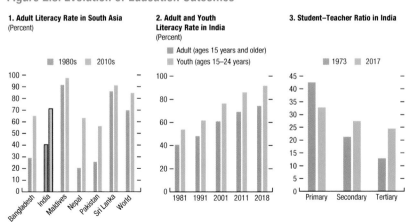

Sources: IMF staff calculations using Sachs and others (2019), IMF FAD Expenditure Assessment Tool (Garcia-Escribano and Liu 2017), and World Bank (2020).
Note: "World" is the simple average across all countries in the world for which the index is available. SDG3 = Sustainable Development Goal 3 (Good Health and Well-Being).

Education

In the past few decades, all countries in South Asia have improved their education outcomes. Since the 1980s, the adult literacy rate has doubled or tripled in Bangladesh, India, Nepal, and Pakistan (Figure 2.3, panel 1). At present, Sri Lanka and Maldives have literacy rates above 90 percent, whereas other countries lag the world's average.

Figure 2.3. Evolution of Education Outcomes

Source: IMF staff calculations using World Bank (2020).
Note: "World" is the simple average across all countries in the world for which the index is available.

India's growth into an emerging market economy has been accompanied by increased levels of education. The share of literacy among all adults increased from 41 percent in 1981 to 74 percent in 2018 (Figure 2.3, panel 2). The economic gains of past decades have gone hand in hand with better education service delivery, including through the reduction in the student–teacher ratio at the primary level (Figure 2.3, panel 3). Still, nearly 45 percent of the population has education only at or below the primary level (National Statistics Office 2019). While the expansion in the participation of youth in higher grade levels is welcome, it has put pressure on service delivery at the secondary and especially tertiary levels, resulting in rises in the student–teacher ratio.

Despite progress, educational outcomes in most South Asian countries lag emerging economy peers (Figure 2.4). South Asian countries span a wide spectrum in educational performance. Only Maldives and Sri Lanka are close to attaining an SDG4 index of 100 and well exceed the emerging economy median of 87.[4] At the same time, two countries—Pakistan and Afghanistan—even fall short of the low-income developing countries median index of 54. India's value at 80.2 falls short of the median index for emerging economies, which is likely related to the relatively large class sizes as well as gaps in preprimary and tertiary enrollment. The student–teacher ratio is higher than in Brazil and China, and the enrollment ratio for the population ages 3–23 years is also below that of Brazil and China. India's own goal is to achieve a 100 percent adjusted net enrollment for grades 1–10 by 2030 (Government of India, NITI Aayog 2018).

Figure 2.4. SDG4 (Education) Index for South Asia
(100 = highest)

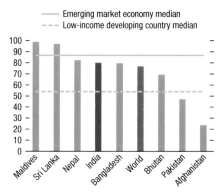

Source: IMF staff calculations using Sachs and others (2019).
Note: "World" is the simple average across all countries in the world for which the index is available. SDG = Sustainable Development Goal.

---

[4] The SDG4 index for non-OECD countries is based on three measures: youth literacy, primary enrollment, and secondary completion rates.

Water and Sanitation

South Asia is rapidly improving access to water and sanitation. South Asian countries have gradually expanded access to basic drinking water, with several of them reaching almost universal access (Figure 2.5). In India, almost 90 percent of its rural population and all its urban population had access to basic water in 2019, a substantial improvement from below 80 percent in both categories in 2000, especially considering the population growth in the past two decades. Likewise, in basic sanitation, India has also seen impressive improvements, with 97 and 98 percent of the rural and urban population, respectively, being served in 2019. Meanwhile, access to safely managed water services in rural areas increased from 40 percent in 2010 to 56 percent in 2019 and urban areas from 73.5 percent in 2010 to 75.1 percent in 2019. Another important achievement in India has been ending open defecation (Government of India, Ministry of Jal Shakti 2019).

However, pockets of hygiene deprivation remain. Many households have only access to public sources of water, and exclusive access to drinking water in the home remains a privilege. The challenge in most South Asian countries is to improve the quality, accessibility, and safety of water and sanitation services (Figure 2.6). There is a persistent 30 to 60 percent gap in access to safely managed

Figure 2.5. Access to Basic Drinking Water in South Asia
(Percent of population)

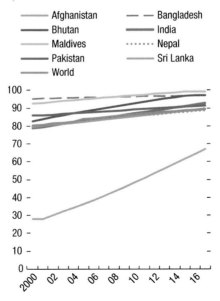

Source: World Bank 2020.
Note: "World" is the simple average across all countries in the world for which the index is available.

Figure 2.6. SDG6 (Water and Sanitation) Index for South Asia
(100 = highest)

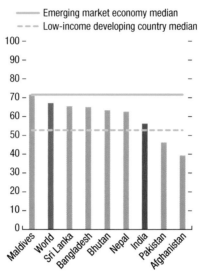

Source: IMF staff calculations using Sachs and others (2019).
Note: "World" is the simple average across all countries in the world for which the index is available. SDG = Sustainable Development Goal.

water and sanitation in the region.[5] In India, there is room for improvement even in basic sanitation, as 29 percent of the rural population and 15 percent of the urban population do not practice basic hygiene nor have access to such services. India lags peers in safely managed water and sanitation, especially in rural areas (Figure 2.7).[6]

Electricity

Access to electricity, a key requirement for a modern economy, has been steadily increasing across South Asia during the past decade (Figure 2.8). During 2002–17, India tripled its installed capacity from 108 to 327 gigawatts. Most of the added installed capacity came from thermal and hydro power plants, with an increasing share of renewable energy sources in recent years. During the same period, the per capita energy consumption increased from 559 to 1,122 kilowatt-hours. Recently, the peak demand not met declined from 12,159 megawatts (9.0 percent of peak demand) in 2012 to 2,608 megawatts (1.6 percent of peak

[5] The SDG6 index synthesizes variables on access to basic drinking water, access to basic sanitation, freshwater withdrawal, groundwater depletion, and treated wastewater. See Sachs and others (2019) for further details.

[6] The fact that the figure for safely managed sanitation is high for India may be related to different definitions used for classification between the Indian authorities and the United Nations.

Figure 2.7. Safely Managed Water and Sanitation in BRICS, 2016
(Percent of population)

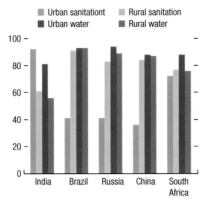

Source: IMF staff calculations based on data from the World Bank (2020).
Note: BRICS = Brazil, Russia, India, China, and South Africa.

Figure 2.8. Access to Electricity in South Asia
(Percent of population with access)

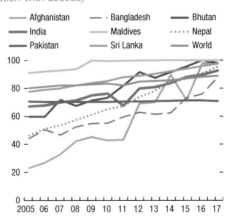

Source: World Bank 2020.
Note: "World" is the simple average across all countries in the world for which the index is available.

demand) in 2017, reflecting a substantial improvement in the quality of electricity service (Government of India, Ministry of Power 2018).

Several South Asian countries display high achievement in the electricity SDG subindex (Figure 2.9). In only one country—Pakistan—is electricity access below 80 percent as well as below the median for emerging market economies. There remains room for most South Asian countries to increase capacity, reliability, and

Figure 2.9. SDG7 (Electricity) Index in South Asia
(Percent of population with access)

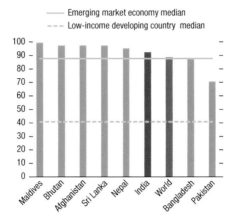

Source: World Bank 2020.
Note: The figure reflects only the subindex of SDG7 capturing the percentage of the population with access to electricity. "World" is the simple average across all countries in the world for which the index is available. SDG = Sustainable Development Goal.

Figure 2.10. GDP and Electricity Consumption Per Capita, 2018 or Latest Year

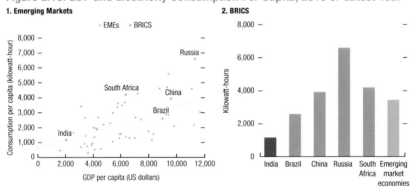

Source: IMF staff calculations based on data from World Bank (2020).
Note: In panel 1, the dotted line represents the fitted line of the relationship between electricity consumption per capita and GDP per capita, calculated using ordinary least squares regression. Data for India are from 2018; data for Brazil, Russia, China, and South Africa are from 2016. BRICS = Brazil, Russia, India, China, and South Africa.

sustainability of electricity provision. For instance, India's electricity consumption per capita falls behind peers. With per capita consumption of 1,181 kilowatt-hours in 2019, India is in line with its expected provision of electricity given its GDP per capita (Figure 2.10, panel 1), but it lags other BRICS (Figure 2.10, panel 2).[7] While India has accomplished practically universal supply of electricity to its approximately 700,000 villages, universal and reliable access has yet to be extended

---

[7] BRICS include Brazil, Russia, India, China, and South Africa.

to every household, with ubiquitous blackouts being one of India's major electricity challenges (Jha, Preonas, and Burling 2021). In addition, India intends to become energy self-sufficient and independent from imported power inputs.

Roads

South Asian countries have undertaken a major effort in extending and upgrading their road systems over the past decade (Figure 2.11). India appears to have made the largest strides, currently exhibiting the world's third largest road network (Road Traffic Technology 2014). In the years 2011–17, India added on average more than 130,000 kilometers per year to its road network (Government of India, Ministry of Road Transport and Highways 2019) with notable efforts including developing roads around industrial corridors and the implementation of rural road programs.

Nevertheless, the quality of road infrastructure remains low across the South Asia region. The infrastructure index places South Asia, except for India, below the world average (World Economic Forum 2019; Figure 2.12).[8] Rural roads in India account for 71 percent of the total road length,[9] but only about 70 percent of the rural population have access to all-weather roads within two kilometers (Figure 2.13). Closing the rural road infrastructure gap and increasing rural access to at least 90 percent will be critical for further development in India as well as in the rest of the South Asian region.

Figure 2.11. South Asia Evolution of Road Infrastructure Index
(Road index score; 1 = lowest, 7 = highest)

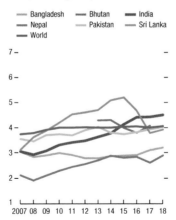

Source: World Economic Forum 2019. Data are not available for Afghanistan and Maldives.
Note: "World" is the simple average across all countries in the world for which the index is available.

---

[8] The survey-based infrastructure index obtains information from expert respondents on the quality of overall infrastructure in a country, and ranges from 1 (worst possible) to 7 (best possible).

[9] Of total roads length, rural roads account for 71 percent, district roads for 10 percent, urban roads for 9 percent, project roads for 5 percent, state highways for 3 percent, and national highways for 2 percent (Government of India, Ministry of Road Transport and Highways 2019).

Figure 2.12. South Asia Road Infrastructure Index, 2019
(Road index score; 1 = lowest, 7 = highest)

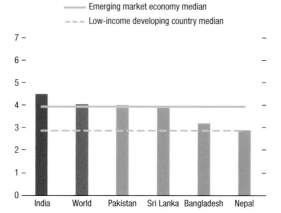

Source: World Economic Forum 2019. Data are not available for Afghanistan, Bhutan, and Maldives.
Note: "World" is the simple average across all countries in the world for which the index is available.

Figure 2.13. Rural Access Index for BRICS and Emerging Market Economies
(percent of rural population within 2 kilometers of an all-weather road)

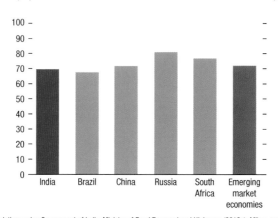

Source: IMF staff calculations using Government of India, Ministry of Road Transport and Highways (2018a); Mikou and others (2019); and World Bank (2020).
Note: BRICS = Brazil, Russia, India, China, and South Africa.

RESULTS ON ADDITIONAL SPENDING IN INDIA NEEDED TO MEET THE SDGS

This section presents the estimates of the additional public and private spending required to make substantial progress toward the SDGs in India following the methodology developed by Gaspar and others (2019). The methodology is based on an input-outcome approach, which assumes that development outcomes are a function of a mix of inputs. For each country, the methodology sets the levels of key inputs and the associated unit costs at the values observed in countries with similar levels of GDP per capita that reach high development outcomes (Gaspar and others 2019). The costing approach used in the paper does not systematically account for cross-sectoral (and cross-country) interdependence and spillovers.[10]

For the health and education sectors, the additional spending is estimated using as a benchmark the input variables (for example, student to teacher ratio in the case of education) in peer countries that exhibit relatively good performance in these two sectors, and also taking into account India-specific factors such as demographics and the level and growth of GDP per capita. Peer countries for India in this analysis are emerging market economies (EMEs), including the other BRICS. The estimates, as indicated in Gaspar and others (2019), are consistent with increasing technical efficiency. Countries that perform well also tend to be among the most efficient. Thus, when assigning the input levels observed in countries that perform well today to India, our spending estimates for high performance assume better spending. Should improvements in efficiency not take place, the spending required to reach the SDGs would be larger.[11] Results are presented as the annual additional spending in 2030 in percentage points of GDP compared with the current level of spending as a share of GDP. For physical capital, additional spending in percentage points of GDP corresponds to the annualized spending required to close infrastructure gaps between 2019 and 2030. The costing estimates for electricity and roads assume a linear 5 percent depreciation and reinvestment rate; for water and sanitation, given its longer depreciation period, a one-off investment in capital stock is assumed. More methodological details for each sector are presented in the annexes.

Health

Enhancing health outcomes in India in line with achieving the health SDGs would require a sizable increase in health spending. Health spending in India currently stands at 3.7 percent of GDP and falls short of levels spent in BRICS and EMEs (Figure 2.14, panel 1). This level of spending reflects a lag in doctors and hospital beds per 1,000 inhabitants (Figure 2.14, panel 2). For India to achieve substantial progress toward the SDGs by 2030, it will need to more than double health sector spending relative to its GDP (Table 2.1). Such additional spending of 3.8 percent of GDP would allow India to expand the number of medical staff, while moderately slowing the growth of personnel compensation, containing the ratio of doctor salaries to GDP per capita from 7.8 to 6.6—the current ratio is higher than for economies in the same income group that are able to achieve strong health

---

[10] For instance, increasing health spending may be useful for school attendance, and increasing spending on physical infrastructure might be helpful for improving health outcomes, for example, through wider access to health facilities. The cross-sectoral and cross-country inter-dependence and spillovers should be addressed with a dynamic stochastic general equilibrium model, which goes beyond the scope of this chapter.

[11] Considering how different levels of allocative efficiency across sectors would affect our results goes beyond the scope of this study, and could be explored in future research.

outcomes.[12] Meanwhile, capital and recurrent spending other than on the health care workers' wage bill should increase as a percent of total health spending. The expansion in health spending would need to be undertaken mostly by the public

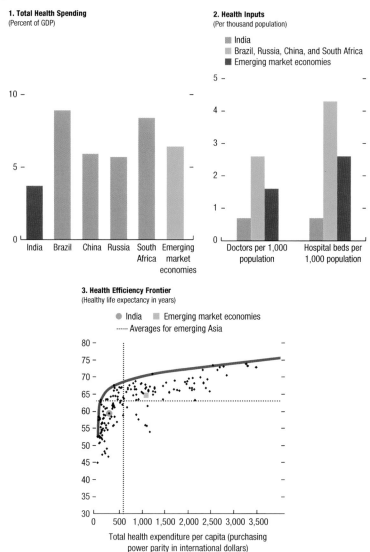

Figure 2.14. Performance in the Health SDG in Income Group and Regional Comparison

Source: IMF staff estimates using Sachs and others (2019) and IMF FAD Expenditure Assessment Tool.
Note: SDG = Sustainable Development Goal.

---

[12] A potential concern of brain drain resulting from slowing the growth of salaries of medical staff is mitigated by the fact that strong-performing peers in the same income group appear not to face this problem substantially.

TABLE 2.1.

Estimated Health Spending Needed for High Performance in India in Health SDG

| | GDP Per Capita $3,000–$6,000 | | | India | |
	All	Low Performers	High Performers	2017	2030
Main factors					
Doctors per 1,000 population	1.2	0.8	1.7	0.7	1.6
Other medical personnel per 1,000 population	6.0	5.6	6.3	2.9	5.4
Share of population <1 year and 60+ years	12.0	10.9	19.0	11.4	14.1
Doctors per 1,000 population age 1–59 years	0.9	0.7	1.2	0.6	1.2
Other medical personnel per 1,000 population age 1–59 years	4.2	4.2	4.1	2.3	4.1
Doctor wages (ratio to GDP per capita)	7.1	7.1	6.6	7.8	6.6
Other current and capital spending (percent of total spending)	62.3	61.1	62.3	54.2	62.3
Results					
Health spending (percent of GDP)	6.9	6.6	7.0	3.7	7.5
Per capita spending (2018 US dollars)	285.6	258.6	350.2	68.9	315.1

Source: IMF staff estimates using Gaspar and others (2019) methodology.
Note: SDG = Sustainable Development Goal.

sector as the country currently relies heavily on private outlays (67 percent of total health spending). The spending increase could help cover an expansion of India's health protection scheme, Pradhan Mantri Jan Arogya Yojana, to prevent non included but vulnerable individuals from falling into poverty because of illness and private health costs[13] (see Annex 2.1 for methodological details).

As stated earlier and illustrated in panel 3 of Figure 2.14, India will need to not only spend more on its health system but also spend more efficiently. Institutional changes and strengthening public financial management could contribute to increasing the efficiency of outlays. Providing greater autonomy to facility managers could foster greater efficiency in the sector. Rigidities imposed on clinic and hospital managers limit their ability to allocate funding in their facility in the most appropriate way for service delivery (Barroy and others 2019). Strengthening budget preparation will also improve health units' absorptive capacity and mitigate the problem of these units often having to return unused funds.

Education

India can achieve better education outcomes by 2030 without increasing the share of GDP devoted to education expenditures. As the student-age population is expected to shrink, India can increase the spending per student even if expenditures as a percentage of GDP decline. Education spending in 2030 as a share of GDP at 4.1 percent (lower than the current expenditures of 5.6 percent) would allow spending per student to increase by 37 percent by 2030—to an annual

---

[13] Today India's health insurance scheme, at about 0.1 percent of GDP, remains small in size and scope.

TABLE 2.2.

Additional Education Spending for High Performance in India in Education SDG

	GDP Per Capita $3,000–$6,000			India	
	All	Low Performers	High Performers	2018	2030
Main factors					
Students per teacher ratio	19.0	20.6	16.5	26.9	16.5
Teacher wages (ratio to GDP per capita)	2.5	3.9	1.7	3.1	1.7
Other current and capital spending (percent of total spending)	38.9	39.0	35.7	52.1	35.7
Student-age population (percent of total population)	39.0	40.9	33.1	38.3	31.9
Enrollment rate (preprimary to tertiary)	68.4	64.3	69.8	59.9	80.1
Results					
Education spending (percent of GDP)	5.7	8.2	3.7	5.6	4.1
Spending per student (US dollars, 2018)	890.8	1,401.6	660.2	491.2	673.6
SDG4 Index	77.8	75.3	88.2	80.2	

Source: IMF staff estimates using Gaspar and others (2019) methodology.
Note: SDG = Sustainable Development Goal.

$674 per student from the current level of $491 (Table 2.2). Such expansion in spending per student might require a larger share of public sector in education, as private spending contributes 27 percent of overall spending—compared with peer countries with a strong sectoral record, with only 5 percent reliance on private spending (see Annex 2.1 for details on the methodology).

While there is no need to spend more in education relative to GDP, India needs to spend more efficiently. Reallocation of resources by reducing wage growth toward bringing on board more teachers will support higher enrollment and reduce class size. The student per teacher ratio is 16.5 in countries with strong education outcomes compared with 27 in India today. As strong economic growth continues, teachers' wages would have to increase at a slower pace than GDP per capita. India's teachers' wages are three times its GDP per capita, which is distinctly higher than teachers' wages in high-performing countries among India's peers that are less than twice the GDP per capita. More effort also needs to be exerted to reduce absenteeism of those teachers already employed if resources are to be used efficiently, for example, through more systematic monitoring—using both top-down (for example, through surprise inspections) and bottom up (through active parent–teacher associations) mechanisms (Muralidharan and others 2017).

Beyond countrywide levels, the geographic and socio-cultural distribution of educational opportunities requires greater attention. The SDG4 India Index across states/union territories ranges widely, from 36 to 87 (Government of India, NITI Aayog 2018). Discrepancies also prevail across social groups. For example, scheduled tribes' gross enrollment rate in higher education is 10 points lower than the overall average (Government of India, Ministry of Finance 2019). Important progress by the government needs to be acknowledged in bringing about gender equity in enrollment. In fact, gross enrollment rates are higher for girls than boys at all levels other than higher education (Government of India, Ministry of Finance 2019). Being attentive to these distributional concerns will both improve targeting of spending for more efficient achievement of India-wide goals, as well as address crucial concerns of equity.

Water and Sanitation

India can achieve universal coverage of water and sanitation with large health externalities at a relatively low cost. Using the World Bank's water, sanitation, and hygiene (WASH) methodology in Hutton and Varughese (2016), we estimate the cost to provide universal safely managed access to water and sanitation at $106 billion over 2020–30, which on an annualized basis is equivalent to 0.17 percent of GDP in 2030, including depreciation. The bulk of the burden comes from sanitation in rural areas (see Annex 2.3 for the methodology).

Beyond resources, institutional and technical capacity constraints need to be addressed. Subnational governments are responsible for water and sanitation, but often do not have the capacity to set the institutional framework, especially in rural areas. Other areas for improvement include enhancing the management of tariffs—unsystematic application of tariffs might be straining the finances of local governments—and improving the mapping of the existing network, which can bring efficiency gains as well as facilitate maintenance and network expansion. In addition, efforts should continue to improve wastewater treatment—only around 30 percent of wastewater is treated—to prevent the deterioration of the groundwater.

Electricity

Generation capacity needs to keep up with population and economic growth to grant full access to electricity (the SDG Indicator 7.1.1 measures the proportion of the population with access to electricity). To provide universal electricity access to a larger population of 1.5 billion and increase electricity per capita consumption to keep up with GDP growth, there will be a need to expand installed capacity (Figure 2.15). The cost of additional generation capacity is estimated at $1,140 per kilowatt (Table 2.3), plus markups of 50 percent for transmission and 50 percent for distribution.[14] The average investment cost per kilowatt of capacity is calculated as the weighted average of unit costs for the different types of energy sources, using the shares of projected installed capacity in the power mix as the weights. At an overall unit cost of $2,280 per kilowatt including generation, transmission, and distribution costs, India will have to invest an aggregate of $469 billion from public and private sources to meet electricity demand, which on an annual basis is equivalent to 1 percent of GDP in 2030, including replacement costs.

---

[14] Based on interviews with experts from India's Ministry of Power and the Central Electricity Authority, the costs in transmission and distribution costs are assumed to add 50 percent each to investment costs in capacity.

Figure 2.15. Electric Power Consumption in India, 2019 and 2030

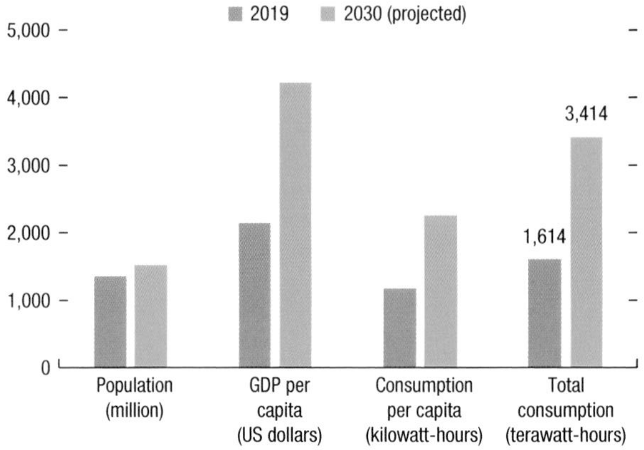

Source: IMF staff calculations.
Note: The electricity consumption forecast of 2,257 kilowatt-hours per capita by 2030 is higher than India's Central Electricity Authority forecast of 1,717–1,777 kilowatt-hours because of our assumption of higher income demand elasticity.

India has embarked on an ambitious program to shift its power mix toward renewable energy. According to the National Electricity Plan (Government of India, Ministry of Power, Central Electricity Authority 2018), renewable energy sources will increase from 23 percent of total installed capacity in 2019 to 44 percent in 2027 (Table 2.3 and Figure 2.16). The major renewable energy sources include solar and wind, both of which will require an investment in battery storage of 136 gigawatt-hours because of their asynchronous (that is, weather-dependent and time-dependent) nature. India is the third-largest CO_2 emitter, after China and the United States (Fleming 2019), thus the environmental advantages of increasing the share of renewables in the energy mix will be substantial at the global level.

Roads

India will have to invest a significant share of its GDP to improve rural roads access. Gradually raising rural access to 90 percent by 2030 will require about 2.4 million additional kilometers of all-weather roads—an increase of 39 percent in road length (Figure 2.17). While construction costs vary by road characteristics (that is, number of lanes and type of surface) and region (for example, a third-tier all-weather road in the north may cost twice as much to build than in the south), we estimate an average cost per kilometer of about $509,000 (Annex 2.4). Thus, extending the road network by 2.4 million kilometers will require an aggregate investment of $1.2 trillion by 2030, which on an annualized basis is equivalent to 2.7 percent of GDP in 2030, including depreciation.

The estimated cost is a lower bound. First, India's goal is to achieve 100 percent of households connected by all-weather roads under the Pradhan Mantri

TABLE 2.3.

Current and Target Installed Capacity Mix in India

Source	2017			2022			2027		
	Megawatts	Percent	Investment Cost per Kilowatt (US dollars)	Megawatts	Percent	Investment Cost per Kilowatt (US dollars)	Megawatts	Percent	Investment Cost per Kilowatt (US dollars)
Conventional									
Coal + lignite	193,001	59	868	217,302	45	1,056	238,150	38	1,285
Gas	25,329	8	514	25,735	5	625	25,735	4	760
Hydro	44,478	14	1,335	51,301	11	1,625	63,301	10	1,977
Nuclear	6,780	2	1,335	10,080	2	1,625	16,880	3	1,977
Subtotal	269,588	82		304,418	63		344,066	56	
Renewable									
Solar power	12,289	4	764	100,000	21	764	150,000	24	764
Wind power	32,280	10	833	60,000	13	833	100,000	16	833
Biomass	8,296	3	792	10,000	2	792	17,000	3	792
Small hydro power	4,380	1	868	5,000	1	1,056	8,000	1	1,285
Subtotal	57,244	18		175,000	37		275,000	44	
Total	326,832	100	905	479,418	100	1,011	619,066	100	1,140

Source: IMF staff calculations based on Government of India, Ministry of Power, Central Electricity Authority (2018).

Figure 2.16. Installed Capacity in India, 2019

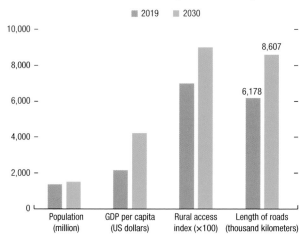

Source: Government of India, Ministry of Power, Central Electricity Authority 2018.
Note: Data correspond to October 2019.

Figure 2.17. Statistics of India's Main Roads, 2019 and Projections

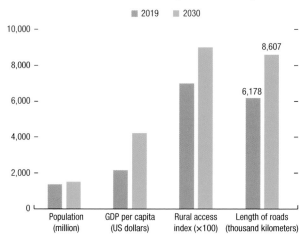

Source: IMF staff calculations based on Government of India, Ministry of Road Transport and Highways (2019).
Note: Projections assume rural access increases to 90 percent.

Gram Sadak Yojana program by 2030 (Government of India, NITI Aayog 2018): that is, the government's goal is more ambitious than the target of 90 percent of the rural population with access, assumed in the IMF's additional spending estimations for EMEs by Gaspar and others (2019). Second, our analysis does not account for the additional investments to make infrastructure resilient to climate change (for example, to more severe floods). The Asian Development Bank has estimated that climate-adjusted costs could add between 1.2 and 1.4 percent of GDP annually to their base estimations (Asian Development Bank 2017).

Land and financing reforms and strengthening subnational institutions are also essential to expedite road infrastructure development. Many infrastructure projects have stalled because of difficulties in land acquisition or the slow pace in obtaining government clearances (Rajan 2019). Addressing these weaknesses could include initiatives such as enhancing procurement practices (that is, increasing openness and transparency and limiting red tape) and improving risk allocation (that is, shifting some of the risks related to land acquisition to the government while maintaining the construction and commercial risks in the private sector). Subnational institutional and technical capacity requires build-up to cope with road network expansion, as about 90 percent of the road budget is administered at the subnational level. While central road agencies are well-equipped and staffed, many state and local level administrations need to increase institutional and technical capacity to accelerate road network development.

The private sector has emerged as a key player in the development of road infrastructure. Many private players are entering the business through the public-private partnership model. In addition, the National Infrastructure and Investment Fund was formed to facilitate international and domestic funding in infrastructure and attract equity capital from both international and domestic sources for infrastructure investments in commercially viable projects. Likewise, the latest budget for 2018–19 highlights the use of innovative monetizing structures such as Toll-Operate-Transfer (TOT) and Infrastructure Investment Trusts (InvITs) to monetize public sector assets, including roads.

RESULTS ON ADDITIONAL SPENDING REQUIRED TO MEET SDGS IN SOUTH ASIA

This section places the results on costs to meet the SDGs in India into a regional context. It compares them with the corresponding costs for other South Asian countries. The analysis for India presented in the previous section is based on an in-depth case study, involving extensive discussions with the authorities and based on the most up-to-date data. For other countries, the estimates follow the same methodology but have not been validated through discussions with and the latest data from the respective country counterparts. Given these estimates are preliminary in nature, Figure 2.18 presents the average for a group of countries including Afghanistan, Bangladesh, Bhutan, Nepal, Pakistan, and Sri Lanka.

Spending to meet the health and electricity goals in India are somewhat comparable to those in the rest of South Asia. The additional expenditures to perform well on the health SDG in India outstrip the corresponding costs associated with any of the other four selected SDGs. This estimate is quite similar to that of other South Asian countries, on average. India's additional spending to achieve a high

Figure 2.18. India: Spending in 2030 in Selected SDG Sectors
(Percent of 2030 GDP)

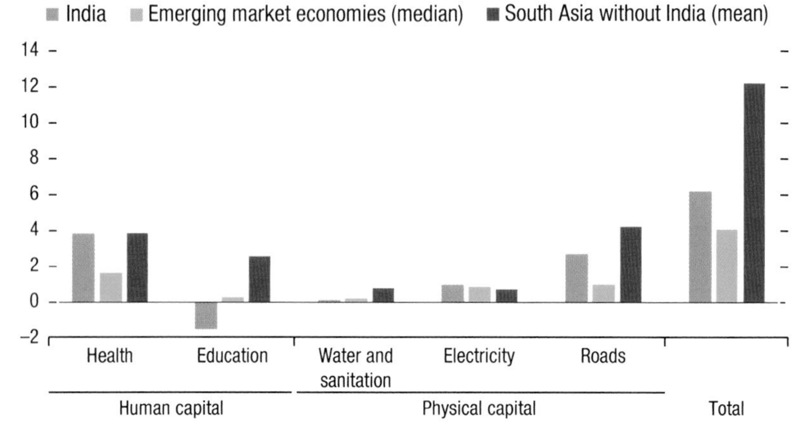

Sources: Gaspar and others 2019; and IMF staff calculations.
Note: South Asia without India consists of Afghanistan, Bangladesh, Bhutan, Nepal, Pakistan, and Sri Lanka. SDG = Sustainable Development Goal.

performance in the electricity sector is also proximate to (and only somewhat higher than) the average across South Asia.

Spending needed for the education, water and sanitation, and roads SDGs are distinctly lower in India than elsewhere in South Asia. On average, South Asian countries' additional costs to meet the education SDG is about 2 percent of GDP, with some countries facing additional costs of more than three times this average. This is higher than for India—which has a lower spending requirement in terms of GDP in 2030 than its current spending—and for the average emerging economy. Overall, additional spending in water and sanitation is relatively low when compared with the spending to meet most other selected goals. Additional spending on water and sanitation is also lower in India and South Asian countries relative to emerging economies. In contrast, the South Asian region will need to make the substantial investments in road infrastructure. The average annual additional spending in the region for roads is about 4.3 percent of GDP, 1.6 percent higher than the additional annual spending required to meet the road SDG estimated for India and more than four times that for emerging economies.

CONCLUSIONS

We estimate that making substantial progress in critical SDG sectors in India would require additional annual spending of about 6.2 percentage points of GDP in 2030. While this is significant in size, it appears moderate when compared with the estimated additional cost in other South Asian countries of about 11.3 percent of GDP. On the other hand, however, additional annual spending in India is above that of the median emerging economy, at about 4 percentage points of GDP (Figure 2.18) as estimated by Gaspar and others (2019).

The estimates assume that India and South Asian countries would be able to combine different inputs efficiently to deliver across the analyzed sectors. This would require important reforms. For example, in education, expanding enrollment in preprimary and tertiary levels as well as reducing class sizes would require increasing the number of qualified teachers. In health, in addition to raising the number of qualified health care workers, it is critical to address the financial vulnerability to health care shocks. In infrastructure, raising institutional and technical capacity remains key, particularly in largely rural states. Broader public financial management reforms are also called for to strengthen the efficiency of spending. For example, while some states have begun to produce medium-term fiscal projections as part of the budget, the central government and all states could do so too, as well as strengthen the performance-orientation of budgeting and develop more forward-looking fiscal strategies.

Because the analysis for this chapter was undertaken before the COVID-19 pandemic, it does not incorporate its potential effect on the spending needed to reach the SDGs. Evidence is already mounting that COVID-19 will have ripple effects for years to come in economies throughout the world, including in South Asia, and, as such, it will also have implications for the SDG agenda. For the first time in more than 20 years, 2020 had an annual rise in the extreme poverty rate, with an estimated additional 119 to 124 million people pushed into poverty—60 percent of whom are in southern Asia (UN 2021). Countries could see a reduction in the available fiscal space to finance the SDGs because of the higher debt, a decline in revenues as economic activity stalls, and higher expenditures to fight the virus and its economic and social consequences, making the achievement of the SDGs in human capital development and infrastructure more challenging (IMF 2021).

Cost estimates for reaching the SDGs may increase because of progress being set back by the pandemic. For instance, school closures are likely to result in children falling behind in learning (especially since homeschooling cannot be done effectively in particular by households lacking skills, means, or time). In India, for example, an estimated 320 million children have been affected by pandemic-induced school closures (Sahni 2020). This will increase the costs to achieve the education SDG. Health personnel and supplies to fight the virus could be diverted from other health needs, and demand for health services could decline when the population fears the risk of contagion in medical facilities. Both factors may compromise progress on critical SDG health indicators. A study on 14 countries, among which six are in South Asia, found that such resource diversion has already shown detrimental effects on the maternal mortality rate (De Beni and Maurizio 2020). Electricity consumption could face a temporary sharp dip because of dropping demand emanating from the lockdowns and cascading effects on stalled economic activity. And the significant resource needs for the emergency health response to the pandemic, for social assistance, and for support to firms, could be expected to temporarily hold back public investment, including in road infrastructure.

On the other hand, emergency financing, debt relief, and budget reallocations that are boosting health-related spending to fight the pandemic, if sustained over time, could accelerate the achievement of some SDG targets. Increases in health spending may improve indicators concerning access to vaccines, health personnel, and mitigating global health risks. Similarly, efforts to contain the virus may lead to advancing progress on the SDG related to water and sanitation by triggering increases in the proportion of the population using safely managed sanitation services, including handwashing facilities with soap and water (WHO 2020).

Future research could usefully update the analysis to account for the pandemic, drawing on additional collected data from 2020 onward on key cost drivers, inputs, and spending in the five sectors and other demographic and economic variables.

The analysis can be expanded in additional ways. Given the cooperative federal structure and the diversity across states and union territories, it would be insightful to review the challenges in achieving the SDGs at the subnational level. To this end, the authorities have taken important steps toward the localization of SDG efforts, including promoting convergent implementation structures and deploying regional monitoring systems. This chapter's analysis discussed qualitatively what reforms may be needed for India to achieve higher levels of efficiency in spending that underlies the costing method. Further work could estimate the effect on spending needs of relaxing assumptions on technical efficiency in spending, and quantify the increases in efficiency commensurate with the stated spending needs to reach the SDGs.

METHODOLOGY AND DATA, BY SECTOR

Annex 2.1. Health Care

Health expenditures (as a percent of GDP), E, can be expressed as an identity:[15]

$$E = 10w\frac{D + 0.5M}{100 - E_{other}} \, ,$$

where w refers to doctors' annual wages as a ratio to GDP per capita, D and M are the numbers of doctors and other medical personnel, respectively, per 1,000 population, and E_{other} pertains to all spending besides the health care workers' wage bill as a percent of total expenditures in education. The number 0.5 in the equation reflects an assumption that wages of other health service providers are about half that of doctors, based on cross-country data[16] on wages of specialists, general practitioners, and nurses (this assumption is also used in Gaspar and others 2019). The rationale behind this equation is that total expenditures are a function of the health service providers wage bill (that is, wages times the supply of personnel) divided by the share of the wage bill in total spending.

The spending needed in 2030 by India to perform well in the health SDG are derived as the level of expenditures that India would incur in light of its projected demographics (in particular, the projected population share of infants and elderly adults) in 2030 and today's levels for the health cost drivers observed in the high-performing countries in the health sector among India's peers (which include emerging markets, as noted in the main text). These cost drivers include doctors' wages, the number of doctors relative to the population size, the number of other medical personnel relative to the population size, and health spending other than the health care workers' wage bill (as a share of total health spending). The approach of matching India's 2030 cost drivers to today's level of the high performers is seen in the corresponding columns of Table 2.1. Annex Table 2.1.1 presents the data sources and computation of demographic factors and cost drivers for India today (latest available are from 2016 to 2017).

---

[15] This is a rearrangement of the equation in Gaspar and others (2019, page 27).

[16] Given limited data availability, this estimate is based on OECD data (OECD 2021), and reflects the average ratio across countries from 2000 to 2020 between specialists' and nurses' wages (0.46) and between general practitioners' and nurses' wages (0.58). The average of these two ratios is 0.52. On the one hand, the two ratios are likely to be lower for lower-income countries, but on the other hand there are usually many more general practitioners than specialists, biasing the simple average of the two ratios upward. The two biases are expected to at least partially cancel each other out.

ANNEX TABLE 2.1.1.

Computation and Data Sources for Variables Used in Health SDG Additional Spending Estimation in India

Variable	Computation or Data Source
D	0.9 * 1000 * number_of_doctors / population
	Assumption that only 90 percent of registered doctors are practicing because of emigration, incapacity, or other factors
No. of doctors	Government of India, Ministry of Health and Family Welfare 2018
Population	Population in 2017 from UN (2019)
M	1000 * (dentists + nurses + Ayush_practitioners) / population
No. of registered dentists	Government of India, Ministry of Health and Family Welfare 2018
Ayush registered practitioners	Government of India, Ministry of Health and Family Welfare 2018
Registered nurses	ANM + RN&RM + LHV
	Government of India, Ministry of Health and Family Welfare 2018
E_{other}	[total_spending − (compensation_of_employees_non_administrative + wage_bill_component_of_current_transfers_to_local_bodies_non_admin)] / total_spending
	Ministry of Statistics and Program Implementation 2019

Note: ANM = auxiliary nurse midwife; LHV = lady health visitor; RM = registered midwife; RN = registered nurse; SDG = Sustainable Development Goal.

Annex 2.2. Education

Education expenditures (as a percent of GDP), E, can be expressed as an identity:

$$E = \frac{w}{STR} e \frac{SAP}{100 - E_{other}} \ ,$$

where w refers to teachers' annual wages as a ratio to GDP per capita, STR is the student–teacher ratio, e signifies the enrollment rate (that is, the number of students as a percentage of the student-age population), SAP indicates the student-age population as a percent of total population, and E_{other} pertains to all education spending besides the teacher wage bill as a percent of total expenditures in education. Total education expenditure is therefore a function of the teachers' wage bill (that is, wages times the supply of teachers) divided by the share of the wage bill in total education spending. The supply of teachers, in turn, is derived as the number of students (enrollment rate times the student-age population) divided by the student–teacher ratio.

The spending needed in 2030 in India to perform well in the education SDG derived taking into account India's projected demographics (student-age population) in 2030 and today's levels of the education cost drivers of the high-performing countries among India's peers. These cost drivers include teachers' wages, the student–teacher ratio, the enrollment rate, and education spending other than the teacher wage bill as a share of total education spending. The approach of matching India's 2030 cost drivers to today's level of the high performers is shown in the corresponding columns of Table 2.2. Annex Table 2.2.1 gives the data sources and computation of demographic factors and cost drivers (latest available are for 2017–18).

ANNEX TABLE 2.2.1.

Computation and Data Sources for Variables Used in the Education SDG Additional Spending Estimation in India

Variable	Computation or Data Source
STR	number_of_students / number_of_teachers
No. of students	pre_primary_students + school_education_students + tertiary_students
No. of teachers	pre_primary_teachers + school_education_teachers + tertiary_teachers
Preprimary students	attendance_rate_of_population_aged_3to5 * population_aged_3to5
School education students	Received from authorities
Tertiary students	Received from authorities
Attendance rate of population ages 3–5 years	Ministry of Statistics and Program Implementation 2019; National Statistics Office 2019
Population ages 3–5 years	UN 2019
Preprimary teachers	Pre-primary_students / 25;
	25 is the student–teacher ratio provided verbally by authorities as a rough estimate, in the absence of data
School education teachers	Received from authorities
Tertiary-level teachers	Received from authorities

(Annex Table 2.2.1 continues on the next page)

Computation and Data Sources for Variables Used in the Education SDG Additional Spending Estimation in India (Continued)

Variable	Computation or Data Source
E_{other}	[total_spending − (compensation_of_employees_non_administrative + wage_bill_component_of_current_transfers_to_local_bodies_non_ admin)] / total_spending
	Ministry of Statistics and Program Implementation 2019
Wage bill component of current transfers to local bodies, nonadministrative, that is, for direct service delivery (Rs.)	current_transfers_to_local_bodies_non_administrative * compensation_of_employees_non_admin / (total_spending_non_ admin − current_transfers_to_local_bodies_non_admin)
	Ministry of Statistics and Program Implementation 2019
SAP	population_aged_3to23 / total_population
Population ages 3–23 years	UN 2019
Total population	Population in 2018 from UN (2019)
e	number_of_students / population_aged_3to23
E	In education:
	(public_spending + private_spending) / GDP
Public spending (Rs.)	total_spending
	Ministry of Statistics and Program Implementation 2019
Private spending (Rs.)	pre_primary + primary + upper_primary_middle + secondary + higher_ secondary + post_higher_secondary
Private education spending, by level (Rs.)	By level:
	out_of_pocket_spending_per_student * number_of_students
Out-of-pocket spending per student, by level (Rs.)	NSO 2019
No. of public school students, by level	By level:
	number_of_students * %_of_students_attending_public_school
No. of private aided school students, by level	By level:
	number_of_students * %_of_students_attending_private_aided_school
No. of private unaided school students, by level	By level:
	number_of_students − number_of_public_school_students − number_ of_private_aided_school_students
Students attending public, private aided, private unaided school (%)	NSO 2019
Total no. of students, by level	gross_enrollment * population_of_corresponding_age_group
Population of corresponding age group	UN 2019
Gross enrollment rate, by level (as %)	NSO 2019
w	Level of teacher wages (as ratio of GDP per capita) that satisfies

$$E = \frac{w}{STR} e \frac{SAP}{100 - E_{other}}$$

Source: IMF authors.

Note: Rs. = rupees; SAP = student-age population; SDG = Sustainable Development Goal; STR = student–teacher ratio.

Annex 2.3. Water and Sanitation

The percentage of served population in rural and urban areas and the cost per capita of providing the service is obtained from different sources and updated data, when available, are provided by government authorities. Annex Table 2.3.1 reports the reviewed statistics of coverage by type of water and sanitation service. The target population unserved in 2030 is extrapolated from the percentage of rural and urban population unserved in 2019, the additional population growth between 2019 and 2030, and the migration from rural to urban areas. This implies, ceteris paribus, an improvement in the coverage ratios by simple migration from unserved rural to served urban areas.

ANNEX TABLE 2.3.1.

Statistics of Coverage, by Type of Water and Sanitation Service in India

	Rural		Urban	
	Coverage (Percent)	Cost Per Capita (US Dollars)	Coverage (Percent)	Cost Per Capita (US Dollars)
End open defecation[1]	100.0	—	100.0	—
Basic water[2]	89.5	15.4	100.0	55.6
Basic sanitation[3]	97.4	37.4	98.5	145.0
Basic hygiene[4]	70.7	21.6	84.8	8.0
Safely managed water[5]	56.1	36.1	81.1	249.6
Safely managed sanitation[6]	61.1	168.5	35.1	122.3

Source: IMF staff calculations using data from UN (2021); World Bank (2020); Government of India, Ministry of Jal Shakti (2019); Government of India, Ministry of Statistics and Program Implementation (2018); and interviews with NITI Aayog officials.

Note: Statistics used for the computation of the Sustainable Development Goal (SDG) additional spending in water and sanitation.

[1] Ending open defecation refers to access to services that remove the need for open defecation—improved or unimproved toilet facility (for example, pit latrines without a slab/platform, hanging latrines, bucket latrines). NITI Aayog considers 100 percent coverage based on the provision of 114 million latrines.

[2] Basic water service is the access to an improved water source within 30 minutes round trip. NITI Aayog considers access to a river, stream, or pond as "basic water."

[3] Basic sanitation service is the access to improved sanitation facilities such as flush toilets or latrines with a slab on household premises.

[4] Basic hygiene service refers to the presence of handwashing stations in the household with soap and water. The actual practice of handwashing after defecation (with soap and water) is lower: 66.8 percent of rural population and 88.3 percent of urban population.

[5] Safely managed water service is the access to an improved water source on household premises. According to NITI Aayog, an urban population of 72.5 million individuals are envisaged to be provided with safely managed water by the government of India.

[6] Safely managed sanitation service is the access to improved sanitation facility on household premises where excreta are safely disposed of in situ or treated off-site. According to the Ministry of Drinking Water and Sanitation, there is no drainage (no formal system of carrying off household wastewater and liquid waste) reported for 38.9 percent of the rural population and 8 percent of the urban population. According to the Ministry of Housing and Urban Affairs and NITI Aayog, 133.5 million people are not covered in small towns (below class 1) and 106.9 million people are not covered in class 1 cities.

Because the goal in water and sanitation is full coverage in each service category (that is, basic water, sanitation and hygiene, safely managed water, and sanitation provision), the cost per type of service and population strata is computed as the product of the population unserved times the cost per capita of providing the service by type of service and population strata.

To avoid double counting and since the services are incremental (that is, populations with safely managed sanitation have access to more basic services such as water and latrines), we compute the total population unserved as the maximum of rural population unserved by type of service plus the maximum of urban population unserved by type of service. Following the WASH methodology developed by the World Bank (Hutton and Varughese 2016), the total cost was calculated as the full cost of providing safely managed water and sanitation services plus half of the cost of providing the basic water and sanitation.

Annex 2.4. Roads

The cost per kilometer by type of road—highway, local, and rural—is taken from the Government of India, Ministry of Road Transport and Highways' (2018b) normative costs. The average cost of road construction was estimated at $509,000 per kilometer. This assumes that future roads are going to follow the same proportion as currently observed between share of highways, local (district, urban, and project) roads, and rural roads as a percent of total roads from the Government of India, Ministry of Road Transport and Highways (2019). Annex Table 2.4.1 provides the input data used for the estimation of the average cost per km of road.

The goal in roads for EMEs is to increase the Rural Access Index (RAI; that is, the share of the population that has access to a road within two kilometers) to at least 90 percent by 2030. Keeping roads constant, the migration from rural to urban areas—assuming a general migration pattern from not connected rural areas to connected rural areas and urban areas—mechanically increases the RAI. We account for population migration to calculate the migration-adjusted RAI in 2030 using the following equation:

$$RAI_{2030}^{migration-adjusted} = 1 - \frac{\overbrace{Rural_{2019} \times (1 - RAI_{2019}^{observed})}^{\text{current rural population not connected}} - \overbrace{(Rural_{2019} - Rural_{2030})}^{\text{migration from rural to urban}}}{\underbrace{Rural_{2030}}_{\text{migration-adjusted rural population witout access to roads}}},$$

where *Rural* is the actual share of rural population in 2019 and projected share of rural population in 2030. Consequently, India's RAI in 2019 increases from 70 to 77 when adjusted for migration dynamics.

We estimate the additional road density needed to increase in the RAI from its current level in India to at least 90 percent by 2030 by estimating the following ordinary least squares regression specification:

$$lg\_cia\_density = \alpha + \beta_1 \times lggdp\_cap + \beta_2 \times lgpop\_density + \beta_3 \times RAI$$
$$+ \beta_4 \times agg\_gdp + \beta_5 \times manu\_gdp + \beta_6 \times urban + \varepsilon,$$

where *lg_cia_density*, *lggdp_cap*, and *lgpop_density* are the natural logarithms of road density, GDP per capita, and population density, respectively, RAI is the Rural Access Index, *agg_gdp* is the aggregated GDP, *manu_gdp* is the ratio of manufacturing to GDP, urban is the share of the urban population in total population, α is a constant, and ε is the error term. The regression is restricted to low-income and developing economies, and EMEs with medium-range road density (that is, for comparability it does not incorporate advanced economies, or countries with too low or too high road density). This approach assumes away contemporaneous reverse causality: that is, road density affects income per capita and population density with a substantial lag (Fay and Yepes 2003).

The additional road length needed to meet the SDG goal is estimated at 2.4 million kilometers. The total cost of the additional road network is computed by multiplying the additional kilometers by the unit cost of constructing 1 kilometer at $509,181 (Annex Table 2.4.1) and accounting for a 5 percent annual depreciation rate.

ANNEX TABLE 2.4.1.

Cost of Road Construction in India

Type	Share of Roads (Percent)	Cost per Kilometer (Indian Rupees, in Crores)	Cost per Kilometer[1] (US dollars)	Reference
National and state highways	4.91	10.87	1,509,722	Greenfield alignment 8-lane, 1.5 meters
District, urban, and project roads	24.44	4.26	591,667	Greenfield alignment 2-lane, 1.5 meters
Rural roads (including Jawahar Rozgar Yojana)	70.65	2.96	411,111	Service road with flexible pavement (10-meter carriageway)
Weighted average			509,181	

Source: IMF staff calculations based on data from the Government of India, Ministry of Road Transport and Highways (2018b).
[1] Costs were converted at a rate of 72 Indian rupees to 1 US dollar.

REFERENCES

Asian Development Bank. 2017. "Meeting Asia's Infrastructure Needs." Asian Development Bank, Manila, Philippines.

Barroy, Helene, Moritz Piatti, Fabrice Sergent, Elina Dale, Sheila O'Dougherty, Gemini Mtei, Grace Kabaniha, and Jason Lakin. 2019. "Let Managers Manage: A Health Service Provider's Perspective on Public Financial Management." World Bank, Washington, DC.

Brollo, Fernanda, and Emine Hanedar. 2021. "Pakistan: Spending Needs for Reaching Sustainable Development Goals (SDGs)." IMF Working Paper 2021/108, International Monetary Fund, Washington, DC.

De Beni, Davide, and Federica Maurizio. 2020. "Coronavirus Is Leaving Pregnant Women with Tough Choices and Bleaker Outcomes." Project Syndicate and World Economic Forum COVID Action Platform.

Fay, Marianne, and Tito Yepes. 2003. "Investing in Infrastructure: What Is Needed from 2000 to 2010?" World Bank, Washington, DC.

Fleming, Sean. 2019. "Chart of the Day: These Countries Create Most of the World's CO_2 Emissions." World Economic Forum, June 7.

Food and Agriculture Organization. 2021. "The State of Food Security and Nutrition in the World 2021." Food and Agriculture Organization, Rome, Italy.

Garcia-Escribano, Mercedes, and Candice Yue Liu. 2017. "Expenditure Assessment Tool (EAT)." Technical Notes and Manuals 17/06, International Monetary Fund, Washington, DC.

Gaspar, Vitor, David Amaglobeli, Mercedes Garcia-Escribano, Delphine Prady, and Mauricio Soto. 2019. "Fiscal Policy and Development: Human, Social, and Physical Investment for the SDGs." IMF Staff Discussion Note 19/03, International Monetary Fund, Washington, DC.

Goretti, Manuela, Daisaku Kihara, Ranil Salgado, and Anne-Marie Gulde-Wolf. 2019. "Is South Asia Ready for Take Off? A Sustainable and Inclusive Growth Agenda." IMF Departmental Paper 19/18, International Monetary Fund, Washington, DC.

Government of India, Ministry of Jal Shakti. 2019. "ODF-Plus Dashboard."

Government of India, Ministry of Health and Family Welfare, Central Bureau of Health Intelligence. 2018. "National Health Profile." Issue No. 13, New Delhi, India.

Government of India, Ministry of Finance. 2019. "Economic Survey 2018–19." Vol. I, New Delhi, India.

Government of India, Ministry of Power, Central Electricity Authority. 2018. "National Electricity Plan—Generation." Vol. I (January), New Delhi, India.

Government of India, Ministry of Road Transport and Highways. 2018a. "Annual Report 2018–19." New Delhi, India.

Government of India, Ministry of Road Transport and Highways. 2018b. "Note on Normative Costs: No. RW/NH-24036/27/2010-PPP." April 25, New Delhi, India.

Government of India, Ministry of Road Transport and Highways. 2019. "Basic Road Statistics of India (2016–17)." New Delhi, India.

Government of India, Ministry of Statistics and Program Implementation. 2018. "Drinking Water, Sanitation, Hygiene and Housing Condition in India." NSS 76th Round, July 2018 – December 2018, National Statistics Office.

Government of India, NITI Aayog. 2017. "Voluntary National Review Report on the Implementation of Sustainable Development Goals." New Delhi, India.

Government of India, NITI Aayog. 2018. "SDG India Index Baseline Report." New Delhi, India.

Government of India, NITI Aayog. 2020. "India VNR 2020: Decade of Action Taking SDGs from Global to Local." New Delhi, India.

Government of India, NITI Aayog. 2021. "SDG India Index and Dashboard 2020–21: Partnerships in the Decade of Action." New Delhi, India.

Hutton, Guy, and Mili Varughese. 2016. "The Costs of Meeting the 2030 Sustainable Development Goal Targets on Drinking Water Sanitation, and Hygiene." The World Bank Group, Washington, DC.

International Monetary Fund (IMF). 2021. "A Fair Shot." *Fiscal Monitor*. International Monetary Fund, Washington, DC, April.

Jha, Akshaya, Louis Preonas, and Fiona Burling. 2021. "Blackouts in the Developing World: The Role of Wholesale Electricity Markets." NBER Working Paper 29610 National Bureau of Economic Research, Cambridge, MA.

Mahler, Daniel G., Nishant Yonzan, Christoph Lakner, R. Andres C. Aguilar, and Haoyu Wu. 2021. "Updated Estimates of the Impact of COVID-19 on Global Poverty: Turning the Corner on the Pandemic in 2021?" Data Blog, World Bank, Washington, DC.

Mikou, Mehdi, Julie Rozenberg, Elco Koks, Charles Fox, and Tatiana Peralta Quiros. 2019. "Assessing Rural Accessibility and Rural Roads Investment Needs Using Open Source Data." Policy Research Working Paper 8746, World Bank, Washington, DC.

Ministry of Statistics and Program Implementation. 2019. "National Accounts Statistics." National Statistics Office, Government of India.

Muralidharan, Karthik, Jishnu Das, Alaka Holla, and Aakash Mohpal. 2017. "The Fiscal Cost of Weak Governance: Evidence from Teacher Absence in India." *Journal of Public Economics* 145: 116–35.

National Statistics Office (NSO). 2019. "Key Indicators of Household Social Consumption on Education in India." NSO 75th Round, Ministry of Statistics and Program Implementation, New Delhi, India.

Organisation for Economic Cooperation and Development (OECD). 2021. Health Care Resources: Remuneration of Health Professionals. OECD.Stat.

Prady, Delphine, and Mouhamadou Sy. 2019. "The Spending Challenge for Reaching the SDGs in Sub-Saharan Africa: Lessons Learned from Benin and Rwanda." Working Paper 19/270, International Monetary Fund, Washington, DC.

Rajan, Raghuram. 2019. "How to Fix the Economy." *India Today*, December 16.

Road Traffic Technology. 2014. "The World's Biggest Road Networks." Global Data, January 12.

Sachs, Jeffrey, Guido Schmidt-Traub, Christian Kroll, Guillaume Lafortune, and Grayson Fuller. 2019. "Sustainable Development Report 2019." Bertelsmann Stiftung and Sustainable Development Solutions Network, New York.

Sahni, Urvashi. 2020. "COVID-19 in India: Education Disrupted and Lessons Learned." Education Plus Development, Brookings Institution, Washington, DC.

Soto, Mauricio, Mariano Moszoro, and Julieth Pico. 2020. "Nigeria: Additional Spending Toward Sustainable Development Goals." IMF Country Report 2020/177, International Monetary Fund, Washington, DC.

United Nations (UN). 2019. "World Population Prospects." Population Division, Department of Economic and Social Affairs.

United Nations (UN). 2021. "Sustainable Development Goals Report 2021." United Nations Department of Economic and Social Affairs.

World Bank. 2020. "World Development Indicators." World Bank Group, Washington, DC.

World Economic Forum. 2019. "Global Competitiveness Report 2019." World Economic Forum, Geneva, Switzerland.

World Health Organization (WHO). 2020. "Water, Sanitation, Hygiene and Waste Management for the COVID-19 Virus." Technical Brief, World Health Organization, Geneva, Switzerland.

CHAPTER 3

Labor Market Reforms for Job-Rich Growth Recoveries in South Asia

Ruchir Agarwal, Andrew Hodge, Racha Moussa, Piyaporn Sodsriwiboon, and Jarkko Turunen

South Asian labor markets have been hit hard by the COVID-19 pandemic. Generating high quality job growth, including expansion of the formal, nonagricultural economy to generate productive, well-paying jobs for their young, growing populations should be a priority to support job-rich recoveries. Current labor market regulations and institutions are largely geared toward protecting jobs in the formal sector, providing little protection to some workers, including those in the informal sector, from shocks such as the COVID-19 pandemic. Empirical evidence presented in this chapter shows that loosening employment protection legislation could lead to an increase in total employment over time, as well as an increase in the share of female employment and lower informality. The chapter also illustrates the need for labor market reforms to increase labor supply. While labor market reforms need to be country specific, there is a strong case for reforms that shift focus toward protecting workers as opposed to jobs and increasing female labor force participation.

INTRODUCTION

South Asian labor markets have been hit hard by the COVID-19 pandemic. The pandemic has hit the mostly informal labor markets hard, with social protection schemes lacking sufficient coverage to be an effective safety net for some. Self-employed workers, employees of small- and medium-sized enterprises, and migrant workers in the informal sector have been badly affected, along with sectors with a relatively high share of female employment, such as hospitality, tourism, and domestic work (see Box 3.1).

South Asian economies need a job-rich recovery from the pandemic to generate productive, well-paying jobs for their young, growing populations. The effect of the pandemic adds to the already-pressing need for job creation in the formal

Shihui Liu provided excellent research assistance. The review of labor market institutions benefited from inputs from the Asia and Pacific Department country teams on Bangladesh, Bhutan, India, Maldives, Nepal, and Sri Lanka. The authors thank participants of the February 2020 workshop in New Delhi for comments.

Box 3.1. COVID-19's Effect on Labor Markets and Policy Responses

South Asian labor markets have been severely affected by COVID-19, making informal workers especially vulnerable. Containment measures including lockdowns and international travel bans disrupted economic activity significantly in all South Asian countries. As in other developing countries with limited telework opportunities and vulnerable informal workers, this resulted in large spikes in unemployment and, in particular for informal sector and migrant workers, loss of livelihoods and displacement (ILO 2020b). For example, in India the strict lockdown imposed in March 2020 left scores of Indian migrant workers without jobs and forced to travel across the country to reach their villages of origin (Bharali, Kumar, and Sakthivel 2020). In Sri Lanka, the ban on international flight arrivals caused tourist arrivals to fall to zero, affecting workers in this critical export industry. The slowdown in the global economy also reduced demand for South Asia's exports, leading to job losses. In Bangladesh, it is estimated that around one quarter of the country's four million garment manufacturing workers had been dismissed or furloughed by March 2020 because of the effect of the pandemic on demand for garment exports (Anner 2020). Overall, ILO estimates indicate that working hours in South Asia fell by approximately 18 percent in 2020 Q2 (year-over-year), compared with a 10 percent decline in East Asia and 14 percent globally (ILO 2020b). Postings on online job matching websites in Bangladesh and Sri Lanka also fell dramatically in April 2020 (Hayashi and Matsuda 2020). The ILO indicates that the sectors most affected by lockdowns and other containment measures include accommodation and food services, particularly relevant for the tourism sector, especially in Maldives and Sri Lanka, and manufacturing, which is of major importance in several economies, including Bangladesh. Wholesale and retail trade are also severely affected. The second COVID-19 wave, which started in March 2021 in India and several South Asian countries, resulted in renewed increases in unemployment and falls in labor force participation, with the potential to contribute to labor market scarring effects that may persist well beyond the pandemic. Scarring effects are made worse also by loss in education and on-the-job training, thus reducing human capital accumulation and the contribution of labor to future potential growth.

Additional protection introduced for workers affected by COVID-19 was low by international standards. Fiscal stimulus measures introduced in every South Asian country, including cash transfers to poor households, have been no more than one percent of GDP, compared with more than two percent of GDP on average in other emerging market and developing economies and five percent of GDP on average in advanced economies (ILO 2020b). This partly reflects limited fiscal space for stimulus in some South Asian countries, particularly India, Maldives, and Sri Lanka. The Indian government announced that the Employees' State Insurance scheme, established in 2018 as a contributory health insurance scheme for formal sector workers, would be used to provide some unemployment insurance to current participants, extending the scheme by one year (to the end of June 2021) and increasing the benefit to 50 percent of the average wage. Around one million workers were reported to be eligible for the scheme when it was established in 2018. Employees in the formal sector will also be able to make withdrawals from their Employees' Provident Fund Organization accounts, which they do not need to refund.

A government stimulus package, included wage support to low-wage workers (in some cases for those still working, and in other cases by easing the criteria for receiving benefits in the event of job loss), increased funds for the rural employment scheme (MNREGA) and provided both cash and in-kind transfers to vulnerable groups, including those working in the informal sectors and migrant workers. State governments also provided support to workers, such as Kerala, which provided food supplies to all households and cash transfers (ILO 2020c). Bangladesh announced Tk 7.6 billion (0.03 percent

(Box 3.1 continues on the next page)

> ### Box 3.1. COVID-19's Effect on Labor Markets and Policy Responses *(continued)*
>
> of GDP) in government support for those who lost jobs as a result of the pandemic. In Sri Lanka, around 0.4 percent of GDP in cash transfers were disbursed to low income groups in March and April 2020, including a $28 per month cash allowance to displaced workers.
>
> Some extraordinary measures were taken in the area of employment protection, offset by lower labor taxes. All employers in the formal sector were directed by the Indian Ministry of Labor not to dismiss their employees or reduce wages in response to the pandemic. Offsetting this, the Indian government would make all contributions to the Employee Provident Fund Organization for three months. Some Indian states also temporarily relaxed labor laws in response to the pandemic (see Box 3.2).

sector, as South Asia's working-age population continues to grow (Goretti, Kihara, and Salgado 2019). The average age in all South Asian countries except Sri Lanka is 25–30 years, below other large emerging market economies including Brazil, Indonesia, and Turkey (CIA World Factbook).[1] The fertility rate in most South Asian countries is approximately 1.9–2.25 live births per female, in line with the average in South East Asian countries, but above the rate in China (1.7), Japan (1.4) and the average in North America (1.75) and Europe (1.6) (United Nations 2019). Estimates by the United Nations suggest that Bangladesh, Bhutan, India, and Nepal will experience a demographic dividend in the coming decades as the working-age population expands (Figure 3.1), whereas Sri Lanka's population will begin to age.

Figure 3.1. UN Estimates on Working-Age Population

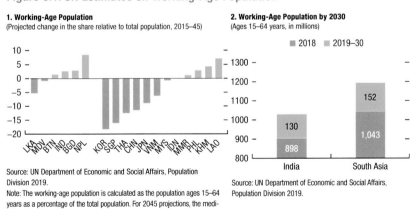

1. Working-Age Population
(Projected change in the share relative to total population, 2015–45)

2. Working-Age Population by 2030
(Ages 15–64 years, in millions)

Source: UN Department of Economic and Social Affairs, Population Division 2019.
Note: The working-age population is calculated as the population ages 15–64 years as a percentage of the total population. For 2045 projections, the medium fertility variant is used. Data labels in the figure use International Organization for Standardization (ISO) country codes.

Source: UN Department of Economic and Social Affairs, Population Division 2019.

---

[1] The share of the working-age population (15–64 years) is 68 percent on average across the region, compared with 65 percent in Organisation for Economic Co-operation and Development (OECD) countries.

High-quality job growth will require an expansion of the formal, nonagricultural economy, which remains small. The informal economy in South Asia is large and accounts for more than 80 percent of employment in Bangladesh and India, more than in East Asian countries and other emerging market economies (Figure 3.2). This reflects in part the still-large share of agriculture in the South Asian economy, much of which is small scale and relatively unproductive: agriculture accounts for around 49 percent of employment in India but only 15 percent of gross value added (NITI Aayog 2018; Figure 3.2). Furthermore, jobs in the informal sector are less secure, often involving self-employment or employment in small- and medium-sized enterprises, without coverage by social assistance and social insurance schemes (NITI Aayog 2018). For example, around half of India's labor force was self-employed in 2016 (Dasgupta and Kar 2018). Informal workers without access to social protection schemes have been particularly vulnerable to the economic effect of COVID-19, including that on self-employed workers. Expanding the formal sector will require both providing continued structural change toward services and manufacturing and increasing the share of formal employment in these sectors.

Low rates of female labor force participation and high youth unemployment also suggest significant barriers to formal employment. Female labor force participation in South Asia is significantly below East Asian peers and other middle-income countries (Figure 3.3), suggesting that there are barriers preventing women from entering the labor market. Women have been particularly vulnerable to the economic impact of COVID-19, accounting for a significant share of employment in hard hit sectors, such as accommodation and hospitality, including tourism, as well as domestic work (ILO 2020b). Youth unemployment is also high, particularly among women in Bangladesh, India, and Sri Lanka. The share of the population ages 15–24 years that are not in education, training, or employment is also significantly above East Asian countries. This correlates with relatively low levels of human capital in South Asia compared with peers, reflected in low student test scores among school students and relatively poor performance in other measures of education quality (World Bank 2018). This suggests that young workers may lack the skills to secure formal sector jobs.

In this chapter, we discuss South Asia's labor market institutions and illustrate potential gains from labor market reform. In the "Need for Jobs" section, we present quantitative estimates of required job growth, given the projected increase in the working-age population. In the "South Asia's Labor Market Institutions" section, we illustrate the main features of labor market institutions, including (1) how wages and conditions are set (collective bargaining rights, restrictions on fixed term contracts, minimum wages); (2) employment protection (including severance payments); (3) social protection (unemployment insurance, pensions); (4) labor taxes (including social security contributions); and (5) support and protection for women in the labor market (including maternity leave entitlements).[2] In the "EPL Reforms

---

[2] A more comprehensive discussion of social protection in South Asia is included in Chapter 4.

Figure 3.2.

1. Informal Employment
(Percent of total employment, latest available)

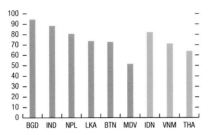

Sources: International Labour Organization and Labor Force
Survey Report 2015.
Note: Data labels in the figure use International Organization for
Standardization (ISO) country codes.

2. Employment, by Sector
(Percent, latest available)

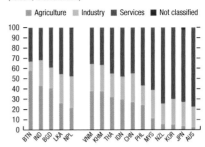

Sources: International Labour Organization and Labor Force Survey
Report 2015.
Note: Data labels in the figure use International Organization for
Standardization (ISO) country codes.

3. Employment and Productivity of Agriculture

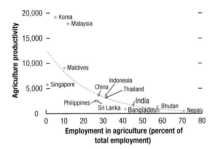

Source: World Bank's World Development Indicators.

**4. Own Account Workers and Contributing Family
Workers**
(Percent of total employment, 2018)

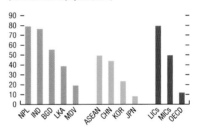

Sources: World Bank Development Indicators and International
Labour Organization.
Note: Data labels in the figure use International Organization for
Standardization (ISO) country codes. LICs = low-income countries;
MICs = middle-income countries; OECD = Organisation for
Economic Co-operation and Development.

5. Value Added in Sectoral Shares in South Asia
(Percent of GDP)

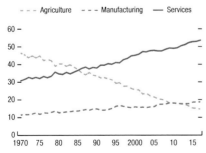

Sources: UN National Account Database; IMF's World Economic
Outlook database; and IMF staff calculations.
Note: The aggregation is weighted by purchasing power
parity GDP.

6. Social Assistance Spending
(Percent of GDP, 2016 or latest year available)

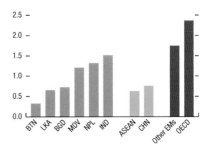

Source: World Bank's ASPIRE Database.
Note: Data labels in the figure use International Organization
for Standardization (ISO) country codes. ASEAN = Association of
Southeast Asian Nations; EMs = emerging markets;
OECD = Organisation for Economic Co-operation and Development.

Figure 3.3.

1. Female Labor Force Participation
(Percent of the female population ages 15+ years, 2018)

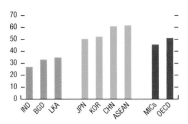

Source: World Bank World's Development Indicators.
Note: Data labels in the figure use International Organization for Standardization (ISO) country codes. ASEAN = Association of Southeast Asian Nations; MICs = middle-income countries; OECD = Organisation for Economic Co-operation and Development.

2. Youth Unemployment
(Percent of labor force ages 15–24 years, 2018)

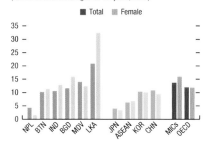

Sources: World Bank's World Development Indicators; and International Labour Organization.
Note: Data labels in the figure use International Organization for Standardization (ISO) country codes. ASEAN = Association of Southeast Asian Nations; MICs = middle-income countries; OECD = Organisation for Economic Co-operation and Development.

3. Share of Population Ages 15–24 Years and Not in Employment, Education or Training
(Percent, latest available)

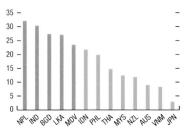

Source: International Labour Organization.
Note: Data labels in the figure use International Organization for Standardization (ISO) country codes.

4. Human Capital Index
(Latest value available)

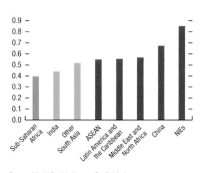

Source: World Bank's Human Capital Index.
Note: ASEAN = Association of Southeast Asian Nations; NIEs = newly industrialized economies.

5. Years of School and Test Scores

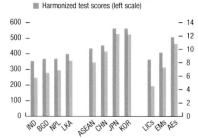

Source: World Bank's Human Capital Index.
Note: Data labels in the figure use International Organization for Standardization (ISO) country codes. AEs = advanced economies; ASEAN = Association of Southeast Asian Nations; EMs = emerging markets; LICs = low-income countries.

Can Support Employment, Productivity, and Reallocation" section, we present empirical evidence that quantifies the potential gains of reforming employment protection legislation (EPL). We also discuss the role of stringent EPL in contributing to misallocation and thus lower productivity growth, using state level evidence in India, as well as the potential effect of automation on labor markets and jobs at risk in South Asia. In the "Reforms to Increase Female Labor Force Participation: An Illustration" section, we illustrate the potential for labor market reforms to increase female labor supply. The focus throughout the chapter is on labor market reforms that protect workers as opposed to jobs and reforms that can support worker reallocation and job-rich growth recoveries in the postpandemic era.

NEED FOR JOBS

A common element of South Asia labor markets is the need to create jobs for young and growing populations. South Asia is the youngest and most densely populated region in Asia. The median age of the population is less than 27 years. As a result, the working-age population in the region is projected to increase over the next 20 years. The working-age population in India for example is expected to peak only in 2040. More than 150 million people are expected to enter the South Asia labor force by 2030. This puts an emphasis on labor market reforms that can support job creation.

Now is the time to reap the growth benefits from the sizable demographic dividend (Figure 3.4). The number of jobs that need to be created to accommodate new entrants is large with the job creation rate (that is, the annual increase in employment consistent with population growth at prepandemic participation

Figure 3.4. Job Creation Rate under the Current Participation Rate in South Asia
(Percent)

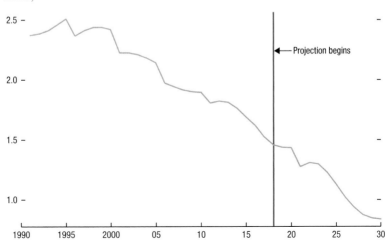

Sources: International Labour Organization; and IMF staff calculations.

rates) amounting to about 1.5 percent. However, while the demographic dividend is large, it is declining over time (India, Bangladesh, and Sri Lanka). India's under-19 population ratio has already peaked because of declines in fertility rates. As a result, the labor force will grow more slowly going forward—at pre–COVID-19 labor force participation rates. Similar patterns hold across South Asia. As a result, the benefits of the potential demographic dividend, including higher potential output growth rates, are also declining over time. The declining demographic dividend calls for some urgency in labor reforms to harness the potential of the demographic dividend.

Moreover, the COVID-19 pandemic shock is likely to adversely affect the job creation rate in the short term. We model the potential effect of the COVID-19 shock as follows. First, we take the Okun's coefficient as 0.25 (as per Ball and others 2019). Second, we take the GDP growth deviation (as per WEO forecast updates) to quantify the size of the COVID-19 shock on the growth trajectory. Given the large shock, we smooth the growth impact on employment growth for more than two years. Combining the two estimates allows us to arrive at a back-of-the-envelope estimate on the potential job losses caused by COVID-19 in the region. Results suggest that in the short term, the job-creation rate in the region could temporarily fall from 1.5 percent to between 0 and 0.5 percent because of the COVID-19 shock. Beyond this temporary impact, there is a growing risk that some of these job losses in the short term may become permanent because of the permanent scarring effects of the deep recession associated with the pandemic.

SOUTH ASIA'S LABOR MARKET INSTITUTIONS

South Asia's labor market regulations and institutions generally do not apply to the large informal sector. For example, in India, up to 90 percent of workers have no written employment contract, which are largely absent in the informal sector, particularly for agricultural workers (Dasgupta and Kar 2018). Informal sector workers in India rarely benefit from union representation, nor from labor laws, except the minimum wage. They are also unlikely to receive long-term contracts that their formal sector counterparts do. Even if labor market regulations are applicable to both formal and informal sectors in principle, as in Nepal, the degree of compliance in the informal sector is unclear.

Minimum wages are low and are unlikely to be a constraint on hiring. Minimum wages in South Asia are low when compared with other developing countries in Asia (Figure 3.4). The ratio of the weighted average of minimum wages in India to the median wage was estimated to be lower than in other large emerging market economies, including Brazil and Indonesia, in the late 2000s (ILO 2016a; Rani and others 2013). Bangladesh has a minimum wages board that reviews the minimum wage periodically, including for the garment sector (ILO 2016b). Pay commissions are also established every few years to review pay and conditions in the public sector. Sri Lanka also has a wages board that sets minimum wages for the private sector, while civil service pay increases are approved by the Cabinet, sometimes on advice from ad hoc commissions. Nepal has a similar arrangement to Bangladesh and Sri Lanka for minimum wages in the private sector. Minimum wages differ by state in India and are set by state governments. An advisory national minimum wage floor has been set since 1996, and the new national wage code legislation allows the central government to mandate a minimum wage (ILO 2018a). However, legally enforceable minimum wages are still not universal, with coverage estimated at 66 percent of wage earners (Rani and others 2013).

In the formal sector, collective bargaining rights are legally protected, supported by restrictions on the use of personalized, fixed term contracts. The right to bargain collectively is protected under the constitutions of India, Bangladesh, and Sri Lanka (ILO 2016b). Collective bargaining power is supported by the right to strike and also by restrictions on fixed term employment contracts in some countries, such as India where they can only be used for employment of a temporary nature, although this may be relaxed by the recently approved Industrial Relations Code. However, the extent of collective bargaining and union power is not clear in practice, with trade union membership relatively low as a share of total employment (Figure 3.5), reflecting that most employment is informal.

Relatively stringent EPL increases the cost of hiring workers in the formal sector. Aggregated measures of the strength of employment protection laws suggest that those in Bangladesh and Sri Lanka are particularly stringent, compared with Asian peers (Figure 3.6). Sri Lanka has the most stringent requirements for dismissal of individual workers, which can only occur if an employee consents or the government approves. Where a group of employees is dismissed for economic reasons, approval must be sought from the government and a decision is required within two months. Severance payments are required for dismissals of those employed for more than five years, at the rate of 14 days of pay for each year of service (ILO 2016b). In Bangladesh, the requirements for dismissal are less stringent but severance payments are more generous. The government and the

Figure 3.5.

1. Monthly Minimum Wage
(2011 purchasing power parity dollars, latest available)

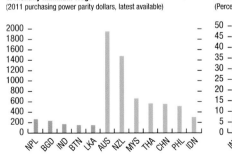

2. Trade Union Membership
(Percent of total employees, latest year available)

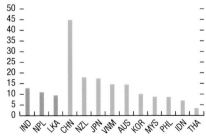

Source: International Labour Organization.
Note: Data labels in the figure use International Organization for Standardization (ISO) country codes.

Sources: International Labour Organization; and country authorities.
Note: Data labels in the figure use International Organization for Standardization (ISO) country codes.

Figure 3.6.

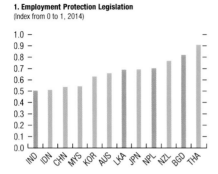

1. Employment Protection Legislation
(Index from 0 to 1, 2014)

2. Coverage of Social Protection Benefits
(Percent of population, latest year available)

Source: Alesina and others 2019.
Note: Data labels in the figure use International Organization
for Standardization (ISO) country codes.

Source: International Labour Organization.
Note: Data labels in the figure use International Organization for
Standardization (ISO) country codes.

relevant union must be notified before a group of employees are dismissed for economic reasons (such as redundancy), but otherwise government approval is not required. Severance payments must be made at the rate of 30 days of pay for each year of service above one year, in cases of redundancy or individual dismissal without reason (ILO 2016b). In India, labor laws differ across states, but government approval is generally required to dismiss an employee who has been employed for more than one year, in a workplace with more than 300 employees, while severance payments are similar to those in Sri Lanka. In India and Bangladesh, there is a "last in, first out" rule for groups of workers dismissed for economic reasons (such as redundancy) and those dismissed must be given priority in future hiring by the employer. Other countries in the region have no requirements for government notification or severance pay, including Bhutan, Nepal, and Maldives. Across the region, dismissed employees can bring a legal challenge and seek reinstatement or compensation if their employer has not complied with employment protection laws.

Social protection for workers is limited for both the formal and informal sectors, with no universal unemployment insurance in South Asia and limited coverage of pension schemes. There is no government-run program of unemployment benefits for the formal or informal sector throughout the region that has wide application. Nepal has introduced a social protection scheme in 2017 that includes unemployment insurance and is potentially universal, but it is not clear if this has been achieved in practice (Danish Trade Union Development Agency 2019). Coverage of other social protection schemes (including cash transfer payments) is well below other developing countries in Asia (Figure 3.5), with South Asia's large informal sector largely excluded from government programs. Coverage of old-age pension schemes is not universal, although India and Nepal have made recent reforms to expand coverage. There are also social assistance payments for some older people, such as in Maldives, sometimes subject to means-testing, as in Bangladesh.

India has made reforms to begin expanding the still limited coverage of its old-age pension system. In India, more than 85 percent of workers have no pension scheme, and less than one quarter of people older than the retirement age receive any pension (NITI Aayog 2018; Anand and Chakraborty 2019). A social assistance payment is available for older people in the general public below the poverty line, but it is relatively small (between $3 and $7 per month) for those over older than 60 years of age, depending on age, and only benefits approximately 16 million people. Around 20 percent of Indians older than 80 years of age are still in employment, according to census data, suggesting that social assistance payments are inadequate (OECD 2019b). For central government civil servants employed before 2004, there is a defined-benefit scheme, funded from government expenditure without employee contributions, allowing civil servants with at least 10 years of service to receive a pension at age 58 years. These employees can also make monthly contributions to the Civil Service Provident Fund, which also operates on a pay-as-you-go basis, giving lump sum payments to employees after 20 years of service (OECD 2019c). Similar arrangements exist for civil servants at the subnational government level. Since 2004, new civil service entrants are enrolled in the National Pension System, which is a defined contribution pension scheme, with matching contributions by the government. For the formal, private sector, the Employees' Provident Fund Organization operates a defined benefit employee pension scheme, to which both employers and the government must make contributions, with pensions payable from retirement at age 58 years. There is also an Employees' Provident Fund Scheme, that is defined contribution with some matching by employers, providing lump sum payments at age 55 years. To expand pension coverage, the National Pension System for civil servants was opened to the general public in 2009 and now has around 13 million members according to the National Pension System Trust, although private sector employers are not required to make matching contributions.

Nepal has also made recent reforms to expand coverage of social protection schemes. Before 2017, Nepal had an Employees' Provident Fund, mostly for civil servants, providing old age benefits that are financed mostly by employers. Other social assistance schemes were in place as a safety net, funded by a tax on payrolls (ILO 2018b). The Contribution Based Social Security Act (2017) establishes a scheme to provide health care, maternity, old age, disability and unemployment benefits, among others, with contributions from both employees and employers. In principle, this scheme is open to all employees in the formal and informal sectors, but coverage in practice is unclear. As of today, government allowances under the Social Security Act (2018) are the main source of social spending. The most generous of the five allocations is the Senior Citizens Allowance, which currently pays 3,000 NPR per month ($25) to all adults older than 65 years (and those older than 60 years from disadvantaged groups/regions). The other four are monthly allowances for some children younger than 5 years, single widows, disabled persons, and certain Indigenous groups.

Other South Asian countries have civil service pensions, contributory savings schemes for the formal private sector and limited social assistance payments as a safety net. In Bangladesh and Sri Lanka, there is a defined benefit civil service pension payable on retirement, funded out of government expenditure. In Bhutan, the civil service pension is partially funded on a pay-as-you-go basis from employee contributions. In Bangladesh, all formal sector employees must contribute 7–8 percent of their base salary to a defined contribution provident fund after one year of service, with a matching contribution by their employer, so that accumulated amounts are payable as a lump sum on retirement. Sri Lanka's Employees' Provident Fund and Bhutan's Provident Fund plan operate in a similar way. Maldives also has the contributory Maldives Retirement Pension Scheme (Sun 2016), although its coverage is unclear. Bangladesh established a social assistance program for elderly adults in 1998 as a safety net, for those with annual income of less than $38, which provides a transfer of around $4 every three months (ILO 2013). Sri Lanka has a similar social assistance scheme and Maldives provides an old age basic pension and senior citizens allowance to those older than 65 years of age (Sun 2016). Sri Lanka also has an Employees' Trust Fund, to which employers in the formal sector make mandatory contributions. It functions as a form of insurance, allowing employees to draw benefits in certain circumstances.

Employer contributions to pension schemes are the main form of labor taxes in South Asia. The defined contribution schemes for the formal private sector, often known as provident funds, in Bhutan, Bangladesh, India and Sri Lanka, all require matching contributions from employers (ILO 2013; OECD 2019c). The new Nepalese contributory social protection schemes will also require employer contributions, and Nepal has a social security tax on payrolls. Sri Lankan employers also must contribute to the Employees' Trust Fund, which provides a form of insurance to employees. In India, employers are required to pay a gratuity to employees on retirement, equivalent to 15 days of their final salary for every year of employment (OECD 2019c). There is also a similar gratuity in Bhutan.

Labor market institutions are not sufficiently supportive of female labor force participation. There is no entitlement to part-time work in South Asian countries, which could be an important driver of higher female labor force participation. Some support to families is provided through childcare facilities. India has made a crèche facility compulsory for establishments with 50 or more employees, likely applicable in the formal sector (OECD 2019a). Sri Lanka issued guidelines establishing national standards for day care centers in 2017. Across the region, there are maternity leave entitlements, of varying degrees of generosity. In Sri Lanka and Maldives, employers in the private sector are required to offer 84 and 60 days paid maternity leave, respectively. Nepalese law requires 60 days of paid maternity leave, some of which is paid for out of labor taxes, although the degree of compliance is unclear in practice. In Bangladesh and Bhutan, civil servants are entitled to six months of paid maternity leave, whereas private sector employees in Bangladesh can access paid maternity leave on one occasion, for 16 weeks, and unpaid leave during subsequent pregnancies (OECD 2013). In India, the Maternity Benefit Amendment Act of 2017 increased the entitlement for paid maternity leave to 26 weeks, for women employed by companies with at least 10 employees, in line with the entitlement for civil servants (OECD 2019b). In all countries, the cost of maternity leave is born entirely by the employer, although this may change under Nepal's new contributory social protection scheme. Labor laws generally prohibit discrimination in hiring and dismissal on the grounds of maternity.

Progress on labor market reform has been modest, with worthwhile reforms in India still in their early stages. In India, the government has proposed amalgamating a range of labor laws into four codes, on wages, safety and working conditions, industrial relations, and social security and welfare, but only the wages code has been approved so far. There remains a complex web of laws and regulations at the central government and state levels. In 2018, the Fixed Term Employment Act required workers on fixed-term contracts to have access to similar conditions as permanent employees, although the use of fixed term contracts remains restricted to where work is of a temporary nature. An income support and pension scheme for farmers was introduced in 2019 (OECD 2019b). The Indian government has also launched a contributory pension system for the informal sector, Pradhan Mantri Shram Yogi Maan-dhan, to cover 100 million workers and provide a monthly pension of around $43, although only around 3 million people were participating in the scheme as of mid-2019 (OECD 2019b). The government will match individual contributions fully. Progress with reforms outside India has been limited. The Bangladesh Labor Act of 2006 was amended in 2013, after the Rana Plaza garment factory collapse, and then again in 2018, with some strengthening of worker rights, including for paid maternity leave, while making it easier to form unions and completely banning child labor in factories. The Nepalese government commenced its contributory social protection scheme for the formal sector in 2018, with contributions required from employees and employers, that would provide an old-age pension and other benefits. Adoption of this new scheme in Nepal so far seems to have been limited. There have been no significant and recent reforms to Sri Lankan labor law.

EPL REFORMS CAN SUPPORT EMPLOYMENT, PRODUCTIVITY, AND REALLOCATION

Stringent EPL contributes to high informality, lower productivity and limits reallocation of workers. As discussed earlier, while unemployment insurance is not a feature of South Asian labor markets, EPL is relatively stringent in several countries (see Table 3.1 and Annex 3.1). This increases the cost of hiring and firing workers, and as a result, EPL serves to protect "insiders" in formal sector jobs, thus exacerbating a dual labor market structure that makes it more difficult for "outsiders"—that is, those in informal employment, unemployment, or outside the labor force—to secure formal sector employment. Stringent EPL also provides an incentive for some firms to remain informal and small. This is the case for firms that are on the margin of being formal but choose to remain informal to bypass stringent EPL. For example, manufacturing firms in India that have more than 100 employees generally need government permission to lay off employees (Government of India 1947). Some firms may choose to limit employment growth to remain below the threshold. There is evidence that

TABLE 3.1.

Snapshot of Labor Market Institutions in South Asia

	Most ▬	Intermediate ▬	Least ▬			
	Bangladesh	Bhutan	India	Sri Lanka	Maldives	Nepal
Restricted work arrangements (restrictions on part-time work and temporary employment contracts)						
Strength of employment protection						
Weakness of social protection (unemployment insurance, pensions)						
Lack of maternity leave and weak protection for women						

Source: IMF staff calculations.

stringent EPL results in a suboptimal level of aggregate employment, and contributes to resource misallocation and low productivity (see Box 3.2). By increasing the cost of reallocating workers across firms, sectors and occupations, stringent EPL may also make it more difficult for South Asian labor markets to respond to shocks, such as the COVID19 pandemic, and to the effect of technological change, such as increasing automation, on production and demand for labor (see Box 3.3).

Informal employment acts as a safety net and can be complementary to formal employment. Given the dearth of social safety nets, informal employment often fills in the gap by acting as a resource for workers who are not able to obtain formal employment but need an income. Informal jobs are generally low-skilled and offer low wages, and for many workers with inadequate skills to obtain formal employment, informal jobs are their only option. Formal and informal employment are often complementary. This is particularly the case in South Asian economies where supply chains include both formal and informal firms. Formal firms can also hire both formal and informal workers. Thus, if looser EPL leads to more formal firms, it may still be the case that these newly formal firms rely on informal firms and informal workers.

We use regression analysis to examine the effect of EPL legislation on employment and informality in South Asia. Following Alesina and others (2020) and IMF (2019) we model changes in employment and informality as follows:

$$y_{i,t+k} - y_{i,t-1} = \alpha_i + \gamma_t + \beta_1 R_{i,t} + \beta_{SA} R_{SA,t} + \theta X_{i,t} + \varepsilon_{i,t},$$

where $y_{i,t+k}$ is the log of employment or share of informal employment,

t is the time dimension,

i is the country dimension,

α_i is the unobserved time-invariant country effect,

y_t is the time dummy,

$R_{i,t}$ is the change in the employment protection legislation (EPL) index,

$R_{SA,t}$ is the change in the EPL index in South Asia (interaction),

$X_{i,t}$ are control variables: two lags of the dependent variable, lagged growth, lagged change in the EPL index.

EPL stringency is measured using the index developed in Alesina and others (2020) and used in IMF (2019). The index is based on three broad indicators measuring the procedural requirements for layoffs, the severance costs associated with layoffs, and valid grounds for dismissal and redress measures in the case that dismissal was unfair, and takes values between 0 to 1, with 1 being the most liberal employment protection legislation. The EPL index covers 88 countries from 1973 to 2014 for most countries and a change in the index represents a labor market reform. Data on various employment indicators are from the ILO's modeled estimates, which include both formal and informal employment and cover 177 countries from 1991 to 2022 for most countries. Data on growth are from the World Economic Outlook database. Data on informality is from the harmonized measure of the share of informal employment from the ILO.[3] Informal employment is defined as the collection of workers who are own account workers (whether for their own enterprise, or for their own final use), contributing family workers, and employees with informal jobs. Informal jobs are characterized by the job not being subject to national labor legislation, income taxation, social protection or benefits such as paid leave and sick leave. Compared with data on total employment, data on informality are available for fewer (65) countries and with less frequent time series observations. To facilitate estimation, we fill gaps by assuming that for each observation, the unobserved informality for previous years is equal to that observation and the most recent observation is carried forward in time. For robustness, we estimate both pooled OLS and fixed-effects models with heteroscedasticity consistent standard errors. Results from both models are qualitatively and quantitively similar. We show pooled OLS results below and fixed effects model results, as robustness check, in Annex 3.2. Regression results for total employment and share of informal employment using pooled OLS are shown in Tables 3.2 and 3.3.

Results show that loosening EPL leads to an increase in total employment over time, despite an initial decline in male employment (Figure 3.7, panels 1, 3, 5, and 7). Each bar measures the change in employment k periods after the loosening of EPL and the difference in employment across bars is measured compared with the same period $y_{i,t-1}$. Our estimates therefore suggest that introduction of looser EPL will increase employment over time. The positive effect on total employment emerges three years after the reform. The positive effect on employment that increases over time is consistent with results in IMF (2019) for emerging markets and low-income countries. However, our results suggest that in the first two years after the reform, loosening of EPL legislation would lead to an initial reallocation of labor and some job losses. We also estimate the impact separately for male and female

---

[3] See the ILOSTAT Database Description: Labour Force Statistics (LFS, STLFS, RURBAN), https://ilostat.ilo.org/resources/concepts-and-definitions/description-informality/.

TABLE 3.2.

Results for Total Employment, Pooled Ordinary Least Squares					
	k=0	k=1	k=2	k=3	k=4
South Asia	−0.001	0.000	0.000	0.000	−0.000
	(0.68)	(0.07)	(0.11)	(0.17)	(0.05)
EPL reform	0.006	0.025	−0.004	−0.005	0.021
	(0.45)	(1.65)	(0.22)	(0.47)	(2.60)*
EPL reform * South Asia	−0.008	−0.103	−0.010	0.088	0.141
	(0.49)	(4.21)**	(0.47)	(5.17)**	(9.13)**
L.EPL reform	0.016	−0.021	−0.024	−0.002	−0.009
	(1.59)	(1.41)	(1.92)	(0.20)	(1.29)
L2.EPL reform	−0.021	−0.034	−0.003	−0.011	0.012
	(1.50)	(3.26)**	(0.18)	(0.80)	(1.10)
L.growth	0.001	−0.001	−0.001	−0.001	−0.001
	(3.88)**	(2.64)*	(2.80)*	(3.64)**	(5.15)**
L2.growth	−0.000	0.000	0.000	0.000	0.000
	(2.31)*	(3.01)**	(2.31)*	(1.72)	(1.42)
L.dependent variable	0.356	1.012	1.153	1.237	1.302
	(7.83)**	(18.18)**	(22.97)**	(27.53)**	(27.60)**
L2.dependent variable	0.163	−0.309	−0.335	−0.351	−0.386
	(5.11)**	(7.63)**	(8.17)**	(9.40)**	(9.17)**
Constant	0.005	0.005	0.010	0.006	0.004
	(5.76)**	(5.27)**	(9.67)**	(3.69)**	(2.12)*
N	1,762	1,762	1,762	1,762	1,762

Source: IMF staff calculations.
Note: EPL = employment protection legislation.
$*p < 0.05; **p < 0.01.$

TABLE 3.3.

Results for Share of Informal Employment, Pooled Ordinary Least Squares					
	k=0	k=1	k=2	k=3	k=4
South Asia	0.002	0.003	0.003	0.001	0.001
	(2.01)	(1.80)	(1.75)	(0.67)	(0.65)
EPL reform	−0.001	0.076	−0.017	0.022	0.004
	(0.27)	(1.90)	(1.74)	(1.23)	(0.36)
EPL reform * South Asia	0.006	−0.056	0.082	−0.015	−0.025
	(0.65)	(1.05)	(3.10)**	(0.51)	(1.39)
L.EPL reform	0.074	−0.016	0.021	0.001	0.007
	(1.89)	(1.33)	(1.01)	(0.10)	(0.68)
L2.EPL reform	−0.035	−0.038	−0.068	−0.063	−0.046
	(2.22)*	(2.37)*	(2.39)*	(1.95)	(1.10)
L.growth	−0.000	0.000	−0.000	0.000	−0.000
	(0.48)	(1.10)	(1.47)	(0.13)	(1.31)
L2.growth	0.000	−0.000	−0.000	−0.000	0.000
	(0.71)	(1.78)	(0.71)	(1.64)	(0.96)
L.dependent variable	0.156	0.876	0.931	1.011	0.993
	(4.51)**	(7.19)**	(17.69)**	(10.06)**	(21.88)**
L2.dependent variable	0.136	−0.339	−0.196	−0.193	−0.124
	(1.35)	(2.62)*	(3.56)**	(2.00)	(2.63)*
Constant	−0.000	0.001	0.001	0.001	−0.001
	(1.21)	(1.60)	(0.96)	(1.27)	(0.97)
N	1,154	1,154	1,154	1,154	1,154

Source: IMF staff calculations.
Note: EPL = employment protection legislation.
$*p < 0.05; **p < 0.01.$

employment. The results show that male employment declines initially, when reform is introduced, before increasing three years after the reform. This is likely driven by the fact that men make up a higher share of the total formal employed that is protected by EPL legislation. Female employment begins to increase when reform is first introduced. Over time, looser EPL legislation will result in the increase of female employment in both absolute terms and relative to male employment, suggesting the strict EPL legislation currently acts as a barrier for increasing female labor force participation in South Asia.

EPL reform can also help reduce informality over time (Figure 3.7, panels 2, 4, 6, and 8). Measures of total employment used in the regression analysis shown earlier include both formal and informal employment. To understand the effect of loosening EPL on informality, we extend the analysis by running the same

Figure 3.7. Effect of Employment Protection Legislation Reform on South Asian Economies

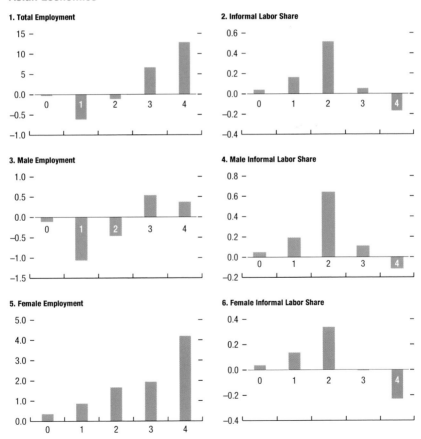

Source: Authors' calculations.
Note: Results show the effect of a 1 standard deviation relaxation in employment protection legislation introduced in period 0.

regression with the share of informal employment as the dependent variable. While the data coverage is more limited, we find evidence that loosening EPL leads to an initial increase in the share of informality before an increase in the share of formal employment over time. Specifically, four years after EPL reform, the initial increase in the share of informality is reversed and the resulting share of formal employees in the economy is higher than before reform. The results confirm the intuition that in the absence of a social safety net and formal unemployment insurance, informal employment acts as a safety valve during periods of job changes and reallocation. Reflecting the larger share of men in formal employment, the impact is more pronounced for men than for women, with the share of informal employment increasing by twice as much as that of women in the initial period.

Box 3.2. Resource Misallocation in India: The Role of Cross-State Labor Market Reform

India's labor market regulations are relatively strict, numerous, and outdated including at the subnational level. The strictness of labor regulations, to a large extent, are attributed to Chapter V-B of the Industrial Disputes Act that requires government approval for layoffs, retrenchments, and closures where this law applies on all factories with 100 or more workers. Before 2017, labor laws at both the center and states in India numbered to around 250 laws are burdensome to businesses. These laws govern different aspects of the labor market such as minimum wages, resolution of industrial disputes, conditions for hiring and firing workers, and conditions for the closure of establishments.

Strict labor market regulations in India can have detrimental economic effects (for example, Besley and Burgess 2004; Dougherty, Frisancho, and Krishna 2011, 2014). India's employment protection is highly restrictive for the organized or formal manufacturing sector, given particularly that it interferes significantly with firms' hiring and severance decisions. High implicit costs of employment especially for large firms have induced many entrepreneurs to start small and stay small.[4] Firms in the unorganized and often informal sector with fewer than 10 or 20 workers are subject to very few labor regulations and can employ casual or contract labor freely. Such high implicit costs of employment have resulted in a suboptimal level of employment, resource misallocation, and low productivity (see Box Figure 3.2).

Empirical analysis suggests that the strict labor market regulations contribute to misallocation in India. Based on Hsieh and Klenow (2009) framework, the analysis identifies the magnitude and key drivers of resource misallocation in the formal sector across Indian states (Annex 3.3). It finds that states with less stringent employment protection have less misallocation. To illustrate the potential effect of labor market reforms, the scenario analysis focuses on the potential total factor productivity (TFP) gains from reallocation resulting from labor reforms, particularly in states with high informality. The effect of labor reforms is calibrated by calculating the impact of advancing labor market reforms of an Indian state to the same level of the best performer (see Figure 3.2.2). The results show that aggregate TFP can be significantly increased, with West Bengal, Maharashtra, and Jharkhand likely to benefit most in terms of absolute TFP gains. These findings suggest that less stringent employment protection would reduce distortions and contribute to both productivity gains and higher long-term growth.

(Box 3.2 continues on the next page)

---

[4] For evidence on low-income countries, see also Hsieh and Olken (2014).

Box 3.2. Resource Misallocation in India: The Role of Cross-State Labor Market Reform *(continued)*

Figure 3.2.1. Misallocation in the United States, India, and China

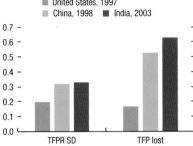

Sources: Annual Survey of Industries database; and authors' calculations for India. China and US statistic are from Hsieh and Klenow (2009).
Note: Measures of misallocation include the variances of revenue productivity or TFPR (logs) from industry means. The TFP lost (percent) was derived by equalizing TFPR within industries. TFP = total factor productivity; TFPR = total factor productivity revenue.

Figure 3.2.2. TFP Gains with Optimal Labor Market Reforms in Indian States with High Informality
(Data in logs as of 2010)

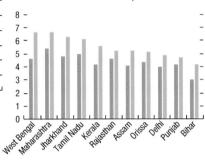

Sources: Annual Survey of Industries database; and authors' calculations.
Note: TFP = total factor productivity.

In recent years, some Indian states have undergone labor reforms to improve labor market flexibility. Rajasthan, Madhya Pradesh, and Haryana in 2014 modified their Industrial Disputes Act to allow automatic retrenchment for a factory with less than 300 workers. Gujarat has allowed automatic retrenchment of workers in any factory in the Specialized Economic Zones, Special Investment Regions, and National Investment and Manufacturing Zones, provided that the employer provides severance payment of 60 days of wages for every year of employment. Maharashtra in 2017 allowed automatic retrenchment for up to 300 workers. Since 2017, the central government has attempted to amalgamate 44 central labor laws into four codes on industrial relations, wages[5], social security and welfare, and safety and working conditions. While some elements of the draft code would create more flexibility, the Chapter V-B of the Industrial Disputes Act has not been altered.

Amid the COVID-19 pandemic, some Indian states have temporarily relaxed their labor laws to stimulate employment and attract foreign investment. Madhya Pradesh provided exemption for new investors from existing labor laws for 1,000 days from the announcement in May 2020. Similarly, Gujarat granted labor-law exemptions for 1,200 days from the start of production of any new venture in the state. Assam, Haryana, Odisha, Punjab, Rajasthan, and Uttarakhand all have announced emergency ordinances to provide similar incentives.

The Indian government has introduced additional labor market reforms during the COVID-19 pandemic. On September 23, 2020, three labor bills were passed, replacing 24 central labor laws. The key changes in the new bills include (1) easing administrative bottlenecks in hiring and firing (by allowing firms with up to 300 workers—compared with

(Box 3.2 continues on the next page)

---

[5] Parliament passed the Code on Wages Bill in August 2019, which gave statutory protection for minimum wages and timely payment of wages to approximately 500 million workers of organized as well as unorganized sector.

Box 3.2. Resource Misallocation in India: The Role of Cross-State Labor Market Reform *(continued)*

only 100 workers in the old law—to wind up businesses or fire workers without central government approval, and reducing administrative steps for layoff and retrenchment of workers); (2) revising the structure for labor union negotiations and union strikes, which is likely to reduce disruption of production; and (3) expanding social security benefits for fixed-term and migrant workers, which is likely to speed up formalization of the labor force. The labor market reforms mark a step forward in reforming the labor market, and will likely ease administrative bottlenecks, support formalization, and expand social security benefits for workers. However, these labor reforms should go hand in hand with a further strengthening of the social safety net for workers, including unemployment insurance, and skills training for workers. Timely implementation of the recently announced measures and a continued push to broaden the structural reform agenda are essential to support the postpandemic recovery.

Looking ahead, labor market reforms remain crucial to help reap the full benefits of the demographic dividend. Addressing distortionary policies such as stringent employment protection legislation is key to helping reduce resource misallocation, thereby raising aggregate productivity, as well as improving growth and employment prospects. Labor market institutions, in addition, should be geared toward protecting workers by providing necessary safety nets against economic shocks.

Source: Based on Mohommad and others 2021.

Box 3.3. Automation in South Asia

On average, 50 percent of workers in South Asia are in occupations where the risk of automation is greater than 70 percent. This estimate is obtained by using the probabilities of automation estimated in Frey and Osborne (2017) and applying them to the occupational categories in our set of countries (Bangladesh, Bhutan, India, Nepal, Maldives, and Sri Lanka). We use data on employment from the latest available labor force survey in each country. One shortcoming is that for most countries, data on employment by occupation are only available for single digit occupations, thus, we average over the probabilities of automation in Frey and Osborne (2017), which are estimated by four-digit occupation codes. The share of workers in occupations at a high risk of automation varies from 26 percent in Maldives, where a lower share of the labor force is in agricultural and elementary occupations, to 65 percent in India.

The automation of tasks is likely to result in profound changes in labor markets, globally and in South Asia. Labor market institutions may distort the effect of automation. For example, strict EPL may act as an additional incentive for firms to favor capital intensive production, including automation, as opposed to more labor-intensive production. It would also inhibit the reallocation of labor to the sectors where it is most productive.

(Box 3.3 continues on the next page)

Box 3.3. Automation in South Asia *(continued)*

Figure 3.3.1. Employment in South Asia, by Occupation
(Percent of total employment)

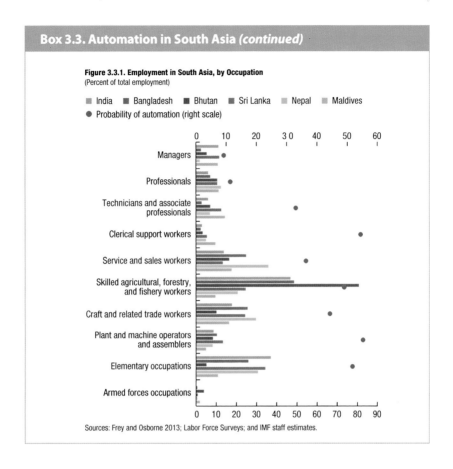

Sources: Frey and Osborne 2013; Labor Force Surveys; and IMF staff estimates.

REFORMS TO INCREASE FEMALE LABOR FORCE PARTICIPATION: AN ILLUSTRATION

Labor market reforms—particularly targeted to increase female labor participation—can help offset the declining growth in labor supply. In an environment of declining demographic dividend and also persistent job losses caused by the COVID-19 pandemic, policies to boost female participation going forward would help increase aggregate labor supply. Labor market institutions in South Asia provide relatively limited support for participation of females in the labor market, for example through policies such as part-time employment, maternity leave and support for child care (see Annex Table 3.1). We undertake a simple scenario analysis to put rough estimates on possible gains from policies to support female participation. We create two scenarios. For the baseline scenario, the labor force participation rate is fixed at the 2018 level for all years between 2018–30. Meanwhile, for the active scenario, we assume that the female participation rate gradually rises from 27.7 percent to 32 percent for the region as a whole between 2018 and 2030 to reflect the positive effect of labor market reforms. Quantitatively, according to ILO data, the region had a similar participation rate in the 2000s, and thus the analysis assumes that active policies restore at least that level of female labor participation (Figure 3.8).

The analysis shows that even such a modest increase in female labor force participation can halt the decline in labor supply in the region (Figure 3.9). In this context, such supply-side policies to boost LFPR are a complementary tool to demand-side labor reforms. Specific policies include improving access and

Figure 3.8. Level and Change of Female Labor Force Participation

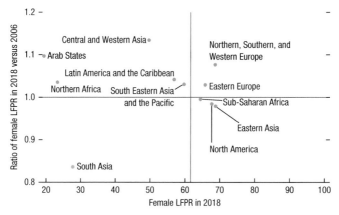

Sources: International Labour Organization; and IMF staff calculations.
Note: Female world LBFR (excluding South Asia) is 61.6 percent. LBPR = labor force participation rate.

Figure 3.9. Job Creation Rate under the Current Participation Rate
(Percent)

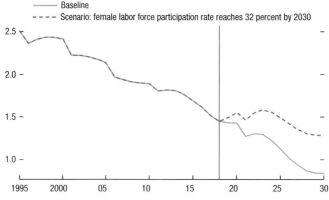

Sources: International Labour Organization; and IMF staff calculations.

information to relevant education and training programs; improving law and order to create a safe public environment for women; investing in safe and accessible transportation; creating more suitable jobs, for example, more part-time jobs; greater possibility for remote work, and so on; strengthening equality-enhancing laws; improving access to child care; and strengthening maternity protection (Verick 2014; Das and others 2015; and Fletcher, Pande, and Moore 2017).

CONCLUSIONS

South Asian labor markets have been hit hard by the COVID-19 pandemic, highlighting the need for labor market reforms to support recoveries. The negative effect has been felt most by self-employed workers, employees of small- and medium-sized enterprises, and migrant workers in the informal sector, along with workers in sectors with a relatively high share of female employment, such as hospitality, tourism, and domestic work. The pandemic has exposed long-standing weaknesses in social protection schemes for workers, while the negative effect on employment and labor force participation adds to the already-pressing need for job creation in the formal sector for the growing working-age population. Furthermore, the possibility of negative scarring effects stemming from bankruptcies, decline in labor force participation and restructuring, underscores the need for labor market institutions that can deliver jobs and facilitate reallocation of workers, while providing social protection.

South Asian economies need high-quality job growth, including expansion of the formal, nonagricultural economy to generate productive, well-paying jobs for their young, growing populations. High-quality job growth requires expanding the formal, non agricultural economy, which remains small. Expanding the formal sector requires continued structural change toward services and manufacturing and increasing the share of formal employment in these sectors. Furthermore, relatively low rates of female labor force participation and high youth unemployment also suggest significant barriers to formal employment.

South Asia's labor market regulations and institutions are geared toward protecting jobs in the formal sector and provide little protection to workers from shocks, such as the COVID-19 pandemic. South Asia's labor market regulations and institutions generally do not apply to the large informal sector. In the much smaller formal sector, collective bargaining rights are legally protected and relatively stringent employment protection legislation results in a high cost of hiring and firing workers. Strict labor market regulations can have detrimental economic effects. For example, in India, high implicit costs of employment—especially for large firms—provide incentives for many entrepreneurs to start small and stay small, contributing to a suboptimal level of employment, resource misallocation, and low productivity. At the same time, social protection for workers is limited for the formal and informal sectors, with no universal unemployment insurance in South Asia.

Empirical evidence shows that loosening EPL leads to an increase in total employment over time, increase in the share of female employment and lower informality. Our estimates from regression analysis for South Asian countries suggest that introduction of looser EPL will increase employment over time, with the positive impact on total employment emerging three years after the reform. However, our results also suggest that in the first two years after the reform, loosening of EPL legislation leads to an initial reallocation of labor and some job losses. The timing of labor market reforms therefore matters. The results also underscore the importance of reform design and sequencing to provide support for those that may be negatively affected in the short term. Novel results that disaggregate the employment impact by gender show that over time, looser EPL legislation results in the increase of female employment in both absolute terms and relative to male employment, suggesting that the strict EPL legislation currently protects the formal, mostly male labor force, and acts as a barrier for increasing female labor force participation in South Asia. There is also some evidence that EPL reform can reduce informality over time.

Despite growing populations, the demographic dividend across South Asia is declining and labor market reforms are needed to increase labor supply. The number of jobs that need to be created to accommodate new entrants is large but declining over time. Moreover, the COVID-19 pandemic shock is likely to adversely affect the job creation rate in the short term. Beyond the temporary short-term impact, there is a growing risk that some job losses may become permanent because of the scarring effects of the deep recession associated with the pandemic, thus reducing the contribution of labor to potential output growth over the medium term. Labor market reforms, particularly targeted to increasing the relatively low levels of female labor participation in the region, can help offset the declining growth in labor supply.

While labor market reforms need to be country-specific, there is a strong case for reforms that shift focus toward protecting workers as opposed to jobs and increasing female labor force participation. In addition to the positive effects on employment, reducing implicit costs of hiring and firing through looser EPL can support needed reallocation of workers in the aftermath of the COVID-19 pandemic. The need for smooth reallocation of workers is further heightened by the profound changes in labor markets that are likely to result from increasing automation of tasks. At the same time, evidence that loosening EPL may result in an initial fall in total employment calls for complementary reforms to strengthen social protection for workers. While the informal sector currently serves as a safety net in South Asian countries, further policy responses to support employment and incomes are likely needed to protect workers during the transition and generate political support for difficult reforms. As labor markets gradually move away from informality there may also be scope to introduce formal unemployment insurance or to extend existing mechanisms, such as the use of National Provident Funds, to protect workers from labor market shocks. A full discussion of social protection reforms is beyond the scope of this chapter (social protection in South Asia is discussed in Chapter 4).

Labor markets reforms should be complemented by other reforms to support sustained growth in output. Although labor market reform can contribute, creating high-quality jobs also requires sustained growth in economic activity. This is likely to require other reforms, including reforms to ease trade restrictions, promoting foreign direct investment, improvements in governance and product market reform. Reform design should also take into account possible interactions between labor and product market reforms, the role of macroeconomic policies in supporting reforms and important political economy considerations.

Annex 3.1. Labor Market Institutions in South Asia

ANNEX TABLE 3.1.1

Snapshot of Labor Market Institutions in South Asia

	Bangladesh	Bhutan	India	Sri Lanka	Maldives	Nepal
Collective bargaining	✓	✓	✓	✓		✓
Part-time work and flexible work arrangements						
Fixed term employment		✓	✓		✓	✓
Restrictions on union membership						
Employment protection legislation: government permission required for dismissal			✓	✓		
Employment protection legislation: severance pay required for dismissal	✓		✓	✓		
Unemployment insurance						✓
Public pension	✓		✓		✓	✓
Government-run savings and/or insurance options for employees	✓	✓	✓	✓		
Employer social security contributions and labor taxes	✓	✓	✓	✓		✓
Maternity leave entitlement	✓	✓	✓	✓	✓	✓
Government-funded maternity leave			✓			✓
Protection against gender discrimination		✓			✓	✓
Protection against sexual harassment		✓	✓	✓		

Source: IMF staff calculations.

Annex 3.2. Fixed-Effects Regression Model Results

Annex Figure 3.2.1. The Effect of Looser Employment Protection Legislation on South Asian Economies

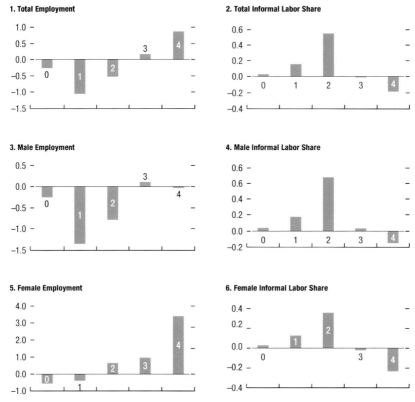

Source: Authors' calculations.
Note: Results show the effect of a 1 standard deviation relaxation in employment protection legislation introduced in period 0.

Annex 3.3. Measuring Resource Misallocation

There is a growing consensus that aggregate productivity is the most important factor in determining income per capita and living standards. Low productivity growth can be a consequence of slow progress in adopting frontier technologies and best practices or the lack of efficiency in allocating productive resources. Institutional features and government policies can have important effects on aggregate productivity and efficiency, as they determine firms' decision making on production, investment, and the allocation of their limited resources.

Some policies may deter factors of production from being allocated to their best use, resulting in so-called resource misallocation, while hindering overall economic performance at the macro level. Examples of such policies include rules and regulations that prevent free market entry, impose limits on firm size—directly or indirectly—or impose heavy burdens on the allocation of factors of production and the distribution of goods and services. Reducing resource misallocation by addressing these distortionary policies would raise aggregate productivity, allowing higher output with the same amount of capital and labor, and the same firm-level technology.

In a simplified framework, we show how firm-level distortions on input and output prices affect resource allocation across firms within a sector and a state. We follow the theoretical approach developed by Hsieh and Klenow (2009). Then, we describe how informality interacts with productivity and misallocation. That methodology uses a standard model of monopolistic competition with heterogeneous firms to illustrate the effect of resource misallocation on aggregate productivity, and firm-specific distortions can be measured by the firm's total factor revenue productivity (TFPR). The main measure of misallocation used is the dispersion of firm TFPR, assuming that firms use a Cobb-Douglas production technology and firms' productivity is jointly lognormally distributed, there is no misallocation if the distribution of TFPR is symmetric. We also construct a measure of aggregate total factor productivity (TFP) and a TFP gap to measure the distance between "efficient" and "observed" output.

In a second step, we use regression analysis to identify potential drivers of the distribution of firm-level distortions. The baseline regression utilizes the derived measures of misallocation and identifies the nature, magnitude, and sources of misallocation. Regressions take the following form:

$$TFP_{sjt} = \beta_0 + \beta_1 \ labor \ reform_s + \beta_2 \ labor \ reform_s * Informality_{st}(d)$$
$$+ \ \beta_3 \ Informality_{st}(d) + \Gamma \ Z_{st} + \varphi_{jt} + \varepsilon_{ikt}$$

The dependent variables are the three measures of misallocation for Indian states by state (s), sector (j) at the three-digit level, and year (t). We use firm-level data from the Annual Survey of Industries, which is compiled by the Central Statistical Organization in India. The survey data is based on India's fiscal years 2003/04, 2006/07, 2008/09, and 2010/11. The "labor reform" index is from OECD's Dougherty (2008), which was computed in 2007 and is time (or sector) invariant. The index is scaled from zero to one, and an Indian state with a higher index is more advanced in labor market reforms at the time of the study. "Informality" is proxied by the size of the unregistered net state domestic product. Other controls (vector Z in the equation shown earlier) include electricity shortage as derived from the share of firms that declared that electricity is an obstacle, use of cell phone, and road density as road per state area. Data are from the World Bank's enterprise survey and the Center for Monitoring Indian Economy.

Empirically, we find that states that made more progress on labor market reforms tend to have lower degree of misallocation as measured by the dispersion of TFPR and its skewness. This result is even more marked in states with a relatively large informal sector. In such states, labor market reforms are also associated with a significant increase in productivity as measured by TFP. We also find that informality has a complex relationship with productivity and resource misallocation. Although it exerts a negative effect on TFP, it appears to reduce the dispersion of TFPR, suggesting that the "positive" effect through the extensive margin is offset by the negative intrafirm effects. Moreover, it tends to increase the negative skewness of the TFPR distribution, implying that high informality is associated with smaller than optimal size firms in the formal sector.

REFERENCES

Alesina, A., D. Furceri, J. Ostry, C. Papagerogiou, and D. Quinn. 2020. "Structural Reforms and Election Evidence from a World-Wide New Dataset." NBER Working Paper 26270, National Bureau of Economic Research, Cambridge, MA.

Anand, R. K., and R. Chakraborty. 2019. "Public Expenditure on Old-Age Income Support in India: Largess for a Few, Illusory for Most." NIPFP Working Paper 253, National Institute of Public Finance and Policy, New Delhi, India.

Anner, M. 2020. "Abandoned? The Impact of COVID-19 on Workers and Businesses at the Bottom of Global Garment Supply Chains." Center for Global Workers' Rights, Penn State University.

Ball, L., D. Furceri, D. Leigh, and P. Loungani. 2019. "Does One Law Fit All? Cross-Country Evidence on Okun's Law." *Open Economies Review* 30 (5): 841–74.

Besley, T., and R. Burgess. 2004. "Can Labor Regulation Hinder Economic Performance? Evidence from India." *Quarterly Journal of Economics* 119 (1): 91–134.

Bharali, I., P. Kumar, and S. Sakthivel. 2020. "How Well Is India Responding to COVID-19?" Brookings Future Development Blog.

Central Intelligence Agency (CIA) World Factbook. https://www.cia.gov/the-world-factbook/.

Dabla-Norris, E., and C. Rhee. 2020. "A 'New Deal' for Informal Workers in Asia." IMF Blog.

Danish Trade Union Development Agency (DTDA) Analytical Unit. 2019. "Nepal Labor Market Profile." https://www.ulandssekretariatet.dk/wp-content/uploads/2020/03/Nepal _lmp_2019.pdf.

Das, S., S. Jain-Chandra, K. Kochhar, and N. Kumar. 2015. "Women Workers in India: Why So Few Among So Many?" IMF Working Paper 15/55, International Monetary Fund, Washington DC.

Dasgupta I., and S. Kar. 2018. "The Labor Market in India since the 1990s." *IZA World of Labor* 2018: 425.

Dougherty, S. 2008. "Labour Regulation and Employment Dynamics at the State Level in India." OECD Economics Department Working Paper 264, Organisation for Economic Co-operation and Development, Paris, France.

Dougherty, S., V. Frisancho, and K. Krishna. 2011. "Employment Protection Legislation and Plant-Level Productivity in India." NBER Working Paper 17693, National Bureau of Economic Research, Cambridge, MA.

Dougherty, S., V. Frisancho, and K. Krishna. 2014. "State-Level Labor Reform and Firm-Level Productivity in India." *India Policy Forum* 10 (1): 1–56.

Fletcher, E. K., R. Pande, and C. T. Moore. 2017. "Women and Work in India: Descriptive Evidence and a Review of Potential Policies." Harvard CID Working Paper 339, Harvard Center for International Development, Cambridge, MA.

Frey, C. B., and M. A. Osborne. 2017. "The Future of Employment: How Susceptible Are Jobs to Computerisation?" *Technological Forecasting and Social Change* 114 (C): 254–80.

Goretti, M., D. Kihara. and R. Salgado. 2019. "Is South Asia Ready for Take-Off? A Sustainable and Inclusive Growth Agenda." IMF Departmental Paper 19/18, International Monetary Fund, Washington, DC.

Government of India (1947). "Industrial Disputes Act 1947 Chapter VB." https://labour.gov .in/sites/default/files/THEINDUSTRIALDISPUTES_ACT1947_0.pdf.

Government of India, "India—Annual Survey of Industries 2016-17." http://microdata.gov.in /nada43/index.php/catalog/145.

Hayashi, R., and N. Matsuda. 2020. "COVID-19 Impact on Job Postings: Real-Time Assessment Using Bangladesh and Sri Lanka Online Job Portals." ADB Brief 135, Asian Development Bank, Mandaluyong, Philippines.

Hsieh, C., and P. J. Klenow. 2009. "Misallocation and Manufacturing TFP in China and India." *Quarterly Journal of Economics* 124 (4): 1403–48.

Hsieh, C., and B. Olken. 2014. "The Missing 'Missing Middle.'" *Journal of Economic Perspectives* 28 (3): 89–108.

International Labour Organization (ILO). 2013. *Decent Work Country Profile: Bangladesh.* International Labour Office, Geneva, Switzerland.

International Labour Organization (ILO). 2016b. *ILO Legal Database on Industrial Relations (IRLex).* International Labour Organization, Geneva, Switzerland.

International Labour Organization (ILO). 2016a. *Global Wage Report 2016/17: Wage Inequality in the Workplace.* International Labour Organization, Geneva, Switzerland.

International Labour Organization (ILO). 2018a. *India Wage Report: Wage Policies for Decent Work and Inclusive Growth.* International Labour Organization, Geneva, Switzerland.

International Labour Organization (ILO). 2018b. *Decent Work Country Programme for Nepal (2018–2022).* International Labour Organization, Geneva, Switzerland.

International Labour Organization (ILO). 2020a. *ILO Monitor—COVID-19 and the World of Work (3rd edition).* International Labour Organization, Geneva, Switzerland.

International Labour Organization (ILO). 2020b. *ILO Monitor—COVID-19 and the World of Work (5th edition).* International Labour Organization, Geneva, Switzerland.

International Labour Organization (ILO). 2020c. "Social Protection Spotlight—Social Protection Responses to the COVID-19 Pandemic in Developing Countries." International Labour Organization, Geneva, Switzerland.

International Monetary Fund (IMF). 2019. *World Economic Outlook.* IMF, Washington, DC, October.

International Monetary Fund (IMF). 2020. Fiscal Monitor. IMF, Washington, DC, April.

Mohommad, A., C. Sandoz, and P. Sodsriwiboon. 2021. "Resource Misallocation in India: The Role of Cross-State Labor Market Reform." IMF Working Paper 21/51, International Monetary Fund, Washington, DC.

National Institution for Transforming India (NITI Aayog). 2018. Strategy for New India at 75.

Organisation for Economic Co-operation and Development (OECD). 2019b. OECD Economic Surveys: India 2019. Organisation for Economic Co-operation and Development, Paris, France.

Organisation for Economic Co-operation and Development (OECD). 2019c. Pensions at a Glance 2019: OECD and G20 Indicators. Organisation for Economic Co-operation and Development, Paris, France.

Organisation for Economic Co-operation and Development (OECD). 2019a. Economic Policy Reforms 2019: Going for Growth. Organisation for Economic Co-operation and Development, Paris, France.

Rani, U., P. Belser, M. Oelz, and S. Ranjbar. 2013. "Minimum Wage Coverage and Compliance in Developing Countries." *International Labour Review* 152 (3–4): 381–410.

Sun, C. 2016. "Universal Old-Age Pensions in Maldives." ILO Social Protection Department, International Labour Organization, Geneva, Switzerland.

United Nations, Department of Economic and Social Affairs, Population Division. 2019. *World Population Prospects 2019* (Online edition, rev. 1).

Verick, S. 2014. "Women's Labour Force Participation in India: Why Is It So Low?" International Labour Organization, Geneva, Switzerland.

World Bank. 2018. *The Human Capital Project.* https://www.worldbank.org/en/publication /human-capital.

CHAPTER 4

Social Protection Reforms in South Asia

Bazlul Haque Khondker and Emmanouil Kitsios

Social protection programs have contributed to poverty reduction and improvement in social outcomes in South Asia. However, a large part of the population still lives in extreme poverty or remains highly vulnerable to shocks such as COVID-19 and spikes in commodity prices. Expanding coverage, strengthening benefit adequacy, and improving efficiency of the social assistance, social insurance, and labor market programs will help build resilience against economic, health, and environmental shocks. Mobilizing resources to sustainably finance higher social protection spending will be critical in facilitating inclusive growth in the region moving forward.

INTRODUCTION

South Asia registered significant economic growth and reduction in head count extreme poverty before the COVID-19 pandemic, while the evolution of inequality has been mixed.[1] Bangladesh, India, and Nepal reduced the share of their population living on less than $1.90 per day by 11, 10, and 35 percentage points within the past two decades (Figure 4.1). However, their head count poverty ratios exceed 14 percent, suggesting that a large segment of their population still lives in poverty. Bhutan, Maldives, and Sri Lanka reduced their poverty head count ratio before the pandemic to less than 2 percent of their population. Most South Asian countries recorded a reduction in the Gini index of inequality before the pandemic. However, the Gini index for Sri Lanka and India increased, with the increase being more pronounced for Sri Lanka that has the highest inequality measure recorded in 2010s among countries in South Asia (Figure 4.2).

The COVID-19 shock combined with the rise in energy and food prices that got exacerbated by Russia's war in Ukraine, have interrupted the momentum on poverty reduction in the region. While reliable indicators of the pandemic impact on monetary poverty are not available for South Asia at the time of this writing, nowcast estimates suggest that poverty rates increased in 2020 with little progress

---

[1] In this article, South Asia comprises Bangladesh, Bhutan, India, Nepal, Maldives, and Sri Lanka.

Figure 4.1. Poverty Head Count Ratio and GDP Per Capita

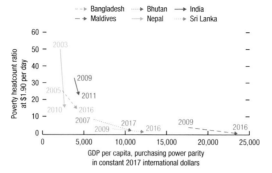

Sources: IMF's World Economic Outlook database; and World Bank's World Development Indicators database.
Note: Poverty head count ratio at $1.90 per day is the percentage of the population living on less than $1.90 per day at 2011 international prices. The figure shows the latest available data over the periods 2000–10 and 2010–20).

Figure 4.2. Gini Index and GDP Per Capita

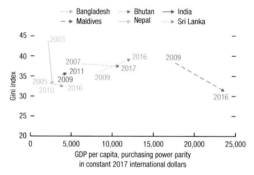

Sources: IMF's World Economic Outlook database; and World Bank's World Development Indicators database.
Note: A Gini index of 0 represents perfect equality of incomes or consumption expenditure among individuals within an economy, and an index of 100 implies perfect inequality.

made as of the middle of 2022 to return to the prepandemic lower levels (Figure 4.3). The poverty impact is estimated to have been more severe for Bhutan, Maldives, and Sri Lanka that are facing higher debt levels and limited fiscal space. Household budgets have been negatively affected by the earnings losses during the pandemic, as well as the hike in commodity prices that started in 2021 and worsened with Russia's war in Ukraine. Higher food and energy prices tend to disproportionately reduce the purchasing power of the poorest as food accounts for a higher share of their consumption basket.

Recent developments have reinforced the importance of social protection systems in protecting the most vulnerable from economic shocks. Social safety nets and social insurance schemes can effectively reduce poverty and inequality by providing income support and consumption smoothing. Countries in South Asia significantly expanded their social protection programs to support livelihoods during the pandemic, including by expanding existing cash transfer programs and providing reductions or

Figure 4.3. Poverty Head Count Ratio Estimates
(Percent of population)

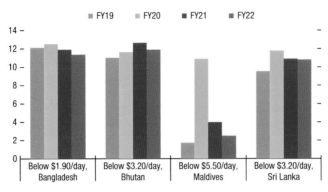

Source: World Bank's Poverty and Equity Briefs, April 2022.
Note: FY19–FY21 refer to nowcast estimates for fiscal years 2019 to 2021. FY22 refers to forecasts for the 2022 fiscal year. Fiscal years for Bangladesh and Bhutan span July 1 to June 30, and fiscal years for Maldives and Sri Lanka span January 1 to December 31. Poverty rate nowcasting estimates are not available for India and Nepal.

waivers for utility bills and financial obligations, such as loan repayments (Table 4.1).[2] New social protection programs and digital tools were also introduced to support poor households and to protect jobs. In Bangladesh, a new database of urban poor was developed during the pandemic with several rounds of cash transfers implemented, that has benefitted more than 9 million people. Bhutan's income support under Kidu (Druk Gyalpo's Relief Kidu) was distributed through the e-PEMS online payment system directly to beneficiaries' bank accounts, and targeted individuals most affected by the COVID-19 pandemic, including those who were laid off, or placed on unpaid leave or faced reduced salary from businesses in tourism and tourism-dependent sectors. The pandemic and surging food and energy prices have made more apparent the need to strengthen social safety nets in South Asia by making them more adequate and efficient in identifying and supporting poor and vulnerable households. This chapter discusses the poverty and inequality challenges of South Asian countries and benchmarks the performance of their respective social protection programs in terms of their coverage, adequacy, and targeting with the view to identify areas for improvement.[3]

---

[2] For example, as part of its stimulus package, the Indian government (1) provided cash support to 35 million beneficiaries under the National Social Assistance Program (NSAP) for elderly adults, widows, and disabled receiving social pensions, (2) made advance payments to 87 million farmers, and (3) provided direct payments for three months to 200 million women with a Pradhan Mantri Jan Dhan Yojana account (IMF 2022).

[3] Social protection instruments include (1) social assistance, (2) social insurance, and (3) labor market programs. Social assistance or social safety net programs are noncontributory transfer programs designed to protect households from poverty and destitution. Social insurance programs include contributory old-age, survivor, and disability pensions, sick leave and maternity/paternity benefits, and health insurance. Labor market programs aim to protect individuals against loss of income from unemployment or to actively help individuals find a job or otherwise enhance their earnings capacity.

TABLE 4.1.

South Asia's Social Protection and Jobs Responses to COVID-19

	Bangladesh	Bhutan	India	Maldives	Nepal	Sri Lanka	Total Worldwide
Social assistance							
Cash-based transfers	✓	✓	✓	✓	✓	✓	204
Public works		✓	✓		✓		48
In-kind support	✓	✓	✓	✓	✓	✓	165
Utility and financial support	✓	✓	✓	✓	✓	✓	187
Social insurance							
Paid leave/ unemployment							124
Health insurance support	✓		✓		✓		51
Pensions and disability benefits			✓			✓	63
Social security contributions (waiver/subsidy)			✓		✓		115
Labor markets							
Wage subsidy	✓	✓					117
Activation (training)				✓	✓		77
Labor regulation adjustment	✓		✓	✓		✓	115
Reduced work time subsidy							89

Sources: World Bank 2022b; and authors' calculations.

POVERTY, INEQUALITY, AND VULNERABILITY IN SOUTH ASIA

Extreme poverty is less pronounced in South Asia when compared with low-income developing countries, but is significantly higher in Bangladesh, India, and Nepal compared with emerging market economies (EMEs). India's population share living below $1.90 per day was 22.5 percent in 2011 and exceeds significantly the 1.1 percent of the population living in poverty in the median of EMEs.[4] In addition to the lowest-income poverty line that is set at $1.90 per day,

---

[4] The 2011 ASPIRE data used for India on poverty, inequality, and social protection is more dated compared with other countries in the analysis, thus rendering cross-country comparisons more difficult. Using more recent unofficial household surveys, Roy and van der Weide (2022) found that inequality and poverty in India have declined since then.

we consider two additional international poverty lines of $3.20 per day and $5.50 per day, that are more applicable to lower- and upper-middle-income countries, respectively. More than 50 percent and 80 percent of the population of Bangladesh, India, and Nepal fall under the $3.20 and $5.50 per day poverty lines, respectively, suggesting that a high share of the population has low purchasing power to address their daily needs. Bhutan and Sri Lanka share similar poverty profiles to each other based on the three international poverty lines as illustrated in Figure 4.4, with the distance to the poverty line of EMEs becoming larger when the highest threshold of $5.50 per day is applied.

South Asian countries tend to have a higher share of the population that is vulnerable to multidimensional poverty relative to their level of GDP per capita. The Multidimensional Poverty Index published by the United Nations Development Program complements the income poverty measures by measuring deprivation across 10 indicators related to health, education, and standard of living. Individuals are counted as multidimensionally poor if they are deprived in one-third or more of these 10 indicators. Population vulnerable to multidimensional poverty refers to the percent of the population at risk of suffering multiple deprivations along these indicators. Figure 4.5 plots the percent of population in each country that is vulnerable to multidimensional poverty against that country's GDP per capita. The more developed a country is, the lower the vulnerable share of the population tends to be.

While poverty rates are high in most of South Asia relative to other countries with similar levels of development, inequality is less stark. The ratio of the share of income between the richest 10 percent and poorest 40 percent, also known as the Palma ratio, is lower for South Asian countries than most low-income

Figure 4.4. Poverty Head Count Ratio
(Percent of population)

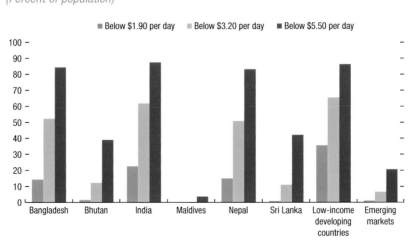

Sources: World Bank's PovcalNet database; and authors' calculations.
Note: Data are for the latest year available.

Figure 4.5. Population Vulnerable to Multidimensional Poverty

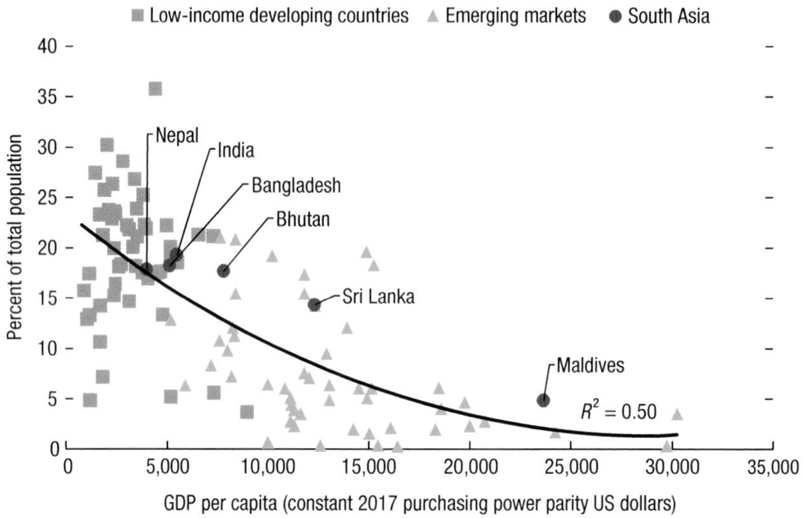

Sources: IMF's World Economic Outlook database; United Nations Development Programme 2021; and authors' calculations.

developing countries (LIDCs). Similarly, most Palma ratios in South Asia are lower than that of the median of EMEs. Bangladesh, Maldives, and Nepal have Palma ratios that are lower than the 25th percentile of the respective Palma ratio distributions of LIDCs and EMEs suggesting that they are more equitable than at least 75 percent of the countries in these income categories (Figure 4.6). Sri Lanka has the highest Palma ratio that is closer to the median of LIDCs and EMEs. Although lower than many other countries, the Palma ratios for South Asia exceed 1, suggesting that they face high inequality as the richest 10 percent receive a larger share of national income than the poorest 40 percent. The COVID-19 pandemic has likely exacerbated inequality during 2020–21 for most countries, while the Gini coefficient in South Asia (Figure 4.7) is higher than the 27 percent threshold that Grigoli and Robles (2017) find inequality to become growth reducing.

Advancing shared prosperity by boosting the incomes of the poorest 40 percent has helped improve the living conditions of poor and vulnerable individuals, but growth has not been sufficiently inclusive across the region (Figure 4.8). Most LIDCs and EMEs registered increased consumption by the bottom 40 percent of their income distribution, indicating that living standards of the relatively less well-off segments of the population have been improving. Relative to the median LIDCs and EMEs, Bangladesh and Bhutan registered smaller annualized growth rates of 1.3 and 1.6 percent, respectively. India, Maldives, and Nepal registered growth rates that exceeded the 75th percentile of the LIDCs and EMEs, while Sri Lanka's growth rate was close to the median of EMEs. As growth in the average

Figure 4.6. Palma Ratio of Inequality

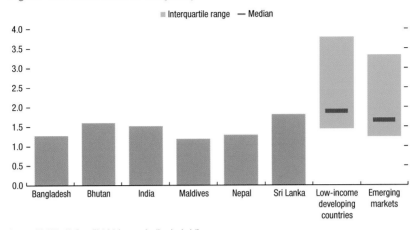

Sources: World Bank's PovcalNet database; and authors' calculations.
Note: The Palma ratio is calculated as the share of income or consumption between the top 10 percent and the bottom 40 percent.
Data are for latest year available.

Figure 4.7. Gini Index of Inequality

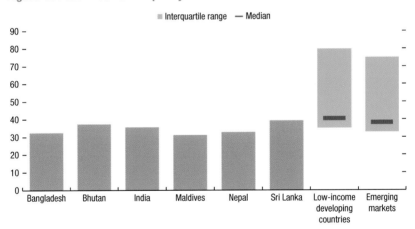

Sources: World Bank's PovcalNet database; and authors' calculations.
Note: Data are for latest year available.

income of the bottom 40 percent of the distribution can result from increases in that segment's share of overall income or from the rising mean income of the overall population, we turn to a measure of whether the income growth of the bottom 40 is growing more quickly than the average population.

While growth has been inclusive, the gains accruing to the poorest are uneven for most countries in the region as the growth in their consumption lags that of the average population. With poverty being prevalent in most of South Asia despite high GDP per capita growth, it is important to track the income or

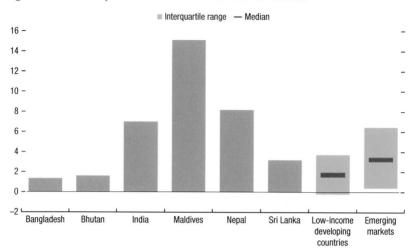

Figure 4.8. Consumption Growth of the Poorest 40 Percent

Sources: World Bank's PovcalNet database; and authors' calculations.
Note: Data shows the annualized growth rate based on the latest two years available.

consumption growth of the poorest 40 percent and compare it to the overall mean to assess whether growth has been inclusive. The difference in growth rates between the bottom 40 and the overall mean is called the shared prosperity premium. Figure 4.9 shows that, on average, inclusive growth has been stronger for EMEs than LIDCs. Most countries in South Asia have recorded a negative shared prosperity premium. India and Sri Lanka had lower shared prosperity premia than most LIDCs and EMEs. The income growth of the poorest 40 percent also grew less quickly than the average in Bangladesh and Bhutan, albeit their negative shared prosperity premium was lower than that observed in most LIDCs. On the other hand, Maldives and Nepal exhibited stronger inclusive growth than most EMEs and LIDCs.

SOCIAL PROTECTION EFFECTIVENESS

Are social protection mechanisms in South Asia strong enough to achieve their objective? This section provides an overview of the key elements of the social protection systems in the region focusing on key aspects such as their coverage, targeting, adequacy, and spending levels.[5] Social protection in the discussion that

---

[5] Data on spending level and composition are only available for social assistance programs in the World Bank's ASPIRE (Atlas of Social Protection Indicators of Resilience and Equity) database. Pretransfer income or consumption without the social protection transfer is used to generate the indicators by quintile, except for the adequacy of benefits indicator for which posttransfer income or consumption is used.

Figure 4.9. Shared Prosperity Premium of the Poorest 40 Percent

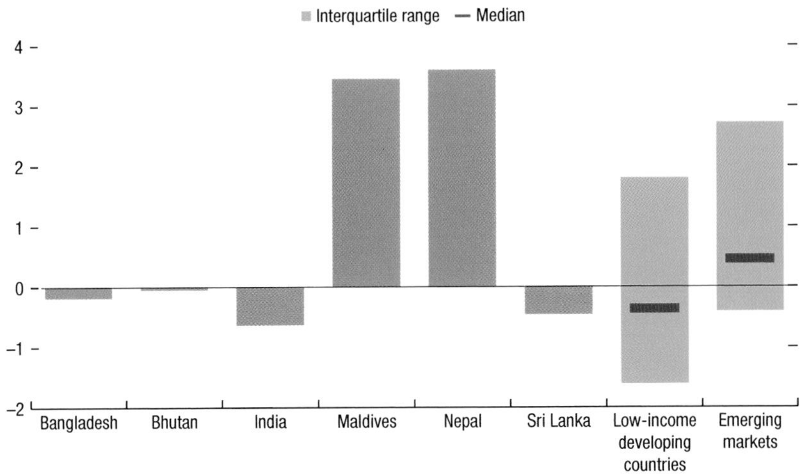

Sources: World Bank's PovcalNet database; and authors' calculations.
Note: Data shows the annualized growth rate based on the latest two years available.

follows consists of any type of social insurance (old-age pension and other social security), labor market programs, and social assistance (unconditional and conditional cash transfers, social pensions, public works, fee waivers and targeted subsidies, school feeding, in-kind transfers, and other social assistance programs).

The coverage of social protection programs in most South Asian countries is lower than that of most EMEs across all quintiles of the income distribution. Coverage is expressed as the percentage of the population receiving a given type of social protection program and includes all household members where at least one member receives a benefit (Figure 4.10). India is the only country in South Asia with a higher share of its population receiving a social protection benefit when compared with most EMEs and LIDCs. On the other hand, Bhutan's coverage ratios are very low.[6] All South Asian countries tend to have higher coverage ratios for their bottom income quintiles suggesting that their social protection systems are geared toward the poorest. However, at least 40 percent of the poorest quintile in most countries in the region do not benefit from a social protection program. The average coverage of the poorest quintile is about 51 percent in South Asia that exceeds the 30 percent coverage in most LIDCs and falls short of the 87 percent coverage reported for most EMEs.

South Asia's social protection programs could be made more progressive by strengthening the allocations provided to the poorest quintiles. Benefit adequacy

---

[6] The low coverage of social protection spending in Bhutan is partly explained by the nonavailability of data on the composition of the country's social assistance spending programs in the ASPIRE database.

Figure 4.10. Social Protection Coverage, by Quintile
(Percent)

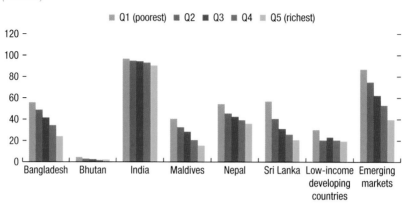

Sources: World Bank's ASPIRE database; and authors' calculations.
Note: Data are for the latest year available. Q = quintile.

is a measure of the total benefit level of social protection programs received by all beneficiaries in a quintile relative to the income or consumption of beneficiaries in that quintile. Many countries in South Asia have a lower adequacy share of benefits in their poorest quintile relative to the median of LIDCs and EMEs, with the adequacy shares of Bangladesh, India, and Nepal being the lowest (Figure 4.11) when posttransfer income or consumption are considered. Average transfer amounts to beneficiaries is likely lower in South Asia, as a result of covering a large pool of beneficiaries with a limited budget allocation. Importantly, many South Asian countries have lower adequacy shares in the bottom quintile relative to higher posttransfer income quintiles. This is the case, for example, in Bangladesh, Bhutan, Nepal, and Sri Lanka, where the social protection system is less generous to beneficiaries belonging to the poorest quintile relative to those belonging to some of the higher ones. Benefit support, therefore, could improve by becoming more progressive to better support poor households.

Most South Asian countries have pro-poor social protection systems in terms of their beneficiary incidence of the lowest quintile. Beneficiary incidence indicates the proportion of program beneficiaries belonging to each quintile of the per capita pretransfer income distribution (Figure 4.12). Social protection is considered pro-poor if more than 20 percent of its total beneficiaries belong to the bottom 20 percent of the distribution. This criterion is met in almost all South Asian countries, except for Bhutan where beneficiary incidence is higher than 20 percent in the fourth and fifth quintiles. All other South Asian countries tend to have progressive social protection systems, as the share of beneficiaries is falling across quintiles and more than 40 percent of total beneficiaries fall under the lowest 40 percent of the distribution. Bangladesh, Maldives, and Sri Lanka have higher beneficiary incidence ratios for their poorest quintiles relative to most LIDCs and EMEs, while India and Nepal are closer to the median of LIDCs.

Figure 4.11. Social Protection: Adequacy, by Quintile
(Percent)

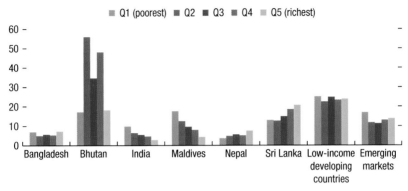

Sources: World Bank's ASPIRE database; and authors' calculations.
Note: Data are for the latest year available. Q = quintile.

Figure 4.12. Social Protection: Beneficiary Incidence, by Quintile
(Percent)

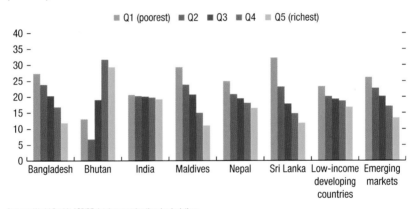

Sources: World Bank's ASPIRE database; and authors' calculations.
Note: Data are for the latest year available. Q = quintile.

While most South Asian countries exhibit pro-poor benefit incidence, the overall progressivity of their social protection system could improve. Benefit incidence measures the proportion of transfers that the poorest quintile receives as a percent of total transfers (Figure 4.13). Except for Maldives, this indicator is above 20 percent for the bottom quintile in the region. Bangladesh, Bhutan, and India have a significantly higher share of the benefits accruing to the bottom quintile than most LIDCs and EMEs. However, the progressivity of the overall social protection system in South Asia could improve considering that the benefit incidence ratio for the richest quintile exceeds that of the second, third, and fourth quintiles for most countries in the region. For example, progressivity could improve to better target poor and vulnerable households in Maldives, Nepal, and

Figure 4.13. Social Protection: Benefits Incidence, by Quintile
(Percent)

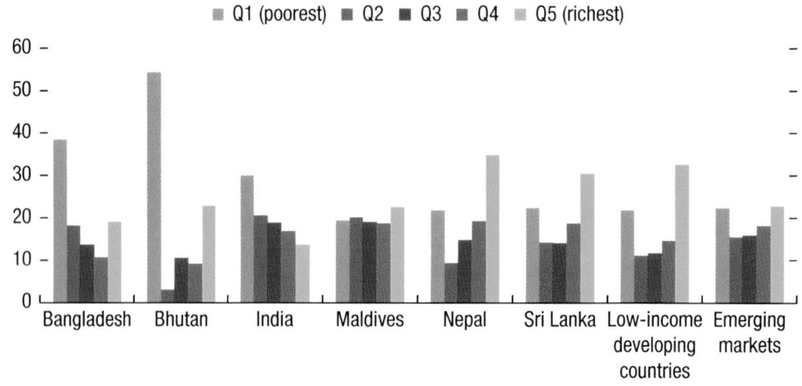

Sources: World Bank's ASPIRE database; and authors' calculations.
Note: Data are for the latest year available. Q = quintile.

Sri Lanka as the benefit incidence in the bottom two quintiles is lower than 40 percent. The higher benefits incidence of social protection observed in the higher quintiles in Nepal and Sri Lanka is mainly attributed to social insurance programs such as contributory pensions. Instead, the benefit incidence of social assistance programs in both countries is the highest for the lowest quintile.

There is significant heterogeneity in the level and composition of social assistance spending across South Asia. Bhutan and Sri Lanka have the lowest social assistance spending shares in the region of about 0.3 and 0.5 percent of GDP, respectively, that are lower than those of most LIDCs and EMEs (Figure 4.14).[7] The rest of the South Asian countries have higher social spending relative to most LIDCs, whereas for India and Nepal social assistance spending exceeds that of most EMEs as well.

It is worth noting that the components of social assistance spending vary within South Asia, but also relative to the median of LIDCs and EMEs (Figure 4.15).[8] Maldives and Nepal allocate more than 80 percent of their social assistance to social pensions, while India allocates about 70 percent of its social assistance to food and in-kind support. Sri Lanka allocates about half of its social assistance support to unconditional cash transfers, while Bangladesh's allocation of 25 percent of its social assistance budget in public works is the highest in the region and across most LIDCs and EMEs. Except for Bangladesh, most South Asian countries tend to concentrate most of their spending on a certain category of assistance, while the countries with the median social assistance spending among EMEs and LIDCs are more diversified across the different types of assistance.

---

[7] In the case of Bhutan, Druk Gyalpois Relief Kidu provided through the National Resilience Fund, as well the Kidu Schemes are provided through nonbudgetary support.

[8] The composition of social assistance spending is not available for Bhutan in the ASPIRE database.

Figure 4.14. Total Social Assistance Spending
(Percent)

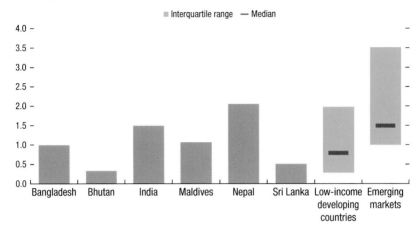

Sources: World Bank's ASPIRE database; and authors' calculations.
Note: Data are for the latest year available. Q = quintile.

Figure 4.15. Social Assistance Spending Composition
(Percent)

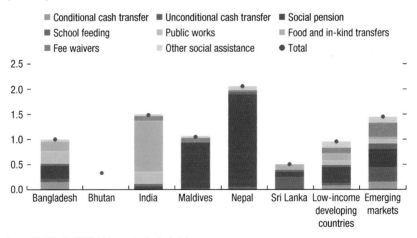

Sources: World Bank's ASPIRE database; and authors' calculations.
Note: Data are for the latest year available. Q = quintile.

Social protection coverage, benefit incidence and adequacy in the poorest quintiles remain low for most South Asian countries, despite improving over time across most urban and rural regions (Table 4.2). Coverage of the poorest quintile increased over time both in the rural and urban areas of South Asia. Coverage exceeded 50 percent of the rural households before the pandemic in Bangladesh, India, Nepal, and Sri Lanka. However, except for India, less than 5 out of 10 urban poor were covered by social protection. Benefit adequacy declined in the

TABLE 4.2.

Social Protection Performance Indicators for the Poorest Quintile
(Percent)

	Coverage		Benefit Incidence[1]		Adequacy[1]	
	Urban	Rural	Urban	Rural	Urban	Rural
Bangladesh						
2010	13.6	27.8	4.0	12.1	6.5	5.7
2016	39.6	55.2	10.9	18.8	5.5	7.4
Bhutan						
2007	1.7	2.9	0.9	18.7	0.7	2.7
2012	3.2	4.9	23.2	2.4	109.2	15.4
India						
2009	4.5	29.0				
2011	93.9	97.2	21.9	19.0	5.3	10.6
Maldives						
2009	24.3	30.3	18.3	18.2	53.1	83.3
2016	31.4	37.7	18.4	13.0	12.2	20.5
Nepal						
2010	36.7	52.5	5.9	9.1	10.0	3.7
Sri Lanka						
2012	38.9	49.1	4.0	6.4	7.5	7.7
2016	40.2	50.8	7.5	9.3	13.1	13.5

Sources: World Bank's ASPIRE database; and authors' calculations.
[1]Data for India are not available for 2009.

urban regions of Bangladesh and Maldives as coverage increased over time. Urban poor across South Asia, mostly employed in the informal sector, were not only among the most vulnerable groups during the COVID-19 lockdowns, but also the most difficult to target.

STRENGTHENING SOCIAL PROTECTION AFTER COVID-19

Tackling rising inequality and poverty has become more urgent for South Asia following the COVID-19 pandemic. This requires safeguarding priority social spending and building a resilient and adaptive social protection system against future shocks. Specific steps that could help strengthen social protection include the following:

- Expanding social protection and labor market programs to improve their adequacy and coverage. The analysis in the previous section documented the need to increase benefit adequacy and expand coverage to better support pro-poor growth in the region both in normal times and during crises such as the COVID-19 pandemic. Additional challenges are posed by the pandemic's "new poor," as considerable financing will be required to broaden the scope of social protection and strengthen the benefit generosity of the offered programs. However, many countries in South Asia are currently facing fiscal constraints from either persistently low revenue or high public indebtedness. Countries with limited fiscal space, therefore, will need to mobilize additional resources to scale up social spending, including by removing inefficient and regressive subsidies, increasing broad-based taxes, and consolidating fragmented programs with duplication of benefits or high administrative costs.

- Addressing inefficiencies in social protection delivery. Informal workers across South Asia were heavily impacted by the pandemic and the lock-downs, as they were more vulnerable to job losses and had lower financial savings. It is important, therefore, to invest in identification and delivery systems that will facilitate (1) reaching out to those currently not covered by social programs, and (2) disbursing social protection benefits in a timely and secure manner. India aims to improve the administrative and targeting per-formance of its social safety nets by integrating its biometric digital citizen identification (ID) system called Aadhaar—that currently covers more than 1.2 billion people—with bank accounts, as well as tax and social program beneficiary databases. This, in turn, enables the government to pursue Aadhaar-based reforms of social programs—such as transforming liquefied petroleum gas subsidies into a direct cash transfer deposited on Aadhaar-linked bank accounts.[9] Similarly, inclusion and exclusion errors in social programs can be reduced by uniquely identifying eligible beneficiaries to mitigate benefit leakages and by setting transparent and simple eligibility criteria to increase enrollment. It is important to note that frontline service providers and enrollment operators need to be adequately trained to resolve authentication exclusion issues or identify and eliminate fraud in the process of program delivery.[10] Better targeting helps improve the effectiveness of social spending, thus benefitting the most countries with limited fiscal space. Well-designed poverty registries could enhance the shock responsive-ness of the social safety net design, which is crucial for preventing climate and other shocks from having a lasting effect on poor households.

- Expanding government-to-person social transfers. Most countries in South Asia employed a variety of payment channels to transfer funds to the benefi-ciaries before the pandemic that included payments through the government treasury, the banking system, and the postal system. These payment systems have often been criticized for (1) delays in beneficiaries receiving funds; (2)

---

[9] Starting in 2013, beneficiaries' Aadhaar numbers were linked to the liquefied petroleum gas program to prevent claims of benefits for ghost beneficiaries or duplication of benefit claims. The government made electronic transfers of the subsidy directly to the Aadhaar-linked bank account of beneficiaries, bypassing dealers who were selling liquefied petroleum gas cylinders to households at a subsidized price under the dual pricing system (see IMF 2018). India's digital infrastructure also enabled the rapid deployment of cash transfers during the pandemic.

[10] In drawing lessons from India's Aadhaar-based reforms, Gelb and Mukherjee (2019) stressed that technology is not infallible and that clear protocols for exception management and clear accountabil-ity for handling cases of technological failure is important to prevent exclusion.

added difficulties for elderly adults, pregnant mothers, child-attending parents, and people with disabilities; (3) high transaction costs; (4) vulnerability to duplication and fraudulent payments; and (5) cash management related fiscal risks. Scaling up government-to-person payments would mitigate such concerns by helping reduce administrative layers and facilitating authenticated and secure payments. Social distancing measures during the pandemic and the large penetration of mobile phones in South Asia have encouraged government-to-person transfers through mobile platforms. However, for government-to-person transfers to be successfully implemented, policymakers and regulators would need to address cybersecurity and digital fraud risks, as well as challenges related to the digital illiteracy and exclusion of the poor and vulnerable segments of the population.

• Better aligning the design of social protection with South Asia's demographic and labor market structure. Children represent a large population group in the region that receives a small share of social assistance spending. On the contrary, a larger share of spending is directed toward elderly adults even though their population share is the lowest among the age groups. Enhancing and rebalancing social spending generosity to better account for the demographic characteristics of the households and the prevalence of poverty in each demographic group may significantly improve the currently weak benefit adequacy of South Asia's social protection systems for the urban poor and certain life cycle groups such as pregnant women, mothers, and children. Moreover, there is a lack of available insurance schemes for the working-age group. Social protection could be strengthened by providing access to affordable unemployment insurance schemes for both formal and informal workers, as well as providing child and adult care services to ensure higher participation of the female workforce in the labor market. Similarly, encouraging the participation of the large pool of informal workers in contributory pension schemes would strongly complement the existing social pension schemes in the region.

CONCLUSIONS

Social protection programs in South Asia will need to be strengthened, given recent and prospective shocks, including to mitigate the scarring effects of the pandemic on the most vulnerable. This chapter has identified strengths and weaknesses in South Asia's social protection systems and has suggested measures that could make them more efficient, to reap the intended benefits of consumption smoothing and further poverty reduction. Preserving the gains in poverty reduction that were realized over the prepandemic period will require expanding the coverage to the new poor not covered by existing programs. Raising benefit adequacy and reducing leakages by improving beneficiary selection would further enhance the social safety net. Enabling South Asia's social protection systems to be easily expandable when adverse shocks occur, would improve their disaster responsiveness moving forward.

REFERENCES

Gelb, Alan, and Anit Mukherjee. 2019. "Building on Digital ID for Inclusive Services: Lessons from India." CGD Notes, Center for Global Development, Washington, DC.

Grigoli, Francesco, and Adrian Robles. 2017. "Inequality Overhang." IMF Working Paper 2017/076, International Monetary Fund, Washington, DC.

International Monetary Fund (IMF). 2018. *Fiscal Monitor: Capitalizing on Good Times.* Washington, DC: IMF, April.

International Monetary Fund (IMF). 2020. *Fiscal Monitor: Policies to Support People during the COVID-19 Pandemic.* Washington, DC: IMF, April.

International Monetary Fund (IMF). 2022. *Fiscal Monitor: Helping People Bounce Back.* Washington, DC: IMF, October.

Sinha Roy, Sutirtha, and Roy van der Weide. 2022. "Poverty in India Has Declined over the Last Decade But Not as Much as Previously Thought." Policy Research Working Paper, World Bank, Washington, DC.

United Nations Development Programme. 2021. *Global Multidimensional Poverty Index 2021: Unmasking Disparities by Ethnicity, Caste and Gender.* New York and Oxford: United Nations Development Programme and Oxford Poverty and Human Development Initiative.

World Bank. 2022a. *COVID-19 in South Asia: An Unequal Shock, an Uncertain Recovery—Findings on Labor Market Impacts from Round 1 of the SAR COVID Phone Monitoring Surveys.* Washington, DC: World Bank.

World Bank. 2022b. "Social Protection and Jobs Responses to COVID-19: A Real-Time Review of Country Measures." Brief, World Bank, Washington, DC.

CHAPTER 5

Improving Gender Equality with Digitalization

Piyaporn Sodsriwiboon

Female labor force participation in South Asia is relatively low, leading to high and widening gender gaps. The COVID-19 pandemic appears to have aggravated existing gender inequalities, leading to job losses and additional burden of care. Today, digitalization is transforming markets quickly and presents important opportunities to support women's workforce participation. This chapter empirically identifies the relationship between digitalization and gender outcomes. Alongside a multidimensional policy approach using a range of fiscal, legal, and structural measures to empower women, digitalization could potentially help facilitate women's workforce participation, thus reducing gender economic gaps.

WOMEN IN SOUTH ASIA: GENDER (IN)EQUALITY

South Asia is arguably one of the most dynamic regions in the world, where it accounts for about a fifth of the world's population and increasingly contributes to the global economy. Yet, a majority of women in South Asia have not been able to become part of this success story, as gaps remain large in many countries in the region on gender equality, both in work and in society. In South Asia, 500 million women are in working age but only about 40 percent of these women participate in the labor force, well below that of other regions (Figure 5.1). The pattern appears to be broadly consistent across countries in South Asia, for instance:

- Bangladesh has made significant progress in gender equality as part of its five-year plans including National Women Development Policy and Gender Responsive Budgeting (IMF 2018a). The World Economic Forum's "Global Gender Gap Report 2017" recognized Bangladesh as South Asia's top performer for improved gender parity. Gender disparity in education has been largely eliminated and maternal mortality has declined substantially. Nevertheless, female labor force participation (FLFP) remained low at about 36.3 percent in 2017, according to the 2016/17 labor force survey (latest data).

This study benefited from comments from Asia and Pacific Department country teams on Bangladesh, India, Maldives, Nepal, and Sri Lanka, and the Indian authorities on an earlier draft of this chapter. The author thanks participants in the regional forum "Fostering Growth in South Asia" in New Delhi, India, for comments.

Figure 5.1. Female Labor Force Participation

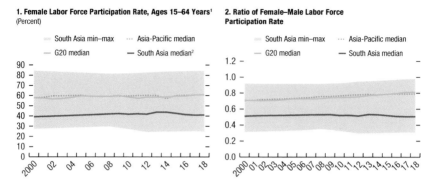

1. Female Labor Force Participation Rate, Ages 15–64 Years[1]
(Percent)

2. Ratio of Female–Male Labor Force Participation Rate

Sources: World Bank's World Development Indicators; Ministry of Statistics and Programme Implementation, Government of India; and IMF staff calculations.
[1]Modeled International Labour Organization estimate.
[2]South Asia median includes Bangladesh, Bhutan, India, Maldives, Nepal, and Sri Lanka.

- In India, women are estimated to account for only 17 percent of GDP, less than half the global average and compared unfavorably with 40 percent of GDP in China (Dixon 2018). Not only is its FLFP comparably low, but it fell sharply from 42.7 percent in FY2004/05 to 23.3 percent in FY2017/18. India also ranks 108th out of 149 countries on the World Economic Forum's "Global Gender Gap Report 2018," with particularly low scores on health and survival and economic participation.

- In Sri Lanka, although gender disparities have largely been eliminated in the key aspects of education and health care, women still face disadvantages in economic and political life (IMF 2018c). FLFP recorded at about 32.1 percent, compared with 71.9 percent for men in 2020. Women's wages in Sri Lanka were comparably low at about 85 percent of men's wages. Sri Lanka's gender outcomes on economic participation and opportunity as well as political empowerment have also been declining in the past decade.

- Nepal's labor force survey of FY2017/18 indicated that FLFP was only about 26.3 percent, well below the male labor force participation rate of 53.8 percent. Nepal's FLFP increased with education level, but only peaked at ages 25–34 years and started to decline at higher ages.

- Bhutan and Maldives, on the other hand, have relatively high FLFP among South Asian countries. Bhutan's FLFP registered around 55.9 percent in 2015 and Maldives' FLFP accounted for about 77 percent in 2019, based on national estimate.

Many women in South Asia participate in low-paid, low-status, and often informal jobs. The informal employment and the associated challenges are high in South Asia (Chapter 3), and these challenges are disproportionately affected women. According to the International Labour Organization (2018), the share of women working in the informal sector is very high, at 96 percent in Nepal, 81 percent in India, and 55 percent in Sri Lanka (Figure 5.2). Such informal employment generally corresponds with low earnings and poor working conditions, as well as a lack of a social safety net and job security. Najeeb, Morales, and Lopez-Acevedo (2020) notes rural female employment is significantly higher than urban, as agriculture primarily accounts for the largest share of female employment in South Asia. Furthermore, women are less likely to own and run businesses in South Asia and women-owned businesses largely prevail in the informal sector with a concentration in small-scale entrepreneurship and traditional sectors such as retail trade and low-skilled services.

A number of structural barriers contributes to gender inequality in economic participation and opportunity in South Asia, where gender norms and other barriers affect both supply and demand for female labor. These include the following:

- *Cultural norms:* These, which include patriarchal attitudes, practice of dowry, and, in India, preference for a male child—viewed to be better able to economically support parents in old age—are intertwined with the status of women and their decision to join the workforce (IMF 2017b). For example, the sex ratio at birth—the number of male-to-female babies born—remains very high in India, leading to a demographic deficit of women (Figure 5.3, panel 1).These norms also create a cycle of low investment in girls' education and health in India, thus resulting in unequal economic opportunities.

- *Education and training:* There has been significant progress in education opportunity, thus contributing to an improved economic opportunity in South Asia (Figure 5.3, panel 2). In Sri Lanka, provision of free state education has resulted in a rapid rise in school enrollment among female students. In Bangladesh, the female enrollments for primary and secondary education have seen a great stride, which, in turn, has made significant contribution

Figure 5.2. Women in Informal Employment

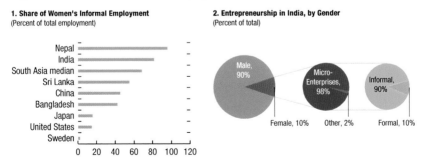

1. Share of Women's Informal Employment
(Percent of total employment)

2. Entrepreneurship in India, by Gender
(Percent of total)

Source: International Labour Organization 2018.

Source: National Sample Survey Organization.

Figure 5.3. Structural Barriers Related to Gender Disparity in South Asia

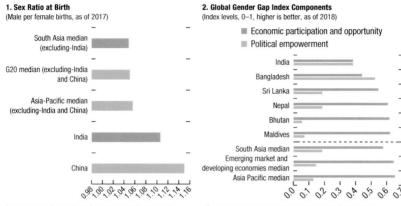

Sources: World Bank's World Development Indicators; and IMF staff calculations.

Sources: World Economic Forum; and IMF staff calculations.
Note: South Asia median includes Bangladesh, Bhutan, India, Maldives, Nepal, and Sri Lanka. Data are sorted based on overall index.

TABLE 5.1.

Are Women Permitted to Do the Same Work as Men?

	Work the Same Night Hours	Work in Mining	Work in Factories	Work in Construction	Work in Agriculture	Work in Water Sector	Work in Transportation	Work in Metalworking
Bangladesh	Yes	No	No[1]	Yes	Yes	No	Yes	Yes
Bhutan	Yes	Yes	Yes	Yes	Yes	Yes	Yes	Yes
India	No	No	No[2]	Yes	Yes	Yes	Yes	No
Maldives	Yes	Yes	Yes	Yes	Yes	Yes	Yes	Yes
Nepal	No	Yes	Yes	Yes	Yes	Yes	Yes	Yes
Sri Lanka	No	No	No[3]	Yes	Yes	Yes	Yes	Yes

Source: Najeeb, Morales, and Lopez-Acevedo 2020, based on Women, Business and the Law Database, World Bank.
[1]Labor Act, Secs. 39, 40, 42, and 87.
[2]Factories Act, Secs. 27, 66, and 87.
[3]Factories Ordinance No. 45 of 1942, Secs. 25, 67, and 67A (2).

in reducing inequalities. Nevertheless, skill gaps remain the key obstacles for women to acquire good quality jobs.

- *Infrastructure:* Poor infrastructure ranging from the lack of water supply, cooking gas, and electricity to public safety facilities and sanitation at the workplace continues to weigh on unpaid home and care burdens of women and prevents women from being part of the workforce.

- *Legal barriers:* Despite strong growth in labor-intensive industries that helped enhance an employment opportunity for women in some South Asian countries (for example, Bangladesh and Sri Lanka), still some legal barriers to female employment continue to disproportionately affect the female labor force (Table 5.1). Strict labor regulations that prevent formal job creation could particularly trap women in low-skill and low-paid jobs in the informal sector, even as the economy grows.

- *Access to finance:* While financial inclusion in many South Asian countries has improved through the availability of bank accounts, the usage of the accounts remains low. Barriers related to access to formal credit continue to hinder the growth of women-owned enterprises. The lack of adequate collateral resulting from social restrictions around inheritance, land ownership rights, and limited financial awareness, often turn women entrepreneurs toward informal financing sources and constrain women's access to formal credit (IMF 2017a). Savings are often stored under the mattress and through informal groups, raising safety concerns and restricting financial intermediation for productive investment.

THE UNEQUAL EFFECTS OF THE COVID-19 PANDEMIC ON WOMEN IN SOUTH ASIA

The COVID-19 pandemic is likely to exacerbate existing economic gender gaps through job losses and reduced working hours. In South Asia, a large share of women are engaged in informal employment, particularly among low-skill services, which were the worst hit by the necessary lockdowns to contain the spread of the disease. Female informal workers therefore were more likely to lose jobs as a result of economic shocks amid the pandemic. Deshpande (2020) found that the decline in employment in India caused by the COVID-19–induced lockdown was not gender neutral. While more men lost employment than women did in absolute terms, women had a 20 percent higher chance than men did to lose jobs, conditional on being employed before the lockdown. Results of the United Nations' Women Rapid Assessment Survey (United Nations 2020) indicated that women in both informal and formal employment were more likely than men were to see their working hours reduced in Bangladesh and Maldives. In Sri Lanka, FLFP fell to its decade low of 32 percent, and labor force participation gap between male and female widened to its decade high of 39.8 percent in 2020.

Women are substantially more likely to carry additional burdens of care, thus preventing them from work during the pandemic and reentering the labor force after the pandemic. Longstanding patriarchal social norms and cultural expectations have put on South Asian women the burden of caring for children, elderly adults, and the household. As a result of the lockdown and the spread of COVID-19, although both women and men face these burdens, women are more likely to perform many of these unpaid care and domestic tasks. In particular, Deshpande (2020) presented early evidence that shows an increase in hours spent on domestic work was significantly higher for women than men in India during the lockdown. Chauhan (2020) found that COVID-19 and the consequent lockdown exacerbated existing gender inequalities and significantly increased the burden of unpaid work for women in urban centers in India.

Gender-sensitive policies are imperative to support female employment amid the economic shock from the pandemic. Early studies have shown the economic costs of the pandemic may be disproportionately borne by women (for example, Deshpande

2020 among others). In Bangladesh, cash transfer programs of 2,500 Bangladeshi taka (US$29.50) per family to support the vulnerable during the pandemic have been rolled out directly from the government to around 8.75 million families through the government-to-person payment system. The substantial part of these beneficiaries are women. The Indian government announced direct cash transfers of 500 rupees (US$6.50) to the women who have a Jan Dhan account—a no-frills bank account opened under the Pradhan Mantri Jan-Dhan Yojana initiative—for three months which helped provide temporary relief, but more needs to be done as many lose their jobs and economic mobility. More broadly, targeted socio economic policies to support female employment and job creation and address women's disproportionate unpaid work and caregiving responsibilities are urgently needed.

WOMEN AND GROWTH: BUILDING AN INCLUSIVE ECONOMY

A growing body of literature shows that women can help to power the growth engine, making vital contributions to enhancing South Asia's growth and making growth more inclusive and sustainable. Studies find greater economic participation of women and reduced gender gaps can lead to significant economic gains. From a cross-country perspective, Cuberes and Teignier (2012) showed that economic gender gaps result in significant output losses ranging from 15 to 30 percent of GDP depending on the initial gaps. According to the International Labour Organization (2017), countries in South Asia could gain about 9 percent in GDP level and 11 percent in employment from reaching gender parity (Figure 5.4). Similarly, IMF (2018b) suggested decreasing gender

Figure 5.4. Gender Equality and Macroeconomic Outcomes

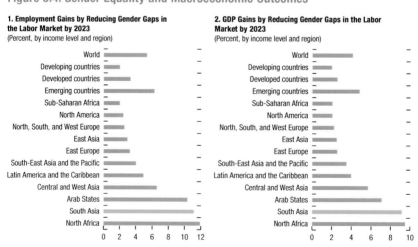

1. Employment Gains by Reducing Gender Gaps in the Labor Market by 2023
(Percent, by income level and region)

2. GDP Gains by Reducing Gender Gaps in the Labor Market by 2023
(Percent, by income level and region)

Sources: ILO 2017; and ILO estimation based on ILO's Trend Economic Models, November 2016.
Note: ILO = International Labour Organization.

discrimination and barriers to FLFP could lead to large potential welfare and output gains. Using analysis for India, Khera (2016 and 2018) found that increased FLFP and female formal employment could improve aggregate economic outcomes in India. Gender-targeted policies on education and safety, along with policies to tackle labor market rigidities, would matter significantly. Likewise, the World Bank's estimate suggests that India's annual GDP growth would rise by 1.5 percentage points, to about 9 percent, if half of Indian women were in the labor force (Dixon 2018).

WOMEN'S WORKFORCE PARTICIPATION AND DIGITALIZATION

Today, new digital technologies are transforming markets quickly and present important opportunities to support women's workforce participation. The rapid increase in mobile phone availability and use can help reduce the costs of obtaining information and other transaction costs. For example, digital marketing platforms can help overcome physical distance and provide access to new markets and revenue opportunities, thus connecting women entrepreneurs with limited mobility in remote areas to markets to sell produce and goods. Digital technology can also serve as a job-matching platform which could improve labor market information flows, cut time for job search, and improve labor market efficiency. This would have particular benefits for people living in remote areas and those looking for part-time work, thus encouraging women to enter the workforce. Mobile and digital financial services could, in addition, help lower the costs of money transfers and financial services and improve access to credit, particularly in areas with large unbanked and underserved populations. Improved access therefore will allow women to make use of financial services to support their economic activities including saving, borrowing, investing, and making payments.

This chapter empirically identifies the relationship between digitalization and gender outcomes and highlights the implications for South Asian countries. In a cross-country setting, this chapter analyzes the relationship between women's workforce participation as well as gender equality and digitalization, taking into account other macro and structural settings. The analysis follows the empirical setup as in Thevenon (2010) that analyzes drivers of FLFP in Organisation for Economic Co-operation and Development countries. Alongside, it will assess the linkages between countries' economic gender gaps and macro-structural circumstances including gender-based legal differences as in IMF (2015). It also follows Watson, Corliss, and Le (2018) in examining the link between Internet use and women's workforce participation in the Indo-Pacific. Panel regressions are estimated as follows:

$$Gender_{it} = \alpha + \sum_{k=1}^{k} \beta_k \, x_{kit} + \gamma \cdot Digital \; usage_{it} + \delta_i + \varepsilon_{it}$$

Gender variables include the FLFP rate in country i at time t and the gender gap—the male labor force participation rate minus the corresponding rate for females—in country i at time t. Digital usage is proxied by the share of survey respondents who used the Internet to pay bills or buy something online or made digital payments over the past year. Other control variables, x_{kit}, include demographics, education, infrastructure, and access to finance. The sample includes data from 158 countries from 2000 to 2017.[1] Data are averaged for more than three consecutive years to remove cyclicality and data gaps. Gender, demographics, and economic data are from the World Bank's World Development Indicators database, years of schooling are from the Barro-Lee database, financial access and digital finance usage data are from the World Bank's Global Findex database, and legal variables are from the World Bank's Women's Legal Rights database.

Digitalization is associated with improving gender outcomes, alongside various socioeconomic factors. Table 5.2 and Figure 5.5 highlight how increasing the use of digital finance has a strong positive and significant correlation with FLFP, as does improved infrastructure as proxied by access to electricity. By contrast, demographics as proxied by fertility is negatively correlated with FLFP, as number of births could negatively affect women's labor supply. Access to finance and

TABLE 5.2.

Determinants of Female Labor Force Participation

Dependent variable	Female Labor Force Participation Rate			
	(1)	(2)	(3)	(4)
Fertility	−0.662***	−0.0537	0.149	0.0354
	(−3.739)	(−0.143)	(0.388)	(0.0908)
Education	0.0144	0.0331	−0.0105	−0.0189
	(0.172)	(0.359)	(−0.134)	(−0.259)
Access to electricity		0.145*	0.230***	0.251***
		(1.751)	(2.956)	(3.213)
Bank account, female	0.0186		−0.0248	
	(0.969)		(−1.134)	
Made digital payments		0.0522**		
		(2.570)		
Used the Internet to pay bills or buy something online			0.0728***	0.0757***
			(4.256)	(4.267)
Constant	67.73***	40.85***	33.69***	35.79***
	(9.049)	(3.462)	(2.928)	(3.234)
Cross-country fixed effects	Yes	Yes	Yes	Yes
Time fixed effects	No	No	No	No
No. of observations	200	119	119	119
R^2	0.132	0.150	0.314	0.325
No. of countries	95	75	75	75

Source: IMF staff estimates.

Note: The sample includes 158 countries from 2000 to 2017. Variables are averaged for more than a three-year period to remove cyclicality and data gaps. Table reports ordinary least squares estimates with robust t-statistics in parentheses. *, **, and *** indicates significance at the 10, 5, and 1 percent level, respectively. Robustness tests for reverse causality between digital usage and female labor force participation, level of economic development, among others, were performed and did not alter the main results.

---

[1] The sample includes Bangladesh, India, Nepal, and Sri Lanka. Because of data limitation, the rest of the South Asian economies are not included.

Figure 5.5. Gender Equality and Digitalization
(Standardized coefficients from univariate regressions)

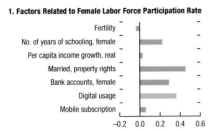

1. Factors Related to Female Labor Force Participation Rate

2. Factors Related to Labor Force Participation Gap

Source: IMF staff estimates.
Note: The sample includes 158 countries from 2000 to 2017.

education appear to be positively correlated with FLFP, but the correlations are nonsignificant. Table 5.3 and Figure 5.5 present consistent findings for economic gender gaps. Increasing use of digital finance is negatively correlated with economic gender gaps. Education and rising income are associated with lower gender gaps, but increasing fertility rate would widen the gaps. Other factors such as the quality of infrastructure, the access to finance gap, and less legal discrimination

TABLE 5.3.

Determinants of the Labor Force Participation Gap

Dependent variable	Labor Force Participation Gap (Male-Female)			
	(1)	(2)	(3)	(4)
Fertility	−0.366	0.403	3.498***	3.061***
	(−0.444)	(0.423)	(4.931)	(2.950)
Education	−0.763*	−0.544	−0.0131	−0.00836
	(−1.915)	(−1.604)	(−0.529)	(−0.180)
Per capita income growth, real	−0.0889**	−0.0646*		
	(−2.023)	(−1.754)		
Getting married, property rights		−0.0104		
		(−0.371)		
Access to electricity				−0.00438
				(−0.147)
Access to finance gap (male-female)		−0.0101		
		(−0.525)		
Made digital payments				−0.0317***
				(−4.067)
Constant	27.34***	24.06***	11.30***	12.73*
	(7.651)	(5.376)	(3.495)	(1.963)
Cross-country fixed effects	Yes	Yes	Yes	Yes
Time fixed effects	Yes	Yes	No	No
No. of observations	839	544	379	248
R^2	0.310	0.282	0.121	0.194
No. of countries	140	136	145	134

Source: IMF staff estimates.
Note: Sample includes 158 countries from 2000 to 2017. Variables are averaged for more than a three-year period to remove cyclicality and data gaps. Table reports OLS estimates with robust t-statistics in parentheses. *, **, and *** indicates significance at the 10, 5 and 1 percent level, respectively. Robustness tests for omitted variables were performed and did not alter the main results.

against women appears to have negative relationships with economic gender gaps, although the correlations are not significant.

Digitalization could potentially support women's workforce participation in South Asia. From the empirical findings (Table 5.1 and Figure 5.6), bringing South Asia's digital usage to the G20 median level is estimated to be associated with about 3 percentage points increase in the female labor force participation rate over a three-year period. The South Asian authorities have recently implemented several policy initiatives to facilitate the digitalization among women that could help sidestep several bottlenecks to women's workforce participation such as the following:

- In India, thanks to recent government initiatives, such as "Digital India" and "JAM trinity" that involves affordable bank accounts and the Aadhaar card for the identification of Indian citizens and mobiles, access to digital technologies and financial services, has expanded. In Bangladesh, the rapid growth of mobile financial services and agent-based banking helped to expand coverage into geographically difficult locations.

- Bangladesh has undertaken a praiseworthy initiative to empower women through the upazila (subdistrict) with positions such as information service officer and information service assistants, popularly known as *Tottho Apa*. A project titled "Tottho Apa: Empowering Women Through ICT Towards Digital Bangladesh Project" was launched to provide e-commerce services to village female entrepreneurs through 492 *upazila* information centers and rendered a full-fledged e-commerce support to the rural women by developing an e-commerce marketplace named "Laalsobuj.com" to sell

Figure 5.6. Scenario Analysis on Gender Equality and Digitalization
(Percent)

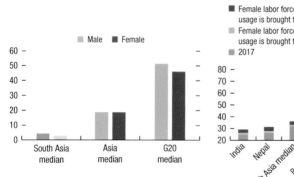
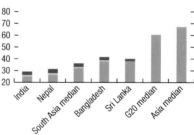

Sources: FINDEX; and IMF staff calculations.
Note: Group medians exclude India. Values indicate the percentage of respondents who reported having used the Internet to pay bills or buy something online in the past year. G20 = Group of 20 countries.

Source: IMF staff estimates.
Note: G20 = Group of 20 countries.

their products. It has also provided extended support to develop the village women as e-commerce entrepreneurs by imparting them e-commerce related knowledge through online training. Initiative has also been taken to provide hands-on support for registering them into the marketplace, uploading their products there and other functions related to the product packaging and delivery. This e-commerce–related activity is creating a lot of employment opportunities in rural Bangladesh, especially helping the village women become self-reliant.

CONCLUSIONS

South Asia has rapidly undergone economic transformation in recent years, but despite its strong economic performance, gender outcomes remain precarious. Evidentially, some South Asian labor markets have low female labor force participation rates, and there is greater likelihood of women being engaged in low-skill, low-paid, and informal employment. Gender norms, lack of basic infrastructure, and legal and institutional barriers account for gender disparity in South Asia. The COVID-19 pandemic appears to have worsened existing gender inequalities related to job losses and additional burdens of care. Expanding productive employment for women, lowering barriers for their entry to take on formal work, and supporting education and skill development are therefore imperative for inclusive growth in South Asia.

This chapter presents cross-country evidence that digitalization could potentially help facilitate women's workforce participation, thus reducing gender economic gaps. Recent experience from the COVID-19 pandemic further emphasizes the role of digitalization, including as a mean of government service delivery in rapid on set emergencies, where digital solutions can help governments deliver cash transfers as well as other services efficiently and quickly to their intended beneficiaries, particularly those in the informal sector. Going forward, digitalization will need to be supported by improving basic and digital infrastructure as well as digital and financial literacy. Expanding the coverage of digital technologies and narrowing gender disparity on digital inclusion will help enhance women's digital connectivity, make use of digital and financial services, expand possibilities for income generation, and improve access to information.

More broadly, digitalization should only be part of broader policies to empower women. Policy priorities include increased labor market flexibility to help create more formal sector jobs, thus allowing more women to be able to find jobs in the formal sector (Chapter 3; and Das and others 2015). Building on recent successful initiatives, supply-side reforms to improve both hard and soft infrastructure as well as digital and financial literacy are crucial to enable more women to enter the workforce. Key measures should include the following:

- Enhancing social spending on health and education and investing in gender-targeted skills training programs to increase female employment in better quality jobs in the formal sector;

- Further expanding the access to and usage of financial services such as providing entrepreneurship development training to unskilled women, creating special mobile and digital platforms for providing business knowledge and financial literacy, bringing the unbanked segment of underprivileged women into the formal financial services, and providing subsidized mobile phones and Internet facilities for poor and underprivileged women;

- Strengthening legal equality for women such as gender-specific labor laws affecting women's decisions to work and women's pay, constraints related to marriage, laws affecting women's work after having children, constraints on women's starting and running a business, gender differences in property and inheritance and laws affecting the size of a woman's pension;

- Implementing gender-responsive budgeting, along with specific and time-bounded targets to ensure the gender-spending efficiency; and

- Further expanding women-friendly public transportation and ensuring security for women, as well as addressing other considerations that could matter for women's decisions to work, such as maternity and parental benefits.

REFERENCES

Chauhan, Priyanshi 2020. "Gendering COVID-19: Impact of the Pandemic on Women's Burden of Unpaid Work in India." *Gender Issues* 38: 395–419.

Cuberes, David, and Marc Teignier 2012. "Gender Gaps in the Labor Market and Aggregate Productivity." Working Paper, Department of Economics, University of Sheffield.

Das, Sonali, Sonali Jain-Chandra, Kalpana Kocchar, and Naresh Kumar. 2015. "Women Workers in India: Why So Few Among So Many?" IMF Working Paper 15/55, International Monetary Fund, Washington, DC.

Deshpande, Ashwini. 2020. "The COVID-19 Pandemic and Lockdown: First Effects on Gender Gaps in Employment and Domestic Work in India." Discussion Paper Series in Economics 30, Ashoka University, Sonipat, India.

Dixon, Annette. 2018. "Women in India's Economic Growth." The Economic Times Women's Forum, Mumbai, India. https://www.worldbank.org/en/news/speech/2018/03/17/women-indias-economic-growth.

Government of Nepal. 2019. "Report on the Nepal Labor Force Survey 2017/18." Central Bureau of Statistics, Nepal.

International Labour Organization. 2017. "The World Employment and Social Outlook: Trends for Women 2017." Labor Market Trends and Policy Evaluation Unit, International Labour Office, Geneva.

International Labour Organization. 2018. "Women and Men in the Informal Economy: A Statistical Picture." International Labour Office, Geneva.

International Monetary Fund (IMF). 2015. "Fair Play: More Equal Laws Boost Female Labor Force Participation." IMF Staff Discussion Note 15/02, Washington, DC.

International Monetary Fund (IMF). 2017a. "India: Selected Issues Paper." IMF Country Report 17/55, Washington, DC.

International Monetary Fund (IMF). 2017b. "India: Staff Report for the 2017 Article IV Consultation." IMF Country Report 17/54, Washington, DC.

International Monetary Fund (IMF). 2018a. "Bangladesh: Staff Report for the 2018 Article IV Consultation." IMF Country Report 18/158, Washington, DC.

International Monetary Fund (IMF). 2018b. "Economic Gains from Gender Inclusion: New Mechanisms, New Evidence." IMF Staff Discussion Note 18/06, Washington, DC.

International Monetary Fund (IMF). 2018c. "Sri Lanka: Selected Issues Paper." IMF Country Report 18/176, Washington, DC.

Khera, Purva. 2016. "Macroeconomic Impacts of Gender Inequality and Informality in India." IMF Working Paper 16/16, International Monetary Fund, Washington, DC.

Khera, Purva. 2018. "Closing Gender Gaps in India: Does Increasing Women's Access to Finance Help?" IMF Working Paper 18/212, International Monetary Fund, Washington, DC.

Najeeb, Fatima, Matias Morales, and Gladys Lopez-Acevedo. 2020. "Analyzing Female Employment Trends in South Asia." IZA Institute of Labor Economics Discussion Paper 12956, IZA Institute of Labor Economics, Bonn, Germany.

Thevenon, Olivier. 2010. "Drivers of Female Labour Force Participation in the OECD." OECD Social, Employment and Migration Working Paper 145, OECD Publishing, Paris, France.

United Nations. 2020. "Surveys Show That COVID-19 Has Gendered Effects in Asia and the Pacific." UN Women's Regional Office for Asia and the Pacific's Rapid Assessment Survey, UN Women Data Hub.

Watson, Timothy, Michael Corliss, and Michelle Le. 2018. "Digitalisation and Women's Workforce Participation in the Indo-Pacific." *Australian Journal of Labour Economics* 21 (1): 45–74.

World Economic Forum. 2017. "The Global Gender Gap Report 2017." World Economic Forum, Geneva.

World Economic Forum. 2018. "The Global Gender Gap Report 2018." World Economic Forum, Geneva.

CHAPTER 6

Digitalization and Public Finances

Emmanouil Kitsios and Sanghamitra Warrier Mukherjee

Digital technologies offer powerful tools that public administrations can leverage to modernize and improve their operational efficiency. South Asian economies have progressively adopted GovTech solutions over the past decade. This chapter discusses their digitization advancements and presents empirical evidence in support of GovTech efforts to improve tax revenue performance, as well as health and education outcomes.

INTRODUCTION

Can South Asian countries increase government efficiency by stepping up their digitalization efforts? Public services are increasingly turning digital across the region, albeit at a different pace for each country. Digitalization can enable governments to improve the efficiency of expenditure and tax policies by facilitating the collection and processing of more reliable, timely, and accurate information on relevant stakeholders. Moreover, the digitalization of public finances can help

Figure 6.1. Government Online Services Index for Years 2010 and 2020

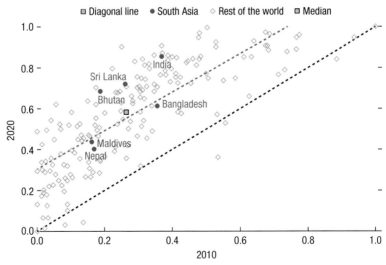

Sources: UN e-Government Survey; and authors' estimates.

enhance access to services and entitlements, reduce errors and frauds, strengthen procurement procedures, and improve tax compliance by simplifying the tax-filing process. By gradually digitalizing their government operations, South Asian countries are incrementally reducing their digital divide to the public administrations of more advanced economies.

The important policy question that arises is whether e-governments are better at mobilizing revenue or spending their resources more efficiently. This question is explored empirically in this chapter using a broad sample of 180 countries at different stages of GovTech development during the period 2008–2019. We focus on three public administration performance areas that digitalization has significant potential to improve (1) government revenue productivity; (2) health outcomes; and (3) educational outcomes. The overall progress in e-government is proxied by the United Nation's Online Service Index that assesses the scope and quality of public sector online services, including online services for tax submission and registration of businesses.[1] We find that building on their recent progress, South Asian countries stand to benefit from further GovTech advancements in terms of public finance efficiency in revenue collection and health and education spending efficiency.

STATE OF GOVTECH IN SOUTH ASIA

Despite the impressive progress made, there is scope to scale up the use of digital technologies in revenue administration, payroll systems, and procurement. Each bullet in this section discusses a set of GovTech indicators for countries in South Asia as of the end of 2020, with the accompanying text tables reflecting the values and implementation year of the corresponding GovTech option. Higher values in the tables indicate more digitally advanced public financial management systems. The horizontal bar charts accompanying the tables document the labels of the indicator values reported in the columns of the tables, along with the number of countries in the world implementing a GovTech solution with similar characteristics.

- *Treasury single account (TSA):* Most South Asian countries benefit from centralized TSA systems that record at least 75 percent of their government's revenue and expenditure transactions.[2] Bangladesh and Bhutan have decentralized TSA systems, with the former recording between 25 to 50 percent of transactions. Most countries worldwide do not have fully centralized TSA systems, although most countries have TSA systems that cover more than 75 percent of transactions (see Table 6.1 and Figure 6.2).
- *Tax Management Information System (TMIS):* Most countries in the region—and worldwide—have fully operational TMISs. Digitalizing the business process of the revenue administration can help minimize the tax

[1] The index is based on data collected from an independent Online Service Questionnaire conducted by the UN Department of Economic and Social Affairs.

[2] TSA operational scope in the text table refers to the revenue and expenditure shares captured by the TSA.

TABLE 6.1.

Treasury Single Accounts in South Asia

Country	Year	Type	Scope
Bangladesh	2008	2	2
Bhutan	2008	2	4
India	1963	3	4
Maldives	2009	3	4
Nepal	2013	3	4
Sri Lanka	2007	2	4

Sources: World Bank Digital Government/GovTech Systems and Services (DGSS) Dataset; and IMF staff calculations.

Figure 6.2. TSA Type and Scope

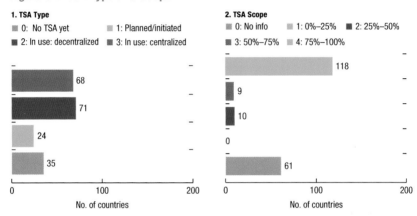

1. TSA Type
- 0: No TSA yet
- 1: Planned/initiated
- 2: In use: decentralized
- 3: In use: centralized

2. TSA Scope
- 0: No info
- 1: 0%–25%
- 2: 25%–50%
- 3: 50%–75%
- 4: 75%–100%

Source: World Bank, Digital Government/GovTech Systems and Services (DGSS) Dataset.
Note: TSA = Treasury single account.

compliance costs and enable the faster processing of returns and payment data, as well improve the communication between taxpayers and the tax authority. Sri Lanka and 29 other countries have connected services or are operating a single-window platform. Implementation of a fully operational and connected TMIS is in progress in Bangladesh, Maldives, and 5 other countries, while 25 countries have not developed a TMIS. Fully integrating a TMIS with existing information systems at other government agencies can help analyze taxpayer information more comprehensively, as well as strengthen the capacity of the revenue authority to assess tax liabilities and monitor compliance (see Table 6.2 and Figure 6.3).

- *e-id and e-signature:* All countries in the region benefit from digitized identification (ID) systems. With more than 1.2 billion residents enrolled, India's Aadhaar unique ID number represents the largest biometrics-based digital ID system in the world. India is also among the 70 countries that implement digital signatures in the public sector for operations and service delivery, backed by relevant digital signature regulation and public infrastructure. Bangladesh, Nepal, and Sri Lanka are among the 36 countries that have developed regulations and infrastructure to support the adoption of digital signatures, while Bhutan has only formulated the supporting

TABLE 6.2.

Tax Administration: Tax Management Information Systems in South Asia

Country	Year	Status	Services
Bangladesh	2018	2	2
Bhutan	2015	3	2
India	1981	3	2
Maldives	—	2	2
Nepal	2010	3	2
Sri Lanka	2014	3	3

Source: World Bank, Digital Government/GovTech Systems and Services (DGSS) Dataset; and IMF staff calculations.

Figure 6.3. TMIS Status and Services

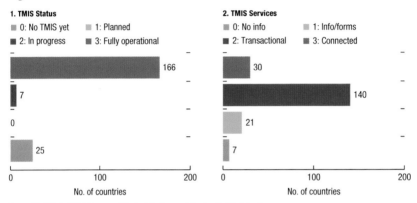

Source: World Bank, Digital Government/GovTech Systems and Services (DGSS) Dataset.
Note: TMIS = Tax Management Information System.

regulatory system. Maldives is among the 52 countries that do not have such digital signature systems and lack the regulation or infrastructure to support them (see Table 6.3 and Figure 6.4).

- *e-filing and e-payment:* Most countries in the region and in the world provide online e-filing services for government to citizens (G2C) or government to businesses (G2B) through their e-tax systems, but do not offer government e-payment solutions. India stands out among South Asian

TABLE 6.3.

e-IDs and e-Signatures in South Asia

	e-ID	Digital Signature	
Country	Status	Year	Status
Bangladesh	1	2009	2
Bhutan	1	2006	1
India	1	2008	3
Maldives	1	—	0
Nepal	1	2012	2
Sri Lanka	1	2013	2

Sources: World Bank Digital Government/GovTech Systems and Services (DGSS) Dataset; and IMF staff calculations.
Note: ID = identification.

Figure 6.4. e-ID and Digital Signature Status

1. e-ID Status

- 0: No   1: Yes

161

37

0	100	200

No. of countries

2. Digital Signature Status

- 0: No digital signature   1: Legal basis only
- 2: System in place   3: Used in practice

70

36

40

52

0	100	200

No. of countries

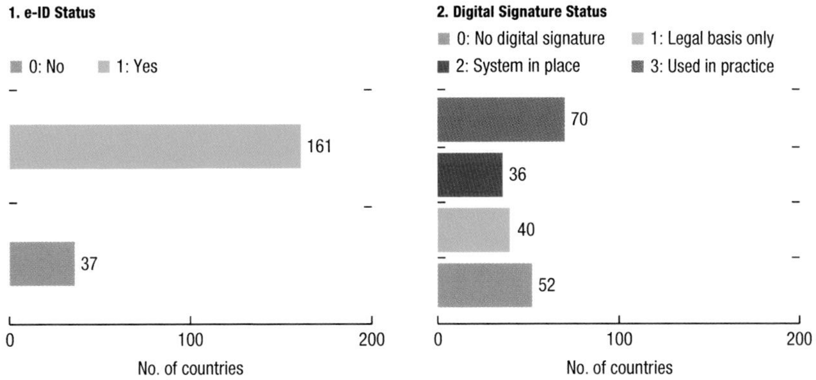

Source: World Bank, Digital Government/GovTech Systems and Services (DGSS) Dataset.
Note: ID = identification.

TABLE 6.4.

e-Filing and e-Payment in South Asia

Country	e-Filing		e-Payment	
	Year	Services	Year	Services
Bangladesh	—	1	2012	1
Bhutan	2009	2	—	0
India	2005	3	2011	1
Maldives	2013	2	—	0
Nepal	2013	2	—	0
Sri Lanka	—	1	2012	2

Sources: World Bank Digital Government/GovTech Systems and Services (DGSS) Dataset; and IMF staff calculations.

countries in offering both e-filing and e-payment options. Sri Lanka implements a centralized e-payment platform. Sri Lanka and Bangladesh provide tax-related information and forms online, but do not yet offer centralized e-filing and e-payment G2C or G2B services (see Table 6.4 and Figure 6.5).

- *Customs Administration Management Information System (CMIS):* All South Asian countries benefit from fully operational online customs systems that offer transactional capabilities but are not operating yet as single windows. Fully operational single-window systems allow traders to submit all import, export, and transit information required by customs and other agencies through a single electronic gateway instead of paper-based processing systems. Most countries in the world operate the CMIS with similar functionalities, whereas 40 countries benefit from more advanced systems (see Table 6.5 and Figure 6.6).

- *Payroll system:* All South Asian countries have fully operational payroll systems. Bhutan, Maldives, Nepal, and Sri Lanka are implementing a centralized payroll platform that is shared across line ministries. Bangladesh and India have not fully centralized their payroll platform. In the case of

Figure 6.5. e-Filing and e-Payment Services

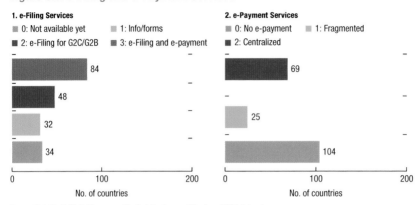

1. e-Filing Services
- 0: Not available yet
- 1: Info/forms
- 2: e-Filing for G2C/G2B
- 3: e-Filing and e-payment

2. e-Payment Services
- 0: No e-payment
- 1: Fragmented
- 2: Centralized

Source: World Bank, Digital Government/GovTech Systems and Services (DGSS) Dataset.
Note: G2C/G2B = government to citizens/government to businesses.

TABLE 6.5.

Customs Administration: Customs Management Information System

Country	Year	Status	Services
Bangladesh	1994	3	2
Bhutan	2015	3	2
India	1997	3	2
Maldives	1994	3	2
Nepal	1998	3	2
Sri Lanka	1994	3	2

Sources: World Bank Digital Government/GovTech Systems and Services (DGSS) Dataset; and IMF staff calculations.

Figure 6.6. CMIS Status and Services

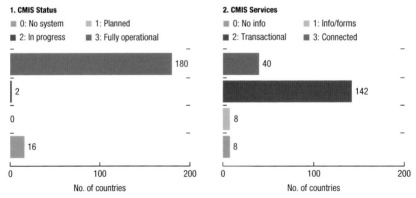

1. CMIS Status
- 0: No system
- 1: Planned
- 2: In progress
- 3: Fully operational

2. CMIS Services
- 0: No info
- 1: Info/forms
- 2: Transactional
- 3: Connected

Source: World Bank, Digital Government/GovTech Systems and Services (DGSS) Dataset.
Note: CMIS = Customs Administration Management System.

Bangladesh, for example, the iBAS++ system currently covers about 96 percent of the payment of salaries and allowances, and its coverage is expected to be completed with the forthcoming inclusion of a few self-accounting entities. Most countries operate fully centralized payroll systems (see Table 6.6 and Figure 6.7).

TABLE 6.6.

Payroll System			
Country	**Year**	**Status**	**Services**
Bangladesh	2016	3	1
Bhutan	2014	3	2
India	—	3	1
Maldives	2010	3	2
Nepal	2004	3	2
Sri Lanka	2012	3	2

Sources: World Bank Digital Government/GovTech Systems and Services (DGSS) Dataset; and IMF staff calculations.

Figure 6.7. Payroll System Status and Services

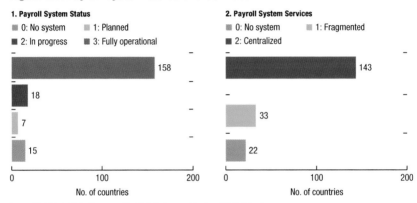

1. Payroll System Status
- 0: No system
- 1: Planned
- 2: In progress
- 3: Fully operational

2. Payroll System Services
- 0: No system
- 1: Fragmented
- 2: Centralized

Source: World Bank, Digital Government/GovTech Systems and Services (DGSS) Dataset.

TABLE 6.7.

e-Procurement System			
Country	**Year**	**Status**	**Services**
Bangladesh	2011	3	2
Bhutan	2017	2	3
India	2007	3	2
Maldives	2011	2	1
Nepal	2014	3	2
Sri Lanka	—	1	0

Sources: World Bank Digital Government/GovTech Systems and Services (DGSS) Dataset; and IMF staff calculations.

- *e-Procurement System:* The electronic procurement systems of Bangladesh, India, and Nepal publish tender and contract information and include bidding documents and contract awards. Their procurement portals, as well as those of most other countries, offer more functionality compared with those of Bhutan and Maldives that only publish tenders. Bhutan's e-procurement system is one of the five in the world that are fully connected, while most other countries' systems either provide bidding documents and contract awards, or include only tender or contract information. Sri Lanka's e-procurement system is among the 43 that do not provide such information (see Table 6.7 and Figure 6.8).

Figure 6.8. e-Procurement Status and Services

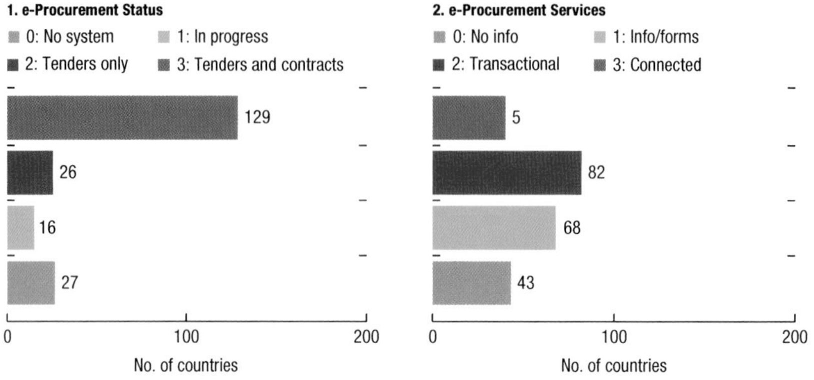

1. e-Procurement Status

- 0: No system
- 1: In progress
- 2: Tenders only
- 3: Tenders and contracts

2. e-Procurement Services

- 0: No info
- 1: Info/forms
- 2: Transactional
- 3: Connected

Source: World Bank, Digital Government/GovTech Systems and Services (DGSS) Dataset.

DIGITALIZATION AND REVENUE COLLECTION EFFICIENCY

Can digitalization help countries in the region improve their revenue efficiency? To explore this question, we estimate the effect of the government digitalization proxy (GovTech) on annual efficiency measures of value-added tax (VAT), personal income tax (PIT), and corporate income tax (CIT).[3] These tax efficiency measures are the dependent variables of interest ($Tax_{i,t}$).[4] Figure 6.9 demonstrates a positive association between the CIT revenue productivity when plotted against the e-government online service index.[5] Advanced and emerging economies tend to have both higher digitalization indices and revenue productivities. Actual CIT revenue productivity is lower than average based on the government digitalization efforts of Bangladesh, India, Nepal, and Sri Lanka. This is likely because of the presence of tax exemptions or revenue administration inefficiencies associated with the economic structure of these countries. To address omitted variable bias, we include in our specification country characteristics that are also likely to affect revenue productivity besides government digitalization (Equation 6.1).

$$Tax_{i,t} = \beta \cdot GovTech_{i,t-1} + \theta \cdot X_{i,t-1} + \alpha_i + \gamma_t + u_{i,t} \qquad (6.1)$$

---

[3] See Kitsios, Jalles, and Verdier (2022) for a study examining the effect of government digitalization on reducing cross-border fraud and increasing trade-related revenue.

[4] VAT productivity is measured as the ratio of VAT revenue to the product of GDP and the standard VAT rate. VAT C-efficiency is measured as the ratio of actual VAT revenues to the product of the standard rate and final consumption expenditure. Similarly, CIT productivity = (CIT revenue as percent of GDP)/(CIT rate) and PIT productivity = (PIT revenue in percent of GDP)/(highest PIT rate).

[5] We use the UN Online Service Index as a proxy for government digitalization because it is significantly correlated with other digitalization indices available—such as the World Bank's GovTech Maturity Index—and it has a broader sample coverage across countries and over time.

Figure 6.9. CIT Productivity and GovTech
(Percent)

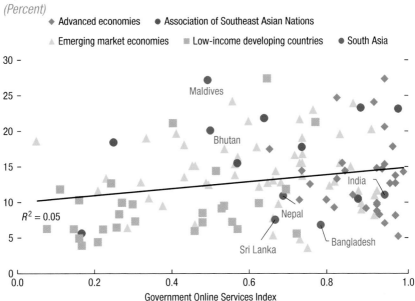

Sources: IMF Government Finance Statistics; IMF Fiscal Affairs Department Tax Rates database; IMF's World Economic Outlook database; OECD Global Revenue Statistics Database; UN e-Government Survey; USAID Collecting Taxes Database; World Bank's World Development Indicators; and IMF staff estimates.

The vector $X_{i,t-1}$ of lagged values of covariates includes (1) GDP per capita to proxy for the level of development; (2) real GDP growth to account for the business cycle effects on revenue performance; (3) agriculture's share of GDP as a proxy for informality; (4) the United Nation's telecommunication index to control for the broader digital technological infrastructure available in the country; (5) the country's nonoil imports and exports shares of GDP as a proxy for trade dependence; (6) the oil trade balance share of GDP to account for oil trade's impact on revenue collection efforts; (7) demographic characteristics impacting the workforce structure, such as population growth and the age dependency ratio; (8) the UN's human capital index to proxy for digital literacy; and (9) an indicator on government effectiveness to account for more effective governments being more likely to adopt GovTech solutions.[6] Country-fixed effects (α_i) are used to capture any time-invariant country-level heterogeneity and year-fixed effects (γ_t) are included to account for cross-country shocks and general trends in revenue performance measures over time.

The estimates suggest that there is a positive association between the GovTech index and revenue efficiency measures (Table 6.1). The results hold when the government effectiveness indicator is used as an additional regressor (columns 2,

---

[6] Similar determinants of revenue efficiency and tax effort are used by Fenochieto and Pessino (2013) and Cevik and others (2019).

Figure 6.10. GovTech Frontier's Effect on Revenue Efficiency
(Change in percent; 2019)

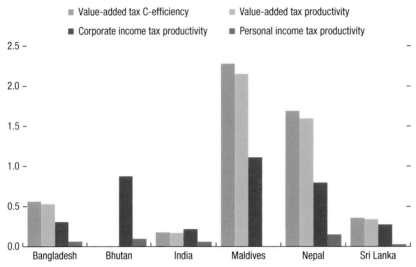

Sources: IMF Government Finance Statistics; IMF Fiscal Affairs Department Tax Rates Database; IMF's World Economic Outlook database; OECD Global Revenue Statistics Database; USAID Collecting Taxes Database; World Bank's World Development Indicators; IMF staff estimates.

4, 6, and 8), though digitalization can also impact revenue efficiency through improving perceived government effectiveness by promoting transparency and reducing corruption vulnerabilities. Revenue efficiency measures on VAT and CIT tend to be higher in periods of higher GDP growth and when overall government effectiveness is stronger. On the other hand, PIT revenue efficiency is negatively associated with agriculture's share of value added in the economy, likely because of the presence of greater informality in the economy. Similarly, VAT and CIT revenue performance measures tend to be lower for more export-dependent economies that may reflect the presence of higher tax incentives for exporters. Countries that have stronger oil trade balances have lower revenue efficiency given that there is likely less pressure on public administration to generate revenue. Revenue performance tends to be lower for economies with a lower proportion of the population participating in the labor force, likely reflecting less economic dynamism.

Bridging the government digitalization divide would result in higher revenue collection efficiency. The estimates of Table 6.8 suggest that if South Asian countries reached the GovTech frontier (that is, government online services index equaled one), then revenue efficiency would improve.[7] For example, VAT productivity and VAT C-efficiency measures would increase by about 0.6 and 0.5 percentage points, respectively, for Bangladesh. Similarly, CIT productivity would

---

[7] Efficiency gains for VAT and PIT are not shown for Bhutan and Maldives, respectively, because of the lack of relevant taxes before 2020.

TABLE 6.8.

Tax Revenue Efficiency

	(1) VAT C-Efficiency	(2) VAT C-Efficiency	(3) VAT Productivity	(4) VAT Productivity	(5) CIT Productivity	(6) CIT Productivity	(7) PIT Productivity	(8) PIT Productivity
GovTech index	0.426** (0.186)	0.401* (0.192)	0.397** (0.185)	0.380** (0.187)	0.453** (0.210)	0.427* (0.209)	0.242* (0.126)	0.233* (0.127)
GDP per capita	0.700*** (0.149)	0.611*** (0.149)	0.569*** (0.152)	0.470*** (0.156)	0.932*** (0.212)	0.806*** (0.206)	-0.078 (0.060)	-0.114 (0.067)
GDP growth	0.010*** (0.003)	0.010*** (0.003)	0.005* (0.003)	0.005* (0.002)	0.019*** (0.004)	0.020*** (0.004)	-0.002 (0.004)	-0.002 (0.004)
Telecommunications index	0.447 (0.298)	0.373 (0.299)	0.545* (0.298)	0.479 (0.303)	0.707 (0.415)	0.635 (0.398)	-0.156 (0.166)	-0.183 (0.159)
Agriculture value added (% GDP)	0.027 (0.075)	0.020 (0.079)	0.108 (0.078)	0.099 (0.083)	0.022 (0.074)	0.014 (0.074)	-0.108** (0.043)	-0.110** (0.044)
Nonoil imports (% GDP)	-0.000 (0.002)	-0.001 (0.002)	0.003 (0.003)	0.003 (0.003)	0.009** (0.004)	0.009** (0.004)	0.008*** (0.002)	0.008*** (0.002)
Nonoil exports (% GDP)	-0.007** (0.003)	-0.007** (0.003)	-0.012*** (0.003)	-0.012*** (0.003)	-0.016*** (0.003)	-0.016*** (0.003)	0.002 (0.002)	0.002 (0.002)
Oil trade balance (% GDP)	-0.016** (0.006)	-0.015** (0.006)	-0.023*** (0.006)	-0.022*** (0.005)	-0.014** (0.005)	-0.013** (0.005)	-0.005* (0.003)	-0.004 (0.003)
Population growth	0.024 (0.027)	0.022 (0.028)	0.012 (0.027)	0.010 (0.028)	-0.021 (0.023)	-0.021 (0.023)	-0.017 (0.016)	-0.019 (0.017)
Age dependency ratio	-0.005* (0.002)	-0.005 (0.003)	-0.007** (0.002)	-0.006** (0.003)	-0.012*** (0.002)	-0.012*** (0.002)	-0.018*** (0.003)	-0.019*** (0.004)
Human capital index		-0.003 (0.348)		-0.256 (0.343)		0.030 (0.242)		0.053 (0.186)
Government effectiveness		0.168** (0.072)		0.176** (0.066)		0.221** (0.093)		0.068 (0.097)
No. of observations	1714	1714	1749	1749	1813	1813	1904	1904
No. of countries	130	130	134	134	134	145	145	141
Country-fixed effects	Yes	Yes	Yes	Yes	Yes	Yes	Yes	Yes
Year-fixed effects	Yes	Yes	Yes	Yes	Yes	Yes	Yes	Yes
Adjusted R^2	0.04	0.04	0.04	0.04	0.06	0.06	0.03	0.03

Sources: IMF Government Finance Statistics; IMF Fiscal Affairs Department Tax Rates database; IMF's World Economic Outlook database; OECD Global Revenue Statistics Database; UN e-Government Survey; USAID Collecting Taxes Database; World Bank's World Development Indicators; and IMF staff estimates.

Note: Robust standard errors are in parentheses. The dependent and independent variables of GDP per capita and agriculture value added are specified in logs. CIT = corporate income tax; PIT = personal income tax; VAT = value-added tax.

$*p < 0.1, **p < 0.05, ***p < 0.01$.

Figure 6.11. GovTech Frontier's Effect on Health Outcomes
(Change in years of life expectancy at birth; change in infant mortality rate)

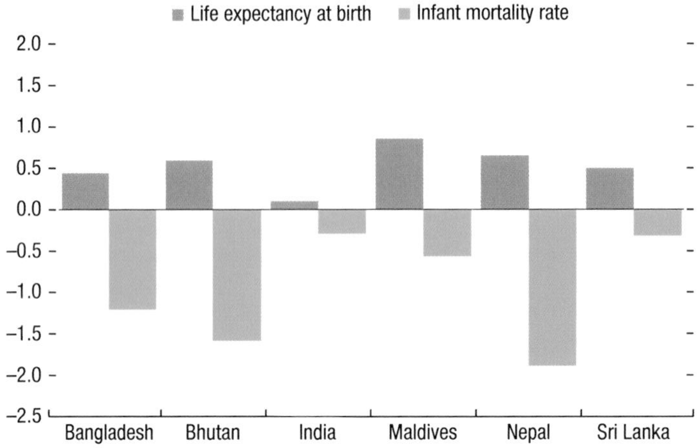

■ Life expectancy at birth   ■ Infant mortality rate

Sources: World Bank's World Development Indicators; and IMF staff estimates.

increase by 0.9 and 0.8 percentage points for Bhutan and Sri Lanka, respectively. The overall impact on revenue is estimated at about 3.3 percent of GDP and 2.5 percent of GDP for Maldives and Nepal, respectively, as their relative distance to the GovTech frontier is higher than other regional peers.

DIGITALIZATION AND HEALTH SPENDING EFFICIENCY

Can digitalization improve the efficiency of health spending execution? Digital payments and e-procurement have the potential to improve the health budget execution process and simplify the provision and management of public health resources. This section uses a stochastic frontier analysis whereby the health system outcomes of average life expectancy at birth and infant mortality rates ($Health_{i,t}$) are regressed on inputs $X_{i,t-1}$, such as the level of resources made available and the level of development (Equation 6.2).[8] The compound error term $\varepsilon_{i,t}$ comprises a normally distributed error term $u_{i,t}$, and a disturbance $v_{i,t}$ representing the distance of each country's error term to the frontier (Equation 6.3).[9] The latter is assumed to follow a truncated normal distribution multiplied by a function of time, t, where T_i is the last period observed in the ith country, and η is a decay parameter (Equation 6.4).[10] The estimated time-varying country-specific

---

[8] Grigoli and Kapsoli (2018) discussed the advantages of stochastic frontier analysis in estimating health spending efficiency.

[9] The stochastic frontier analysis estimates a frontier of best-performing countries that obtain higher outcomes for a given level of inputs. The method then yields efficiency scores for each country by comparing its outcome and inputs to the reference set of the best-performing countries.

[10] See Battese and Coelli (1992) for further details on the estimation procedure used.

technical efficiency is obtained through $TE_{i,t} = \exp\{(-v_{i,t})\}$ $\varepsilon_{i,t}$, and is regressed upon potential determinants of health spending efficiency that include the GovTech index, the telecommunication infrastructure index ($Tcom_{i,t}$), and predetermined variables $Z_{i,t-1}$, such as GDP per capita, the ratio of births attended by skilled health staff, the urban population share, the income Gini index, and the universal health coverage index. Country-fixed effects are included to capture the possibility of time-invariant heterogeneity in efficiency (Greene 2004).

$$Health_{i,t} = \alpha_i + X_{i,t-1} \cdot \theta + \varepsilon_{i,t} \qquad (6.2)$$

$$\varepsilon_{i,t} = u_{i,t} + v_{i,t} \qquad (6.3)$$

$$v_{i,t} = \exp\{-\eta(t-T_i)\} \cdot v_i \qquad (6.4)$$

$$TE_{i,t} = \alpha_i + \beta \cdot GovTech_{i,t} + \gamma \cdot TCom_{i,t} + \theta \cdot Z_{i,t-1} + u_{i,t} \qquad (6.5)$$

The results suggest that both government digitalization as well as telecommunication infrastructure quality are positively correlated with the estimated efficiency in health spending (Table 6.9). All else being equal, better e-government services are associated with higher efficiency of health spending in increasing life expectancy and lower inefficiency of health spending in reducing infant mortality. The accompanying figure shows the estimated gains in health outcomes from bridging the gap to the GovTech frontier. Maldives and Nepal would obtain the highest increase in life expectancy by about 0.9 and 0.7 years, respectively. Similarly, Nepal and Bhutan would benefit the most among South Asian countries in reducing their infant mortality rates by 1.9 and 1.6 percentage points, respectively. Higher GDP per capita and higher health spending are associated with better health outcomes (frontier equation). Health systems tend to be more efficient in countries that are more developed or have a greater share of their population living in urban areas (efficiency equation). Also, health spending efficiency is higher for countries that deploy more skilled health staff to attend births or cover a greater share of essential health services as proxied by the universal health coverage index.[11]

DIGITALIZATION AND EDUCATION SPENDING EFFICIENCY

Are e-governments better at providing access to education? Digital approaches to remote learning during the pandemic underscored the need to promote e-education along with e-government. In this section, we examine whether e-governments tend to be more efficient in administering education spending to achieve better education outcomes. The stochastic frontier analysis described in the previous section is used with education spending per capita and GDP per

---

[11] The results are in line with the data envelopment analysis of Garcia-Escribano, Juarros, and Mogues (2022) who also documented that increasing universal health coverage coverage improves health spending efficiency.

TABLE 6.9.

Stochastic Frontier Analysis: Health Spending Efficiency

Frontier Equation

	Life Expectancy				Infant Mortality			
	(1)	(2)	(3)	(4)	(5)	(6)	(7)	(8)
Health spending per capita	0.006***	0.006***	0.006***	0.006***				
	(0.002)	(0.002)	(0.002)	(0.002)				
GDP per capita	0.028***	0.028***	0.028***	0.028***				
	(0.002)	(0.002)	(0.002)	(0.002)				
Health spending per capita					-0.045***	-0.045***	-0.045***	-0.045***
					(0.012)	(0.012)	(0.012)	(0.012)
GDP per capita					-0.200***	-0.200***	-0.200***	-0.200***
					(0.022)	(0.022)	(0.022)	(0.022)
No. of observations	1891	1891	1891	1891	1967	1967	1967	1967

Efficiency Equation

	Life Expectancy				Infant Mortality			
	(1)	(2)	(3)	(4)	(5)	(6)	(7)	(8)
GovTech index	0.023***	0.018***	0.006	0.008**	-0.000***	-0.000***	-0.000***	-0.000***
	(0.006)	(0.006)	(0.004)	(0.004)	(0.000)	(0.000)	(0.000)	(0.000)
Telecommunications index	0.074***	0.063***	0.041***	-0.004	-0.001***	-0.001***	-0.000***	-0.000
	(0.008)	(0.009)	(0.006)	(0.006)	(0.000)	(0.000)	(0.000)	(0.000)
GDP per capita		0.025**	0.012**	0.026***		-0.000**	-0.000***	-0.000
		(0.011)	(0.006)	(0.008)		(0.000)	(0.000)	(0.000)
Skilled health staff			0.000***	0.000***			-0.000***	-0.000***
			(0.000)	(0.000)			(0.000)	(0.000)
Urban population rate			0.108***	0.048			-0.000***	-0.000**
			(0.036)	(0.054)			(0.000)	(0.000)
Universal health coverage index				0.000*				-0.000**
				(0.000)				(0.000)
Gini index				0.000				-0.000
				(0.000)				(0.000)
No. of observations	1886	1886	1005	85	1963	1963	1038	85
No. of countries	173	173	164	51	180	180	168	51
Country-fixed effects	Yes	Yes	Yes	Yes	Yes	Yes	Yes	Yes
Adjusted R^2	0.43	0.45	0.67	0.74	0.43	0.46	0.72	0.79

Source: IMF staff calculations.

Note: Robust standard errors are in parentheses. The dependent and independent variables of health spending, GDP per capita, and urban population rate are expressed in logs.

*$p < 0.1$, **$p < 0.05$, ***$p < 0.01$.

Figure 6.12. GovTech Frontier Impact on Education Outcomes
(Change in the ratio of total enrollment)

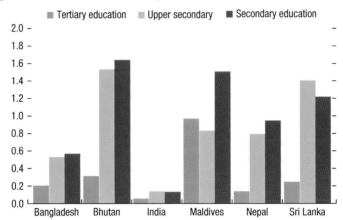

Sources: World Bank's World Development Indicators; and IMF staff estimates.

capita as the main inputs to generate education outcomes, such as school enroll-ment in secondary, upper secondary, and tertiary education (Equation 6.6). The estimation is carried out following a similar structure to Equations (6.3)–(6.5). The technical efficiency estimates obtained from Equation (6.6) are regressed upon determinants of education spending efficiency that include the GovTech index, the telecommunication infrastructure index, the level of development, the share of the population with access to basic sanitation, the urban population share, and the income Gini index.[12]

$$Education_{i,t} = \alpha_i + X_{i,t-1}\,\theta + \varepsilon_{i,t} \qquad (6.6)$$

Countries with stronger e-governments tend to have higher efficiency of edu-cation spending in enrolling secondary, upper secondary, and tertiary students (Table 6.10). Gross enrollment rate refers to the ratio of total enrollment to the population of the age group that officially corresponds to the level of education shown. Higher education spending and level of development are associated with better education outcomes. More advanced government digitalization is correlat-ed with lower inefficiency in education spending for a given level of development and telecommunication infrastructure. The results are statistically significant for gross enrollment ratios in secondary and upper levels of education, while they are less strong for primary education students, where countries have already achieved higher enrollment rates. The estimated gains in education outcomes from bridg-ing the gap to the GovTech frontier are shown in Figure 6.12. These gains are among the highest in the region for Bhutan, as its gross enrollment ratios in secondary and upper secondary education would increase by about 1.6 and 1.5 percentage points, respectively. Similarly, Maldives would increase its gross

---

[12] See Grigoli (2014), Herrera and Pang (2005), Herrera and Abdoulaye (2018), and Wagstaff and Wang (2011) for including similar determinants of education spending efficiency.

TABLE 6.10.

Stochastic Frontier Analysis: Education Spending Efficiency

Frontier Equation

	Secondary			Upper Secondary			Tertiary		
	(1)	(2)	(3)	(4)	(5)	(6)	(7)	(8)	(9)
Education spending per capita	0.033	0.033	0.033						
	(0.021)	(0.021)	(0.021)						
GDP per capita	0.191***	0.191***	0.191***						
	(0.025)	(0.025)	(0.025)						
Education spending per capita				0.021	0.021	0.021			
				(0.037)	(0.037)	(0.037)			
GDP per capita				0.346***	0.346***	0.346***			
				(0.042)	(0.042)	(0.042)			
Education spending per capita							0.152***	0.152***	0.152***
							(0.044)	(0.044)	(0.044)
GDP per capita							0.399***	0.399***	0.399***
							(0.055)	(0.055)	(0.055)
No. of observations	531	531	531	535	535	535	518	518	518

Efficiency Equation

	Secondary			Upper Secondary			Tertiary		
	(1)	(2)	(3)	(4)	(5)	(6)	(7)	(8)	(9)
GovTech index	0.036***	0.024**	0.011*	0.042***	0.027**	0.017**	0.040***	0.020*	0.006
	(0.006)	(0.010)	(0.005)	(0.006)	(0.011)	(0.006)	(0.008)	(0.011)	(0.008)
Telecommunications index	0.057***	0.028	−0.035	0.088***	0.052**	−0.012	0.105***	0.056**	0.040**
	(0.020)	(0.020)	(0.024)	(0.022)	(0.020)	(0.025)	(0.020)	(0.021)	(0.018)
GDP per capita		0.067**	0.075***		0.083**	0.079**		0.092***	0.093***
		(0.028)	(0.018)		(0.032)	(0.029)		(0.022)	(0.020)
Urban population rate			0.060			0.159			0.005
			(0.129)			(0.125)			(0.074)
Gini index			−0.001			−0.001			0.001
			(0.001)			(0.001)			(0.001)
Basic sanitation			0.082***			0.079***			0.057**
			(0.022)			(0.026)			(0.024)
No. of observations	152	152	53	152	152	53	114	114	39
No. of countries	28	28	20	28	28	20	21	21	14
Country-fixed effects	Yes	Yes	Yes	Yes	Yes	Yes	Yes	Yes	Yes
Adjusted R^2	0.50	0.59	0.84	0.57	0.66	0.89	0.70	0.81	0.93

Source: IMF staff calculations.

Note: Robust standard errors are in parentheses. The dependent variables of gross enrollment rates, the independent variables of education spending, GDP per capita, and urban population rates are expressed in logs.

$*p < 0.1$, $**p < 0.05$, $***p < 0.01$.

enrollment ratio in tertiary education by 1 percentage point. The estimates also suggest that countries with better access to basic sanitation services and more advanced telecommunication infrastructure tend to have better education spending efficiency.

CONCLUSIONS

Scaling up the use of GovTech solutions by South Asia's public administrations offers significant potential in transforming service delivery and mobilizing resources. Countries with more digitalized government services tend to have higher efficiency in generating fiscal revenue and achieving higher outcomes from their health and education spending. The COVID-19 pandemic has accelerated the e-government transition that was already underway in the region. However, to reap the full dividends of the GovTech revolution, it is important that institutional frameworks are in place to safeguard against risks related to cybersecurity, digital exclusion, fraud, and privacy infringement.

REFERENCES

Battese, George, and Timothy Coelli. 1992. "Frontier Production Functions, Technical Efficiency and Panel Data: With Application to Paddy Farmers in India." *Journal of Productivity Analysis* 3 (1): 153–69.

Cevik, Serhan, Jan Gottschalk, Eric Hutton, Laura Jaramillo, Pooja Karnane, and Mousse. Sow. 2019. "Structural Transformation and Tax Efficiency." *International Finance* 22 (3): 341–79.

Fenochietto, Ricardo, and Carola Pessino. 2013. "Understanding Countries' Tax Effort." IMF Working Paper 2013/244, International Monetary Fund, Washington, DC.

Garcia-Escribano, Mercedes, Pedro Juarros, and Tewodaj Mogues. 2022. "Patterns and Drivers of Health Spending Efficiency." IMF Working Paper 2022/048, International Monetary Fund, Washington, DC.

Greene, William. 2004. "Distinguishing between Heterogeneity and Inefficiency: Stochastic Frontier Analysis of the World Health Organization's Panel Data on National Health Care Systems." *Health Economics* 13: 959–80.

Grigoli, Francesco. 2014. "A Hybrid Approach to Estimating the Efficiency of Public Spending on Education in Emerging and Developing Economies." IMF Working Paper 2014/019, International Monetary Fund, Washington, DC.

Grigoli, Francesco, and Javier Kapsoli. 2018. "Waste Not, Want Not: The Efficiency of Health Expenditure in Emerging and Developing Economies." *Review of Development Economics* 22: 384–403.

Herrera, Santiago, and Abdoulaye Ouedraogo. 2018. "Efficiency of Public Spending in Education, Health, and Infrastructure: An International Benchmarking Exercise." World Bank Policy Research Working Paper 8586, World Bank, Washington, DC.

Herrera, Santiago, and Gaobo Pang. 2005. "Efficiency of Public Spending in Developing Countries: An Efficiency Frontier Approach." World Bank Policy Research Working Paper 3645, World Bank, Washington, DC.

Kitsios, Emmanouil, João Tovar Jalles, and Geneviève Verdier. 2022. "Tax Evasion from Cross-Border Fraud: Does Digitalization Make a Difference?" *Applied Economics Letters*. https://www.tandfonline.com/doi/ref/10.1080/13504851.2022.2056566.

Wagstaff, Adam, and L. Choon Wang. 2011. "A Hybrid Approach to Efficiency Measurement with Empirical Illustrations from Education and Health." World Bank Policy Research Working Paper 5751, World Bank, Washington, DC.

CHAPTER 7

Climate Change: Further Need for Mitigation and Adaptation in South Asia

Ruchir Agarwal, Vybhavi Balasundharam, Patrick Blagrave, Eugenio Cerutti, Ragnar Gudmundsson, and Racha Moussa

The South Asia region is a large contributor to climate change and one of the regions that is most vulnerable to climate change. This chapter provides an overview of the region's vulnerabilities, national commitments to mitigate emissions, and national policies to adapt to a changing climate. It also discusses policy measures that may be needed to make further progress on mitigation and adaptation. The analysis suggests that while substantial progress is being made, there remains scope to adopt a more cohesive strategy to achieve the region's goals—including by improving the monitoring and tracking of adaptation spending and by laying the groundwork to equitably increase the effective price of carbon while protecting low-income and vulnerable households in the region.

INTRODUCTION

As one of the world's regions most vulnerable to climate change, there is an urgent need to further pursue policies which mitigate the region's contribution to global warming and adapt to the fallout from more frequent severe weather events, sea-level rise, and less predictable rainfall and agricultural output. These events matter, not only because of the physical risks they present, but also because of their potential deep impact on issues such as food security, migration, and the sustainability of livelihoods in affected areas.

This chapter provides an overview of South Asia's circumstances in relation to climate change—its contributions to carbon emissions, and its vulnerabilities—and presents policy commitments already made to both mitigate emissions and adapt to a changing climate, and highlights areas where more action is required.

Decreasing the human contribution to climate change requires mitigation policies. In South Asia, while India is a substantial carbon emitter, other countries

---

This chapter is summary of Agarwal and others (2021). Also, this chapter covers Bangladesh, Bhutan, India, Maldives, Nepal, and Sri Lanka. These are the 6 South Asian countries covered by the IMF's Asia and Pacific Department.

in the region contribute relatively little to the global stock of greenhouse gas emissions, and Bhutan is the only country in the region which is carbon neutral. Hence, although each country in South Asia has a role to play in curbing emissions, the role of India is crucial at a global level.

In the face of a changing climate, countries must put in place adaptation policies. Even assuming full global coordination on mitigation polices, global warming will not be reversed,[1] and countries need to take steps to protect their citizens and ready their economies for a changing climate. There are numerous types of adaptation measures that would result in increased resilience to climate change. This chapter presents a novel stock-taking analysis of the measures already taken by countries in the South Asia region and highlights the need for a comprehensive framework when analyzing investment plans. This framework needs to include the investment impact of regular or climate change–resilient projects on future economic prospects, as well as a strategy for funding sources (including donor support), especially in the presence of limited fiscal space in the region.

Our analysis reveals that South Asian countries are making substantial progress in adapting to the new reality of climate change, as well as in terms of mitigation. However, there is a lack of cohesive strategy to achieve all their goals, and insufficient monitoring and tracking of their adaptation spending. In addition, learning and adopting best practices and experiences from other regions and countries on adaptation and mitigation will be essential. The analysis of both adaptation and mitigation plans and needs also highlight the large financing resources that would be required to tackle climate change in the region, and the essential role of the international community in supporting these efforts, which may prove fiscally challenging, especially for low-income countries.

The chapter is organized as follows: the first section presents the risks and vulnerabilities to climate change faced by South Asia, the third and fourth sections present the mitigation and adaptation analysis, respectively, and the final section concludes.

CLIMATE CHANGE RISKS AND VULNERABILITIES IN SOUTH ASIA

Climate change is a reality we are all facing. The surface average global temperature—a summary statistic that is largely influenced by the stock of CO_2 (Hsiang and Kopp 2018)—indicates that the planet is warming at a rate that has not been seen in the past 20,000 years. Moreover, projections indicate that temperatures will increase even further by the end of the next century. Although considerable uncertainty surrounds temperature projections, the scientific consensus predicts that without action to tackle climate change, average temperatures

---

[1] As reviewed in the next section, the mitigation policies embedded in the Paris Agreement seek to decrease the speed of global temperature increases, which would significantly decrease some of the consequences of climate change.

could rise by 4.4°C by the end of the century (SSP5-8.5), and by 2.7°C in a more likely scenario (SSP2-4.5) capturing current weak mitigation policies (Stocker and others 2013; Masson-Delmotte and others 2021). Very substantial cuts to current emissions—levels consistent with mitigation required to meet Paris goals—will be needed to limit warming to less than 1.5°C (SSP1-1.9).[2]

The effect of climate change in South Asia could be substantial and will affect countries differently (Intergovernmental Panel on Climate Change 2014). The region encompasses several different climatic conditions spread over a wide and diverse geographic area. Landscapes in the region include arid areas subject to severe droughts, low-lying coastal areas subject to flooding and coastal erosion, islands whose continued existence is threatened by the projected rise in sea levels, tropical zones subject to increasingly frequent and devastating cyclones, and mountainous ranges affected by the melting of glaciers.

Overall, the South Asia region is among the world's most vulnerable to fallout from climate change, as many of its countries have substantial portions of their population living in coastal areas (Climate Central 2019)—making them more vulnerable to sea-level rise and severe weather events. With a high population density and high poverty levels, the region is generally considered highly vulnerable to natural disasters. World Bank (2009) noted that more than 50 percent of South Asians had suffered from at least one natural disaster in the preceding two decades, leading to the loss of more than 200,000 lives and damages amounting to about US$45 billion. Table 7.1 illustrates that Bangladesh, India, Nepal, and Sri Lanka have been particularly exposed to extreme weather-related events over the past 20 years. In contrast, the effect of glacier melting on Bhutan and Nepal and of the rise in sea levels on Maldives is likely to become more intense over the medium and long term.

The retreat of glaciers in the Himalayas is set to affect more than 1.5 billion people who live in the floodplains of major rivers, not only because of flooding risks, but also because of the long-term depletion of water supplies which could severely undermine agricultural activity. Sea-level rise and coastal erosion would not only eventually submerge much of Maldives; it is also projected to lead to a loss of 17 percent of land surface and 30 percent of food production by 2050 in Bangladesh (Harris 2014). The combination of extreme weather and unpredictable rainfall patterns in the context of rapid population growth and urbanization is also projected to lead to growing competition for scarce water resources, loss of ecosystems and biodiversity, and a significant reduction in food production (Stocker and others 2013; Havlik and others 2015; Knox and others 2015). In a context of demographic growth, such trends present clear risks in terms of income

---

[2] The Intergovernmental Panel on Climate Change has constructed possible scenarios using alternative greenhouse gas concentration assumptions, land use, and air pollutant futures to project likely ranges of temperatures over the 21st century. While the five scenarios in their latest 2021 report are called "shared socioeconomic pathways", the four scenarios in the previous 2013 report, based on a narrower range of greenhouse gases, land use and air pollutant futures, were called "representative concentration pathways."

TABLE 7.1.

South Asia Vulnerabilities			
Climate Risk Rank 2018[1]	Climate Risk Rank 1999–2018[1]	Global Risk Rank[2]	Natural Disaster Risk Rank[3]
India (5)	Bangladesh (7)	Bangladesh (22)	Bangladesh (10)
Sri Lanka (6)	Nepal (9)	India (29)	Sri Lanka (73)
Nepal (20)	India (17)	Nepal (46)	India (85)
Bangladesh (98)	Sri Lanka (22)	Sri Lanka (97)	Nepal (116)
Maldives (118)	Bhutan (103)	Bhutan (115)	Bhutan (143)
Bhutan (135)	Maldives (175)	Maldives (136)	Maldives (169)

Sources: INFORM Global Risk Index 2019; Global Climate Risk Index 2019; and UN-World Risk Index 2020.
Note: [1]The Global Climate Risk Index 2020 ranks the climate risk indices of 181 countries for year 2018, and for the period 1999–2018. The index takes into account the number of deaths per 100,000 inhabitants, the sum of losses in US dollars in purchasing power parity, as well as losses per unit of GDP. The lower the rank (number in parentheses next to country name), the higher the risk.
[2]The INFORM Global Risk Index 2019 ranks 191 countries at risk from humanitarian crises and disasters that could overwhelm national response capacity. The index is made up of three dimensions: hazards and exposure, vulnerability, and lack of coping capacity. The lower the rank, the higher the risk.
[3]The World Risk Index 2019 ranks the disaster risk of 180 countries in the world. The index takes into account disaster exposure, vulnerability, susceptibility, lack of coping capacities, and lack of adaptive capacities. The lower rank, the higher the risk.

and food security, which in turn may prompt an acceleration in migration flows, both nationally and internationally (Chen and Mueller 2018).

A recent study (World Bank 2018a) looks at the effect on South Asian countries of temperature and precipitation changes at the 2050 horizon. It indicates that temperatures in the region are expected to increase by 1.6°C relative to 1981–2010 in a climate-sensitive scenario that assumes collective global action in line with commitments made under the 2015 Paris Agreement. In a carbon-intensive scenario that assumes no global action, temperatures are expected to increase by 2.2°C. Average monsoon precipitation is projected to increase by 3.9 percent in the climate-sensitive scenario and 6.4 percent in the carbon-intensive scenario.

Because they will exacerbate the intensity and frequency of glacier melting, flooding, cyclones, and coastal erosion, these weather changes are expected to prompt a decrease in living standards in the region, and to have a marked negative effect on Bangladesh, India, and Sri Lanka. While a warmer climate might have a positive effect on productivity in cold, mountainous areas in Bhutan or Nepal, it would notably reduce agricultural productivity elsewhere and increase the propagation of infectious diseases, leading to lower labor productivity. In India, the increased risk of flash droughts could have significant negative effects on food production, irrigation needs, and livelihoods in rural areas (Mishra, Aadhar, and Shwarup Mahto 2021). The decline in per capita income under the carbon-intensive scenario is by 2050 projected to reach 6.7 percent in Bangladesh, 2.8 percent in India, and 7 percent in Sri Lanka. In hotspots—areas where changes in weather are expected to have a disproportionately large impact—the reduction in per capita income is projected to reach 14.4 percent for Bangladesh, 9.8 percent for India, and 10 percent for Sri Lanka (World Bank 2018a).

MITIGATION EFFORTS IN SOUTH ASIA

A key global coordination mechanism in reducing carbon emissions is the Paris Agreement, and countries' nationally determined contributions (NDCs) to lower emissions. As the largest carbon emitter in South Asia and one of the largest emitters in the world, India has a key leadership role to play.

Global Coordination Mechanism for Mitigation

The Paris Agreement entered into force on November 4, 2016 and aims to keep global temperature rise this century well below 2°C above preindustrial levels and to pursue efforts to further limit warming to 1.5°C. In addition, the agreement aims to strengthen the ability of countries to deal with the effects of climate change and includes enhanced support to assist developing countries. Under the agreement, all Parties are required to put forward their best efforts through NDCs and to strengthen these efforts in the years ahead. This includes requirements that all Parties report regularly on their emissions and on their implementation efforts.

As of 2019, 184 parties had submitted their first NDCs, including all six South Asian countries covered here (Bangladesh, Bhutan, India, Maldives, Nepal, and Sri Lanka). Table 7.2 summarizes the key pledges and targets for the six countries based on information from the respective NDCs. Unconditional targets refer to targets that the countries have pledged to in their NDCs without any conditions attached. By contrast, conditional targets refer to targets a given country has pledged to achieve only conditional on international support (typically in the form of grants, financing, or technology transfer).

Bhutan is notable for being one of two countries in the world that is already carbon neutral (with Suriname being the other). Bhutan made the commitment to remain carbon neutral in 2009 despite their status as a small, mountainous developing country. Consistent with this, their NDC renewed this commitment to remain carbon neutral going forward, and it is expected to adhere to this commitment for the foreseeable future.

NDC pledges should be evaluated against the huge human and economic effort that is needed to meet the Paris Agreement goal to limit warming well below 2°C by 2100. According to the estimates in the UN Emissions Gap 2018 report, to prevent warming of 2°C by 2100, we will have to make sure that global emissions do not exceed 40 gigatons of CO_2 equivalent by 2030. By comparison, to limit warming to 1.8°C by the end of the century, emissions would have to be cut even further, not exceeding 34 gigatons of CO_2 equivalent by 2030. And to prevent 1.5°C of temperature rise by 2100, our total emissions will have to stay below 24 gigatons of CO_2 equivalent.

Even if countries follow through on all their unconditional climate pledges, the planet's average temperature is expected rise by about 2.1°C to 3.5°C by 2100—well beyond the goal of Paris Agreement. Therefore, to avoid damaging levels of climate change, countries will need to be bolder in their climate commitments with material action to make those commitments a reality.

TABLE 7.2.

Paris Agreement Pledges and Targets

	India	Bangladesh	Nepal	Sri Lanka	Bhutan	Maldives
Ratified	Yes	Yes	Yes	Yes	Yes	Yes
Share of 2012 greenhouse gases	5.73%	0.35%	0.09%	0.06%	0.01%	0.00%
2017 emissions per capita relative to the United States	11%	3%	2%	7%	9%	22%
unconditional target	33–35% reduction in emissions intensity by 2030, compared with the 2005 levels	6.73% reduction in greenhouse gas emissions by 2030, compared with business-as-usual levels, in the power, transportation, and industry sectors	None	By 2030, an unconditional 4% emissions cut in the power, transport, industry, waste, agriculture, and forestry sectors, compared with business-as-usual projections	Remain carbon neutral so that emissions of greenhouse gases do not exceed carbon sequestration by forests	None
Conditional target	40% of cumulative electricity installed capacity from non–fossil fuel-based resources by 2030 with the help of transfer of technology and low cost international finance including from the Green Climate Fund	Further 15.12% reduction, conditional upon international support in the form of finance, investment, technology development and transfer, and capacity building	By 2050, to achieve net-zero greenhouse gas emissions	Conditional on international support, a further 10.5% emissions cut in the six sectors, compared with business-as-usual projections	None	26% reduction of emissions by 2030 (under BAU), in the context of sustainable development, enabled by financial support, technology transfers, and capacity building. With extensive support, the goal would be net-zero emissions by 2030.
LULUCF	Increase tree cover, creating an additional carbon sink of 2.5 to 3 billion tonnes of CO_2 equivalent by 2030	None	Maintain 40% of the total area of the country under forest cover	Increase the forest cover of Sri Lanka from 29% to 32% by 2030	Maintain current levels of forest cover	None

Source: IMF staff calculations based on individual NDCs that can be accessed at the NDC public registry maintained by the United Nations Framework Convention on Climate Change Secretariat as of August 2021.

Note: LULUCF = land use, land-use change, and forestry; NDC = nationally determined contributions.

Figure 7.1. World Fossil CO$_2$ Emissions, 1970–2018
(Million tonnes CO$_2$/year)

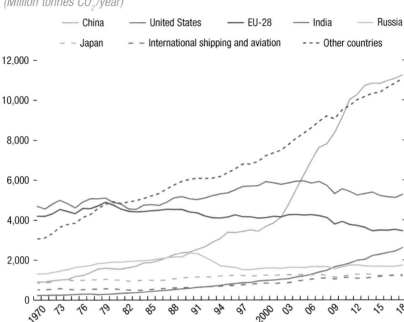

Source: Emissions Database for Global Atmospheric Research (EDGAR).
Note: EU-28 = Austria, Belgium, Bulgaria, Croatia, Cyprus, Czech Republic, Denmark, Estonia, Finland, France, Germany, Greece, Hungary, Ireland, Italy, Latvia, Lithuania, Luxembourg, Malta, The Netherlands, Poland, Portugal, Romania, Slovenia, Slovakia, Spain, Sweden, and the United Kingdom.

All countries need to reduce emissions, but the biggest global impact will come from the top four emitters—China, the United States, the European Union, and India. These four regions account for more than 56 percent of all the greenhouse gases that were emitted over the past decade. As of 2018, China is currently the largest contributor, accounting for 27 percent of all emissions (and has committed to reach carbon neutrality by 2060); the United States and the European Union account for slightly more than 20 percent of the global greenhouse gas emissions; and India's emissions represent about 6 percent (Figure 7.1). However, it must be noted that India's emissions per capita remain significantly below that of advanced countries (Figure 7.2).

Thus, among the South Asian countries, much of the focus is on India with respect to mitigation, given its relatively large share of greenhouse gas emissions. As of 2012 (a date for which comparable data are available for all six countries), India accounted for almost 6 percent of global CO$_2$ emissions, despite its low per capita emissions and large needs for better living standards for a sizable fraction of the population (Figure 7.6). By contrast, Bangladesh accounted for 0.33 of a percent; and the others accounted for less than 0.1 percent of global greenhouse gas emissions (see Table 7.2). In this context, India's mitigation policy is of central interest to the global community focused on combatting climate change. This is the focus of the next section.

Figure 7.2. CO$_2$ Emissions Per Capita
(Tonnes)

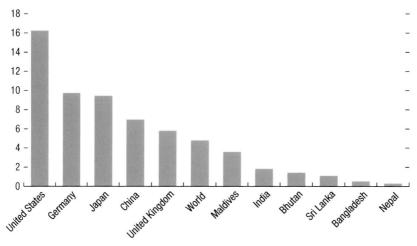

Source: Our World in Data (https://ourworldindata.org).

India's Mitigation Path

While India's emissions are projected to grow as the country's economy develops, its commitments may be compatible with the 2°C goal set in Paris. India is emerging as a leader in renewable energy, with significant investments in renewable energy (in addition to still-sizable investments in fossil fuel). According to the 2018 UN Emissions Gap Report, India is one of the few G20 members where the emissions under current policies are projected to be more than 10 percent below their unconditional NDC targets for 2030.

India is expected to achieve both its 40 percent nonfossil target and its emissions intensity target by 2030. India's NDC commits it to reducing its emissions intensity of GDP by 33–35 percent below 2005 levels by 2030 and increasing the share of nonfossil energy in total power generation capacity to 40 percent (with help of international support). Estimates by the Climate Action Tracker (CAT)—an independent scientific analysis under a collaboration between Climate Analytics and New Climate Institute that tracks government climate action—suggest that India can achieve its NDC target with currently implemented policies. In particular, the CAT projects that its share of nonfossil power generation capacity will reach 60–65 percent in 2030. Thus, under current policies, India is projected to achieve both its 40 percent nonfossil target and its emissions intensity target. These reported estimates from CAT India are consistent with the findings of the 2018 UN Emission Gap Report and several other studies.[3]

---

[3] Other studies, including Dubash and others (2018), analysis by The Energy and Resources Institute (COMMIT 2018), the International Energy Agency's World Energy Outlook (International Energy Agency 2017), Mitra and others (2017), Vishwanathan and Garg (2020), come to the same conclusion that India is likely to meet its NDC targets and even overachieve its emissions intensity reduction target.

Figure 7.3. Carbon Emissions in India, by Energy Source
(MT CO$_2$)

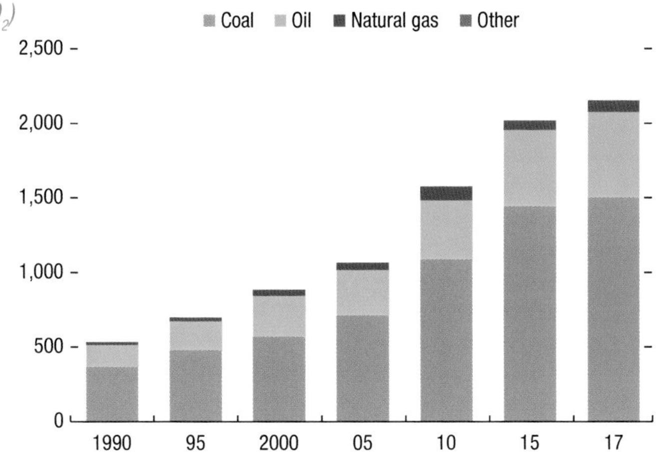

Source: International Energy Agency, CO$_2$ Emissions from Fuel Combustion database.

India's progress offers it an opportunity to become a leader on the world stage by taking bolder steps toward the more ambitious 1.5°C goal set in Paris. Going forward, India will have an opportunity to strengthen their mitigation goals. One priority for India could be to phase out its reliance on unabated coal-fired power plants.[4] By energy source, carbon dioxide emissions in India come primarily from coal (Figure 7.3).

The generation of electricity in India is still heavily coal-dependent for a variety of reasons, including its historical cost advantage and an abundance of domestic (see Tongia and Gross, 2019 for a fuller discussion).[5] In addition to emitting substantial amounts of carbon, India's thermal power sector is much more dependent on water than are renewables, and a relative lack of water since 2013 has reduced the efficiency of coal-fired-plant operations (Luo, Krishnan, and Sen 2018).

Over the past decade, there are signs of a gradual shift away from thermal power generation toward renewable sources. A decade ago, power generation came primarily from thermal sources (about 64 percent) with just under 10 percent from renewables. As of the end of 2019, the role of thermal had barely declined, but renewables (mainly solar and wind) accounted for nearly a quarter of India's power generation. Among renewables, solar and energy have come to play a dominant role, with a smaller share attributed to hydropower generation. Perhaps more encouraging has been the trend over the past two years, wherein marginal additions to power generation capacity have been dominated by renewables (Figure 7.4).

---

[4] "Unabated" here refers to plants without carbon, capture, and storage capacities.

[5] Worrall and others (2019) provide suggestive evidence on the lack of spatial correlation between coal thermal power plants and energy access in India.

Figure 7.4. Marginal Additions to Power-Generation Capacity in India
(Percent)

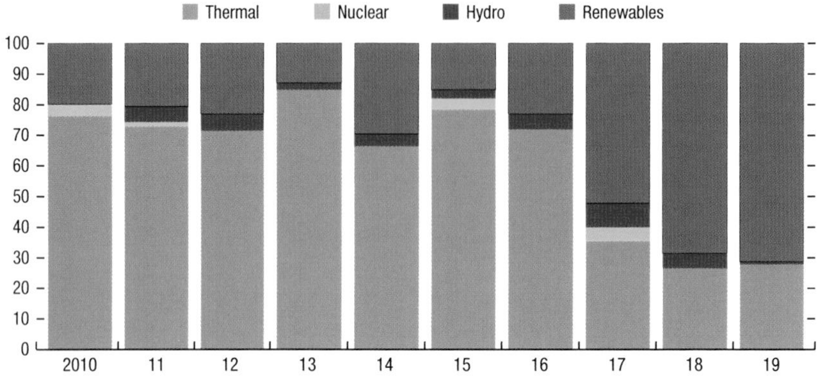

Sources: Central Electricity Authority; and IMF staff calculations.
Note: Renewable energy sources includes wind, small hydro project, biomass gasifier, biomass power, urban and industrial waste power, and solar power.

Going forward, with a large population and a rapidly growing economy, demand for energy in India will increase markedly. To limit carbon emissions associated with this increase in demand for energy, the transition away from fossil fuels toward renewables generation is vital. In addition, measures targeting greater energy efficiency of appliances and lighting, and green building construction can play a role in limiting any unnecessary growth of electricity usage.

India's latest Electricity Plan (Central Electricity Authority 2018) still envisions several new coal-fired power plants. While several advanced countries are envisioning a similar phasing out (for example, Canada by 2030), India also has an opportunity to embark on a similar goal and demonstrate leadership at the world stage. This will also benefit the local population by reducing local air pollution and incentivize a shift toward cleaner and potentially job-rich renewable technologies.

Some Mitigation Policy Considerations

The recent strong increase in renewable power generation capacity is being facilitated by a rise in government subsidies to renewables (Abhinav and others 2018), illustrating the important role for policy in durably reducing carbon emissions. Going forward, one approach to reduce emissions rapidly and substantially is to meaningfully change the relative cost of electricity generation through renewables, relative to nonabated coal-fired production. This can be achieved either by further lowering the cost of renewables through greater subsidization or technological innovation (for example, a rapid decline in price of solar or wind energy because of technological advancements), or by increasing the cost of thermal production.

Existing policies in India have elements of both approaches. Recognizing the need to partly internalize the externalities associated with the generation of electricity using thermal sources, especially coal production, a coal cess tax was enacted in 2010.[6] Nevertheless, the efficacy of this cess in discouraging coal production and usage in power generation is dampened by large subsidies which remain in place throughout the value chain benefitting coal mining and the operation of coal-fired power plants (Abhinav and others 2018). The elimination of these subsidies would also help shore up India's fiscal position, including in the context of the current COVID-19 pandemic.

Levying a direct tax on fossil-fuel production, in proportion to their carbon content and ultimately their carbon emissions (a so-called carbon tax) would accelerate the shift away from thermal power generation while also providing a fiscal dividend. As discussed in IMF (2019c, 2021), the enaction of a carbon tax is an important mechanism in reducing emissions. As an example, a $50/ton carbon tax would reduce carbon dioxide emissions by about 35 percent below a no-policy-change baseline scenario, by 2030.[7] Unlike subsidization which carries a fiscal cost, a carbon tax could provide a large fiscal boon to India. IMF (2019c) estimates that a $50/ton carbon tax would generate between 1.5 and 2 percent of GDP in additional fiscal revenues by 2030. If this boost to revenues were put toward reducing the country's deficit, it would play a large role in counteracting the deterioration in India's fiscal position associated with the COVID-19 pandemic and necessary fiscal support measures. Alternatively, higher fiscal revenues could be partly used to increase fiscal transfers to lower income households, thereby offsetting any negative distributional impact that the carbon tax itself may imply (for a discussion of household compensation using cash transfers, see Jain and others 2018). In addition, a well-designed carbon pricing reform can support distributional and poverty objectives. In this regard, analysis in the IMF's *Fiscal Monitor* suggests that a carbon tax may in fact have a similar or smaller incidence on lower-income households than on those with higher incomes, due largely to the fact that electricity is either less available or less consumed by rural households in India (IMF 2019c). In addition, using part of carbon pricing revenues to increase fiscal transfers to lower-income households would make the reform more progressive and could result in net benefits among poorer households. Doing so could make the reform both pro-equity and pro-poor (IMF 2021). In addition, it could also help with improving air quality and mitigating pollution.

Overall, while raising the carbon tax further in the future can bring several benefits, several design issues and implementation timing need to be considered to mitigate the effect on vulnerable individuals. Further work is needed in each South Asian country to evaluate, assess, and design the practical aspects of the

---

[6] The "clean energy cess" was first enacted at a rate of 50 rupees/ton in 2010 and has been increased three times since it was enacted. With the enaction of the goods and services tax in 2017, the clean energy cess was replaced by the goods and services tax compensation cess (a tax on coal production), at a rate of 400 rupees/ton, since unchanged.

[7] As empirical evidence on the elasticity of carbon emissions with respect to prices is relatively limited, these estimates are subject to considerable uncertainty. For one empirical study, see Rafaty and others (2020), which indicates a positive link between carbon prices and emissions reductions.

policy implementation to ensure vulnerable and low-income households are protected and adequately covered by the various fiscal transfers. Moreover, more thought will need to be given to the effect of carbon taxes on growth and inflation as policy makers are likely to be worried about this. Options to enhance protection of vulnerable households are discussed further in IMF (2021).

The COVID-19 shock has already led to sectoral reallocation away from some dirty-energy-intensive sectors, which could help reduce transition costs on the path to a greener economy. Some sectors that rely intensively on carbon—such as airlines, transportation, and so on—have been particularly impacted by the COVID-19 shock, and the adverse effect is expected to last for several years. While in the short-term this has led to sizable pain for the workers and businesses operating in these sectors, over the medium term this provides an opportunity for job creation in less pollution-prone sectors. In this context, over the mediumterm, a well-designed carbon tax package—that is combined with complementary product and labor market policies—could support the reallocation of capital to and reskilling of labor in more productive and cleaner sectors.

ADAPTATION STRATEGY IN SOUTH ASIA

Adaptation is the other main policy response to climate change and consists of improving the resilience of people's behavior and the country's infrastructure to the consequences of climate change. Adapting to climate change takes many forms. In addition to making physical infrastructure more resilient to climate shocks, adaptation involves improving policymaking processes to be more agile in the face of climate shocks, internalizing climate risk in areas such as land use laws and procurement, and educating households and firms on their role in adapting to climate change and providing support in the effort (Global Commission on Adaptation 2019; Hallegatte and others 2020). South Asia has made strides in adapting to climate change and there is scope for more action.

Different Types of Adaptation Policies

Early warning systems for cyclones in the North Indian Ocean are a good example of adaptation through policy. These cyclones routinely devastate the coastline and are often deadly and destructive. Improvements in early warning systems and evacuation exercises have helped save the lives of thousands of people as demonstrated in comparing two category 5 cyclones from 1991 and 2020 in the North Indian Ocean (Figure 7.5). The 1991 Bangladesh cyclone was a category 5 tropical cyclone and among the strongest and deadliest cyclones in the North Indian Ocean with more than 138,000 deaths and an estimated US$1.78 billion in damages (EM-DAT 2020). Most recently, on May 20, 2020, another category 5 cyclone, Amphan, made first landfall and impacted the coasts in Bangladesh and West Bengal and that also affected Sri Lanka and Bhutan (Ellis-Petersen and Ratcliffe 2020). Amphan is the costliest cyclone ever recorded in the North Indian Ocean, with estimated damages of more than US$13 billion

Figure 7.5. Deaths, by Climate-Related Disaster

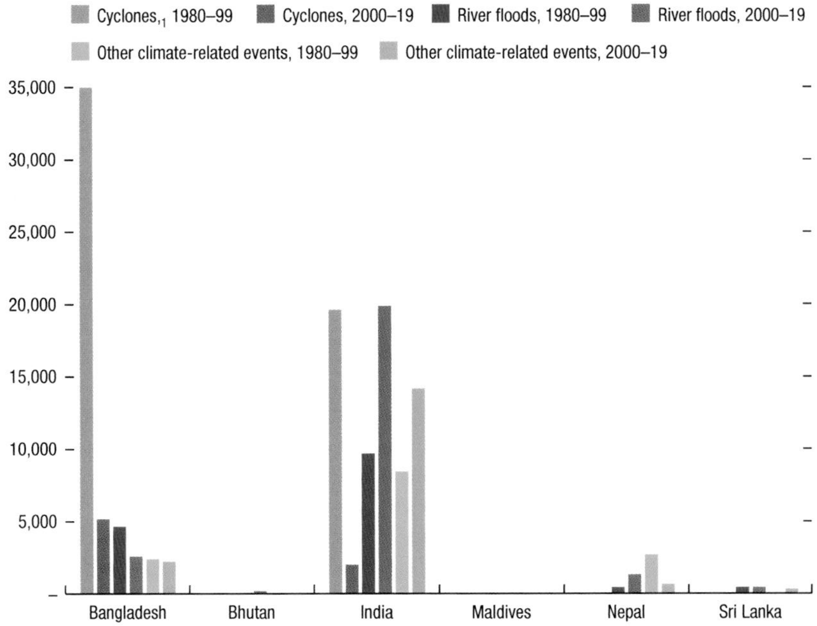

■ Cyclones,₁ 1980–99   ■ Cyclones, 2000–19   ■ River floods, 1980–99   ■ River floods, 2000–19
■ Other climate-related events, 1980–99   ■ Other climate-related events, 2000–19

Source: EM-DAT 2020.
¹158,531 deaths; the 1991 cyclone in Bangladesh alone claimed more than 138,000 lives.

and 128 lives lost. With improvements in early warning systems and evacuation efforts, 2.4 million Bangladeshis were evacuated before the storm made landfall, saving thousands of lives (International Federation of Red Cross and Red Crescent Societies 2020).

In addition to adaptation policies that trigger benefits by educating the public and changing people's attitudes, the need to improve physical infrastructure is also a key element in effective adaptation. Physical infrastructure needs in South Asia are well documented, even before considering the need for infrastructure to be resilient to climate change. A recent study by Rozenberg and Fay (2019) estimated that to achieve their development goals, low- and middle-income countries need to spend between 2 and 8 percent of GDP annually until 2030. The estimates vary based on spending efficiency and development goals. In the scenario where the Sustainable Development Goals are attained and full decarbonization is achieved around 2050, the average annual capital cost and maintenance cost for South Asia would be 4.8 and 2.7 percent of regional GDP up to 2030.

To maximize the benefits of the needed infrastructure, new infrastructure should be resilient to climate shocks to the extent possible. Satisfying infrastructure needs requires a comprehensive analysis of investment plans, their impact on future economic prospects, as well as a strategy for funding sources, especially in the presence of limited fiscal space in the region. Using the example of Maldives,

Box 7.1 illustrates through a general equilibrium framework how the choice between standard- and adaptation-capital is intertwined with decisions on how to finance the additional investment, whether with debt or through other sources. More generally other studies have also highlighted that South Asian economies can still stand to gain from improving their adaptability to climate change, including in terms of infrastructure (Agarwal and others 2021).

Box 7.1. Enhancing Infrastructure Resilience to Climate Change in Maldives

The increased likelihood of adverse climate-related shocks calls for building adaptation (resilient) infrastructure. Satisfying these infrastructure needs requires a comprehensive analysis of investment plans, their impact on future economic prospects, as well as a strategy for funding sources, especially in the presence of limited fiscal space. This box presents the results of an analysis precisely illustrating these challenges, through calibrating the model of Marto and others (2018) to Maldivian data and using it as a general equilibrium framework to analyze the effects of climate change-related shocks, public investment, and its financing sources.

Climate change-related shocks can affect the economy by damaging both public and private capital and by temporarily hampering productivity, but the investment in adaptation capital could make the economy more resilient to these shocks. To consider those dynamics, the general equilibrium growth model is tailored to small-open economies prone to natural disasters, with firms that use different types of capital and labor to produce traded and nontraded goods and services. The modeling of natural-disaster shocks allows us to analyze the implications of alternative public investment decisions, such as the choice between standard and adaptation infrastructure. The choice between standard and adaptation capital is intertwined with decisions on how to finance the additional investment, whether with debt or through other sources. The model allows us to underscore critical margins that influence both types of decisions.

The financing strategy is crucial in the case of Maldives, given its limited fiscal space. To this aim, illustrative experiments are set up along two main dimensions: investment options and financing. For the sake of simplicity, the assumption is that authorities use the same budget envelope of 1 percent of GDP for 5 consecutive years for building standard or adaptation infrastructure, and a natural disaster occurs as soon as this investment plan is completed. The experiments help address three main questions: (1) What are the gains associated with adaptation infrastructure in the face of a natural disaster? (2) How does the outcome change when the government finances the initial investment with international grants, rather than by raising taxes? (3) What are the financing needs for reconstruction in the aftermath of a disaster, depending on whether the government has invested in standard or adaptation capital? And what does this mean for international donors?

Three scenarios are considered: (1) investment in standard infrastructure; (2) investment in adaptation infrastructure financed by higher taxation; and (3) investment in adaptation infrastructure financed by international grants. These simulations, for simplicity, assume that the postdisaster reconstruction is financed by increased taxation, under the assumption that Maldives has no fiscal space for deficit-financed spending. It is, however, possible that donors would intervene also with postdisaster grants.

The natural-disaster shock is assumed to destroy 10 percent of capital and to trigger a symmetric productivity drop in both the tradable and nontradable sectors. While the

(Box 7.1 continues on the next page)

Box 7.1. Enhancing Infrastructure Resilience to Climate Change in Maldives *(continued)*

Figure 7.1.1. Infrastructure Resilience to Climate Change in Maldives

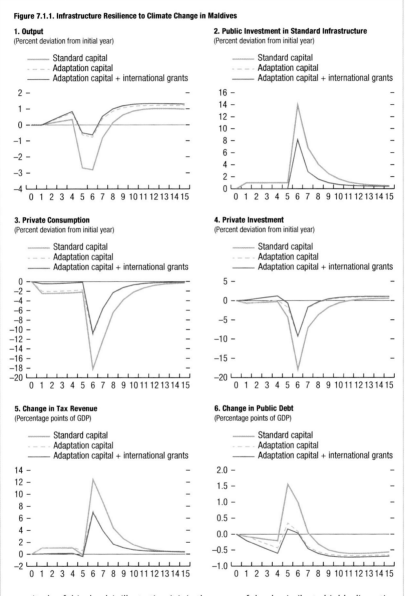

1. Output
(Percent deviation from initial year)

2. Public Investment in Standard Infrastructure
(Percent deviation from initial year)

3. Private Consumption
(Percent deviation from initial year)

4. Private Investment
(Percent deviation from initial year)

5. Change in Tax Revenue
(Percentage points of GDP)

6. Change in Public Debt
(Percentage points of GDP)

magnitude of this shock is illustrative, it is in the range of shocks similar to highly disruptive floods observed in island countries. The results highlight the following:

- *Effect of the shock on GDP.* Building resilient infrastructure in Maldives can halve the losses in terms of GDP at the trough triggered by the natural disaster. Note that, investing in resilient infrastructure yields a dividend even before the disaster occurs, as its greater

(Box 7.1 continues on the next page)

gross rate of return and durability imply that its net return is higher (the greater durability is captured by a smaller depreciation rate of resilient infrastructure relative to that of standard infrastructure). The additional tax pressure required for the reconstruction in the case of standard infrastructure would be (politically) difficult. The supplementary increase in tax revenues should be about 6–7 percentage points of GDP, in the aftermath of the shock (difference between blue and black/red lines in the tax revenue chart).

- *Financing.* Financing public investment (in standard or adaptation infrastructure) with higher taxation would lead to a sacrifice in terms of GDP, and private consumption and investment in the ramp up of the investment effort. Grant-financing can reduce this cost (or eliminate it if it covers the investment plan in full, as in the example provided).

Donors' considerations. The large increase in tax revenue required to support the reconstruction underscores the large financing gaps that authorities could face with worsening climate conditions. Very likely, donors might have to financially support the country during the reconstruction phase. The experiment underscores the tradeoff faced by the international community: financing the initial investment in adaptation infrastructure with prospects of much smaller postdisaster disbursements or wait for the disaster to occur and sustain the reconstruction in the case of standard infrastructure, with potentially twice-as-large disbursements (difference between the black and blue line in the tax revenue chart, in the aftermath of the shock).

Source: Prepared by Giovanni Melina and Marika Santoro (both in the IMF's Research Department), based on Melina and Santoro (2021).

The incidence and effect of COVID-19 in the region also highlights the importance of strengthening preparedness to respond to future pandemics and increases the need to design adaptation policies with a view to addressing the risk of future pandemics. Evidence suggests that climate change, along with changes in land use driven by urbanization, deforestation, and increased demand for food, reduces biodiversity and exacerbates the risk of the emergence of new diseases and their transmittal to humans. It is important to maintain surveillance of at-risk areas to protect the habitat of pathogen-carrying species and ensure that interaction with humans and other animals is limited; also, environmental impact assessments can take health risks into account (Keesing and others 2010; World Health Organization and Secretariat of the Convention on Biological Diversity 2015).

Current State of Adaptation in South Asia

South Asian countries have advanced to different degrees in their adaptation to climate change in relation to nonstructural interventions, structural resilience building, fiscal actions, financial actions, and risk management.

Nonstructural Interventions and Structural Resilience Building

First, all South Asian countries have developed national climate change action and disaster management plans (Table 7.3). These nonstructural interventions involve

TABLE 7.3.

Survey of Nonstructural Interventions and Structural Resilience Building in South Asia

	Bangladesh	Bhutan	India	Maldives	Nepal	Sri Lanka
National Climate Change Action Plan	✓	✓	✓	✓	✓	✓
National Disaster Management Plan	✓	✓	✓	✓	✓	✓
Enact laws and regulations to address climate change impacts						
Adaptation capital and climate-resilient green growth initiatives	✓	✓	✓	✓	✓	✓
Climate risk financing strategy						

Source: Authors, based on the status of these respective adaptation categories as of July 2021. See the Annex in Agarwal and others (2021) for details on each category, by country.

developing guidelines, operating frameworks, and action plans to help guide both ex ante resilience building and postdisaster resilience. These plans are quite granular in nature, invariably containing sectoral action plans for each vulnerable sector.[8]

In line with the proposals in many of the action plans, nearly all South Asian countries have started to build adaptive capacity. Examples include improving crop and livestock production practices for higher food security and farmer income; safeguarding communities in coastal areas; and enhancing early-warning systems, climate-resilient building measures and water management. However, South Asian countries have only recently started to transition from planning to implementation, and they would require more investment in adaptation capital and climate resilient green growth initiatives in the coming years, given their high exposure to climate risks.[9] The countries should also promote inclusive growth strategies given that poverty and the lack of access to basic services are strong predictors of vulnerability to climate change (Hallegatte, Rentschler, and Rozenberg 2020).

Apart from taking early steps for climate change adaptation, as highlighted in Table 7.3, no South Asian country has enacted any laws or regulations to directly address climate change adaptation. Examples of such policies in other countries include National Building Codes that stipulate natural-disaster-proof physical infrastructure and land regulations to prevent land degradation. Starting in 2019, both Sri Lanka and Maldives have taken initiatives to strengthen the safety and resilience of their built environment through participation in the Building Regulation for Resilience Program. As part of the program, the current level of

---

[8] The national adaptation plans of Bangladesh, Bhutan, India, Maldives, Nepal, and Sri Lanka incorporate plans to address the increase in diseases because of climate change. Most plans focus on vector-borne diseases, but plans also include pathogenic diseases, diarrheal diseases, and heatstroke. Details of the plans vary but tend to cover research, monitoring, prevention, and education.

[9] IMF (2021) showed that many South Asian countries currently have low adaptive capacity, even after controlling for income levels.

building regulatory capacity of both countries will be assessed and tailored recommendations will be provided and incorporated into the existing regulatory framework. Utilizing such programs and updating laws and regulations could play a critical role in building adaption capital. In addition, none of the South Asian countries have a cohesive and holistic climate risk financing strategy.[10] Resilience building would require consistent spending over the next decades that would be facilitated by formulating a financing roadmap.[11]

Fiscal Actions

Fiscal policies could play a vital role in financing resilience building. Most South Asian countries have limited fiscal space to deal with natural disasters and other climate change shocks to the economy (Table 7.4). With potentially increasing frequency and severity of natural disasters because of climate change, coping with shocks such as the COVID-19 pandemic and other crisis situations will become more challenging. Some South Asian countries have established contingent budgets or reserve funds to cover disaster expenses, usually financed by annual appropriations and drawn down in the event of a disaster. These funds are generally limited in scope and size to cover small and recurring losses from natural disasters such as local floods and landslides (World Bank 2017). Given the vulnerability to severe natural disasters, such funds might not offer sufficient buffers against climate change. Relying on new loans and donations from the international community following a disaster is risky as it is often inadequate in providing timely assistance and recovery. Therefore, South Asian countries could have high returns

TABLE 7.4.

Survey of Fiscal Actions in South Asia

	Bangladesh	Bhutan	India	Maldives	Nepal	Sri Lanka
Setting fiscal policies and targets	✓		✓	✓		
Climate change expenditure tagging system	✓				✓	
Climate/green fund for adaptation	✓	✓	✓	✓		
Natural disaster–related reserves (contingency funds)		✓	✓			
Fiscal space	Moderate	Moderate	Limited	Limited	Moderate	Limited

Source: Authors, based on the status of these respective adaptation categories as of July 2021. See the Annex in Agarwal and others (2021) for the details on each category by country.
Note: Fiscal space assessments are estimated based on the IMF Article IV debt sustainability assessments performed before COVID-19 and do not reflect the developments since the outset of the pandemic. The pandemic has generally further constrained the fiscal space for countries.

---

[10] Bangladesh is currently developing the "Mujib Climate Prosperity Plan," a strategic investment framework to mobilize financing for implementing renewable energy and climate resilience initiatives, including the US$ 37 billion worth of projects identified in the Bangladesh Delta Plan 2100.

[11] See IMF (2021) for estimates of public adaption costs as share of GDP annually in South Asia.

from investing in risk reduction and adopting other risk-coping strategies such as self-insurance, risk-transfer instruments, and ex-ante financing arrangements.

For risk-reduction purposes, a majority of the South Asian countries have started to allocate budget or create a resilience fund for adaptation building. An example is Bangladesh's Climate Fiscal Framework where about 2 percent of the national budget was allocated to resilient infrastructure building in 2017. Alternatively, Maldives levied from 2016 a green tax of US$6 per person per day from resorts, vessels, and hotels and US$3 per person per day from guest houses, and this revenue could be used for resilience building. However, only Bangladesh and Nepal have adopted a climate change expenditure tagging system to monitor and track climate-related expenditures in the national budget system and publish citizen climate budgets to present the government's budget plans to raise and spend public money to address climate change and its effects (World Bank 2021).[12] Using such public financial management tools to monitor and track climate-related expenditures would help the governments identify financing gaps, effectively mobilize investment to attain the national action plans, evaluate the climate financing activities, enhance transparency, and improve accountability (Guzmán, Guillén, and Manda 2018; Micale, Tonkonogy, and Mazza 2018). Given the capacity constraints in South Asian countries, adaptation strategies are likely to be cost-effective and efficient when built into, funded from, and made an integral part of the existing schemes and programs, rather than trying to create new ones and find additional resources for the same.

TABLE 7.5.

Survey of Risk-Sharing Instruments and Financing in South Asia						
	Bangladesh	**Bhutan**	**India**	**Maldives**	**Nepal**	**Sri Lanka**
Climate/green finance	✓		✓			✓
Catastrophe bonds						
Contingency credit lines (for example, Cat DDO)		✓		✓	✓	✓
Green bonds	✓		✓			
Macro-level national disaster risk insurance						✓
Micro-level index insurance	✓		✓		✓	✓
Meso-level index insurance	✓		✓			
Concessional financing for adaptation (GCF, GEF, etc.)	✓	✓	✓	✓	✓	✓

Source: Authors, based on the status of these respective adaptation categories as of July 2021. See the Annex in Agarwal and others (2021) for the details on each category by country.
Note: Cat DDO = Catastrophe Deferred Drawdown Option; GCF = Green Climate Fund; GEF = global environment facility.

---

[12] The state of Odisha in India is the first subnational government to apply a specific climate budget tagging methodology (World Bank 2021).

Financial Actions and Risk Management

South Asian countries generally have an underinsurance problem whereby few people have adequate protection in the event of natural disasters. Sri Lanka has the only public national insurance program in South Asia, the National Natural Disaster Insurance Scheme launched in 2016 (Table 7.5). In addition, no South Asian country currently has a sovereign parametric insurance scheme or has issued catastrophe bonds (Cat bonds) to tackle the increasing costs from climate change. A Cat bond is a security that pays the issuer when a predefined disaster risk is realized. This lack of take-up in insurance can primarily be attributed to the high costs and high barriers to access. Pooling insurance or issuance of Cat bonds by multiple countries in a region such as that of Pacific Alliance Countries Cat Bonds (Chile, Colombia, Mexico, and Peru) can overcome these challenges through economies of scale for insurers, better costs, and diversification for investors (World Bank 2018b).

Larger countries in the region such as India and Bangladesh can generally absorb the impact of adverse natural events since the affected region can be subsidized by revenues from unaffected regions. However, for smaller states such as Bhutan and Maldives, pooling arrangements stretching beyond their borders would be critical to sustaining the increasing costs of natural disasters (Linnerooth-Bayer and Mechler 2009).

Besides mobilizing domestic revenue for adaptation, South Asian countries are not leveraging funding from external sources as effectively as countries in other regions. Various sources and channels of climate financing are available. While there has been some action in terms of accessing multilateral concessional financing such as the Green Climate Fund for adaptation, it has been limited. In fact, East Asia and Pacific remains the primary destination region for climate finance, accounting for US\$ 238 billion per year (53 percent of all flows) on average during 2017–18 whereas South Asia only received US\$ 31 billion per year (7 percent of all flows). The conditions to access climate finance vary but generally require a robust public financial management system. This highlights the need for South Asian countries to continue strengthening public financial management and public investment management efficiency, and to improve project planning and prioritization to access the available climate financing. The international donor community can foster resilience building by continuing to mobilize more funds, defining conditions more clearly, and improving accessibility.

Even within climate finance, mitigation receives 93 percent of the available funds. Adaptation received minimal private funding, primarily from the multilateral climate funds (Buchner and others 2019). This reflects a continued dependency on public funds among developing countries for resilience building, as well as a need to further attract private investors to bring about a larger-scale shift in adaptation financing. The newest instruments for mobilizing private sector investments are green finance and green bonds. The larger South Asian countries, India, Bangladesh, and Sri Lanka, are actively encouraging their commercial banks and financial institutions to lend to green projects and setting up targets. For example, Bangladesh Bank requires every commercial bank and financial institutions under its jurisdiction to disburse 5 percent of its total loaned amount to green projects (IMF 2019b). Until recently, only India had an active green bonds market, owing to its relatively large and developed financial capital market.[13] In April 2021, Bangladesh approved its first green bond (Islam 2021).

While projects are funded with climate benefits, there is a lack of clarity on what constitutes climate financing amongst the financial sector. Bangladesh Bank has developed a Sustainable Finance Policy for Banks and Financial Institutions in 2020 that covers sustainable and green taxonomy to classify economic activities based on their contribution to climate change objectives, and Central Bank of Sri Lanka has developed a Roadmap for Sustainable Finance in 2019 to address the climate finance challenges. These could serve as models for other South Asian countries that are looking to expand and standardize climate financing. Even within climate financing, encouraging projects on climate change adaptation can help to accelerate resilience building through the private sector.

South Asian countries are making substantial piecemeal progress in adapting to the new reality of climate change. However, there is a lack of cohesive strategies to achieve all their goals, and insufficient monitoring and tracking of their adaptation spending. In addition, learning and adopting best practices and experiences from other regions and countries on adaptation will be essential. The international community, particularly the international financial institutions, could be pivotal in guiding climate change adaptation in South Asia by continuing to develop diagnostic tools such as the World Bank's Country Climate and Development Report, IMF's Climate Macroeconomic Assessment Program, risk sharing instruments such as the Catastrophe Deferred Drawdown Option (Cat DDO)[14] and mobilizing funds through the Global Climate Fund, Climate Investment Funds, and other multilateral, regional and sovereign funds.[15]

CONCLUSIONS

South Asia is one of the world's most vulnerable regions to climate change. It features varied landscapes that include arid areas subject to severe droughts, low-lying coastal areas subject to flooding and coastal erosion, islands whose continued existence is threatened by the projected rise in sea levels, tropical zones subject to increasingly frequent and devastating cyclones, and mountainous ranges

---

[13] The Reserve Bank of India joined the Central Banks and Supervisors' Network for Greening the Financial System in April 2021 as an avenue to benefit from membership in the Network for Greening the Financial System by learning and contributing to global efforts on green finance. The Reserve Bank of India is currently the only Network for Greening the Financial System member from South Asia.

[14] A World Bank Cat DDO is a contingent financing line that provides immediate liquidity to countries to address shocks related to natural disasters and/or health-related events.

[15] The Country Climate and Development Report and the Climate Macroeconomic Assessment Program are successors to the Climate Change Policy Assessment. The Climate Macroeconomic Assessment Program's structure is similar to that of the Climate Change Policy Assessment, following the NDC framework, covering climate risk and preparedness, national strategy, mitigation, risk management, adaptation, macroeconomic implications of climate policy, and national processes (such as public financial management).

affected by the melting of glaciers. Mitigation policies have a vital role to play in reducing carbon emissions, and in turn the human impact on the climate, whereas adaptation policies can make the population and the economy more resilient in the face of a changing climate—action on both fronts is urgently needed.

Regarding mitigation, the region, and especially India, can play a leading global role by pursuing policies which seek to limit carbon emissions more aggressively. Over the medium term, the most promising policy option is to increase the cost of thermal power production, likely through the enaction of a carbon tax—such a policy would have the additional benefit of generating a fiscal windfall, which could help support the government budget, or could be used to offset the impact on lower-income households from higher electricity prices. Further work is needed in each South Asian country to evaluate, assess, and design the practical aspects of the policy implementation to ensure vulnerable and low-income households are protected and adequately covered by the various fiscal transfers. Moreover, more thought will need to be given to the impact of carbon taxes on growth and inflation as policy makers are likely to be worried about this. In addition, considerations of equity between nations will need to be considered, especially since South Asian countries currently have significantly lower emissions per capita compared with advanced countries. Advanced nations will also need to find ways to facilitate technology and knowledge transfer to accelerate the tipping points at which renewables become cost-competitive with fossil fuels.

Adaptation policies are multifaceted, and a comprehensive approach is needed. Countries in South Asia have shown progress in terms of planning as well as promoting climate resilient green growth. However, implementation is lacking as they have not enacted any regulations to directly address climate change, nor do they have concrete financing plans. As in many countries in the larger Asia-Pacific region, South Asia's ability to adapt to climate change may prove fiscally challenging, especially for low-income countries (IMF 2021).

The transformation of South Asia into greener resilient economies would touch 1.5 billion people in a region with already many development needs. The financing needs for achieving successful mitigation plans in the region are large and conditional on extensive support and assistance from the international community. Similarly, as highlighted in the chapter, although the costs of infrastructure adaptation are hard to pin down, the financing needs are not only large but also their use often cost-effective—both from the perspective of an individual country and for the international community. Hence, climate finance and technology transfers from developed countries to the region would be essential for both South Asia's adaptation and mitigation strategies to succeed.[16]

The challenges stemming from climate change need to be addressed at all levels. At the national level, individual comprehensive country actions are

---

[16] The UN report by the Independent Expert Group on Climate Finance (Averchenkova and others 2020) highlights that meeting the pledge by developed countries to mobilize at least US$100 billion a year to support developing countries in mitigating and adapting to climate change—lagging even before the COVID-19 pandemic—requires urgent action.

particularly important to the extent that the nature of climate change challenges varies from country to country. Nonetheless, there is also much to be gained from a coordinated regional approach to building climate-resilient economies, in areas including river management, development of drought-resistant crops, harnessing hydropower potential, or pooled insurance mechanisms to better address the impact of more frequent natural disasters.

REFERENCES

Ivetta Gerasimchuk, Christopher Beaton, Vibhuti Garg, Abhinav Soman, Harsimran Kaur, and Karthik Ganesan. 2018. "India's Energy Transition: Subsidies for Fossil Fuels and Renewable Energy 2018 Update." International Institute for Sustainable Development, Winnipeg, Manitoba.

Agarwal, Ruchir, Vybhavi Balasundharam, Patrick Blagrave, Eugenio M. Cerutti, Ragnar Gudmundsson, and Racha Mousa. 2021. "Climate Change in South Asia: Further Need for Mitigation and Adaptation." IMF Working Paper 2021/217, International Monetary Fund, Washington, DC.

Averchenkova, Alina, Amar Bhattacharya, Richard Calland, Lorena González, Leonardo Martinez-Diaz, and Jerome van Rooij. 2020. "Delivering on the $100 Billion Climate Finance Commitment and Transforming Climate Finance." Independent Expert Group on Climate Finance. https://www.un.org/sites/un2.un.org/files/100_billion_climate_finance _report.pdf.

Buchner, Barbara, Alex Clark, Angela Falconer, Rob Macquarie, Chavi Meattle, Rowena Tolentino, and Cooper Wetherbee. 2019. "Global Landscape of Climate Finance 2019." Climate Policy Initiative.

Bündnis Entwicklung Hilft. 2020. "World Risk Report 2020: Forced Displacement and Migration." Bündnis Entwicklung Hilft and Ruhr University Bochum – Institute for International Law of Peace and Armed Conflict.

Central Electricity Authority, Government of India, Ministry of Power. 2019. "CEA Annual Report 19-20." https://cea.nic.in/old/reports/annual/annualreports/annual_report-2020.pdf.

Chen, Joyce J., and Valerie Mueller. 2018. "Coastal Climate Change, Soil Salinity, and Human Migration in Bangladesh." *Nature Climate Change* 8 (11): 981–85.

Climate Central. 2019. "Flooded Future: Global Vulnerability to Sea Level Rise Worse Than Previously Understood." Climate Central, Princeton, NJ. https://sealevel.climatecentral.org /research/reports/flooded-future-global-vulnerability-to-sea-level-rise-worse-than-previously/.

Dubash, Navroz K., Radhika Khosla, Narasimha D. Rao, and Ankit Bhardwaj. 2018. "India's Energy and Emissions Future: An Interpretive Analysis of Model Scenarios." *Environmental Research Letters* 13 (7): 074018.

Eckstein, David, Marie-Lena Hutfils, and Maik Winges. "Global Climate Risk Index 2019: Who Suffers Most from Extreme Weather Events? Weather-Related Loss Events in 2017 and 1998 to 2017." German Watch Briefing Paper. https://www.germanwatch.org/sites/default /files/Global%20Climate%20Risk%20Index%202019_2.pdf.

Ellis-Petersen, Hannah, and Rebecca Ratcliffe. 2020, May. "Super-cyclone Amphan hits coast of India and Bangladesh." *The Guardian.* https://www.theguardian.com/world/2020 /may/20/super-cyclone-amphan-evacuations-in-india-and-bangladesh-slowed-by-virus.

Global Commission on Adaptation. 2019. "Adapt Now: A Global call for Leadership on Climate Resilience." Report, Global Commission on Adaptation, Rotterdam, The Netherlands. https://gca.org/wp-content/uploads/2019/09/GlobalCommission_Report _FINAL.pdf.

Guzmán, Sandra, Tania Guillén, and Joanne Manda. 2018. "A Review of Domestic Data Sources for Climate Finance Flows in Recipient Countries." Latin American and Caribbean Climate Finance Group (GFLAC) and United Nations Development Programme (UNDP),

New York, NY. https://www.undp.org/sites/g/files/zskgke326/files/migration/asia_pacific _rbap/RBAP-DG-2018-Review-of-Domestic-Data-Sources-for-Climate-Finance-Flows.pdf.

Hallegatte, Stephane, Jun Rentschler, and Julie Rozenberg. 2020. "The Adaptation Principles: A Guide for Designing Strategies for Climate Change Adaptation and Resilience." Report, World Bank, Washington, DC.

Havlik, Petr, Hugo Valin, Mykola Gusti, Erwin Schmid, David Leclère, Nikolas Forsell, Mario Herrero, Nikolay Khabarov, Aline Mosnier, Matthew Cantele, and Michael Obersteiner. 2015. "Climate Change Impacts and Mitigation in the Developing World, An integrated Assessment of the Agriculture and Forestry Sectors." Policy research Working Paper 7477, World Bank, Washington, DC.

Intergovernmental Panel on Climate Change. 2014. *Climate Change 2014: Impacts, Adaptation, and Vulnerability. Part B: Regional Aspects*. Cambridge, UK, and New York, NY: Cambridge University Press.

Hsiang, Solomon, and Robert E. Kopp. 2018. "An Economist's Guide to Climate Change Science." *Journal of Economic Perspectives* 32 (4): 3–32.

INFORM. 2019. "INFORM Report 2019: Shared Evidence for Managing Crises and Disasters." https://reliefweb.int/report/world/inform-report-2019-shared-evidence-managing -crises-and-disasters.

Stocker, Thomas F., Dahe Qin, Gian-Kasper Plattner, Melinda M. B. Tignor, Simon K. Allen, Judith Boschung, Alexander Nauels, Yu Xia, Vinecnt Bex, and Pauline M. Midgley, eds. 2013. "Climate Change 2013: The Physical Science Basis." Intergovernmental Panel on Climate Change Report, Cambridge, UK, and New York, NY, Cambridge University Press.

Masson-Delmotte, Valérie, Panmao Zhai, Anna Pirani, Sarah L. Connors, Clotilde Péan, Yang Chen, Leah Goldfarb, Melissa I. Gomis, J. B. Robin Matthews, Sophie Berger, Mengtian Huang, Ozge Yelekçi, Rong Yu, Baiquan Zhou, Elisabeth Lonnoy, Thomas K. Maycock, Tim Waterfield, Katherine Leitzell, and Nada Caud, eds. 2021. "Climate Change 2021: The Physical Science Basis." Intergovernmental Panel in Climate Change Report, Cambridge, UK, and New York, NY: Cambridge University Press.

International Federation of Red Cross and Red Crescent Societies. 2020. "Cyclone Amphan, Operation Update Report, July." IFRC, Bangladesh.

International Monetary Fund (IMF). 2019a. "Bangladesh Selected Issues: Climate Change Mitigation and Adaptation in Bangladesh." IMF, Washington, DC.

International Monetary Fund (IMF). 2019b. "Building Resilience in Developing Countries Vulnerable to Large Natural Disasters." IMF Policy Paper, Washington, DC.

International Monetary Fund (IMF). 2019c. *Fiscal Monitor: How to Mitigate Climate Change*. International Monetary Fund, Washington, DC, October.

International Monetary Fund (IMF). 2021. "Fiscal Policies to Address Climate Change in Asia and the Pacific." IMF Departmental Paper 2021/007, Washington, DC.

Islam, Syful. 2021. "Bangladesh Launches First Green Bond." *PV Magazine*. https://www.pv -magazine.com/2021/04/12/bangladesh-launches-first-green-bond/

Jain, Abhishek, Shalu Agrawal, and Karthik Ganesan. 2018. "Lessons from the World's Largest Subsidy Benefit Transfer Scheme: The Case of Liquefied Petroleum Gas Subsidy Reform in India." *In The Politics of Fossil Fuel Subsidies and Their Reform*, edited by Jakob Skovgaard and Harro van Asselt, eds. Cambridge: Cambridge University Press, 212–28.

Keesing, Felicia, Lisa K. Belden, Peter Daszak, Andrew Dobson, C. Drew Harvell, Robert D. Holt, Peter Hudson, Anna Jolles, Kate E. Jones, Charles E. Mitchell, Samuel S. Myers, Tiffany Bogich, and Richard S. Ostfeld. 2010. "Impacts of Biodiversity on the Emergence and Transmission of Infectious Diseases." *Nature* 468: 647–52.

Knox, Jerry William, Tim Hess, Andre Daccache, and Tim Wheeler. 2012. "Climate Change Impacts on Crop Productivity in Africa and South Asia." *Environmental Research Letters* 7 (3): 034032.

Linnerooth-Bayer, Joanne, and Reinhard Mechler. 2009. "Insurance against Losses from Natural Disasters in Developing Countries." DESA Working Paper 85, UN Department of Economic and Social Affairs, New York, NY.

Luo, Tianyi, Deepak Sriram Krishnan, and Shreyan Sen. 2018. "Parched Power: Water Demands, Risks, and Opportunities for India's Power Sector." Working Paper, World Resources Institute, Washington, DC.

Marto, Ricardo, Chris Papageorgiou, and Vladimir Klyuev. 2018. "Building Resilience to Natural Disasters: An Application to Small Developing States." *Journal of Development Economics* 135: 574–86.

Melina, Giovanni, and Marika Santoro. 2021. "Enhancing Resilience to Climate Change in the Maldives". IMF Working Paper 2021/96, International Monetary Fund, Washington, DC.

Micale, Valerio, Bella Tonkonogy, and Federico Mazza. 2018. "Understanding and Increasing Finance for Climate Adaptation in Developing Countries." CPI Report, Climate Policy Initiative. https://www.climatepolicyinitiative.org/publication/understanding-and-increasing -finance-for-climate-adaptation-in-developing-countries.

Mishra, Vimal, Saran Aadhar, and Shanti Shwarup Mahto. 2021. "Anthropogenic Warming and Intraseasonal Summer Monsoon Variability Amplify the Risk of Future Flash Droughts in India." *npj Climate and Atmospheric Science* 4 (1): 1.

Mitra Apurba, Katie Ross, Juan-Carlos Altamirano, Taryn Fransen, and Puneet Chitkara. 2017. "Pathways for Meeting India's Climate Goals." Working Paper, World Resources Institute, Washington, DC.

Harris, Gardiner. 2014, March. "Facing Rising Seas, Bangladesh Confronts the Consequences of Climate Change." *The New York Times.* https://www.nytimes.com/2014/03/29/world/asia /facing-rising-seas-bangladesh-confronts-the-consequences-of-climate-change.html

Nordhaus, William D. 1993. "Reflections on the Economics of Climate Change." *Journal of Economic Perspectives* 7 (4): 11–25.

Rafaty, Ryan, Geoffroy Dolphin, and Felix Pretis. 2020. "Carbon Pricing and the Elasticity of CO_2 Emissions." INET Working Paper 140, Institute for New Economic Thinking, New York, NY.

Rozenberg, Julie, and Marianne Fay, eds. 2019. Beyond the Gap: How Countries Can Afford the Infrastructure They Need while Protecting the Planet. Washington, DC: World Bank.

Tongia, Rahul, and Samantha Gross. 2019. "Coal in India: Adjusting to Transition." Brookings Paper 7, Brookings Institution, Washington, DC.

United Nations Development Programme. 2018. "Landscape of Climate-Relevant Land-Use Finance in Papua New Guinea: A Review of Financial Flows Related to Land-Use Mitigation and Adaptation." United Nations, New York, NY. https://www.undp.org/sites/g/files /zskgke326/files/migration/pg/cdc37d86d1580852119e56f7a4327f9a946cac5bdc18b 52d3edd8a92cc1393e2.pdf. New York, NY.

Vishwanathan, Saritha S., and Amit Garg. 2020. "Energy System Transformation to Meet NDC, 2° C, and Well Below 2° C Targets for India." *Climatic Change* 162: 1–15.

Worrall, Leah, Shelagh Whitley, Vibhuti Garg, Srinivas Krishnaswamy, and Christopher Beaton. 2018. "India's Stranded Assets: How Government Interventions Are Propping Up Coal Power." Overseas Development Institute Working Paper 538, London, UK.

World Bank. 2009. *South Asia: Shared Views on Development and Climate Change.* Washington, DC: World Bank.

World Bank. 2017. *Sovereign Climate and Disaster Risk Pooling: World Bank Technical Contribution to the G20.* Washington, DC: World Bank.

World Bank. 2018a. *South Asia's Hotspots: The Impact of Temperature and Precipitation Changes on Living Standards.* Washington DC: World Bank.

World Bank. 2018b. "Webinar on Demystifying Catastrophe Bonds for Debt Managers." World Bank, Washington, DC.

World Bank. 2021. *Climate Change Budget Tagging: A Review of International Experience.* Washington DC: World Bank.

World Health Organization and Secretariat of the Convention on Biological Diversity. 2015. *Connecting Global Priorities: Biodiversity and Human Health, a State of Knowledge Review.* World Health Organization: Geneva, Switzerland.

CHAPTER 8

A Diversification Strategy for South Asia

Weicheng Lian, Fei Liu, Katsiaryna Svirydzenka, and Biying Zhu

Diversification and structural transformation play important roles in the process of economic development. There is growing evidence that until an economy reaches advanced economy status, higher per capita income is broadly associated with greater export product diversification and economic complexity. IMF (2014) and Cadot and others (2011) found a positive relationship between export diversification on the one hand and per capita income and growth on the other hand for countries at lower levels of development. Hausmann and others (2011) and Anand, Mishra, and Spatafora (2012) found a similar link for economic complexity.

Diversification contributes to growth and economic development directly when resources move from low-to high-productivity sectors and the economy accumulates know-how. Indirectly, diversification lifts growth and income levels by shifting resources from sectors where prices are highly volatile and correlated, such as mining and agriculture, to less volatile sectors, such as manufacturing, resulting in greater macroeconomic stability and lower vulnerability to adverse terms of trade shocks (Koren and Tenreyro 2007; Haddad and others 2013).

This chapter documents South Asia's progress on diversification and explores policy options to promote greater export diversification and economic complexity. While South Asia's liberalization path has been associated with greater diversification of exports in several of the countries, there is substantial scope to diversify further. To do so, South Asia needs to invest in infrastructure, education, and research and development (R&D), facilitate bank credit to productive companies, and increase openness to trade. Other factors—such as a stable macroeconomic environment and the level of investment—could also potentially assist this process. Given the COVID-19 pandemic, adopting and investing in digital technologies as part of the infrastructure push and improving education are of even greater importance to facilitate the ability to work remotely and assist resource reallocation away from the less viable sectors.

See Lian and others (2021) for more details on the diversification strategy for South Asia.

SOUTH ASIA'S PROGRESS ON DIVERSIFICATION

As South Asian economies liberalized in the 1980s and 1990s, creating space for the private sector to grow and opening to trade, their export structure underwent rapid transformation, moving from exporting raw products to exporting garments and services (Figure 8.1).

Figure 8.1. Diversification in South Asia Improved Over Time, 1972–2016
(Share of different sectors in export basket)

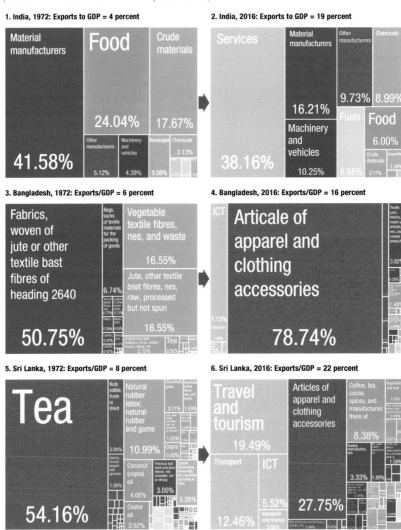

Source: Atlas of Economic Complexity.
Note: This figure shows exports of goods and services, while diversification and complexity indices presented in Figures 8.3 and 8.4 are based on data for goods exports only, because services data are only available from 1980.

Figure 8.1. Diversification in South Asia Improved Over Time, 1972–2016 (Continued)

(Share of different sectors in export basket)

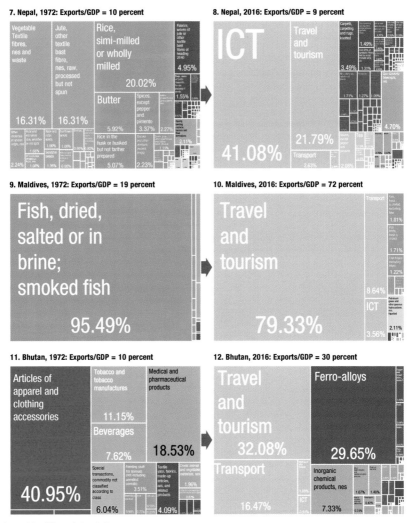

Source: Atlas of Economic Complexity.

India's pro-business reforms in the late 1980s and early 1990s led to a significant reduction in tariffs and eased controls on the domestic private sector, while the emphasis on tertiary education created a highly educated labor force. As a result, India managed to transition from exporting tea and fabrics in 1970s to a more sophisticated export basket of car parts, capital goods, and pharmaceuticals, and laid the foundation for its remarkable service sector-led growth. Annex I models key economic channels behind India's structural change.

In Bangladesh, reforms and trade liberalization attracted FDI in the readymade garment sector. This facilitated technology transfer to domestic entrepreneurs, helping Bangladesh diversify from exporting jute and tea to labor-intensive garments, catalyzing export-led growth. Eventually, the export basket became highly concentrated again, with garments accounting for around 80 percent of exports.

Smaller South Asian economies shifted from exporting raw food products and agricultural produce to tourism and information and communications technology (ICT). Maldives moved from fish to tourism, Nepal from raw food products (jute and rice) to information and communications technology and tourism, and Sri Lanka from tea to tourism and garments. Bhutan benefited from exporting hydropower electricity, which now accounts for 30 percent of its exports.

While several South Asian countries increased the diversity and complexity[1] of their exports, there is still substantial scope to improve further (Figures 8.2 and 8.3). India is the most diverse in South Asia, with the diversity of its export basket similar to that of China and ahead of that of the Association of Southeast Asian Nations (ASEAN). Nepal is a close second, with export diversification higher

Figure 8.2. Export Diversification

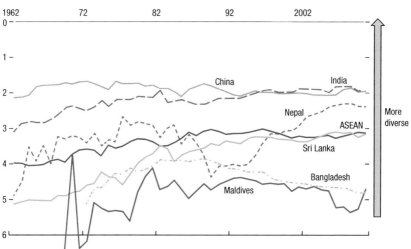

Source: IMF 2014.
Note: ASEAN = Association of Southeast Asian Nations.

---

[1] Export diversification captures how varied a country's export basket is in terms of its products. It is constructed using the Theil index, which sums the extensive and intensive margins of diversification (IMF 2014). Economic complexity captures both the diversity and complexity of a country's exports. It is a term popularized by Hausmann and others (2011) and is developed from the concept of revealed comparative advantage. Economic complexity is a combination of the diversity of an economy (defined as the number of products in which the economy has revealed comparative advantage) and the ubiquity of these products (captured by the number of countries that have revealed comparative advantage in this product). Economic complexity is thus a measure of the knowledge in an economy as expressed in the products it makes. Both measures are based on trade in goods.

Figure 8.3. Economics Complexity

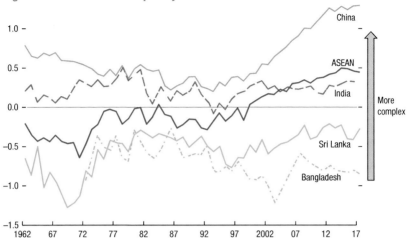

Source: The Atlas of Economic Complexity.
Note: ASEAN = Association of Southeast Asian Nations.

than that of the ASEAN. However, when one takes account of complexity, China has surpassed India starting from early 2000s, even though both countries had similar levels of complexity for two prior decades. Other countries lag even further, so it will be important not only to diversify, but also move into more complex products.

One way to improve export complexity is to move up the value chains. South Asia has a lot of room to climb up the global quality ladder[2] (Figure 8.4). Producing higher quality varieties of existing products, building on comparative advantage, is easier than diversifying into completely new areas. For example, in Bangladesh, the complexity of the ready-made garment industry remains relatively low. In India, there is scope to further close the technology gap in the auto component industry.

Another way to improve economic complexity is to move the production structure into similar but more complex products. India, Nepal, and Sri Lanka are especially well positioned to improve the complexity of their exports as captured by the economic complexity outlook index (Figure 8.5). The index measures the average complexity of products that are close to the country's current set of productive capacities. It captures the complexity of products into which it is feasible for the country to diversify into—that is, how strategically positioned a country is in its product space. Given the current production structures, it will be easier for India, Nepal, and Sri Lanka to diversify because they have many complex products near their current set of productive capabilities. India has the highest diversification potential in the world.

---

[2] This is calculated as the unit value of exported goods adjusted for differences in production costs and for selection bias stemming from relative distance (Henn, Papageorgiou, and Spatafora 2013).

Figure 8.4. Quality Ladder, 2014

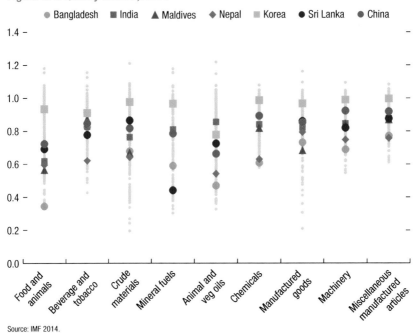

Source: IMF 2014.

Figure 8.5. Economic Complexity Outlook Index, 2016

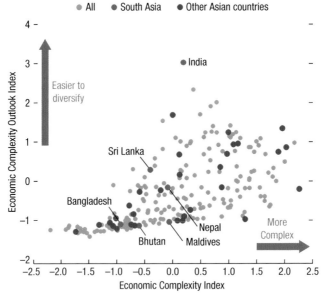

Source: The Atlas of Economic Complexity.
Note: The Economic Complexity Index measures how diversified and complex a country's export basket is. The Economic Complexity Outlook Index measures the ease of diversification for a country, captured by how many complex products are near a country's current set of productive capabilities.

Figure 8.6. The Product Space in India and Bangladesh

1. India: Product Space, 2016

Other parts and accessories, for vehicles of headings 722, 781-783 ! (7849 SITC4)

2. Bangaladesh: Product Space, 2016

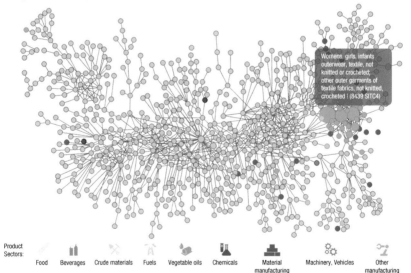

Womens, girls, infants outerwear, textile, not knitted or crocheted; other outer garments of textile fabrics, not knitted, crocheted ! (8439 SITC4)

| Product Sectors: | Food | Beverages | Crude materials | Fuels | Vegetable oils | Chemicals | Material manufacturing | Machinery, Vehicles | Other manufacturing |

Source: The Atlas of Economic Complexity.
Note: A colored node is a product the country exports. The size of the node is the share of this product in the country's exports.

This is more intuitively seen through a visualization called product space (Figure 8.6). The product space depicts the connectedness between products, based on the similarities of know-how required to produce them. For example, India exports several products at the core of the product space, such as cars parts, ships, and mobile phones. In other words, India has revealed comparative advantage in exporting various manufacturing products that are related to more complex goods. The existing facilities make it easier for India to diversify into similar products. On the other hand, although Bangladesh has been successful in dominating the garments sector, it has a lower complexity outlook because the ready-made garment sector is less connected to other, more complex industries. As a result, it would be harder for Bangladesh to move up the complexity scale without concerted policy measures.

Improving economic diversification and complexity requires different strategies tailored to country-specific circumstances. For countries such as India, Nepal, and Sri Lanka, who are well positioned in their product space, this will involve expanding their existing technological know-how. For countries with relatively clustered product space, such as Bangladesh, Bhutan, and Maldives, it will require taking a longer-term view, expanding product space by addressing bottlenecks and integrating an economic diversification strategy into the national development plans. The next section studies what policies could be more conducive in these efforts.

WHICH POLICIES COULD FOSTER DIVERSIFICATION IN SOUTH ASIA?

A Conceptual Framework

Many routes lead to a more diversified economy. A fundamental force is structural transformation, with resources shifting from agriculture toward manufacturing and further toward services as the country develops (Hansen and Prescott 2002; McMillan and Rodrik 2011; Herrendorf, Rogerson, and Valentinyi 2014). Some may even leapfrog manufacturing altogether (Carmignani and Mandeville 2010; Rodrick 2016). IMF (2019) argued that South Asia, especially India, should grow all sectors of the economy in a balanced way, including increasing agricultural productivity, expanding manufacturing in a sustainable way, and building on the relatively strong position of high-skill services, to cope with the challenge of 150 million people entering the labor market by 2030.

What policies could foster export diversification and economic complexity in South Asia? In our regression analysis, we use the following conceptual framework to try to disentangle the intertwined and often mutually reinforcing economic factors (Figure 8.7). Many of the diversification drivers are similar to the drivers of economic growth. The availability of the needed factor inputs—physical capital and infrastructure, human capital, and technological know-how—as well as their quality and cost determine whether you can engage in a new production process. It is hard for countries to create products that require capabilities they do not have. To produce semiconductors, a manufacturing facility needs the know-how to start out and R&D to keep up with competitors, but also access to power, water, chemicals, and other raw materials, it needs complex machinery and an educated labor force to operate it, and road and port infrastructure to be able to export the final product.

With the factor inputs in place, the ease of resource reallocation determines how fast economic diversification and improvements in complexity take place. Openness to trade and finance, and more broadly financial development, have the potential to contribute to both factor accumulation and the reallocation of

Figure 8.7. What Factors Drive Diversification and Complexity

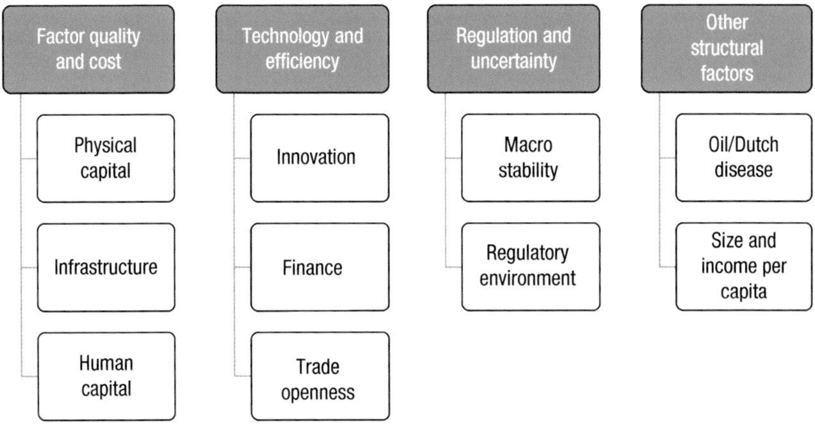

Factor quality and cost	Technology and efficiency	Regulation and uncertainty	Other structural factors
Physical capital	Innovation	Macro stability	Oil/Dutch disease
Infrastructure	Finance	Regulatory environment	Size and income per capita
Human capital	Trade openness		

Source: Authors.

resources to more productive activities by bringing in the foreign know-how, financing investment, and giving a boost to competition. Macroeconomic and political stability and the regulatory environment—including low inflation and public debt, absence of conflict and ease of doing business—create an enabling environment, within which firms operate and can either impede or facilitate creative destruction. Presence of a large extractive sector, such as oil and gas, can impede diversification by absorbing the resources that could be used otherwise and inflating the price of nontradables, leading to Dutch disease. One would also expect that diversification is easier in larger economies and at higher income per capita levels; this factor is important to control for reverse causality.

Multiple studies show that the quality of institutions, innovation and technology adoption, trade openness, political stability, and the right mix of macroeconomic policies are generally associated with higher growth (Acemoglu and Robinson 2008; Ostry and others 2009; Christiansen and others 2013; Prati and others 2013). Nonetheless, important caveats exist, for example, such positive association was found to exist only in middle-income countries (Christiansen and others 2013) and was shown to be highly heterogeneous and to be influenced by a country's constraints on the authority of the executive power and by its distance from the technology frontier (Prati and others 2013. There were also significantly different growth effects across alternative reform sequencing strategies (Ostry and others 2009).

With regard to the effect of these factors on diversification, the economic debate continues. Bayesian model averaging in Giri and others (2019) found that accumulating human capital, reducing barriers to trade, improving quality of institutions, and developing the financial sector lead to greater diversification. Macroeconomic stability, access to credit, good infrastructure, a conducive regulatory environment, human capital, and income equality are associated with higher economic diversification (IMF 2017) and export complexity (Ding and Hadzi-Vaskov 2017). Oil dependency tends to reduce the degree of diversification (IMF 2017).

Other studies are less conclusive. For example, on trade openness, many studies find a positive relationship with export diversification, but such a relationship exists with some degree of ambiguity. In an empirical analysis on a wide panel of countries at different levels of development, Di Giovanni and Levchenko (2009) find that trade openness is associated with higher specialization and volatility in countries at lower levels of development. Makhlouf and others (2015) find that the effect of openness on specialization depends on the type of political regime for developing countries, in autocracies openness is linked with specialization, whilst in democracies it is related to export diversification.

Similarly, though domestic financial reforms are found to be robustly associated with economic growth (Ostry and others 2009; Christiansen and others 2013), financial development does not have a statistically significant relationship with export diversification in Agosin and others (2012). Nonetheless, in the same paper but based on event studies, Agosin and others find that the trend toward export diversification accelerates after episodes of financial reform, but not in the case of trade reform. Giri and others (2019) find that although credit to the private sector is not associated with diversification for the sample of all countries, it is associated with increase in diversification among the emerging market and developing countries, but only along the intensive margin.

The effect of research and development (R&D) spending on diversification is less clear. Intuitively, R&D leads to innovation and contributes to the production of complex products. Nonetheless, it is also possible that as a country develops, R&D leads to concentration in specific product lines, which occupy resources and hence reduce diversification. Empirical research in this area is relatively scarce. Using firm-level data, Peyrefitte and Brice (2004) find a negative relationship between product diversification and relative R&D intensity, supporting a hypothesis that diversified firms lower R&D investment as they realize economies of scope in R&D activities.

The departure of this chapter from the existing literature is two-fold. First, we explore a large set of structural indicators jointly, which is in spirit closer to Giri and others (2019). Second, we assess the drivers of both export diversification and complexity, building on the literature exploring export complexity (Hausmann and others 2011; Ding and Hadzi-Vaskov 2017).

We rely on a number of indicators and data sources to capture the role of these factors on export diversification and economic complexity based on annual data for 189 countries from 1962 to 2018. We explore their role using the following econometric model (see Lian and others 2021, for more details):

$$D_{i,t}^k = \sum_{j=1}^{J} \beta^{k,h,j} Z_{i,j,t} + \gamma^{k,h} M_{i,h,t} + \delta_t^{k,h} + \varepsilon_{i,t}^{k,h}, \tag{1}$$

where $D_{i,t}^1 \left(D_{i,t}^2 \right)$ is export diversification (economic complexity) of country i in year t. $\left\{ Z_{i,j,t} \right\}_{j=1}^{J}$ is the selected list of structural indicators for country i in year t. $M_{i,h,t}$ is one of four control variables: a constant, GDP, population size, and GDP per capita. $\delta_t^{k,h}$ is time fixed effects.

The specification controls for GDP, population size, and GDP per capita, one at a time; as diversification may vary significantly across countries with different market size, population, or development stage. This specification does not control for country-fixed effects because structural indicators are slow moving over time and there is not enough within-country variation to capture the effect of structural indicators on diversification and complexity.

Drivers of Export Diversification and Economic Complexity

The results suggest that more developed infrastructure and better educated labor force help not only to diversify the economy, but also to improve the sophistication of products (Tables 8.1 and 8.2). This is consistent with the findings in the literature and a casual observation that advanced economies tend to have infrastructure of higher quality and more skilled labor force. With the normalization

TABLE 8.1.

Impact of Structural Factors on Economic Complexity

Variable	Economic Complexity Index			
	(1)	(2)	(3)	(4)
Railway density	0.0466***	0.0589***	0.0623***	0.0338***
	(0.00819)	(0.00776)	(0.00623)	(0.00728)
R&D expenditure	0.359***	0.329***	0.217***	0.204***
	(0.0305)	(0.0284)	(0.0239)	(0.0292)
Trade openness	0.00133**	0.00218***	0.00362***	0.00180***
	(0.000621)	(0.000592)	(0.000482)	(0.000554)
Average inflation	−0.00371	−0.00608***	−0.00684***	−0.00289
	(0.00245)	(0.00230)	(0.00185)	(0.00219)
Log(credit to GDP)	0.606***	0.316***	−0.288***	0.0258
	(0.105)	(0.103)	(0.0909)	(0.102)
Log(external debt to GDP)	−0.103	0.0973	0.0755	−0.332***
	(0.0638)	(0.0631)	(0.0487)	(0.0588)
Oil share in exports	−1.116***	−1.064***	−1.268***	−1.487***
	(0.0945)	(0.0880)	(0.0730)	(0.0901)
Years of schooling	0.104***	0.130***	0.0933***	0.0407***
	(0.0120)	(0.0115)	(0.00908)	(0.0117)
Log(population)		0.138***		
		(0.0160)		
Log(GDP in US dollar)			0.249***	
			(0.0117)	
Log(GDP in US dollar per capita)				0.340***
				(0.0239)
Constant	−1.019**	−1.662***	−1.687***	−0.357**
	(0.504)	(0.475)	(0.135)	(0.160)
Time fixed effect	Yes	Yes	Yes	Yes
No. of observations	594	594	593	593
R^2	0.718	0.752	0.837	0.776

Note: A higher economic complexity index value means higher complexity. Robust regression. Standard errors are in parentheses. R&D = research and development.
***$p < 0.01$; **$p < 0.05$; *$p < 0.1$.

TABLE 8.2.

Impact of Structural Factors on Export Diversification

Variable	Export Diversification			
	(1)	(2)	(3)	(4)
Quality of infrastructure	−0.257***	−0.239***	−0.211***	−0.224***
	(0.0677)	(0.0615)	(0.0584)	(0.0631)
R&D expenditure	0.0304	0.133*	0.240***	0.202***
	(0.0803)	(0.0741)	(0.0715)	(0.0765)
Trade openness	0.00460***	0.00335**	0.00311**	0.00448***
	(0.00147)	(0.00135)	(0.00127)	(0.00133)
Average inflation	0.0194	0.0246**	0.00861	−0.0129
	(0.0120)	(0.0109)	(0.0104)	(0.0116)
Investment to GDP	−0.0100	−0.00400	−0.00784	−0.0169**
	(0.00764)	(0.00696)	(0.00653)	(0.00695)
Log(external debt to GDP)	0.345***	−0.00579	0.159	0.660***
	(0.124)	(0.124)	(0.109)	(0.122)
Oil share in exports	3.089***	3.014***	3.654***	4.217***
	(0.259)	(0.235)	(0.231)	(0.291)
Years of schooling	−0.126***	−0.138***	−0.0776***	−0.0273
	(0.0258)	(0.0235)	(0.0228)	(0.0292)
Log(population)		−0.237***		
		(0.0328)		
Log(GDP in US dollar)			−0.258***	
			(0.0284)	
Log(GDP in US dollar per capita)				−0.427***
				(0.0740)
Constant	4.244***	5.004***	4.836***	3.881***
	(0.355)	(0.342)	(0.309)	(0.336)
Time fixed effect	Yes	Yes	Yes	Yes
No. of observations	250	250	250	250
R^2	0.527	0.608	0.653	0.612

Note: Lower values of dependent variable mean higher diversification. Robust regression. Standard errors are in parentheses.
***$p < 0.01$; **$p < 0.05$; *$p < 0.1$.

mentioned in the previous paragraph, the quantitative impact of these indicators is among the largest, when compared with those of other structural indicators.

It is not always the case that structural reforms benefit both export diversification and complexity in the same way. Some dimensions of structural change improve export complexity but hurt export diversification or the other way around. Opening to trade tends to lead countries to specialize, rather than diversify their export baskets, but at the same time helps them move up the value chain into more complex products. A more open capital account, on the other hand—as captured by the size of external debt relative to GDP—leads countries to specialize more, but access to foreign capital does not seem to have a significant effect on export sophistication. Higher R&D expenditure and domestic bank credit to the private sector help increase export complexity, without having a significant impact on diversification. The latter might be caused by the offsetting effects of specialization and the country gaining new export varieties.

Several structural indicators have a more nuanced impact on economic complexity and diversification. For example, a more stable macroeconomic environment—proxied by lower inflation—contributes to product upgrading and export diversification. The impact, however, is not significant, unless we control for either economic size or income per capita. Investment improves export diversification, but the impact is also not significant, unless we control for income per capita.

Figures 8.8 and 8.9 show standardized coefficients of our baseline specification in the first column of the two tables to gauge the economic significance of the variables. The normalization is done by multiplying the coefficient of a structural indicator by one standard deviation of the structural indicator's distribution in the sample across countries and time and further dividing it by one standard deviation of the distribution of the diversification or complexity index. The figures show improvement in diversification and complexity in terms of standard deviation as a result of one standard deviation improvement in the dependent variable. We focus on the first column of the two tables, and the results are broadly unchanged in columns two to four.

In terms of the magnitude of their impact, R&D expenditure and education seem to offer the greatest bang for the buck in terms of helping to improve economic complexity, followed by bank credit and infrastructure as measured by

Figure 8.8. Impact of Structural Indicators on Economic Complexity Relative to One Standard Deviation of the Distribution of the Economic Complexity Index

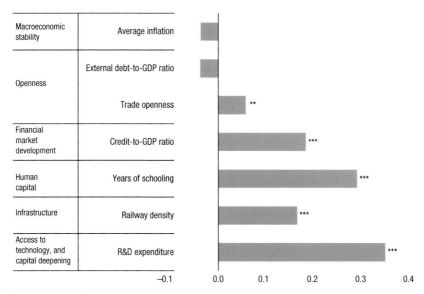

Source: Authors' calculations.
Note: Positive values mean the factor leads to higher complexity. R&D = research and development.
***$p < 0.01$; **$p < 0.05$; *$p < 0.1$.

Figure 8.9. Impact of Structural Indicators on Export Diversification Relative to One Standard Deviation of the Distribution of the Export Diversification Index

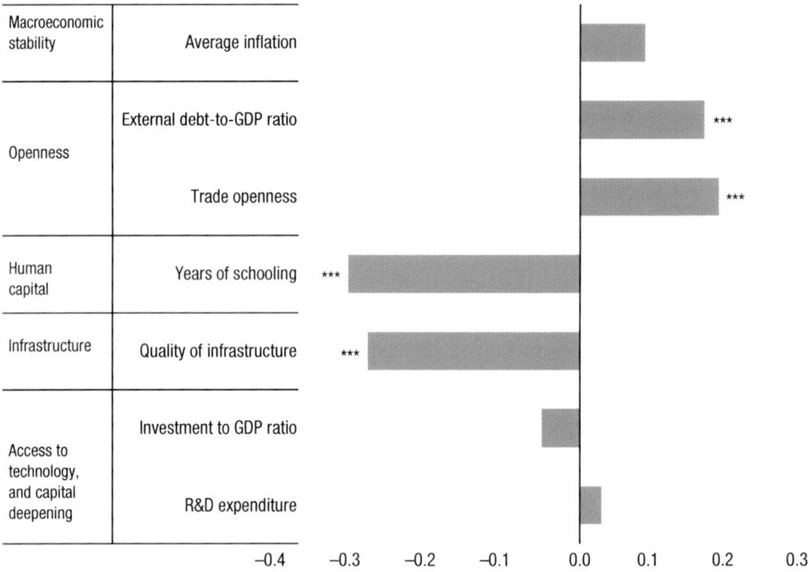

Source: Authors' calculations.
Note: Negative values mean the factor leads to higher diversification. R&D = research and development.
***$p < 0.01$; **$p < 0.05$; *$p < 0.1$.

railway density, followed by trade openness (Figure 8.8). For export diversification, improvements to education and quality of infrastructure tend to have the greatest impact (Figure 8.9).

What do these findings imply for South Asia? As previous studies have found, higher per capita income is broadly associated with greater export diversification and complexity before an economy reaches an advanced economy status. Along its journey to higher income status, South Asia needs to step up its reform efforts to improve the diversity and complexity of its exports. Compared with advanced economies such as Korea and Japan, and other emerging economies such as China and ASEAN, South Asia lags behind in terms of the structural indicators associated with greater diversity and complexity (Figure 8.10). For example, average years of schooling and trade openness in India are roughly half of the levels in Korea, and spending on R&D was about 0.5 percent of GDP, compared with 4.5 percent of GDP in Korea. The region has room to further open to trade, invest in infrastructure and education, and promote R&D spending.

How would improvements in the underlying structural indicators translate to improvements in economic diversification and complexity? To help gauge the potential impact, Figure 8.11 shows illustrative scenarios of the potential impact if South Asian countries close 50 percent of the gap on economic fundamentals relative to the frontier. The frontier is defined as the average performance of the

Figure 8.10. Selected Structural Indicators in South Asia

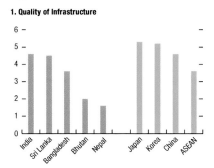

1. Quality of Infrastructure

Source: World Bank's World Development Indicators.
Note: Data reflect latest year available. ASEAN = Association of Southeast Asian Nations.

2. R&D Spending

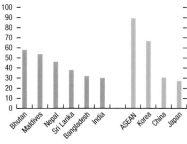

Source: OECD ANBERD (Analytical Business Enterprise R&D) database.
Note: Data reflect latest year available. ASEAN = Association of Southeast Asian Nations; R&D = research and development.

3. Years of Schooling

Source: Barro-Lee Educational Attainment Dataset.
Note: Data reflect latest year available. ASEAN = Association of Southeast Asian Nations.

4. Trade Openness

Sources: IMF World Economic Outlook database; and IMF staff calculations.
Note: Data reflect latest year available. ASEAN = Association of Southeast Asian Nations.

top three countries in terms of their economic complexity in 2017 (Japan, Korea, and Switzerland) and export diversification in 2014 (Austria, Italy, and Poland). In Figure 8.11, panels 1 and 3 shows the estimated quantitative effects, and panels 2 and 4 shows the contribution from each of the underlying structural indicators.

It is not surprising that the quality of infrastructure plays a key role for greater diversification, and improving R&D spending would contribute the most to greater economic complexity, while educational outcomes are instrumental to both dimensions. It is important to interpret the policy implications with caution: the larger contributions do not necessarily imply a sequence of the reforms—a country can start with the reforms that are expected to generate the largest impact, or with the reforms that are easier to implement. Increasing spending on infrastructure can lead to higher quality of infrastructure, but improving the efficiency of spending and tackling the infrastructure bottlenecks are equally important. The potential positive effects stemming from interactions among the various structural

Figure 8.11. Potential Gains from Improvements in Underlying Structural Indicators

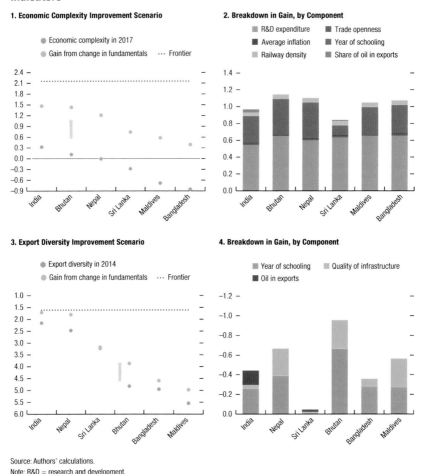

Source: Authors' calculations.
Note: R&D = research and development.

improvements are not captured here. Last, it is worth noting that these references are drawn based on the analysis from a broader sample of countries with South Asia included. While the regression coefficients are not South Asia specific per se, the quantified impacts are and so are policy implications.

More broadly, policies that encourage climbing up the quality ladder are instrumental in promoting diversification. As found in Cherif and Hasanov (2014), a focus on competing in international markets and an emphasis on technological upgrades and improving quality are crucial, among other policies. Though their study was based on a sample of oil exporters, the need to climb up the quality ladder equally applies to South Asian countries whose goods exports concentrate to a large degree on clothing and garments.

Encouraging vertical diversification can be complementary to the structural reforms discussed earlier. For example, India not only exports products such as cars parts, ships, and mobile phones, but also it has developed domestic capabilities in downstream and upstream activities around these exports. Going forward, the emphasis could be on building linkages with the rest of the economy, technological transfer and upgrades, and expanding products along the current product space. Bangladesh has successfully developed the garments sector, and future development could involve creating networks of suppliers around the existing exporting industries and upgrading to more sophisticated products, following the example of Italy's high-end garments and fashion.

Overall, a more diversified economy in terms of exports can better withstand shocks and is associated with better economic outcomes. Because it is hard to know in advance which sectors could be the winners, in this chapter we do not recommend policies targeting specific sectors, but rather focus on creating the enabling environment where many sectors can flourish. During the diversification process, consideration should be given to developing sectors with higher value added and encouraging the climb up the quality ladder.

DIVERSIFICATION IN TIMES OF COVID-19

The challenges posed by the COVID-19 pandemic give an even greater impetus for countries to diversify their economies and export structures to become more resilient to shocks. At the same time, as the permanent impact on sectors becomes clearer, there is also the need to facilitate the reallocation of resources from less viable to more viable sectors.

One aspect of choosing which sectors are more viable is by looking at how easy it is to work in that sector remotely. To study this, we rely on the newly created database by Brussevich and others (2020) that quantifies how feasible it is to work from home in different industries based on a sample of 35 advanced and emerging market economies. They find that it is harder to work remotely in sectors such as accommodation and food services, construction, and transportation. Sectors best suited for teleworking include ICT, finance, and other professional services that require less physical proximity and rely more on digital tools and technologies.

As it happens, South Asia's factor endowments and policy environment are well suited to ICT services trade, and the region saw its export basket successfully diversify into ICT over time. India, in particular, has been the poster child for services-led export diversification. In the early 1980s, the Indian government recognized that the large number of low-wage, high-skilled engineers, fluent in English, boded well for the country's potential in information technology services (Saxenian 2001). The emerging sector was proactively liberalized, with a new computer policy in 1984 and the creation of software technology parks in the early 1990s providing the ecosystem for attracting private investment. The global adoption of a new technology platform Unix created saving opportunities for big corporations in the United States and Europe to replace high-cost onshore information technology service contracts with low-cost offshore ones in countries such as India, Israel, and Ireland (Dossani 2006). Now, ICT is the largest export sector in India, contributing more than 9 percent to India's GDP, employing more than 4 million people, and making India one of the top 10 global service exporters, well known for its exports of business process outsourcing and support services for finance and medicine. Bangladesh, Nepal, and Sri Lanka also have emerging ICT sectors and should look to lessons from the successful India experience.

The ability to provide services remotely is important not only when virus mutations prompt new quarantine requirements, but also more broadly, as we rethink the nature of work and potentially move to hybrid work models. The ability to provide services remotely will determine to what extent countries can benefit from the next wave of globalization, this time increasingly driven by services trade, both because of the technological shift toward teleworking as part of the "third unbundling" (Baldwin 2016) and because trade in services could be less amenable to direct policy restrictions such as tariffs and quotas. Indeed, there seems to be a positive relationship between economic complexity and tele-workability (see Lian and others 2021), indicating that they go hand in hand.

Figure 8.12. Internet Use in South Asia Within the Past 3 Months, 2017
(Percent of population)

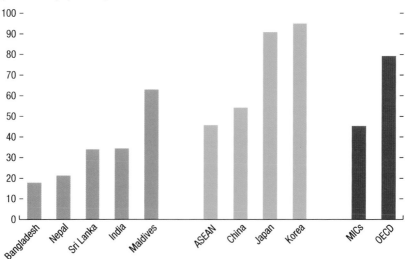

Source: World Bank's World Development Indicators.
Note: ASEAN = Association of Southeast Asian Nations; MICs = middle-income countries; OECD = Organisation for Economic Co-operation and Development.

What factors could help improve teleworkability? The ability to work remotely seems to be related to fixed bandwidth subscription, years of schooling, and mobile phone subscriptions (Lian and others 2021). As a result, adopting and investing in digital technologies and improving education will be key to prepare the workforce for the challenges of the new economy. As it happens, these are also the factors that support growth and poverty reduction, enhance productivity, business opportunities, and greater diversification and complexity through better access to information and a wider range of goods and services at lower prices.

Going forward, investing in sectors such as ICT to strengthen the needed infrastructure for digital development that has been in high demand since the COVID-19 crisis would be needed. Although digitalization and financial technologies have grown in South Asia, investing in infrastructure will be key given that a large share of the population still lacks internet access (Figure 8.12). Sectoral policies to further support the ICT sector could include in-house training and skill upgrades in new technologies—such as big data analytics, cloud computing, artificial intelligence, and machine learning—developing high value-added product software, engineering, and research and development services to move up the value chain and capture a larger share of the growing digital economy segment. These sectoral policies are complementary to the horizontal policies analyzed in our empirical analysis.

CONCLUSIONS

Economic development, diversification, and complexity are mutually reinforcing processes. The process of creative destruction and dynamic reallocation of resources from less productive to more productive sectors boost growth, and more diversified economies tend to show greater resilience to shocks and exhibit lower volatility.

While South Asian countries have gone a long way diversifying their economies, there is substantial scope to do more. Some countries—such as India, Nepal, and Sri Lanka—can build on their existing production facilities; others where product space is clustered in specific industries—such as Bangladesh, Bhutan, and Maldives—would need to undertake a more concerted push.

While it is hard to pick specific winner industries, South Asia can draw lessons from other countries on the enabling environment that can foster the process of greater diversification and complexity. South Asia needs to invest in infrastructure, education, and R&D, facilitate bank credit to productive companies, and increase openness to trade. Other factors—such as a stable macroeconomic environment and the level of investment more broadly—could also potentially assist the process of increasing diversification and complexity of exports. Given the COVID-19 pandemic, adopting and investing in digital technologies as part of the infrastructure push and improving education are of even greater importance to facilitate the ability to work remotely and assist resource reallocation away from the less viable sectors.

Box 8.1. Structural Change in India: A Model-Based Approach

Structural change—the reallocation of production and employment across sectors of the economy (Herrendorf and others, 2014)—has followed a unique pattern in India compared with East Asian economies. Since India began economic reforms in the early 1990s, the services sector has grown more rapidly than manufacturing, while agriculture's share in the economy has declined (see also Adhikari 2019; Dehejia and Panagariya 2010). This differs from the experience in Korea and ASEAN economies, where the services sector has been comparatively stable as a share of the economy since the 1970s. China has also followed a different path, developing a much larger manufacturing sector than India, although also with significant expansion in services.

Figure 8.1.1. Sectoral Shares, Services, and Manufacturing

1. Sectoral Shares, Value Added
(Percent of GDP)

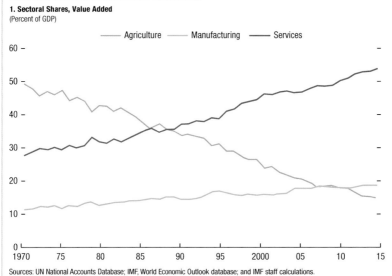

Sources: UN National Accounts Database; IMF, World Economic Outlook database; and IMF staff calculations.

2. Services
(Percent of value added)

Source: UN National Accounts Database.

3. Manufacturing
(Percent of value added)

Source: UN National Accounts Database.

(Box 8.1 continues on the next page)

Box 8.1. Structural Change in India: A Model-Based Approach
(continued)

Economic theory suggests that there are several key channels through which structural change toward the services sector can occur:

- *Consumer preferences.* Consumers may spend a larger share of their income on services as living standards rise (*nonhomothetivc* preferences), accompanied by an increase in demand for workers able to perform high-skilled services (for example, see Kongsamut and others 2001; Buera and Kaboski 2009; and Comin and others 2021).
- *Technological change.* Rapid technological progress can reduce the price of manufactured goods relative to services, raising the share of services in nominal production and consumption. See for example Ngai and Pissarides (2007). Technological progress can also reduce the need for unskilled labor in the manufacturing sector, including by substituting machinery for unskilled labor because of automation, allowing labor to move into the services sector (for example, see Buera, Kaboski, and Rogerson 2015).
- *Capital deepening.* An increase in the capital–labor ratio in the economy—capital deepening—can raise the relative price of services, if capital is used less in this sector. This raises the share of services in nominal production and consumption, with labor moving toward the services sector (for example, see Acemoglu and Guerrieri 2008).

All of these channels reflect "skill-biased technological change" to some extent, whereby labor moves toward the services sector, either because of increased demand for high-skilled services, or greater displacement of labor from other sectors because of technological progress or capital deepening. It is notable that the share of services in India's private final consumption expenditure has risen in recent decades, as has the total share of employment in the services sector. Given that India began economic reforms later than some East Asian economies, the ability to import manufactured goods and machinery at declining prices, facilitated by trade liberalization, may have contributed to automation substituting for labor in the manufacturing sector and the shift in employment toward the services sector. This could support a growth strategy that is more focused on services than were those of Korea or China in the past.

A multicountry economic model allowing for all of the channels described earlier (Kanasheuski 2021) is able to distinguish between the rapid growth in India's services sector since the 1990s and the relative stability of the sector's share in some other East Asian economies. Allowing openness to trade in the model is important for capturing the rapid growth in both unskilled and skilled services in the Indian economy during 1995–2007 before the global financial crisis, relative to the declining share of manufacturing. In the case of Korea, the model is able to capture the relative stability of the manufacturing sector's share during this period, as well as the shift from unskilled to skilled services. These results imply that the ability to import technology through manufactured goods, while exporting high-skilled services is important to explaining India's experience of structural change.

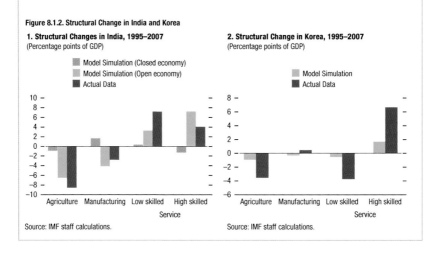

Figure 8.1.2. Structural Change in India and Korea

Source: IMF staff calculations.

REFERENCES

Acemoglu, Daron, and James Robinson. 2008. "The Role of Institutions in Growth and development." Commission on Growth and Development, World Bank Working Paper 10, Washington, DC.

Adhikari, Santosh. 2019. "Structural Transformation of India: A Quantitative Analysis." *Indian Economic Journal* 1–22.

Agosin, Manuel R., Roberto Alvarez, and Claudio Bravo-Ortega. 2012. "Determinants of Export Diversification Around the World: 1962–2000." *World Economy* 295–315.

Anand, Rahul, Saurabh Mishra, and Nikola Spatafora. 2012. "Structural Transformation and the sophistication of Production." IMF Working Paper 12/59, International Monetary Fund, Washington, DC.

Baldwin, Richard. 2016. *The Great Convergence: Information Technology and the New Globalization.* Cambridge, MA: Belknap Press of Harvard University Press.

Brussevich, Mariya, Era Dabla-Norris, and Salma Khalid. 2020. "Who Will Bear the Brunt of Lockdown Policies? Evidence from Tele-workability Measures Across Countries." IMF Working Paper 20/88, International Monetary Fund, Washington, DC.

Buera, Francisco, and Joseph Kaboski. 2009. "Can Traditional Theories of Structural Change Fit the Data?" *Journal of the European Economic Association* 7(2–3) 469–77.

Buera, Francisco, Joseph Kaboski, and Richard Rogerson, 2015, "Skill-Biased Structural Change," NBER Working Paper 21165, National Bureau of Economic Research, Cambridge, MA.

Cadot, Olivier, Céline Carrère, and Vanessa Strauss-Kahn. 2011. "Export Diversification: What's behind the Hump?" *Review of Economics and Statistics* 93 (2): 590–605.

Carmignani, Fabrizo, and Thomas Mandeville. 2010. "Never Been Industrialized: A Tale of African Structural Change." *Structural Change and Economic Dynamics* 31: 124–37.

Cherif, Reda, Fuad Hasanov, and Lichen Wang. 2018. "Sharp Instrument: A Stab at Identifying the Causes of Economic Growth." IMF Working Paper 2018/117, International Monetary Fund, Washington, DC.

Cherif, Reda, and Fuad Hasanov. 2014. "Soaring of the Gulf Falcons: Diversification in the GCC Oil Exporters in Seven Propositions." IMF Working Paper 2014/117, International Monetary Fund, Washington, DC.

Christiansen, Lone, Martin Schindler, and Thierry Tressel. 2013. "Growth and Structural Reforms: A New Assessment." *Journal of International Economics* 89: 347–56.

Comin, Diego, Lashkari, Danial, and Marti Mestieri. 2021. "Structural Change with Long-Run Income and Price Effects." *Econometrica* 89 (1): 311–74.

Dehejia, Rajeev, and Panagariya, Arvind. 2010. "Services Growth in India: A Look Inside the Black Box." Columbia Program on Indian Economic Policies, Working Paper 2010–04, School of International and Public Affairs, Columbia University.

Dossani, Rafiq. 2006. "Origins and Growth of the Software Industry in India." Asia-Pacific Research Center, Stanford University, Stanford, CA.

Di Giovanni, Julian, and Andrei A. Levchenko. 2009. "Trade Openness and Volatility." *Review of Economics and Statistics* 91 (3): 558–85.

Ding, Xiaodan, and Metodij Hadzi-Vaskov. 2017. "Composition of Trade in Latin America and the Caribbean." IMF Working Paper 17/42, International Monetary Fund, Washington, DC.

Giri, Rahul, Saad Quayyum, and Rujun Yin. 2019. "Understanding Export Diversification: Key Drivers and Policy Implications." IMF Working Paper 19/105, International Monetary Fund, Washington, DC.

Haddad, Mona, Jamus Jerome Lim, Cosimo Pancaro, and Christian Saborowsk. 2013. "Trade Openness Reduces Growth Volatility when Countries are Well Diversified." *Canadian Journal of Economics* 46: 765–90.

Hansen, Gary D., and Edward C. Prescott. 2002. "Malthus to Solow." *American Economic Review* 92 (4): 1205–17.

Hausmann, Ricardo, César A Hidalgo, Sebastián Bustos, Michele Coscia, Sarah Chung, Juan Jímenez, Alexander Simoes, and Muhammed A. Yildirim. 2011. *The Atlas of Economic Complexity: Mapping Paths to Prosperity.* Cambridge, MA: Harvard University.

Henn, Christian, Chris Papageorgiou, and Nicola Spatafora. 2013. "Export Quality in Developing Countries" IMF Working Paper 2013/108, International Monetary Fund, Washington, DC.

Herrendorf, Berthold, Richard Rogerson, and Akos Valentinyi. 2014. "Growth and Structural Transformation." *Handbook of Economic Growth* 2: 855–941.

Imbs, Jean, and Romain Wacziarg. 2003. "Stages of Diversification." *American Economic Review* 93: 63–86.

International Monetary Fund (IMF). 2014. "Sustaining Long-Run Growth and Macroeconomic Stability in Low-Income Countries—The Role of Structural Transformation and Diversification." IMF Policy Paper, International Monetary Fund, Washington, DC.

International Monetary Fund (IMF). 2017. *Regional Economic Outlook: Sub Saharan Africa— Fiscal Adjustment and Economic Diversification.* International Monetary Fund, Washington, DC.

International Monetary Fund (IMF). 2019. "Is South Asia Ready for Take Off? A Sustainable and Inclusive Growth Agenda." IMF Departmental Paper 2019/016, International Monetary Fund, Washington, DC.

Kanasheuski, Eugene. 2021. "A Model of Structural Change in India." Unpublished manuscript. Washington, DC.

Kongsamut, Piyabha, Sergio Rebelo, and Danyang Xie, 2001. "Beyond Balanced Growth." *Review of Economic Studies* 68: 869–82.

Koren, Miklós, and Silvana Tenreyro. 2007. "Volatility and Development." *Quarterly Journal of Economics* 122: 243–87.

Lian, Weicheng, Fei Liu, Katsiaryna Svirydzenka, Biying Zhu. 2021. "A Diversification Strategy for South Asia." IMF Working Paper 2021/202, International Monetary Fund, Washington, DC.

Lucas, Robert. 1993. "Making a Miracle." *Econometrica* 61 (2): 251–72.

Makhlouf, Yousef, Neil M. Kellard, Dmitri Vinogradov. 2015. "Trade Openness, Export Diversification, and Political Regimes." *Economics Letters* 136: 25–7.

McMillan, Margaret S., and Dani Rodrik. 2011. "Globalization, Structural Change, and Productivity Growth." NBER Working Paper 17143, National Bureau of Economic Research, Cambridge, MA.

Ngai, Rachel L., and Christopher A. Pissarides. 2007. "Structural Change in a Multisector Model of Growth." *American Economic Review* 97: 429–43.

Ostry, Jonathan, Alessandro Prati, and Antonio Spilimbergo. 2009. "Structural Reforms and Economic Performance in Advanced and Developing Countries." IMF Occasional Paper 268, International Monetary Fund, Washington, DC.

Papageorgiou, Chris, Nikola Spatafora, and Ke Wang. 2015. "Diversification, Growth, and Volatility in Asia." World Bank Policy Research Working Paper 7380, World Bank, Washington, DC.

Peyrefitte, Joseph, and Jeff Brice. 2004. "Product Diversification and R&D Investment: An Empirical Analysis of Competing Hypotheses." *Organizational Analysis* 12 (4): 379–94.

Prati, Alessandro, Massimiliano Gaetano Onorato, and Chris Papageorgiou. 2013. "Which Reforms Work and under What Institutional Environment? Evidence from a New Data Set on Structural Reforms." *Review of Economics and Statistics* 95 (3): 946–68.

Rodrik, Dani. 2016. "Premature Deindustrialization." *Journal of Economic Growth* 21 (1): 1–33.

Saxenian, AnnaLee. 2001. "Bangalore: The Silicon Valley of Asia?" Stanford Center for International Development Working Paper 91, Stanford University, Stanford, CA.

CHAPTER 9

Boosting Trade and Value Chain Participation to Sustain Growth in South Asia

Shanaka Jayanath Peiris, Weicheng Lian, Pragyan Deb, Patrick Blagrave, and Naihan Yang

India and South Asia's opening up to external trade in the 1990s accelerated growth in the region, but the benefits are beginning to wane. However, the disruptions to key industries in the rest of Asia as a result of COVID-19 and the broader technology realignments and trade tensions provide opportunities for South Asia if it can put in place the necessary structural conditions through further liberalization and regulatory reforms. India needs to leverage its existing strength in services exports and extend it to job-rich manufacturing export by deepening its global value chain participation and complementary structural reforms that can boost productivity, formal employment, and exports, thereby creating a virtuous cycle of productivity growth and strong export performance. Trade and investment reforms, by reducing tariffs and nontariff barriers, for both goods and in particular high value services such as professional services, will be pivotal to raise competitiveness and establish regional supply chains that would benefit it and the rest of South Asia.

INTRODUCTION

The South Asian region's growth accelerated since the 1990s, led by India's opening up to external trade. But this is beginning to taper and requires a boost to sustain the post–COVID-19 recovery. As India started to undertake reforms in the 1980s and 1990s, growth increased steadily—averaging 7 percent over the past decade—making India one of the fastest growing countries in the world and helping lift about 200 million people out of poverty (IMF 2019). Although the growth takeoff of India and Bangladesh has been comparable to those of most Association of Southeast Asian Nations (ASEAN) economies[1] at a comparable development stage, it has not fully mirrored the sustained takeoffs in Korea and

---

[1] ASEAN comprises Brunei, Cambodia, Indonesia, Laos, Malaysia, Myanmar, the Philippines, Singapore, Thailand, and Vietnam. ASEAN-5 refers to Indonesia, Malaysia, the Philippines, Singapore, and Thailand, and ASEAN-6 adds Vietnam to the group. ASEAN+3 includes all ASEAN countries plus China, Japan, and Korea.

Figure 9.1. Growth Index, Years from Reform Commencement
(Year 0=100)

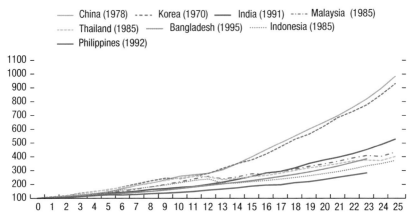

Sources: World Economic Outlook database; and IMF staff calculations.

Figure 9.2. Growth, Trade Liberalization, and Deregulation in South Asia

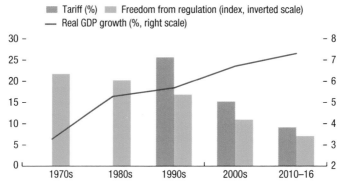

Sources: Fraser Institute, Human Freedom Index; World Integrated Trade Solution database; World Economic Outlook database; and IMF staff calculations.

China and has begun to falter recently (Figure 9.1). Structural reforms and open-ing up the economy in the rest of South Asia also gathered pace in the 1990s, which helped accelerate economic growth rates supported by a more vibrant Indian economy to trade with (Figure 9.2).[2] Trade liberalization and regulatory reforms were an important ingredient of India's and South Asia's growth takeoff, and further reforms will be essential to sustain growth (Figure 9.3 and 9.4).

This is particularly important given the devastating impact of the COVID-19 pandemic and the associated scarring, which is likely to result in a permanent loss

---

[2] Sri Lanka was an outlier by starting to liberalize the economy in 1978 but growth and reform momentum was affected by the internal conflict between 1983 and 2009.

Figure 9.3. Real GDP Per Capita Relative to the United States
(Percent, 1970 versus 2014)

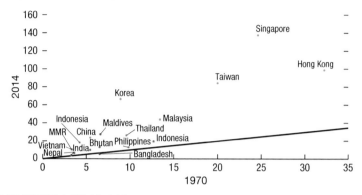

Sources: Penn World Tables; and IMF staff calculations.
Note: Purchasing power parity exchange rates.

Figure 9.4. Human Freedom Index Freedom from Regulation

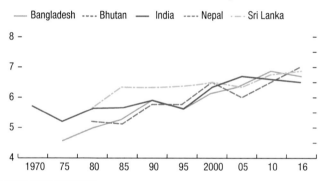

Source: Fraser Institute, Human Freedom Index.
Note: Score out of 10.

in output and lower potential growth. Employment is also taking a big hit and while part of the decline is cyclical, labor force participation has declined, suggesting potential scarring effects in the labor market. In particular, contact-intensives services sectors are likely to take longer to recover, posing an additional challenge for service-oriented South Asian economies and further highlighting the need to boost manufacturing and deepen GVC integration. Nevertheless, the disruptions to key industries in the rest of Asia as a result of COVID-19 and the broader technology realignments and trade tensions, provides opportunities for South Asia if it can put in place the necessary structural conditions through further liberalization and regulatory reforms.

Despite strong services trade, manufacturing exports growth remained tepid in India even before the effect of COVID-19, reflecting India's muted global value chain (GVC) participation. COVID-19 has depressed global demand for goods across the globe and is directly (and indirectly) leading to substantial realignments in GVCs, and thus designing policies to boost trade integration and participate in evolving and new supply chains will be all the more urgent. Trade disruptions and export restrictions on critical goods (for example, health, high-tech) could lead countries to reduce reliance on GVCs to build greater resiliency going forward, including through reshoring of production, greater regionalism, and diversion away from China. This realignment and China-US trade tensions provide a potential opportunity for India and the rest of South Asia to emerge as a global manufacturing hub, in a similar way that China's rise and regional supply chains with ASEAN reshaped Asia over the last few decades. Potential technological decoupling of China from the United States and other high-tech hubs could impede the global knowledge frontier and diffusion across countries (see Cerdeiro and others 2021). However, there may also be opportunities for India and the rest of South Asia to emerge as knowledge hubs and enhance labor productivity, especially in high-tech sectors that are likely to thrive in a post COVID-19 world.

India's export basket has gradually become more complex, with significant potential now for expansion to new industries if accompanied by steadfast and coherent reforms (see Chapter 8). Greater regional integration and investment in soft and hard infrastructure (Chapter 10) would also help develop regional supply chains within South Asia and potentially link up the rest of South-east Asia and beyond. Although no single reform can deliver rapid trade integration, existing evidence and analysis in this chapter suggests that the key focus needs to be on deepening GVC integration and implementing complementary structural reforms that can boost productivity and exports, thereby creating a virtuous cycle of productivity growth and strong export performance. Unleashing such a cycle would require a new wave of trade liberalization in India given the high trade barriers in critical areas as well as regional integration and policies to support such a reallocation of labor across India and the region.

The existing strengths in services exports and the new wave of technological innovations need to be harnessed to advance India's edge in the digital age and benefit from the region's demographics. Going forward as global incomes converge, the demand for services is expected to grow faster[3] than that for manufactured goods, supported by ongoing technological innovations (for example, artificial intelligence, big data, and machine learning) and efforts to lower trade barriers in services (World Trade Organization 2019). COVID-19 has also accelerated this transition to a high-tech and low-contact service economy where India's past performance on "outsourcing" may provide an advantage. India's services still have room for further diversification and for productivity enhancement, especially by lowering the high NTBs and investment restrictions in service sectors. South Asia as a whole will be one of the few regions with a young population and thus a growing workforce, that could be harnessed to cater to the new

---

[3] Globally, services exports have expanded at three times the growth rate of goods exports in the past decade and constitute 40 percent of global trade in value-added content. So far, the global rise of services has been led by financial services and information and computer services, a trend India has benefitted from.

technology global economy through human capital investment (Chapter 2) and deeper service, investment and people-to-people integration in the region.

PROGRESS AND CHALLENGES

India's growth convergence accelerated since the 1990s. For more than three decades following its independence, India was mired in a low-growth equilibrium, struggling to achieve growth rates above 4 percent. This tepid pace of economic expansion reflected substantial state intervention and other restrictive policies, which stifled trade, innovation, and investment activity. Momentum for liberalization efforts began in the 1980s, laying the groundwork for more extensive reforms from mid-1991 onward. The key elements of the reforms undertaken in the 1990s focused on deregulation of industry and liberalization of external trade—a thorough summary of the reforms undertaken in the 1980s and 1990s is available in Panagariya (2004). As reform momentum increased, India's average GDP growth rate accelerated from the so-called "Hindu rate of growth"—about 3.5 percent—to above 5 percent in the 1990s and between 6 and 7 percent from 2000 onward.

The rest of South Asia followed a similar trajectory supported by structural reforms but with different growth models. In Bangladesh, reforms and trade liberalization attracted FDIs in the ready-made garment sector, which in turn facilitated technology transfer to domestic entrepreneurs and catalyzed export-led growth. Maldives diversified from fish into tourism, while Nepal diversified from raw food products to information and communications technology (ICT) and tourism. Bhutan benefited from exporting hydropower electricity, which now accounts for 30 percent of its exports. Sri Lanka was an early reformer transforming from a plantation-based economy to niche manufacturing (garments) and tourism, but the strong growth trajectory was derailed by the three decades of civil war and bouts of macro-instability.

Trade-liberalization efforts in India were associated with higher productivity growth across the entire economy, though the acceleration has been most evident in services (Figure 9.5). Indeed, high-skill services (business, financial, and telecommunication services) have been the country's productivity-growth leader over the most recent postreform period, followed closely by low-skill services (hotels and restaurants, trade and transportation, and storage services). Gains relative to the preliberalization period are also evident in manufacturing, mining, and agriculture, suggesting the benefits of liberalization were widespread. Productivity growth also accelerated in most of South Asia as structural reforms took hold and the counties benefited from greater knowledge diffusion from the global technology frontier as their economies integrated to the global economy, albeit with setbacks during times of civil unrest (Figure 9.6).

The importance of boosting productivity growth is hard to overstate—South Asia remains at an early stage of catch-up growth, with per capita income, even on PPP terms, a fraction of the level of the United States and gains small relative to those achieved by the Asian Tigers (Figure 9.7). Sustained high productivity growth is the key channel through which the region can achieve convergence from its still-low level of per capita income toward that in middle-income and

Figure 9.5. Productivity Growth across Sectors in India
(Percent)

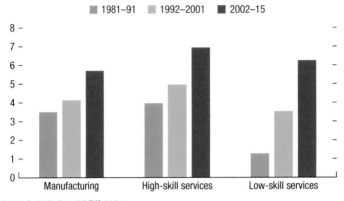

Sources: Reserve Bank of India; and KLEMS database.

Figure 9.6. Labor Productivity Growth
(Percent)

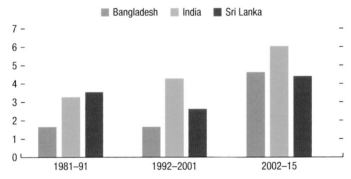

Sources: The Conference Board; and IMF staff calculations.
Note: The bars are calculated by the average of labor productivity growth in the period.

advanced economies. Achieving catch-up will be all the more challenging in the current context, given the permanent loss in output already seen and the likely persistent or even permanent scarring effects of COVID-19 on potential growth in the region (see Asia and Pacific *Regional Economic Outlook,* October 2021). In addition, with a large population entering the labor force in the next few decades, productivity gains will be key to creating jobs and harnessing the demographic dividend (Chapter 3). This is particularly urgent since the COVID-19 pandemic risks exacerbating inequality with high frequency labor surveys showing that the pandemic is having particularly adverse effects on people that are economically more vulnerable, including younger workers and women. Previous evidence of crises and pandemics suggest that these effects can be persistent in the absence of adequate policy support (see the Asia and Pacific *Regional Economic Outlook,*

October 2020, Chapter 4), highlighting the criticality of ensuring that productivity gains are achieved, particularly for low-wage workers. Therefore, a more proactive set of policies to raise productivity growth and create quality is needed—this chapter's central argument is that greater trade liberalization and integration into regional value chains can play a key role in this regard (see the Asia and Pacific *Regional Economic Outlook,* October 2021, Chapter 4).

Figure 9.7. Purchasing Power Parity GDP Per Capita Relative to the United States
(Percent)

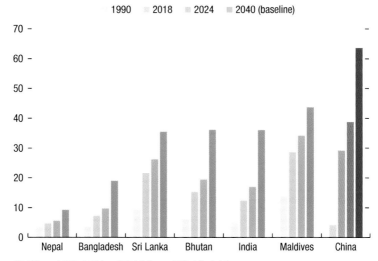

Sources: World Economic Outlook database; United Nations; and IMF staff calculations.

Figure 9.8. Trade Openness in Asia
(Index)

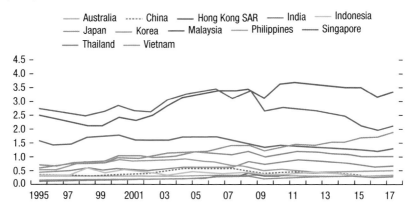

Sources: IMF, World Economic Outlook database; IMF, Direction of Trade database; and IMF staff calculations.

Figure 9.9. Export Intensity
(Exports of goods and services as a percent of GDP)

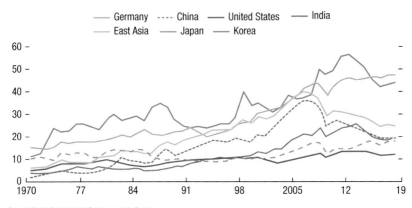

Source: World Bank's World Development Indicators.

Figure 9.10. Manufacturing Export Intensity
(Export of manufacturing goods as a percent of GDP)

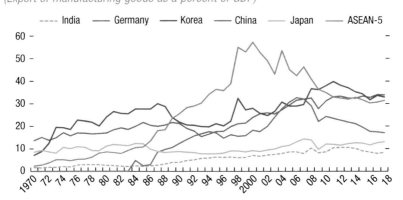

Sources: World Bank's World Development Indicators; and IMF staff calculations.
Note: ASEAN-5 = Indonesia, Malaysia, Philippines, Singapore, and Thailand.

Trade openness and the exports of goods and services are a key ingredient of higher productivity growth, which South Asia has not fully harnessed unlike its Eastern neighbors. The sharp rise in trade openness since 1992, when India began liberalizing its trade regime, has begun to taper and remains significantly below other export-led Asian economies (Figure 9.8). While the recent fall in trade openness is common across many Asian economies attributed largely to the muted pace of trade liberalization (and rising protectionism), onshoring in China and maturation of global value chains (IMF 2015; IMF 2018b), the trend is even more worrisome for India and rest of South Asia as the exports of goods and services to GDP (export intensity) ratio never reached the levels of the Asian Tigers and China, even after including the dynamic service export sector (Figure 9.9).

Figure 9.11. Cross-Country Job Creation
(Percent of increase in the working-age population, as of 2018)

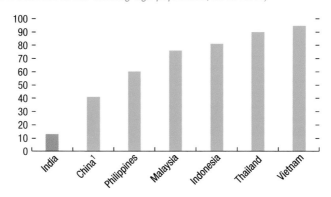

Sources: United Nations *World Population Prospects 2019*; International Labour Organization; and IMF staff calculations.
Note: Data are calculated as the change in employees in 2018 or the latest over 2000 as a percent of change in the working-age population (15–64 years) in 2018 over 2000.
¹As of 2017.

Manufacturing goods export intensity is low and has fallen since 2014, despite the "Make in India" initiative (Figure 9.10). After 1992, when India began liberalizing its trade regime, India's share of world goods exports rose from 0.5 percent to 1.7 percent in 2018, though stagnating over the past decade. Over the same period, China's share of world merchandise exports rose from 1.8 percent to 12.7 percent (Gopinath and Lahiri 2019).[4] Tepid manufacturing export growth has been associated with weak productivity and formal employment growth in India. Productivity growth in manufacturing has been slower than in formal or informal services, with firm sizes remaining small.[5] And formal job creation has not kept pace with the growth in working-age population, as the ability to generate jobs is significantly greater for manufacturing than services, especially the high-skill services that India exports (Figure 9.11).[6]

India has a significant comparative advantage in services exports and has secured market share, albeit concentrated and with some services at risk of automation (Figure 9.12). The world export share of the Indian services sector rose

---

[4] According to the Report of the High-Level Advisory Group (Ministry of Commerce and Industry, Government of India 2019), India's ranking in export growth declined in all major export sectors during 2012–17, relative to the high trade growth period of 2003–11.

[5] Firms with less than 100 workers, despite being more than ten years old, account for more than half of all organized firms in manufacturing by number; their contribution to employment is only 14 percent and to productivity is a mere 8 percent. In contrast, large firms (more than 100 employees) account for three-quarters of such employment and close to 90 percent of productivity despite accounting for about 15 percent by number (Ministry of Finance Economic Survey 2019).

[6] Cross-country estimates (based on a panel data of 43 countries, 2000–16) show that the employment elasticity to gross exports (percentage change in employment associated with a 1 percentage change in gross exports) is five times higher for manufacturing than in services (Goretti, Kihara, and Salgado 2019).

Figure 9.12. Revealed Comparative Advantage of One-Digit Service Categories

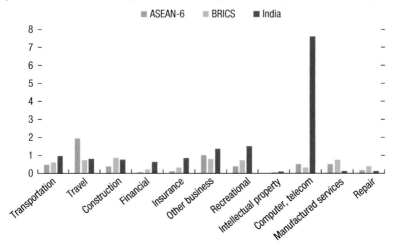

Sources: IMF International Services Trade Database; and IMF staff calculations.
Note: Revealed comparative advantage is calculated as the ratio between the country's export share in a given sector to the world's average share in that sector. Greater than 1 implies revealed comparative advantage. ASEAN-6 = Indonesia, Malaysia, Philippines, Singapore, Thailand, and Vietnam; BRICS = Brazil, Russia, India, China, and South Africa.

Figure 9.13. Correlation between Trade Openess and Global Value Chain Linkages
(Percent of GDP)

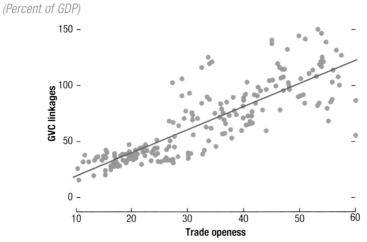

Source: IMF staff calculations.
Note: Correlation = 0.83.

from 0.5 percent to 3.1 percent during 1992–2018. Computer services alone account for about half of India's total services exports. Other business services including manufacturing-related services and charges for intellectual properties are relatively low, partly reflecting the underperformance of manufacturing exports. The concentration and the level of complexity of service exports in India make it

Figure 9.14. GVC Participation of Goods and Services Sectors

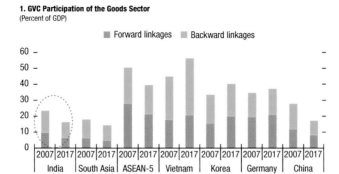

1. GVC Participation of the Goods Sector
(Percent of GDP)

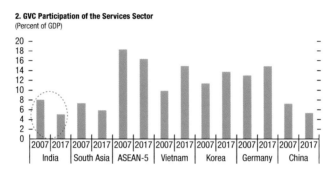

2. GVC Participation of the Services Sector
(Percent of GDP)

Source: Asian Development Bank database.
Note: ASEAN-5 = Indonesia, Malaysia, Philippines, Singapore, and Thailand; GVC = global value chain.

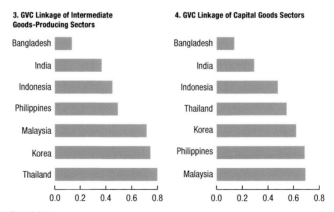

3. GVC Linkage of Intermediate
Goods-Producing Sectors

4. GVC Linkage of Capital Goods Sectors

Source: IMF staff calculations.
Note: The figure shows total GVC linkages in 2017. GVC = global value chain.

relatively vulnerable to possible disruptive technological changes, including automation and robotization (see the Asia and Pacific *Regional Economic Outlook*,
October 2020, Chapter 4). Diversification and moving into higher technological
sectors that have benefitted more as a result of COVID-19 is therefore necessary
to maintain comparative advantage and generate further opportunities.

Low export intensity and trade integration also reflect limited GVC participation. GVC participation and trade openness are closely related across countries, with a correlation coefficient of more than 0.83 (Figure 9.13). Strong export growth in many rapidly growing economies has been accompanied by rising GVC participation, improving productivity, and formal job creation (Figure 9.14). GVCs foster specialization and promote the diffusion of technology, increasing productivity and income growth (World Bank 2020). While the rise of GVCs has been observed across the globe, the expansion has been particularly pronounced in China, Korea, Japan, and the ASEAN.[7] India's GVC integration in both goods and services remains low (Athukorala 2014; Veeramani and Dhir 2017) and lags significantly behind the ASEAN-6, which have emerged as a manufacturing hub. Perhaps more surprising is that even GVC participation in services remains relatively weak in India.

Given its stage of development and focus on manufacturing exports, India needs to deepen its backward linkages. IMF research (Raei, Ignatenko, and Mircheva 2019) found that manufacturing exports are associated with sizeable backward linkages (Table 9.1). Policy measures that limit backward linkages, for example, tariffs on intermediate goods, adversely affect the emergence of a vibrant

TABLE 9.1.

GVC Participation and Position, by Sector, 2013

Sector	Share in World Exports		GVC Participation Index[1]	
	Value-Added Concept	Gross Concept	Backward Linkage	Forward Linkage
Manufacturing				
Electrical and machinery	37.7	46.7	32	15
Petroleum and chemical products	15.0	15.3	33	25
Transport equipment	5.2	8.1	37	10
Metal products	5.1	4.3	29	35
Textiles and wearing apparel	3.8	4.5	27	11
Food and beverages	1.1	1.4	23	9
Wood and paper	0.9	0.7	26	30
Other manufacturing	0.4	0.6	28	7
Services				
Financial and business services	20.7	5.7	8	91
Transport	3.0	1.6	19	38
Wholesale trade	1.7	0.6	10	88
Retail trade	0.6	0.2	12	76
Post and telecommunications	0.3	0.1	14	63
Hotels and restaurants	0.2	0.1	13	23

Source: Raei, Ignatenko, and Mircheva 2019.
[1]Backward linkages refer to foreign value added in gross exports. Forward linkages refer to parts of domestic value added exports that are further re-exported. Both as share of gross exports.
[2]Downstream index refers to number of previous stages embodied in the exports of particular country or sector. Upstream index refers to number of additional steps to final consumer.

---

[7] Recent studies better differentiate activities in GVCs, where countries either source foreign inputs for export production or provide inputs to foreign partners for their export production. These two types of GVC activities have been called the "backward" and "forward" linkages, respectively.

and globally competitive manufacturing sectors that can be scaled up including for job creation, the essence of the vision behind the Government's "Make in India" initiative. Services, including business and financial services and wholesale trade, have very high forward linkages reflecting that they are intermediate inputs in their export destinations, and have limited backward linkages reflecting that the production of business and financial services uses limited foreign inputs.

The participation of South Asia in the GVCs of intermediate goods and capital goods is also relatively low.[8] Cheaper intermediate goods enhance the competitiveness of an economy by lowering production costs.[9] Moreover, trade in intermediate goods, or intraindustry trade, accounts for the largest share of GVC participation since capital goods production tends to be concentrated among a few countries, with most EMDEs being mainly importers of these goods. Still, being part of the GVCs of capital goods through trade in intermediates can improve productivity, likely through improved allocation of resources and capital deepening (Lian and others 2020). Therefore, low integration of SA into the GVCs of intermediate and capital goods could have impeded their economic convergence and are indicative of the presence of significant barriers for GVC expansion in this region. An analysis of the drivers of GVCs later in the chapter points to a need to conduct structural reforms, especially to reduce tariffs and nontariffs trade barriers, to strengthen South Asia's position in these key sectors' GVCs.

POLICIES TO SUSTAIN GROWTH IN THE POST–COVID-19 ERA

Speeding Up Convergence of South Asia by Raising Productivity Growth

The section revisits convergence through growth regressions for EMDEs given the impact on potential growth of the COVID-19 pandemic (Asia and Pacific *Regional Economic Outlook* 2020, Chapter 2; *World Economic Outlook,* April 2021). Trade openness and FDI are important determinants of the speed of economic convergence in EMDEs in addition to the traditional drivers of growth such as

---

[8] Intermediate goods are defined as those whose outputs are mainly used by other sectors as intermediate inputs based on the Eora database (they include basic metals and fabricated metal; chemicals and chemical products; coke, refined petroleum, and nuclear fuel; electricity, gas, and water supply; mining and quarrying; other nonmetallic minerals; pulp, paper, paper products, printing, and publishing; rubber and plastics; and wood and products of wood and cork). The definition of capital goods producing sectors is consistent with that used in Lian and others (2020), and the sectors classified as capital goods producing ones include electrical and optical equipment; machinery; and transport equipment.

[9] Raei, Ignatenko and Mircheva (2019) found that it is mostly trade in intermediate goods as well as the share of GVC-related trade flows, rather than conventional trade, that contribute to a country's income per capita

human and physical capital (Dabla-Norris and others 2013). Empirically, the literature finds a close link between the reduction of trade costs, trade expansion and productivity, particularly through participation in GVCs (Criscuolo and Timmis 2017; Raei, Ignatenko, and Mircheva, 2019, and Chapter 4 of the October 2016 *World Economic Outlook*). The significant scarring on potential growth in South Asia from the COVID-19 pandemic and the role policies could play to raise potential growth will be critical over the short- to medium-term.

Trade, investment, and knowledge flows that underpin GVCs, including FDI largely explain growth dynamics in EMDEs. Growth regressions show a statistically significant positive association between FDI inflows and growth, as well as between tariff reductions and growth, while controlling for external demand. These findings hold both in a global sample of countries and one relating just to Asia and Pacific countries. This is consistent with other findings in the literature studying the relationship between structural factors and growth for EMDEs, including Rajan and Zingales (1998), Djankov and Murrell (2002), Caselli and Gennaioli (2008), and Christiansen, Schindler, and Tressel (2013), among others. One possible channel for tariff-reduction to boost productivity growth is through a specialization of goods countries have greater comparative advantage, as revealed by the chapter on economic and trade diversification in this book. Table 9.2 suggests that the benefit goes beyond diversification, and after controlling for it, the impact of tariff reduction and FDI remains significant.[10] Bilateral GVC participation measures and bilateral FDI volumes are also positively related, and thus indicate that GVC participation associated with lower tariffs and FDI may be a key driver of growth in EMDEs and Asia over the last few decades.

The well-established link between trade liberalization and productivity growth is also validated at the sectoral level. Reducing tariffs can significantly enhance productivity at the sector level, a finding established by exploiting sector-level variation in import tariffs. The rich variation in tariffs at the sector level allows us to alleviate endogeneity concerns by controlling for country-by-year and country-by-sector fixed effects. Such fixed effects account for shocks common across sectors and time-invariant factors specific for a sector in a country. Table 9.3 suggests that tariff is a significant force driving productivity.[11]

Improvement of productivity at the sector level is also significantly associated with the sector's integration into global supply chains, as regression results in Table 9.4 suggest. This finding is robust to controlling for import tariffs at the sector level. This is an important finding, as it shows that GVC participation and trade liberalization leads to higher productivity gains within sectors of a country rather than through a change in the sectoral composition of the economy alone.

---

[10] As we control for several structural indicators in column (5), the coefficient of import tariff becomes even larger than its coefficient in column (1), when only income, external demand, country, and period-fixed effects are controlled.

[11] The data come from the World Input-Output database, and an experiment using sector-level FDI yields nonsignificant coefficients for FDI measures. It is possible that the key variation over time for FDI is common across sectors and hence absorbed by country-by-year fixed effects.

TABLE 9.2.

Growth Regressions for EMDEs and Asia

Variable	(1) All	(2) All	(3) All	(4) All	(5) All	(6) All	(7) APD Only	(8) APD Only
Tariff rates	-0.038**				-0.045***		-0.077***	
	(0.015)				(0.015)		(0.016)	
Foreign direct investment inflows		0.150***			0.122***			0.314***
		(0.036)			(0.046)			(0.046)
Export diversification			0.372		-0.046			
			(0.271)		(0.585)			
Economic opportunity index				0.619***	0.151			
				(0.206)	(0.373)			
Foreign direct investment restrictions						-0.616		
						(2.411)		
Log(income)	6.099*	0.764	-1.124	-2.987	10.500**	-0.174	0.124	-7.083
	(3.359)	(1.950)	(2.398)	(2.237)	(4.725)	(3.734)	(5.633)	(4.005)
External demand	74.671***	43.531***	48.051***	43.826***	63.335***	93.340***	0.330	2.101
	(11.645)	(10.133)	(9.639)	(9.501)	(15.338)	(20.155)	(19.772)	(10.666)
Country fixed effects	Y	Y	Y	Y	Y	Y	Y	Y
Period fixed effects	Y	Y	Y	Y	Y	Y	Y	Y
No. of observations	987	1,130	1,520	1,674	719	423	166	162
R^2	0.472	0.374	0.329	0.321	0.615	0.628	0.672	0.575

Sources: IMF World Economic Outlook dataset; RES Structural Indicators; and IMF staff estimation.
Note: Standard errors in parentheses are clustered at the country level. The dependent variable is the growth of real GDP per capita compared with the previous year. The sample consists of 178 countries from 1988 to 2017, and is unbalanced. EMDEs = emerging markets and developing economies.
$***p < 0.01, **p < 0.05, *p < 0.1.$

TABLE 9.3.

Impact of Sector-Specific Import Tariff on Sectoral Productivity: Controlling for Country-by-Year and Country-by-Sector Fixed Effects

Variable	(1) Log(productivity)
Tariff rates	−0.027***
	(0.0044)
Country-by-year fixed effects	Yes
Country-by-sector fixed effects	Yes
No. of observations	16,057
R^2	0.992

Sources: World Input-Output database; and IMF staff estimation.
Note: Robust standard errors are in parentheses. The dependent variable is defined as the log of real value added per employee, and the sample consists of 40 countries and manufacturing industries defined at the three-digit level of the Interational Standard Industrial Classification from 1995 to 2014. Two vintages of the World Input-Output database are merged together to create this sample.
***$p < 0.01$, **$p < 0.05$, *$p < 0.1$.

TABLE 9.4.

Are the Benefits of Global Value Chains, and Why Do Countries Participate?

Variable	(1) Productivity All	(2) Productivity All	(3) Productivity Tradable	(4) Productivity All	(5) Productivity All	(6) Productivity Tradable
Forward linkage	55.89***	37.57***	38.34***	55.15***	38.36***	38.40***
	(11.43)	(10.92)	(12.01)	(11.36)	(11.10)	(12.05)
Backward linkage				25.23*	22.30*	33.02***
				(13.06)	(12.59)	(12.27)
Import tariff	−1.536***	−1.540***	−0.454	−1.437***	−1.464***	−0.359
	(0.521)	(0.471)	(0.551)	(0.517)	(0.466)	(0.549)
Year fixed effects	Y			Y	Y	Y
Country-year fixed effects		Y			Y	
Country-sector fixed effects	Y	Y	Y	Y	Y	Y
Clustered at the country-sector level	Y	Y	Y	Y	Y	Y
Constant	674.5***	678.4***	667.2***	669.2***	673.5***	657.3***
	(2.689)	(2.521)	(4.119)	(4.162)	(4.166)	(6.357)
No. of observations	2,911	2,911	1,305	2,911	2,911	1,305

Source: IMF staff calculations.
Note: Robust standard errors are in parentheses.
***$p < 0.01$, **$p < 0.05$, *$p < 0.1$.

What's Holding Back Trade Integration?

India and the rest of South Asia under-trades at the global level, because of high trade and investment barriers. Gravity models show that India under-trades in goods (that is, exports less than predicted by natural endowments and geography) by a wide margin relative to most other regions and the rest of Asia (IMF 2018b). India over-trades services as expected but intraregional South Asian trade of goods and services are less than predicted. Gravity-based estimates of trade barriers show that India's trade barriers (including natural, tariff, and nontariff barriers) are high not only for merchandise imports, but across the board (Figure 9.15).

Trade liberalization is an unfinished agenda in India and could be further broadened in the rest of South Asia. Although tariffs have been reduced from 70 percent on average in India since the early 1990s, they are still relatively high and characterized by pronounced disparities between the World Trade

Figure 9.15. Tariff-Equivalent Importing Costs
(Percent)

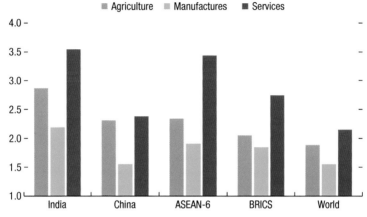

Sources: Boz, Li, and Zhang 2019; and IMF staff estimates.
Note: The figure presents gravity-based estimates of tariff-equivalent costs of imports for agriculture, manufactures, and services, respectively, in 2014. The gravity specification follows Eaton and Kortum 2001. ASEAN-6 = Indonesia, Malaysia, Philippines, Singapore, Thailand, and Vietnam; BRICS = Brazil, Russia, India, China, and South Africa.

Figure 9.16. Services Trade Restrictiveness Index: Computer Services
(Percent)

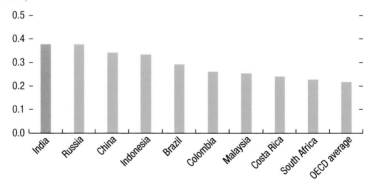

Source: OECD Services Trade Restrictions Database.
Note: STRI quantifies restrictions across five policy categories: restrictions on foreign entry, restrictions to movement of people, other discriminatory measures, barrier to competition, and regulatory transparency. OECD = Organisation for Economic Co-operation and Development; STRI = Services Trade Restrictiveness Index.

Organization's bound rates and the most favored nation applied rates, which increases trade policy uncertainty.[12] The Indian government has also imposed other nontariff barriers (NTBs) on imports. Comparing the degree of NTB restrictiveness with a single measure is difficult given the broad range of NTB instruments used and the heterogeneity in their impacts. Cerdeiro and Nam (2018) adopted a multi-indicator approach that highlights India high service sector barriers to foreign entry and competition as well as foreign investment restrictions. Overall, costs to import are twice as high as those in China and other manufacturing hubs. In addition, restrictions to foreign competition are higher in India than those in other non-OECD countries and the OECD average including for India's "champion" exporting sector, computer services (Figure 9.16). The rest of South Asia has a more liberal trade regime comparable to EMDEs in merchandise goods trade and FDI but falls behind in terms of agriculture and service sector restrictions (Figures 9.17 and 9.18).

Intraregional trade within South Asia and with the rest of Asia has also remained low compared with its East Asian neighbors (Figure 9.19). Asia has been the engine of global trade driven by subregional trade (among China, Korea, and Japan) and interregional trade between Southeast Asia and East Asia (ASEAN+3 regional supply chains) as well as to the rest of the world. Intra–South Asian trade is negligible even compared with intra-ASEAN trade. In terms of composition, intra-South Asian trade is mainly related to intermediate manufacturing goods, with consumption and capital goods trade at a relatively low level.

India needs to strategically approach and leverage its plurilateral, regional, and bilateral trade agreements to foster GVC integration. Research shows that the depth and content of preferential trade agreements have a larger impact on GVC-intensive sectors, and regional/free trade agreements are found to be more effective in the short term in promoting the expansion of GVCs, when their membership is consistent with regional production networks (OECD 2015). For example, a preferential trade agreement with the European Union could ease access of some of India's major exports such as textiles, which are currently excluded from the European Union's Generalized System of Preferences, unlike those from Bangladesh or Vietnam. The latest Economic Survey by the Ministry of Finance shows that, contrary to popular perceptions, India has gained from FTAs a 0.7 percent increase per year in the trade surplus with partner countries for manufactured products and 2.3 percent per year for total merchandise. A more strategic approach to regional arrangements, whether it is the Bay of Bengal Initiative for Multi-Sectoral Technical and Economic Cooperation, the Regional Comprehensive Economic Partnership, or the South Asian Association for Regional Cooperation, while further deepening bilateral FTAs including with

---

[12] India's World Trade Organization bound tariff rates averaged 48.5 percent, while its applied most-favored-nation tariff for 2017 (latest data available) averaged 13.8 percent. Many of India's bound tariff rates on agricultural products are among the highest in the world, averaging 113.5 percent and ranging as high as 300 percent.

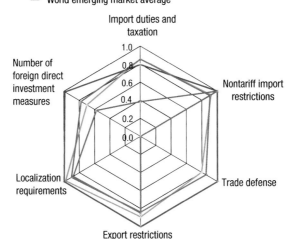

Figure 9.17. Overall Trade and FDI Regime of Emerging Market Economies

Source: IMF staff calculations.
Note: FDI = foreign direct investment.

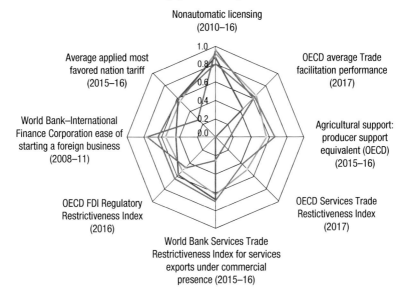

Figure 9.18. Trade Restrictive Measures since 2008*

Source: IMF staff calculations.
Note: Measures are in effect as of the end of January 2018. Years of data appear in parentheses. FDI = foreign direct investment; OECD = Organisation for Economic Co-Operation and Development; STRI = Services Trade Restrictiveness Index

Figure 9.19. Asia's Subregional and Interregional Trade
(Percent of global trade)

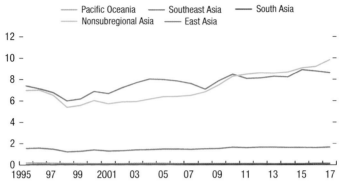

Sources: IMF's World Economic Outlook database; IMF, Direction of Trade database; and IMF staff calculations.

South Asian partners outlined in Chapter 10, should aim to benefit from mutual preferential access and develop regional supply chains with East Asia and integrate the rest of South Asia (Figure 9.19).

What Policies Can Boost GVC Integration?

Reducing high trade costs and investment barriers would foster GVC participation and manufacturing exports. The extensive GVC literature (OECD 2012; Blackman and others 2016; World Bank 2020) highlights the association between tariffs and a country's integration into global value chains and studies the relative importance of structural indicators in driving GVC integration (Figure 9.20). We examine GVC participation, both in terms of backward and forward linkages, and use the Eora database and a global supply chain database compiled by the Asian Development Bank. The Eora database provides country-level measures for 168 countries from 1990 to 2015. Sector-level information is available in the Asian Development Bank's global supply chain dataset for 54 economies between 2007 and 17.[13] In terms of differentiating from the extensive empirical literature assessing the drivers of GVC participation globally, our analyses focus not only on backward and forwards linkages at the country level but also on sectors more relevant to South Asia and on a sample more representative for Asia.

---

[13] The 54 countries are mainly Asian countries and include Australia, Austria, Bangladesh, Belgium, Bhutan, Brazil, Brunei Darussalam, Bulgaria, Cambodia, Canada, Croatia, Cyprus, Czech Republic, Denmark, Estonia, Fiji, Finland, France, Germany, Greece, Hungary, India, Indonesia, Italy, Japan, Kazakhstan, Kyrgyz Republic, Latvia, Lithuania, Luxembourg, Malaysia, Maldives, Malta, Mexico, Mongolia, Nepal, Netherlands, Norway, Pakistan, the Philippines, Poland, Portugal, Singapore, Slovak Republic, Slovenia, Spain, Sri Lanka, Sweden, Switzerland, Thailand, Turkey, the United Kingdom, and the United States.

Figure 9.20. Interregional Trade
(Percent)

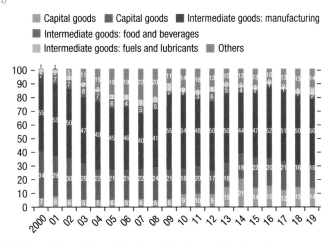

Sources: IMF's World Economic Outlook database; IMF, Direction of Trade database; and IMF staff calculations.

Figure 9.21. Global Value Chain Linkages, 2017

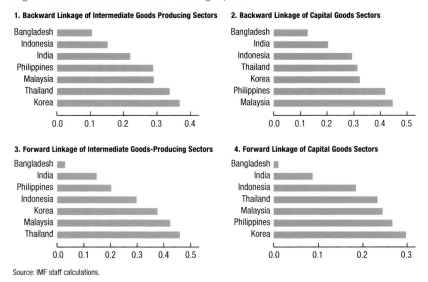

Source: IMF staff calculations.

A low participation of South Asia in the GVCs of intermediate and capital goods is manifested in both backward and forward linkages of these sectors (Figure 9.21). For both metrics, India and Bangladesh has fallen behind Indonesia, Korea, Malaysia, Thailand, and the Philippines significantly (Figure 9.22). One natural conjecture is that trade frictions may stand behind to explain the difference between these countries, given the sensitivity of GVC expansion to trade barriers (OECD 2012).

Figure 9.22. Global Value Chain Linkages, 2017

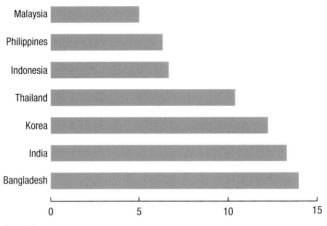

Source: IMF staff calculations.

TABLE 9.5.

Association between Tariffs and Global Value Chain Linkages						
	(1)	(2)	(3)	(4)	(5)	(6)
		Backward Linkages			Forward Linkages	
		Intermediate Goods	Capital Goods		Intermediate Goods	Capital Goods
Variable	Country	Sectors	Sectors	Country	Sectors	Sectors
Import tariffs	−0.218**	−0.543***	−0.519***	−0.160*	−1.111***	−0.967***
	(0.0846)	(0.189)	(0.179)	(0.0813)	(0.119)	(0.245)
Constant	1.301***	2.293***	2.577***	1.023***	1.951***	2.243***
	(0.111)	(0.145)	(0.163)	(0.0947)	(0.0975)	(0.150)
No. of observations	3,231	4,825	1,618	3,242	1,614	4,802
R^2	0.038	0.310	0.096	0.028	0.332	0.296

Source: IMF staff calculations.
Note: Robust standard errors are in parentheses.
***$p < 0.01$, **$p < 0.05$, *$p < 0.1$.

South Asia indeed has relatively high import tariffs, which could hurt its GVC development. Simple regressions of the backward and forward linkage on import tariffs point to significantly negative associations between tariffs and GVC integration, which are reported in Table 9.5. The negative association holds not only for the GVC integration at the country level, but also for those of intermediate goods and capital goods producing sectors. Despite being an association, which does not necessarily imply a causal relationship, the coefficient of the tariff is economically large. It implies that if India could reduce the tariff by 9.7 percent, it could have closed half the distance in the backward linkage between India and Korea.

Association between Tariffs and Nontariff Barriers and GVC Linkages						
	(1)	(2)	(3)	(4)	(5)	(6)
		Backward Linkages			Forward Linkages	
		Intermediate Goods	Capital Goods		Intermediate Goods	Capital Goods
Variable	Country	Sectors	Sectors	Country	Sectors	Sectors
Import tariffs	−0.388*	−0.511**	−0.170	−0.574***	−0.976***	−1.041***
	(0.207)	(0.232)	(0.218)	(0.168)	(0.231)	(0.149)
Nontariff barriers	−0.186***	−0.247**	−0.363***	−0.205***	−0.309***	−0.210***
	(0.0607)	(0.0975)	(0.0856)	(0.0600)	(0.0714)	(0.0606)
Constant	0.187	0.522	−0.145	−0.0285	0.0533	0.427
	(0.411)	(0.753)	(0.651)	(0.441)	(0.553)	(0.452)
No. of observations	1,192	4,169	1,398	6,332	4,149	1,395
R^2	0.131	0.368	0.205	0.242	0.401	0.384

Source: IMF staff calculations.
Note: Robust standard errors are in parentheses.
***$p < 0.01$, **$p < 0.05$, *$p < 0.1$.

The role of NTBs in affecting GVC integration is less well studied but appears to be a significant factor.[14] As Table 9.6 suggests, the associations between NTBs and the GVC measures, whether at the country level or at the sector level, are all significant. Moreover, controlling for NTBs does not weaken the association between tariffs and the GVC measures, suggesting that tariffs and NTBs capture different forces that drive the GVC integration.

As other structural forces in the economy can also impede GVC expansion, we explore their roles through the following empirical framework:

$$GVC_{i,t} = \alpha_t + \rho\tau_{i,t} + \varphi NTB_{i,t} + \beta_1 Z_{i,t} + \varepsilon_{i,t},$$

where $GVC_{i,t}$ is one of the two metrics: backward or forward linkages. Given structural indicators being slow-moving, we aggregate the data into 5-year cohorts. In addition, as the main variation we are going to exploit to estimate the model is the cross-country variation, we do not control for country fixed effects. Therefore, the analysis conducted here is suggestive and points to an association rather than any causal link. α_t denotes year fixed effects, $\tau_{i,t}$ is the import tariff, NTB is the nontariff barrier, and $Z_{i,t}$ refers to the following structural indicators: FDI, external debt to GDP ratio (proxy for availability of external debt financing), infrastructure quality (proxied by shipping or mobile phone coverage), and the average number of years of schooling (proxy for quality of labor force or skill level).

[14] NTBs are based on surveys conducted by the World Economic Forum and defined as follows: in your country, to what extent do nontariff barriers (for example, health and product standards, technical and labeling requirements, and so on) limit the ability of imported goods to compete in the domestic market? [1 = strongly limit; 7 = do not limit at all]. We multiply it by −1 in the regression analysis.

The thinking behind the choice of these variables goes as follows: the theory of offshoring suggests that the relative factor cost difference is a key motivation for offshoring to occur (Grossman and Rossi-Hansberg 2008), and therefore, a better access to international capital market and lower transportation costs should encourage offshoring and GVC expansion. We include FDI here as a de-facto measure of the quality of the business environment and expect a positive association between FDI and GVC integration. However, one caveat could be that foreign firms may choose to invest directly in the country to gain access to its market if there are significant trade barriers. If this incentive is strong, the association between FDI and GVC integration is not necessarily positive. Better infrastructure and better skilled labor force are conducive to GVC formation. We control for income levels and the size of the country.

Table 9.7 reports the estimation results for backward GVC linkages. The results confirm our hypothesis—all the structural factors considered are statistically significant in encouraging backward linkages. When taken together, we find that factors such as infrastructure, external debt, and labor quality play a significant role. FDI is significant in univariate regressions, but loses its significance in the presence of other factors. It is important to recognize that these results are obtained while we control for import tariffs and nontariff barriers, and therefore, these structural indicators capture forces orthogonal to direct trade barriers.[15] Results continue to hold if we replace NTB with ease of doing business, which captures elements of NTBs along with other factors. As expected, we obtain qualitatively similar, but weaker results for forward linkages.

To summarize, the findings in this section clearly point to the importance of lowering tariffs and nontariff trade barriers, improving the business environment (proxied by FDI), enhancing the access to international capital market, strengthening the infrastructure for GVC integration and improving the skill level of the labor force. While these patterns are broadly in line with what the literature has established, confirming their importance not only for the overall economy but also for intermediate goods and capital goods producing sectors is an innovation in this chapter, which further suggests the robustness of such findings.

Scope for and Benefits of Greater Trade Integration

The potential gains from further tariff reduction in goods and NTB in services is large, given the high trade barriers and important role they play in GVC participation. India's tariffs on imports of goods are high compared with other major economies in the Asia-Pacific (Figure 9.23). It is interesting that India has similar tariffs across goods used as intermediates and goods used in final demand, unlike most other countries in the region that tend to have lower tariffs on goods for

---

[15] It is worth noting that results from this step are likely to be different from a direct regression of NTBs on structural indicators, because the latter does not necessarily mean that variables with significant coefficients in that specification will have significant impact on GVC integration.

TABLE 9.7.

Associations between Tariffs and Structural Indicators and Global Value Chain Linkages

Backward Linkages	(1)	(2)	(3)	(4)	(5)	(6)	(7)
Infrastructure (shipping)	0.000995***						0.000838*
	(0.000356)						(0.000454)
Years of schooling		0.00983***					0.00905***
		(0.00190)					(0.00268)
External debt			0.0611***				0.0657***
			(0.0179)				(0.0209)
Foreign direct investment				0.592***			0.0186
				(0.150)			(0.0113)
Tariffs					-0.00245***		-0.000487
					(0.000618)		(0.00101)
Nontariff barrier						-0.0536***	-0.0238**
						(0.0115)	(0.00910)
Per capita income							-0.0232***
							(0.00730)
Population							-0.00910**
							(0.00443)
Constant	0.0749***	0.0276**	0.0715***	0.0792***	0.131***	-0.127**	0.117*
	(0.00746)	(0.0133)	(0.00873)	(0.00700)	(0.00994)	(0.0488)	(0.0612)
No. of observations	548	705	887	686	912	420	164
R^2	0.146	0.169	0.071	0.135	0.079	0.187	0.558

Source: IMF staff calculations.
Note: Robust standard errors are in parentheses.
***$p < 0.01$, **$p < 0.05$, *$p < 0.1$.

intermediate use compared with those on goods for final demand. India also imposes high NTBs on imports of services.[16]

The long-term output gains from a reduction in India's trade barriers are quantified using a sectoral, computable general equilibrium trade model (Caliendo and others 2017). The general equilibrium model includes two features that are important to explain international trade: heterogeneity in firms' productivity and cross-border production chains under some simplifying assumptions (such as frictionless movements of labor across firms and ease of firm entry/exit).

Two potential scenarios in which India reduces its trade barriers are analyzed.

Under the first scenario, tariffs on imports of intermediate goods are lowered to the 25th percentile of major economies in the Asia-Pacific. The second scenario assumes NTBs on imports of services are lowered to the 25th percentile of the same group.[17] The second scenario involves much larger reductions in trade costs than in the first scenario and is harder to implement.

India sees significant aggregate gains under both liberalization scenarios (Figure 9.24). Real GDP and real exports increase by around 2 percent and 37 percent, respectively, in the first scenario and by 2 percent and 36 percent,

---

[16] NTBs on services are those estimated by Fontagné, Mitaritonna, and Signoret (2016) for 2011.

[17] NTBs are considered in construction, wholesale and retail trade, transportation, and communication, and financial and other services.

Figure 9.23. Average Effective Tariffs and Tariff-Equivalent Nontariff Barriers

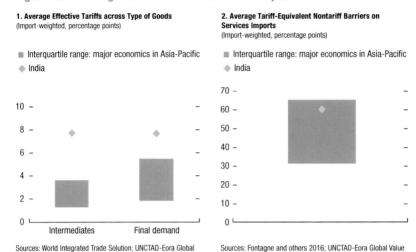

1. Average Effective Tariffs across Type of Goods
(Import-weighted, percentage points)

■ Interquartile range: major economics in Asia-Pacific
◆ India

2. Average Tariff-Equivalent Nontariff Barriers on Services Imports
(Import-weighted, percentage points)

■ Interquartile range: major economics in Asia-Pacific
◆ India

Sources: World Integrated Trade Solution; UNCTAD-Eora Global Value Chain database; and IMF staff estimates.

Sources: Fontagne and others 2016; UNCTAD-Eora Global Value Chain database; and IMF staff estimates.

respectively, in the second scenario. The first scenario indicates that reducing tariffs on intermediate goods would disproportionately favor export-driven sectors, particularly those that benefit from cheaper inputs, while the second scenario shows a stronger expansion of goods-producing sectors with strong linkages to services and a mild contraction of some services sectors.

Within India, gains are unevenly distributed across sectors.

- Under scenario 1, sectors with strong input linkages to intermediate goods see their sectoral real GDP and real exports rise in the same direction. Sectors producing mostly intermediate inputs face increased competition from abroad and grow relatively less (for example, mining, which contracts, or wood and paper). At the same time, mid/downstream sectors such as metals, oil and chemicals, textiles, and transport equipment, which includes autos and airplanes, thrive with strengthened comparative advantage. Some services also expand strongly, such as construction and wholesale and retail trade, because of their strong links to goods-producing sectors.

- Under scenario 2, the value added of several services industries falls such as in business services (included in other services) and transport and communication because of increased international competition. Some goods-producing sectors such as transport equipment, oil and chemicals, metals, or mining see large increases in their real value added and exports because of their strong linkages with now more efficient services, particularly logistics (wholesale and retail trade).

The sectoral export and GDP gains highlighted by the trade model simulations are only possible with costless reallocation of labor across sectors (and firms and firm entry/exit). Structural reforms can support manufacturing exports and

Figure 9.24. Scenarios on Sectoral Effects on Real GDP and Exports

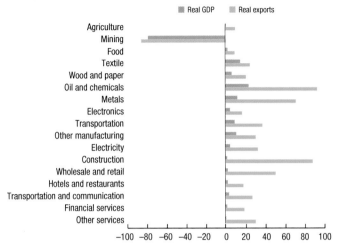

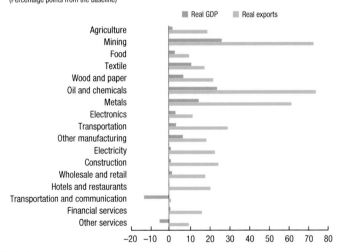

Source: IMF staff estimates.

job creation by reducing policy-induced frictions, preventing resource reallocation from less productive (sectors or firms) to more productive units. Relative to
its emerging market peers in the Asia-Pacific region, India has stricter market
regulations across most areas, including labor regulations (Figure 9.25). Realizing
the gains from reducing NTBs in service sectors and facilitating the "servicification" of manufacturing would also require further opening up sectors to FDI
where restrictions are particularly severe.

Figure 9.25. Indicators of the Stringency of Market Regulations in India versus the Average of the Top Two Emerging Markets in Asia-Pacific with Least Stringent Regulations

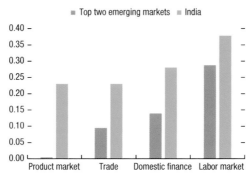

Source: IMF staff calculations.

Trade liberalization in India would provide a conducive environment for deeper regional integration in South Asia and the formation of regional supply chains as observed in East Asia and ASEAN+3 countries. Tariffs are higher in India than rest of South Asia, thus preferential trading arrangements with South Asian neighbors provide those economies access to the larger Indian market, especially for consumption goods. However, the high NTBs in India may still hinder intra-regional trade. It is important to note that integration to GVCs would be impeded as India would not be able to play the role of a hub for regional supply chains as China, Germany, and the United States do because of higher trade costs, although the rest of South Asia may be competitive in supplying the intermediate goods.

CONCLUSIONS

Boosting trade and value chain participation will be critical for India and South Asia to overcome the scarring of COVID-19 on potential growth and provide jobs to the growing working-age population in the post–COVID-19 global economy. Despite strong services trade, job-rich manufacturing export growth has remained tepid, reflecting India's muted GVC participation and lack of regional supply chains within South Asia. That said, India's export basket has gradually become more complex, with significant potential now for expansion to new industries if accompanied by steadfast and coherent reforms.

Deepening GVC integration and complementary structural reforms can boost productivity, formal employment, and exports, thereby creating a virtuous cycle of productivity growth and strong export performance. Trade and investment reforms in India will be pivotal to raise competitiveness and act as a hub for regional supply chains in South Asia and integration to the global economy as the ASEAN+3 economies achieved. The China-US trade and technology tensions and post–COVID-19 realignments in GVCs provide added opportunities especially in manufacturing and high-technology sectors. Realizing South Asia's century would require the following:

- Reducing tariffs and nontariff barriers, while minimizing trade policy uncertainty. In particular, lowering tariffs (customs duties) on intermediate goods would increase GVC integration through backward linkages and lift competitiveness of exports such as autos, chemicals, electronics, and industrial machinery.

- NTBs on services in India and the rest of South Asia are comparatively high, and a coordinated reduction could unleash regional supply chains and benefit from the post–COVID-19 remote technology economy and servicification of manufacturing.

- Creating an ecosystem for GVC participation along with deeper backward linkages to broaden the focus from "Make in India for India," to "Make in India for the World." Accordingly, energy, logistics, port facilities, and customs will need to be aligned to attract foreign companies to locate in India.

- Revisiting India's approach to plurilateral, regional, and bilateral trade agreements to link with global and regional supply chains as well as market access for key products.

- Accelerating ongoing efforts to increase labor market flexibility, including to shift employment regulations to protect workers instead of jobs, to facilitate a reallocation of labor.

REFERENCES

Athukorala, Prema-Chandra. 2014. "How India Fits into Global Production Sharing: Experience, Prospects and Policy Options." *India Policy Forum* 57–116.

Boz, Emine, Nan Li, and Hongrui Zhang. "Effective Trade Costs and the Current Account: An Empirical Analysis." IMF Working Paper 2019/008, International Monetary Fund, Washington, DC.

Caliendo, Lorenzo, Robert C. Feenstra, John Romalis, and Alan Taylor. 2017. "Tariff Reductions, Entry, and Welfare: Theory and Evidence for the Last Two Decades." CEPR Discussion Paper, Centre for Economic Policy Research, London, UK.

Caselli, Francesco, and Nicola Gennaioli. 2008. "Economics and Politics of Alternative Institutional Reforms." *Quarterly Journal of Economics* 123 (3): 1197–1250.

Christiansen, Lone, Martin Schindler, and Thierry Tressel. 2013. "Growth and Structural Reforms: A New Assessment." *Journal of International Economics* 89 (2): 347–56.

Cerdeiro, Diego A., and Rachel J. Nam. 2018. "A Multidimensional Approach to Trade Policy Indicators." IMF Working Paper 18/32, International Monetary Fund, Washington, DC.

Cerdeiro, Diego A., Rui Mano, Johannes Eugster, Dirk V. Muir, and Shanaka J. Peiris. 2021. "Sizing Up the Effects of Technological Decoupling." IMF Working Paper 2021/069, International Monetary Fund, Washington, DC.

Criscuolo, Chiara, and Jonathan Timmis. 2017. "The Relationship Between Global Value Chains and Productivity." *International Productivity Monitor* 32: 61–83.

Dabla-Norris, Era, Giang Ho, Kalpana Kochhar, Annette J. Kyobe, and Robert Tchaidze. 2013. "Anchoring Growth: The Importance of Productivity-Enhancing Reforms in Emerging Market and Developing Economies." IMF Staff Discussion Note 2013/008, International Monetary Fund, Washington, DC.

Djankov, Simeon, and Peter Murrell. 2002. "Enterprise Restructuring in Transition: A Quantitative Survey." *Journal of Economic Literature* 40 (3): 739–92.

Eaton, Jonathan, and Samuel Kortum. 2002. "Technology, Geography, and Trade." *Econometrica* 70: 1741–79.

Fontagné, Lionel, Cristina Mitaritonna, and José E. Signoret. 2016. "Estimated Tariff Equivalents of Services NTMs." CEPII Working Paper 2016–20, Centre d'Etudes Prospectives et d'Informations Internationales, Paris, France.

Gopinath, Gita, and Amartya Lahiri. 2019. "India's Exports." In *What the Economy Needs Now*, edited by Abhijit Bannerjee, Gita Gopinath, Raghuram Rajan, and Mihir Sharma. New Delhi, India: Juggernaut.

Goretti, Manuela, Daisaku Kihara, and Ranil Salgado. 2019. "Is South Asia Ready for Take Off? A Sustainable and Inclusive Growth Agenda." IMF Departmental Paper 19/18, International Monetary Fund, Washington, DC.

Grossman, Gene M., and Esteban Rossi-Hansberg. 2008. "Trading Tasks: A Simple Theory of Offshoring." *American Economic Review* 98 (5): 1978–97.

International Monetary Fund (IMF). 2015. "Reaping the Benefits from Global Value Chains." In *Regional Economic Outlook: Asia and Pacific* (Chapter 2). International Monetary Fund, Washington, DC.

International Monetary Fund (IMF). 2018c. "Scenario Box 1: Global Trade Tensions." *In World Economic Outlook, Challenges to Steady Growth.* Washington, DC: IMF, October.

International Monetary Fund (IMF). 2018b. "Regional Economic Outlook: Asia and Pacific Background Paper No. 2—The Evolving Role of Trade in Asia: Opening a New Chapter." IMF, Washington, DC.

International Monetary Fund (IMF). 2018a. "Is Productivity Growth Shared in a Globalized Economy?" In *World Economic Outlook: Cyclical Upswing, Structural Change.* Washington, DC: IMF, April.

International Monetary Fund (IMF), World Bank, and World Trade Organization. 2017. *Making Trade an Engine of Growth for All: The Case for Trade and for Policies to Facilitate Adjustment.* Washington, DC: International Monetary Fund.

International Monetary Fund (IMF), World Bank, and World Trade Organization. 2019. *The Future of Services Trade.* Washington, DC: International Monetary Fund.

Kinda, Tidiane. 2019. "E-commerce as a Potential New Engine for Growth in Asia." IMF Working Paper 201919/135, International Monetary Fund, Washington, DC.

Lian, Weicheng, Natalija Novta, Evgenia Pugacheva, Yannick Timmer, and Petia Topalova. 2020. "The Price of Capital Goods: A Driver of Investment under Threat." *IMF Economic Review* 68 (3): 509–49.

Mercer-Blackman, Valerie, and Christine Ablaza. 2018. "The Servicification of Manufacturing in Asia: Redefining the Sources of Labor Productivity." ADBI Working Paper Series 902, Asian Development Bank Institute, Tokyo, Japan.

Ministry of Commerce and Industry, Government of India. 2019. "Report of the High-Level Advisory Group." New Delhi.

Ministry of Finance, Government of India. 2019. "Nourishing Dwarfs to become Giants: Reorienting policies for MSME Growth." Economic Survey 2019–20. New Delhi. https://www.indiabudget.gov.in/budget2019-20/economicsurvey/doc/vol1chapter/echap03_vol1.pdf.

Ministry of Finance, Government of India. 2020. "Creating Jobs and Growth by Specializing to Exports in Network Products." Economic Survey 2019–20, New Delhi, India.

Panagariya, Arvind. 2004. "Growth and Reforms during 1980s and 1990s." *Economic and Political Weekly* 39 (25): 2581–94.

Raei, M.F., Ignatenko, A. and Mircheva, M., 2019. Global Value Chains: What are the Benefits and Why Do Countries Participate? International Monetary Fund.

Rajan, Raghuram, and Luigi Zingales. 1998. "Financial Development and Growth." *American Economic Review* 88 (3): 559–86.

Organisation for Economic Co-operation and Development (OECD). 2012. "Trade, Growth and Jobs." Summary of the OECD/ICITE Report on Policy Priorities for International Trade and Jobs, OECD, Paris, France.

Organisation for Economic Co-operation and Development (OECD). 2015. "The Participation of Developing Countries in Global Value Chains: Implications for Trade and Trade-Related Policies." OECD Trade Policy Paper 179, OECD, Paris, France.

Veeramani, C. and Garima Dhir. 2017. "Domestic Value-Added Content of India's Exports: Estimates for 112 Sectors, 1999–2000 to 2012–13. Mumbai, India: Indira Gandhi Institute of Development Research.

World Bank. 2020. *World Development Report 2020: Trading for Development in the Age of Global Value Chains.* World Bank.

World Trade Organization. 2019. "World Trade Report 2019: The Future of Services Trade." Geneva: World Trade Organization.

CHAPTER 10

Fostering Regional Trade Integration between South Asia and East Asia for COVID-19 Recovery

Ganeshan Wignaraja

Since the 1990s, South Asia–East Asia trade and free trade agreements have accelerated as India's trade realigned toward East Asia. As regional trade recovers after the COVID-19 pandemic, South Asian economies have opportunities to participate in global value chains and services trade. Regional trade integration across Asia can be encouraged by gradually reducing barriers to goods and services trade and investing in modern special economic zones, supported with adjustment financing and technical assistance to losing sectors to reallocate factors of production. Pursuing comprehensive free trade agreements eventually leading to the Regional Comprehensive Economic Partnership can provide for regional rules-based trade to help insure against rising protectionist tendencies. A reinvented trade-focused Bay of Bengal Initiative for Multi-Sectoral Technical and Economic Cooperation (BIMSTEC) may catalyze more effective regional cooperation for small and large economies alike. Narrower geographical coverage between South Asian and Southeast Asian economies could act as a building block for eventual trade integration across Asia. To avoid potential backlash against regionalization, special attention should also be paid to ensuring actual gains from trade for South Asia's smaller and poorer economies.

INTRODUCTION

Historically, South Asia is described as having one of the lowest levels of trade integration in the world and the South Asian Free Trade Area (SAFTA) is believed to have had little success in facilitating intraregional trade (Jain and Singh 2009; Kathuria 2018). The backlash against open trade and economic disruptions during

The author is most grateful for comments from IMF staff, particularly Rahul Anand, Ritu Basu, Eugenio Cerutti, Abdul Mannan, Racha Moussa, Shanaka Peiris, Ranil Salgado, and Fan Qi. Vaishali Ashtakala and Chatuni Pabasara deserve thanks for efficient research assistance. The views expressed here are solely those of the author and not to be attributed to the institutions to which I am associated.

the COVID-19 pandemic has also stifled nascent regionalism in South Asia. Sri Lanka reviewed its free trade agreement (FTA) with Singapore in February 2020 after domestic concerns. Underlying India's unease about trade with China, it withdrew from Regional Comprehensive Economic Partnership (RCEP) negotiations in November 2019 (Gupta and Ganguly 2020). Maldives restricted trade with China since 2018 and is talking about Scrapping its landmark FTA with China. The pandemic has exposed the fragility of apparel value chains in South Asia (for example, sickness among workers and intermediate goods shortages) that were recalibrating to vulnerabilities of global value chains (GVCs) (Castañeda-Navarrete, Hauge, and López-Gómez 2021). Nonetheless, signs of a recovery in Asia's trade have renewed interest in regional trade integration across Asia (WTO 2021).

Recent developments have reignited a policy debate on fostering closer regional trade integration involving South and East Asian economies for COVID-19 recovery. Important questions are: What is the state of play in regional trade integration? What policies aid regional trade recovery? Can South Asia gain from integrating with East Asia? This chapter addresses these questions in regional trade integration across Asia in COVID times by examining trends, obstacles, and model-based studies.[1] The second section looks at the history of regional economic integration, regional trade flows and free trade agreements (FTAs), and the outlook. The third section analyze obstacles to regional trade integration in areas such as trade barriers, special economic zones (SEZs), FTAs, and regional institutions. The fourth section reviews the findings from model-based studies. The final part concludes. South Asia is defined here as the eight members of the South Asian Association for Regional Cooperation (SAARC): Afghanistan, Bangladesh, Bhutan, India, Maldives, Nepal, Pakistan, and Sri Lanka. East Asia consists of the 10 members of the Association of Southeast Asian Nations (ASEAN), China, Japan, Korea, Taiwan Province of China, and Hong Kong Special Administrative Region.

TRADE INTEGRATION BETWEEN SOUTH ASIA AND EAST ASIA: STATE OF PLAY

A Brief History of Regional Trade Integration

South and East Asia had divergent views of the benefits of globalization after the Second World War. After independence from British colonial rule in 1947, India and Pakistan adopted import-substituting industrialization strategies with high import tariffs and pervasive state intervention. Business and exports were shackled by an antiexport bias in the trade regime. Influenced by prevailing anti-globalization economic philosophy, the smaller South Asian economies, to varying degrees, also adopted a similar development strategy. Growth and trade in inward-oriented South Asia largely stagnated. Meanwhile, after a short import

---

[1] The analysis in this chapter draws from Francois, Rana, and Wignaraja (2009); Wignaraja (2014); and Plummer, Morgan, and Wignaraja (2016).

substitution period, East Asian economies (initially Korea and Taiwan Province of China, and then ASEAN) switched to outward-oriented market-friendly development strategies in the 1960s and 1970s. By embracing globalization, East Asia experienced the so-called "Asian economic miracle" of rapid growth, a shift into manufacturing for export and rising living standards (World Bank 1993).

The relative isolation between South Asia and East Asia meant that regional trade integration was not on the agenda (Rana and Dowling 2009). Regional trade flows were limited, and the 1975 Asia-Pacific Trade Agreement (APTA) was the only FTA between the two regions. The absence of ties is because of a lack of political signals to foster South Asia–East Asia integration, trade and investment barriers, poor regional connectivity, and cultural and linguistic barriers.

The period since 1990 was marked by intensifying efforts at regional integration across Asia. Several factors explain the shift in regionalism priorities (Francois, Rana, and Wignaraja 2009; Dasgupta, Pitigala, and Gourdon 2012; Rana and Chia 2015; McKinsey Global Institute 2019; De 2020).

First, South Asia's adoption of more outward-oriented development strategies encouraged greater global and regional trade ties. Sri Lanka was the earliest in South Asia to undertake reforms in 1977 in an attempt to promote FDI and exports. Bangladesh began implementing reforms in the early 1980s while Pakistan's major reforms came in 1988. Although India began partial reforms in the 1980s, major reforms started only in 1991. Afghanistan, Bhutan, Nepal, and Maldives undertook various partial reforms in the 1990s and 2000s. Studies (for example, Rana and Chia 2015) have argued that the first generation of reforms in many South Asian countries focused on macroeconomic issues such as monetary, fiscal, and exchange rate management. However, they were not followed by the so-called second-generation reforms, that is more micro-economic reforms involving deregulation at a sectoral level as well as measures to improve governance and institutions. Accordingly, the first generation of reforms soon ran out of steam with business being hampered by red tape, rent seeking behavior as well as law and order issues.

Second, India's adoption of a "Look East Policy" and an outward-orientated economy in 1991 marked the start of a new phase in regional ties. India's Look East Policy signaled its intent to revitalize its cultural, defense and economic relations with globally important East Asia. India's Act East Policy took effect when Prime Minister Narendra Modi at his maiden visit to ASEAN-India Summit in 2014 emphasized on practicing more action-oriented policy toward ASEAN and the wider East Asia. The Act East Policy is more akin to a deepening of the Look East Policy rather than a strict foreign policy shift. India's moves have catalyzed policy interest in Asian integration. Several FTAs have taken effect to liberalize intra-Asian trade and investment including the historic 2010 ASEAN-India Comprehensive Economic Cooperation Agreement. These agreements were motivated by a desire to advance trade liberalization beyond World Trade Organization (WTO) disciplines and increasing recognition in South Asia of the market opportunities in dynamic East Asia.

Third, financial crises have encouraged widespread economic restructuring particularly in East Asia. In the decade after the 1997–98 Asian financial crisis,

East Asia reemerged into the global economy characterized by rapid growth, high productivity, significant flows of export-oriented FDI, and increasingly localized GVCs geared toward regional markets. After the global financial crisis of 2008–09, East Asian and South Asian economies have attempted to rebalance trade and FDI toward faster growing regional economies and away from slower growing advanced economies. China and India have increased their bilateral economic ties and have acted as growth poles in their respective subregions. ASEAN has become increasingly internally integrated, at least in trade in goods through the ASEAN Free Trade Agreement (AFTA) and has played a growing role as a regional economic integration hub with larger neighbors.

Fourth, China's offshoring of GVCs to other parts of Asia. Supplies of cost-competitive skilled labor and falling trade costs amid technological progress and productivity gains have helped spur the fragmentation of manufacturing activities throughout East Asia through GVCs and trade in intermediate goods. The first wave of GVC activity involved Japanese firms offshoring segments of automotive and electronics manufacturing to economies such as Korea, Malaysia, Taiwan Province of China, and Thailand. A second wave of GVC activity followed China's opening to export-oriented FDI and membership of the WTO in 2001. Regional GVC activity naturally gravitated to a rapidly growing Chinese economy that emerged as Asia's central assembly hub. A third and more recent wave of GVC activity was driven by rising labor costs in China and an intensifying US–China trade war, which is encouraging offshoring of some labor-intensive segments of GVCs from China to lower wage parts of Asia including Bangladesh, India, and Sri Lanka.

The other part of the China trade story with South Asia are trade spillovers from China's 2013 Belt and Road Initiative (BRI). India is not a part of the BRI, reflecting the complex nature of China–India relations, which have both competitive and cooperative elements. India has also expressed concerns about the economic and geopolitical implications of BRI projects in its South Asian neighborhood. This ambitious transcontinental connectivity initiative is financing important infrastructure projects throughout the rest of South Asia. Such projects seek to strengthen the trade capacity of South Asian countries (such as the building of ports, roads, bridges, and power plants).[2] However, the fiscal sustainability of BRI projects with long gestation periods could raise the risk of debt distress in some borrowers such as Nepal, Pakistan, and Sri Lanka (see the country papers in Pant and Saha 2021). Another study shows that Sri Lanka's external debt problems stem from borrowing from international capital markets rather than Chinese BRI projects per se (see Wignaraja and others 2020). Nonetheless, the same study also highlights the high content of capital and intermediate goods imports by Chinese state-owned enterprises operating in Sri Lanka, which has spurred rising trade imbalances between Sri Lanka and China. Further research is needed to unpack the trade effects of BRI projects in South Asia.

---

[2] Examples included the Gwadar Port in Pakistan as a part of the ambitious China–Pakistan Economic Corridor Hambantota Port and Industrial Zone in Sri Lanka and the Sinamale Bridge in Maldives.

Figure 10.1. Total Merchandise Trade between South Asia and East Asia, 1990–2023F

(US billion dollars)

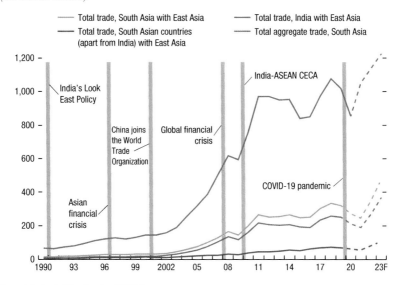

Source: Author's calculations based on IMF (2021).
Note: The "F" indicates a forecast. The 2020 and 2021 forecasts for total trade were calculated using percentage change in trade during the periods of 2008–09 and 2009–10, respectively. ASEAN = Association of Southeast Asian Nations; CECA = Comprehensive Economic Cooperation Agreement.

Mapping Regional Trade Integration

South Asia–East Asia trade has been one of the most dynamic areas of world trade over the past three decades. Although from a small base, total merchandise trade between South Asia and East Asia (in US dollar terms) grew rapidly at 10.2 percent per year between 1990 and 2020 to reach $271.4 billion in 2020 (see Figure 10.1).[3] Reflecting fluctuations in business cycles, this trade experienced spurts in inter-global economic crisis periods. In the decade between the Asian and global financial crises, the value of South Asia–East Asia trade steadily expanded from $28.3 billion (1998) to $164.6 billion (2008). The decade between the global financial crisis and the COVID-19 economic crisis saw a more volatile regional trade expansion, which peaked at $331.7 billion (2018). The initial onset of the COVID pandemic, however, marked a watershed moment, causing trade between South Asia and East Asia to fall by $47.2 billion between 2019 and 2020. The outlook for regional trade integration is discussed in the following paragraphs.

It is not surprising that South Asia's trade integration with East Asia has been led by South Asia's largest and most dynamic economy. In 1990, India accounted for 51.5 percent of the value of South Asia's total trade with East Asia. By 2020, India's

---

[3] Merchandise trade is exports and imports of goods. Estimated using the compound annual growth rate method.

role in such trade increased to 78.0 percent. The collective share of the next three major economies (Pakistan, Bangladesh, and Sri Lanka) halved from 43.2 percent to 20.2 percent over the same period. Meanwhile, the collective share of the region's four smallest economies (Nepal, Maldives, Afghanistan, and Bhutan) fell from 5.3 percent to 1.8 percent. These economies may suffer from a potential disadvantages of small country size reflected in tiny domestic markets with little purchasing power or production capacity as well as adverse geographical circumstances such as being sea-locked (as in Maldives) or landlocked (as in the case of the other three).

South Asian exports from East Asia have significantly lagged the growth of its imports from East Asia resulting in a widening trade gap between the two sub-regions. Table 1 shows that the value of South Asia's exports to East Asia amounted to $74.7 billion in 2020 (up from about $5 billion in 1990). Meanwhile, the value of South Asia's imports from East Asia amounted to $196.8 billion in 2020 (up from $9.9 billion in 1990). The share of South Asia's total exports to East Asia increased modestly from 18.1 percent to 21.9 percent between 1990 and 2020 while there was a notable rise in the share of total imports from 25.4 percent to 39.6 percent.

Underlying South Asia's tilt toward trade with East Asia is a significant realignment of India's trade toward East Asia and away from other world markets. In 1990, trade with East Asia accounted for 18.3 percent of India's exports and 18.2 percent of its imports (see Table 10.1). By 2020, these shares had increased to 24.7 percent of India's exports and 39.0 percent of its imports. India's experience points to trade with East Asia offering a potentially dramatic enlargement of its economic horizons, making available a far greater regional market with which it can integrate. South Asia's other three major economies (Pakistan, Bangladesh, and Sri Lanka) have an increasing reliance on East Asia as a source of imports but have had difficulty exporting to East Asia. Meanwhile, the region's smallest economies (for example, Afghanistan, Bhutan, and Nepal) are at the early stages of trading with East Asia but are characterized by high import shares and volatile export shares.

In East Asia, Japan and China have swapped places as engines of South Asia–East Asia trade (see Table 10.2). In 1990, Asia's only developed economy, Japan, was prominent, providing 36.5 percent of East Asia's total exports to South Asia and absorbing 57.2 percent of East Asia's imports from South Asia. By 2020, Japan's shares had declined to 6.2 percent of the region's exports to South Asia and 8.7 percent of its imports from South Asia. In 1990, China was a much smaller trader with 9.9 percent of its region's exports to South Asia and 4.3 percent of its region's imports from South Asia. However, China's global rise had propelled its export share to 52.4 percent and its import share to 32.4 percent. Adding Hong Kong Special Administrative Region raises the combined China and Hong Kong Special Administrative Region share in their region's exports to as much as 60.5 percent and 42.8 percent of their region's imports.

Another notable development has been the rise of other East Asian players in regional trade over the past 30 years, including Indonesia, Korea, Singapore, and Malaysia. The value of trade with South Asia of each of these economies was similar to that of Japan in 2020.

Furthermore, growing trade with South Asia has resulted in only a small tilt in East Asia's direction of trade over time. Thus, in 2020, South Asia accounted

TABLE 10.1.

Merchandise Trade between South Asia and East Asia

(Millions of dollars)

	South Asia Exports to East Asia				South Asia Imports from East Asia			
	1990	2008	2019	2020	1990	2008	2019	2020
South Asia	**4,945.0**	**50,631.3**	**82,229.5**	**74,680.0**	**9,859.1**	**113,941.8**	**236,364.1**	**196,762.9**
India	3,263.4	47,203.1	74,728.5	68,179.9	4,359.4	86,165.6	175,829.4	143,373.8
Pakistan	1,262.0	2,102.1	3,614.2	3,204.3	2,073.4	11,767.3	20,154.5	20,755.5
Bangladesh	171.1	544.2	2,405.4	2,096.6	1,466.9	10,132.0	25,524.4	20,563.7
Sri Lanka	211.9	667.5	1,309.7	1,016.8	1,207.4	3,463.8	8,894.1	7,226.0
Nepal	16.7	38.0	68.2	42.8	335.6	807.4	2,712.4	2,235.5
Maldives	17.2	69.4	68.2	80.7	100.8	570.3	1,290.6	767.1
Afghanistan	2.6	2.3	32.6	56.3	315.7	939.8	1,867.9	1,708.3
Bhutan	-	4.7	2.6	2.6	-	95.5	90.8	132.9
	East Asia Share of Total South Asia Exports (%)				East Asia Share of Total South Asia Imports (%)			
	1990	2008	2019	2020	1990	2008	2019	2020
East Asia	**18.1**	**21.1**	**20.6**	**21.9**	**25.4**	**27.9**	**37.5**	**39.6**
India	18.3	24.2	23.0	24.7	18.2	26.8	36.6	39.0
Pakistan	22.6	10.4	15.5	14.4	28.1	27.8	40.3	45.3
Bangladesh	10.2	4.0	6.7	6.8	40.1	42.5	46.3	44.8
Sri Lanka	11.2	7.5	10.9	9.4	45.8	29.3	44.5	45.1
Nepal	7.9	4.2	7.0	4.9	57.2	22.3	20.7	20.4
Maldives	33.0	54.2	43.2	49.5	73.1	41.0	44.7	41.7
Afghanistan	2.0	0.4	3.8	7.3	65.9	31.0	27.6	26.1
Bhutan	-	0.9	0.5	0.7	-	17.6	3.4	5.4

Source: IMF 2021.
Note: Direction of Trade Data on Taiwan Province of China is limited. Taiwan Province of China is not listed as a reporting economy.

for 4.0 percent of China's exports and 1.2 percent of its imports and 1.9 percent of Japan's exports and 1.0 percent of its imports. These shares have increased modestly over figures for 1990. Likewise, Korea, Singapore, and Malaysia also conducted relatively small amounts of their global trade with South Asia. However, Indonesia is an exception, particularly on the export side, with South Asia accounting for 11.8 percent of its exports[4] and 2.8 percent of its imports in 2020.

The commodity composition of trade between South Asian and East Asian economies tends to reflect inter-country differences in factor endowments[5]

---

[4] Indonesia's exports of commodities and processed raw materials to India dominates its exports to South Asia. In 2020, Indonesia's exports to India consisted of petroleum and petroleum products ($3.7 billion), animal and vegetable oils ($3.1 billion), chemicals ($705.2 million), and metals ($464.1 million). See https://tradingeconomics.com/indonesia/exports/india.

[5] The analyses of Scollay and Pelkmans-Balaoing (2009) and Dasgupta, Pitigala, and Gourdon (2012) analyze revealed comparative advantages at the product level in South and East Asian trade. They concluded that South Asian economies exhibit a relatively narrow range of comparative advantages compared with East Asia.

TABLE 10.2.

Merchandise Trade between East Asia and South Asia

(Millions of dollars)

Reporting Economy	East Asia Exports to South Asia				East Asia Imports from South Asia			
	1990	2008	2019	2020	1990	2008	2019	2020
China	973.1	44,253.5	114,968.2	103,057.5	213.4	21,548.5	21,307.5	24,194.5
Hong Kong SAR	809.7	8,016.6	18,332.1	15,949.2	914.9	8,132.4	10,490.2	7,747.3
Taiwan Province of China	597.8	3,718.2	5,827.7	5,298.4	130.6	1,853.8	1,745.4	1,673.7
Japan	3,602.7	10,742.8	14,377.8	12,222.3	2,827.0	6,128.5	7,489.9	6,514.8
Korea	1,152.0	11,645.7	17,554.5	14,331.9	482.4	7,442.9	6,489.4	5,639.4
ASEAN	**3,680.2**	**42,903.7**	**67,132.3**	**52,469.6**	**1,942.1**	**21,259.7**	**31,471.7**	**27,637.6**
Brunei Darussalam	1.2	338.3	610.9	418.0	1.4	21.5	120.2	79.5
Cambodia	3.2	5.9	74.0	65.0	1.9	110.7	244.9	176.7
Indonesia	201.2	9,337.4	16,115.2	14,821.8	289.9	3,042.1	4,810.5	4,063.7
Lao P.D.R.	0.4	0.8	3.3	2.5	0.3	4.7	32.2	30.0
Malaysia	873.1	10,399.3	13,648.0	10,522.5	260.9	3,333.1	6,416.8	6,464.6
Myanmar	63.1	1,053.1	793.1	823.8	3.5	193.1	757.7	753.5
Philippines	7.3	319.4	655.0	634.8	148.3	783.1	2,168.7	2,307.6
Singapore	2,226.8	15,789.2	17,175.0	10,964.9	550.5	8,704.9	6,768.7	4,395.7
Thailand	283.6	5,088.2	10,089.1	7,677.5	681.1	2,878.1	5,391.3	4,632.4
Vietnam	20.3	572.1	7,968.7	6,538.6	4.3	2,188.4	4,760.8	4,733.9

Reporting Economy	South Asia Share of Total East Asia Exports (%)				South Asia Share of Total East Asia Imports (%)			
	1990	2008	2019	2020	1990	2008	2019	2020
China	1.6	3.1	4.6	4.0	0.4	1.9	1.0	1.2
Hong Kong SAR	1.0	2.2	3.4	2.9	1.1	2.1	1.8	1.4
Taiwan Province of China	0.8	1.2	1.2	1.0	0.3	0.9	0.7	0.6
Japan	1.3	1.4	2.0	1.9	1.2	0.8	1.0	1.0
Korea	1.7	2.8	3.2	2.8	0.6	1.7	1.3	1.2
ASEAN	**2.5**	**4.3**	**4.7**	**4.0**	**1.2**	**2.3**	**2.2**	**2.2**
Brunei Darussalam	0.1	3.2	8.4	6.3	0.1	0.8	2.4	1.5
Cambodia	7.6	0.1	0.5	0.4	3.4	2.5	1.2	0.9
Indonesia	0.8	6.8	9.6	9.0	1.3	2.4	2.8	2.8
Lao P.D.R.	0.6	0.1	0.1	0.0	0.2	0.2	0.4	0.5
Malaysia	3.0	5.2	5.7	4.5	0.9	2.1	3.1	3.4
Myanmar	15.4	13.4	4.4	4.8	0.5	3.8	4.1	4.3
Philippines	0.1	0.7	0.9	0.9	1.1	1.3	1.8	1.7
Singapore	4.2	4.7	4.4	3.8	0.9	2.7	1.9	1.7
Thailand	1.2	2.9	4.1	3.3	2.0	1.6	2.3	2.2
Vietnam	0.8	0.9	3.1	2.3	0.2	2.7	1.9	1.7

Source: IMF 2021.
Note: Direction of Trade Data on Taiwan province of China is limited. Taiwan is not listed as a reporting economy.

(natural resources, capital, labor, and technology) and levels of industrial development. With an abundance of natural resources and labor, South Asia's exports to East Asia tend to be weighted toward such products. Meanwhile, South Asia's imports from East Asia mainly consist of finished and high-technology goods reflecting an abundance of capital and technology. Differences in factor endowments are not the only cause of trade, scale economies and imperfect competition need to be included in explaining South Asia–East Asia trade patterns.

TABLE 10.3.

South Asia's Top Traded Commodities with East Asia
(Share of total exports)

		India		Pakistan		Sri Lanka	
HS Commodity Code	Commodity Description	2000	2019	2003	2019	2000	2019
52	Cotton	7.0	3.0	47.1	29.0	1.0	0.1
27	Mineral fuels, mineral oils, and products of their distillation	0.0	16.3	6.8	3.8	4.9	6.4
3	Fish and crustaceans	12.6	4.0	4.8	10.7	21.6	4.8
10	Cereals	0.2	0.3	4.1	11.7	0.0	0.1
29	Organic chemicals	1.0	10.0	3.6	0.0	0.0	0.0
84	Nuclear reactors, boilers, machinery, and mechanical appliances; parts thereof	0.1	6.7	0.4	1.5	23.6	0.6
89	Ships, boats, and floating structures	0.0	5.4	0.0	1.0	0.0	6.0
9	Coffee, tea, mate, and spices	0.9	1.4	0.1	0.1	7.2	11.0
62	Articles of apparel and clothing accessories not knitted or crocheted	2.7	0.7	1.3	1.6	2.4	9.5
61	Articles of apparel and clothing accessories knitted or crocheted	0.6	0.3	0.6	2.9	1.5	10.1

		India		Pakistan		Sri Lanka	
HS Commodity Code	Commodity Description	2000	2019	2003	2019	2000	2019
85	Electrical machinery and equipment and parts thereof	10.6	21.6	6.2	17.9	10.7	10.9
84	Nuclear reactors, boilers, machinery, and mechanical appliances; parts thereof	13.4	16.2	14.9	14.3	11.5	10.1
87	Vehicles; other than railway or tramway	2.2	2.2	13.5	6.9	12.5	8.9
15	Animal or vegetable fats and oils	4.5	3.5	16.0	9.0	1.5	1.4
27	Mineral fuels, mineral oils, and products	5.7	8.7	1.3	4.1	6.2	13.5
29	Organic chemicals	3.9	8.2	8.6	5.8	0.7	1.4
39	Plastics and articles thereof	3.7	5.1	4.5	3.7	4.5	3.2
72	Iron and steel	6.8	4.4	2.6	5.2	1.4	2.6

Source: Author's calculations based on UN (2021) and Export Development Board, Sri Lanka (2021).
Note: HS refers to the Harmonized System (standardized international system to classify globally traded products).

To illustrate this pattern of trade, Table 10.3 provides the leading items in India, Pakistan, and Sri Lanka's trade with East Asia since 2000. The exports of Pakistan and Sri Lanka conform to the expected pattern of South Asian exports to East Asia. Pakistan's exports to East Asia are heavily concentrated in a handful of natural resource products (mineral fuels, cotton, fish, and cereals) and some labor-intensive products (apparel). Sri Lanka's leading exports are oriented toward natural resource products (mineral fuels, fish, and tea), labor-intensive products (apparel), and one technology intensive product (ships). Compared with the other two South Asian economies, however, India's exports to East Asia have become somewhat broad-based over time. Such exports include a mix of natural resource-intensive products (mineral fuel, cotton, fish, tea and coffee, cereals), labor-intensive products (apparel), and some technology-intensive products (chemicals, ships, and machinery).

In contrast, leading imports from East Asia to South Asia feature mainly technology-intensive products such as computers and integrated circuits; TV, radio, and telecommunications equipment; motor vehicles and motor vehicle parts; and chemicals and fuels. Where there is two-way trade in the same industry, partly reflecting the presence of large multinational firms engaged in GVC activities, East Asian exports are at a higher level of processing. For the steel industry, India's leading exports to East Asia include ferro-alloys, pig iron, and rolled steel; East Asia's leading imports from South Asia include rolled steel of a heavier grade.

While data on regional merchandise trade is readily available from international sources (such as the IMF Direction of Trade Statistics Database), data on regional services trade is limited. Kaur, Khorana, and Kaur (2020) using revealed comparative advantage indices, suggest that there is significant regional services trade potential particularly in South Asia. Thus, according to the authors, India has a competitive advantage in ICT and other business services; Maldives and Nepal in travel services; Bangladesh has competitiveness in government services; and Pakistan and Sri Lanka in transport services.

FTA-led regionalism is a recent development in South Asia–East Asia trade relations (Scollay and Pelkmans-Balaoing 2009). APTA—previously known as the Bangkok Agreement signed in 1975—was the first agreement to link South Asia and East Asia. Its six members include Bangladesh, India, and Sri Lanka in South Asia and China, Korea, and Lao PDR in East Asia. Mongolia is set to become the seventh member in the future. As a sign of the lack of interest in cross-regional FTAs, however, it took another two decades for the next such agreement (the India-Singapore Comprehensive Economic Agreement) to take effect in 2005. Since then, there has been a modest increase in FTA activity to link the two regions.

Figure 10.2 provides a breakdown of FTA activity between the two regions since the mid-1970s according to their legal status[6]: (1) FTAs signed and in effect means that the provisions of FTAs have become effective or tariff rates have been liberalized, (2) FTAs only signed means the parties have signed the agreement but it is not yet in effect, (3) FTAs under negotiation means parties are engaging in formal negotiation or have signed framework agreements, and (4) FTAs proposed and under consultation means parties have jointly established working groups or conducted feasibility studies on FTAs. Annex Table 10.1 lists the individual agreements by legal status. Items (1) and (2) are defined as concluded FTAs while items (3) and (4) are future FTAs.

At the advent of the global financial crisis, there were only four South Asia–East Asia FTAs in 2008. This figure rose to 11 concluded FTAs by August 2021. The last such FTA was concluded in 2018 between Singapore and Sri Lanka. Thus, no new regional FTAs were concluded during the pandemic.

The awaking of interest in FTA-led regionalism between the two regions in the 2000s can be attributed to a combination of political and economic factors. The political factors include the desire of countries to strengthen bilateral

---

[6] This follows the classification shown in Kawai and Wignaraja (2011), page 7.

Figure 10.2. Growth in FTAs between South Asia and East Asia, by Legal Status
(Number of FTAs)

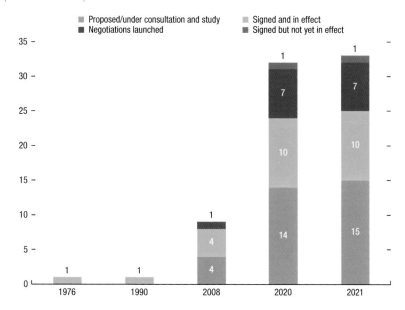

Source: Asian Development Bank 2021.
Note: See Annex Table 10.1 for definitions of FTA status. FTA = free trade agreement.

political and diplomatic relations across Asia (as exemplified by India's Look East Policy) and as a response to rising FTA activity in the Americas and Europe. The economic factors include an attempt to insure against rising protectionism globally in the wake of the stalled multilateral liberalization process under the WTO, a means to achieve liberalization of barriers to trade and GVCs in Asia beyond levels attainable under the WTO, and a strategic attempt by China and India to secure market access in dynamic Asian markets.

Of the 11 concluded FTAs, two are regional agreements (covering several countries in the two regions) while another nine are bilateral agreements (involving just two countries in South Asia and East Asia). The two regional agreements are APTA and the ASEAN India Comprehensive Economic Cooperation Agreement.

The larger economies in the two regions have been instrumental in the recent trend toward FTA-led regionalism. India is involved in six FTAs including four bilaterals with Japan, Korea, Singapore, and Malaysia and the two regionals with APTA members and ASEAN members. Pakistan has three bilaterals with China, Malaysia, and Indonesia. Sri Lanka is a member of APTA and has South Asia's most recent bilateral with Singapore (2018). Bangladesh's sole FTA is as a member of APTA.

Maldives signed a bilateral FTA with China in 2017, but it is not in effect Ministry of Commerce 2017). Its ratification by Maldives Parliament appears stalled because of internal political developments. Motivated by a more India-leaning new government, Maldives has expressed concerns about the lack of gains from the trade pact for Maldives.

There are also another 22 future South Asia–East Asia FTAs in August 2021 (see Annex Table 10.1). Proposing bilateral agreements with Malaysia and Thailand, Bangladesh is signaling its interest in FTAs with East Asian countries. Many of these future FTA talks, however, have been ongoing for some time with little visible progress in reaching agreement on difficult trade opening provisions beyond tariffs and moving the process toward signature.

COVID-19 and Regional Trade Integration

The onset of the COVID-19 pandemic in 2020 has precipitated an ongoing global economic crisis disrupting trade and the world economy in unimaginable ways. A sharp trade recovery followed by a slowdown is expected from the pandemic. The latest WTO projections released in October 2022 suggest that the volume of world merchandise trade increased by 9.7 percent in 2021 having fallen by 5.2 percent in 2020 (WTO 2022, Table 1). A revival in the world economy in the first half of 2021 raised merchandise trade above its prepandemic peak, partly linked to a strong rebound in Asia's trade. In 2021, Asia's exports grew at 13.3 percent and its imports at 11.1 percent. This is significantly up from Asia's 2020 figures. While world trade growth could slow to 3.5 percent in 2022, Asia's trade rebound is expected to spill over into South Asia–East Asia trade, but WTO (2022) does not provide regional trade projections.

One simple, intuitive projection method is to compare the economic shock of COVID-19 with the 2008–09 global financial crisis. Fortunately, data on the value of regional merchandise trade can be readily computed from the IMF Direction of Trade Statistics Database. The two crises have similarities but also differences. As with the global financial crisis, economies in South Asia and East Asia have implemented stimulus and social protection measures to tackle the fallout of COVID-19. The global financial crisis originated outside Asia and was transmitted to the region through the finance and trade channels. The COVID-19 pandemic was first identified in December 2019 in Wuhan, Hubei, China, and spread globally through travel and trade patterns. Closure of airports, quarantine measures, and lockdowns during the pandemic have produced a synchronized, global, sudden stop in economic activity and the shutdown of many sectors not seen during the global financial crisis.

As Figure 10.1 shows, the pandemic caused a hit on South Asia–East Asia trade. which contracted from $319 billion to $271.4 billion between 2019 and 2020. India-East Asia trade declined from $250.6 billion to $211.6 and that of the rest of South Asia–East Asia from $68.4 billion to $59.8 billion. Short-term projections for 2021–23 were obtained by applying the same trajectory in South Asia–East Asia trade as during the global financial crisis (see Figure 10.1). A V-shaped regional trade recovery scenario is suggested by this method underpinned by strong assumptions such as a relatively short pandemic (or at least a decline in infections) and an effective policy response. Under an optimistic scenario, South Asia–East Asia trade could increase to $478.9 billion around 2023. India–East Asia trade could amount to $368 billion and the rest of South Asia–East Asia trade for $110.9 billion. Thus, the value of regional trade could exceed to prepandemic levels within a couple of years.

This forecast indicates an upside scenario for regional trade integration across Asia. However, the reality could be different to the forecast as significant uncertainty exits. The duration of the pandemic, the emergence of new variants such as Omicron, and possible future lockdowns continue to be the biggest risks. Rising oil prices, supply-side disruptions to global supply chains in Asia (for example, semiconductor scarcity and port backlogs), trade and technology tensions between the United States and China, the economic fallout from the Russia–Ukraine conflict and debt distress in some South Asian countries (for example, Sri Lanka and Pakistan) could also unsettle regional trade integration.

OBSTACLES TO REGIONAL TRADE INTEGRATION

While some of these risks may be beyond the scope of public policy, important policy-related obstacles also exist at a national and regional level, including barriers to goods and services trade, gaps in SEZs, emerging challenges of FTAs, and institution-lite regionalism. Tackling these obstacles will help to support COVID-19 recovery in South Asia–East Asia trade integration.

Barriers to Goods and Services Trade

Asia's development experience over the past 50 years suggests that outward-oriented trade regimes are more conducive to global and regional trade integration than the alternatives (World Bank 1993; ADB 2008). Among other advantages, openness to goods and services trade encourages specialization according to comparative advantage, enables economies of scale, fosters FDI inflows and technology transfer and regionalization of supply chains.

With several economies initiating unilateral trade liberalization under economic reform programs, South Asia typically experienced falling import tariffs through the 1990s and early 2000s. Tepid global GDP growth after the global financial crisis coincided with sluggish global trade growth. Fears of unemployment in declining sectors have led to mounting public pressures for protectionism. As Table 10.4 shows, there is evidence of an intensification of tariff protection in South Asia since the global financial crisis. Between 2008 and 2019, India significantly raised its high tariffs on agricultural goods from 32.2 percent to 38.8 percent and on manufactured goods from 10.1 percent to 14.1 percent. Afghanistan followed suit. Bangladesh, Nepal, and Bhutan either raised or kept unchanged their high agricultural tariffs. Sri Lanka also raised agricultural tariffs but ramped up overall import protection by banning all nonessential imports in 2020 (such as vehicles and some food imports) in a bid to manage a foreign exchange crisis.[7] Meanwhile, Pakistan and Maldives lowered tariffs on both agricultural and manufactured goods. Two outliers in East Asia significantly raised agricultural tariffs with Korea's from 49 percent to 56.8 percent and Thailand's from 25.2 percent to 29 percent. The Philippines kept its low tariffs unchanged. It is striking, however, China lowered its tariffs on agricultural and manufactured goods (reflecting two decades of accession to the WTO). More generally, overall levels of tariff protection in South Asia in 2019 are generally higher than in East Asia.

Murky, nontariff measure (NTM)-based protection has accompanied rising tariffs. Measurement of NTMs is problematic as only head count data are available, which gives no indication of protective impacts of various measures. Interestingly, there seems to be a greater incidence of NTM-based protection in East Asia than in South Asia in recent years inclusive of the pandemic. During 2017–20, the numbers of NTMs implemented against global trading partners were 284 in China, 153 for Korea, 121 for the Philippines, and 88 in Thailand (see Table 10.4). In South Asia, however, only India (n=177) and Pakistan (n=45) were active users of NTM protection.

Rising protectionism is occurring against a backdrop of restricted trade in services in both regions. Measuring services trade restrictiveness is a difficult undertaking beset by data gaps and subjective judgments.[8] Keeping this qualification in mind, the data point to barriers inhibiting trade in services between the regions as indicated by a Services Trade Restrictiveness Index in Table 10.4. India[9] has greater restrictions on trade in services than large East Asian economies do, such as China, Japan, and Korea. Services trade restrictions in Bangladesh, Nepal, and Sri Lanka are slightly lower (or comparable) with levels in the Philippines, Indonesia, Thailand, and Malaysia. While some regulatory reforms have taken place in certain service sectors (such as telecommunications) in South Asia over the past decade, many restrictions still remain. The major change in these service sectors has been the reductions in constraints imposed on foreign equity participation in South Asia. Limited opening of services trade, particularly in South Asia, reflects concerns about the large costs of adjustment to liberalization of services trade on unemployment, poverty, and loss of universal access to basic

---

[7] Prolonged protection could have two adverse effects on Sri Lanka's trade. One is that it could misallocate resources and hinder exporting activities. Another is that it risks violating WTO rules and inviting retaliation from trading partners.

[8] The data for developing countries were collected using surveys in 2012, while OECD countries covered were taken from various publicly available sources such as General Agreement on Trade in Services commitments and offers, WTO reports, and Economic Intelligence Unit reports, among others. This attempts to capture the policies and regulations that discriminate against foreign services or foreign service providers as well as certain key aspects of the overall regulatory environment that have a notable impact on trade in services. A high score means greater restrictiveness.

[9] According to WTO (2011), ownership limits were a particular impediment to the development of financial services in India. FDI up to 100 percent was permitted in other major services sectors in India. But, "specific market access conditions or permits were applicable, which in some cases may be more restrictive than an explicit cap on foreign ownership" (WTO 2011, xiii).

TABLE 10.4.

Barriers to Goods and Services Trade

	Simple Average MFN-Applied Tariffs				Nontariff	Services Trade
	Agriculture (%)		Manufactures (%)		Measure Implemented,	Restrictiveness
Country	2008	2019	2008	2019	2017–20[3]	Index (MRE)
India	32.2	38.8	10.1	14.1	177	65.7
Pakistan	15.4	13.5	13.2	11.9	45	28.3
Bangladesh	17.6	17.5	34.4	13.4		44.2
Sri Lanka	25.5	27.1	9.0	6.4	5	38.2
Maldives	18.3	10.8	20.7	13.3		–
Nepal	14.8	14.6	12.4	11.8	6	42.9
Afghanistan	5.8	9.4[2]	5.5	6.0[2]		–
Bhutan	41.4[1]	41.9	18.9[1]	18.9		–
China	15.6	13.9	8.7	6.5	284	36.6
Korea	49	56.8	6.6	6.6	153	23.1
Indonesia	8.5[1]	8.7	6.7[1]	8.0	49	50.0
Thailand	25.2[1]	29.0	8.2[1]	7.2	88	48.0
Malaysia	14.7	7.7	8.0	5.3	24	46.1
Philippines	9.7	9.8	5.7	5.5	121	53.5
Vietnam	24.2[1]	17.2	15.7[1]	8.4	43	41.5

Sources: World Trade Organization 2009, 2020; and World Bank 2012.
Note: MFN = most favored nation; MRE = most recent estimate.
[1] Most recent estimates from 2007.
[2] Most recent estimates from 2018.
[3] Includes all nontariff measures (initiated and in force) imposed on all members from January 1, 2017, to January 6, 2020.

services (see Kelegama 2009). Most South Asian economies have thus adopted a cautious approach to services trade liberalization.

Amid an uneven recovery during the pandemic and rising protectionism, little appetite exists for trade liberalization in either region.[10] Nonetheless, regional economies should explore rationalizing import structures by streamlining irrational protection on essential food supports to ensure food security for poor households and intermediate goods imports to mitigate disruptions in supply chains. When the recovery is firmly rooted, regional economies can embark on gradual trade liberalization and export promotion programs. Implementing competition policy frameworks to facilitate productivity improvement in the services sector and addressing issues related to monopoly power will help cement the gains from trade reform. Significant cooperation is also required to improve the quality of data on services trade in South Asia particularly in ICT services and e-commerce, which have expanded during the pandemic.

Gaps in SEZs

Efficient and seamless infrastructure has been the backbone of regional trade integration in Asia (ADB and ADBI 2015). It powers the movement of goods,

---

[10] For assessments of the progress in trade and other reforms in South Asia, see Dee (2012) and Kathuria (2018).

services, technology, and people across borders. Furthermore, it contributes to reducing trade costs, encourages business competitiveness, and promotes the spread of GVCs and digital trade. Within the broad spectrum of trade-related infrastructure, SEZs stand out for their potential impact on South Asia–East Asia trade integration.

An SEZ is defined as a geographically distinct area within which a government assists manufacturing activity using fiscal incentives, light regulations, and infrastructure support.[11] The world's first SEZ was probably set up in Shannon, Ireland, in 1954 and then spread through the developed world. In the 1980s and 1990s, SEZs proliferated in the developing world with the adoption of outward-oriented development strategies emphasizing attracting export-oriented FDI and job creation. The spread of SEZs can be attributed to factors such as the relative ease of providing attractive investment climates though SEZs in countries where implementing trade and investment reforms has been difficult, the perceived low cost of setting up SEZs, and heighted competition to attract export-oriented FDI.

UNCTAD (2019) estimates that there are nearly 5400 SEZs globally with more than two thirds of these located in Asia. East Asia—which makes up about half the global total—is reputed to have some of the world's most successful SEZs in China, Korea, and Singapore. SEZs in these countries have played an important role in East Asia, becoming the world's factory through attracting FDI, spreading sophisticated GVCs, fostering domestic linkages and supporting a dense network of trade in parts and components. A recent study on Asian economies suggests that the number and presence of SEZs is positively related to overall export performance and the volume of inward FDI. On average, a 10 percent increase in the number of SEZs increases manufacturing exports by 1.1 percent (ADB 2015).

A relative latecomer to the gathering momentum toward SEZs globally and in East Asia, South Asia has somewhere between 456 to 645 SEZs (or 8.5 percent to 12.0 percent of the global total of SEZs).[12] Recent examples of SEZs focusing on manufacturing include the Cochin SEZ in India, Gwadar Free Zone in Pakistan, the Mirsarai Economic Zone in Bangladesh, and the Hambantota Industrial Zone in Sri Lanka. Dedicated SEZs for services, such as the Colombo Port City SEZ, are less common. Table 10.5 provides an evaluation of SEZs in South Asia by ADB (2015) with updated data on FDI inflows and some data for Nepal. The available data suggests that the performance of SEZs in South Asia has been mixed. Such SEZs have typically failed to attract significant FDI inflows and create large numbers of jobs. FDI inflows as a percentage of GDP

---

[11] Here, the terms "SEZ" and "export processing zone" are used synonymously. In the strict sense, however, export processing zones focus on promoting manufactured exports while SEZs are open to all business sectors (for example, manufacturing, trading, and services).

[12] UNCTAD (2019) estimates that South Asia has 456 SEZs while ADB (2015) suggests a higher figure of 645. These differences might reflect different definitions of SEZs, data collection methods, and time periods.

TABLE 10.5.

Evaluating SEZs in South Asia

	Total (No. of Zones), 2015	By Modality		By Linkage to Domestic and Global Economy				Benefits (Most Recent Estimates)[3]
		Public (%)	Private (%)	Enclave	GVC	Logistics/Services	Border Areas	
India	615[1]	26	74	•	•	•	•	• Annual average FDI inflows $44.7 billion (2017–19) • FDI inflows as a percent of GDP were 1.7 percent in 2019 • SEZs accounted for 26 percent of exports and 4 percent of employment in 2014
Pakistan	7[1]	100	0	•				• Annual average FDI inflows $2.2 billion (2017–19) • FDI inflows as a percent of GDP were 0.9 percent in 2019
Bangladesh	8[1]	89	11	•				• Annual average FDI inflows $1.3 billion (2017–19) • FDI inflows as a percent of GDP were 0.5 percent in 2019 • SEZs accounted for 8 percent of total investment (foreign and domestic) and 17 percent of national exports in 2013 • SEZs credited with development of garments industry
Sri Lanka	14	94	6	•				• Annual average FDI inflows $2.5 billion (2017–19) • FDI inflows as a percent of GDP were 0.9 percent in 2019 • SEZs accounted for 69 percent of national exports in 2017 and 6 percent of the total labor force between 2008–17 • SEZs credited with development of garments industry
Nepal	1[2]	Not available	Not available	•				• Annual average FDI inflows $150 million (2017–19) • FDI inflows as a percent of GDP were 0.6 percent in 2019

Sources: Asian Development Bank 2015; Board of Investment Pakistan 2021; Board of Investment, Sri Lanka 2017; and UNCTAD 2021.

Note: FDI = foreign direct investment; GVC = global value chain; SEZ = special economic zone.

[1] Includes zones that have a public-private partnership component.

[2] 2020.

[3] Unless specified, the FDI figure refers to FDI into the whole country.

ranged from 0.5 percent in Bangladesh to 1.7 percent in India. They only created 4 percent of employment in India and 6 percent in Sri Lanka. Nonetheless, SEZs have made a notable contribution to exports in some South Asian economies, particularly in the development of the garment industry, accounting for 69 percent of Sri Lanka's total exports, 26 percent of India's, and 17 percent of Bangladesh's.

One can speculate on the reasons as to why SEZs in South Asia did not perform as expected. They mainly operate as public sector entities, which means it becomes expensive for South Asian economies to bear the full costs of establishing and running them, particularly while offering generous fiscal incentives. In addition, with the exception of India, SEZs in South Asia function as enclaves with few domestic economic linkages such as those with local suppliers, small and medium enterprises and the domestic goods market. A negative image problem linked to long-running civil conflicts repels actual investment in SEZs, as Nepal and Sri Lanka have discovered to great cost. The hidden costs of SEZs could include misallocated resources, the encouragement of rent-seeking, and distraction of policy makers from carrying out more effective economic reforms.[13]

Furthermore, the odds are stacked against SEZs in small South Asian economies with difficult geographical circumstances. For instance, land-locked Nepal and Bhutan are hampered by a lack of sea connectivity, high transit costs involved in international border crossings, gaps domestic infrastructure, and cumbersome bureaucratic approvals. Although Nepal's first SEZ in Bhairahawa was inaugurated in 2014 at considerable state expense, only three factories were in operation three years later (Prasain 2020). Nepal's experience suggests that feasibility of SEZs in small economies should be carefully studied and policy lessons drawn.

More generally, some South Asian economies suffer from gaps in their national competitiveness as indicated by World Economic Forum's Global Competitiveness Index 2019, which adversely affects their attractiveness to FDI in SEZs.[14] India, in 68th place in the rankings, was South Asia's best ranked economy while Pakistan in 110th place, was the worst. In between come Sri Lanka (in 84th place), Bangladesh (in 105th place) and Nepal (in 108th place).

Drawing on East Asia's successful experience, some policy lessons may be gleaned for South Asian SEZs (see ADB 2015 and UNCTAD 2019). First, SEZs are an important development policy tool not only for promoting inward investment but also for facilitating industrial clustering. Notable spillovers can be gained from sharing resources and costs by locating related industrial activities in given geographical locations. Second, regulatory and governance frameworks should be adaptable. The role of government is to set regulatory frameworks for SEZs. But the development and ownership of SEZs could be public, private, or a public-private

---

[13] An interesting political economy take on SEZs can be found in Moberg (2017).

[14] Using a mix of hard data and survey data, WEF (2019) measures national competitiveness defined as a set of institutions, policies, and factors which determine the level of productivity. Unfortunately, data was not available for Afghanistan, Bhutan, and Maldives.

partnership. Third, competitive fiscal incentives are important to initial investments in industrial ventures along with institutional factors (such as an efficient SEZ governing authority, a supporting legal framework, and a flexible labor market). But there is an ongoing debate on the economic costs and benefits of certain fiscal incentives such as long tax holidays. Fourth, improving incentive climates by implementing behind-the-border regulatory reforms are necessary condition for exploiting gains from investments in SEZs. Political stability is essential to attract foreign investors into SEZs. Investing overseas is a long-term activity and risks of domestic conflicts and violence of any kind tends to deter investment in SEZs.

Emerging Challenges of FTAs

In the absence of unilateral and multilateral liberalization, policy makers have been studying the economic benefits of FTAs to participating economies (Kawai and Wignaraja 2013; Suominen 2019). FTAs can not only lower import tariffs but also deal with behind-the-border barriers that hamper goods and services trade. Furthermore, by eliminating entry restrictions they can facilitate inward investment and technology transfer as well as improve trade rules on new trade issues such as competition, government procurement, intellectual property, and e-commerce.

As discussed earlier, there was an uptick in emerging South Asia–East Asia FTA activity since the global financial crisis. Assuming that all the future FTAs are concluded, there may be more than 30 FTAs connecting South Asia and East Asia over the next decade. Thus, market-based regionalism through trade flows between South Asia and East Asia may become increasingly policy-led through FTAs over time. Furthermore, the handful of agreements in October 2021 means there is little current risk of crisscrossing FTAs in the trade policy architecture between South Asia and East Asia—which Bhagwati famously called a "spaghetti bowl" of trade deals (Bhagwati 1995, 2008). His powerful insight suggested that the discriminatory trade liberalization occurs under multiple, overlapping FTAs and that this causes the international trading system to become chaotic and raises transactions costs for business. As the number of crisscrossing FTAs significantly rise in the future, however, it is possible that detrimental spaghetti bowl effects could begin to affect South Asia–East trade.

While this systemic issue is a future agenda item for regional trade policy, the evidence points to two emerging challenges in the current FTA architecture between South Asia and East Asia. First, a mixed picture of the use of tariff preferences in South Asia–East Asia FTAs is visible in the limited data. This overarching indicator of the effectiveness of regional FTAs is ideally measured by the share of export value covered by tariff preferences. The source of such data can be found in certificates of origin filed by firms with customs authorities or authorized bodies. However, such information is not available from official data sources. Table 10.6 provides some information for various years from secondary studies on export value using FTA preferences for four FTAs (India–Korea FTA, Thailand–India FTA, ASEAN–India FTA, and Pakistan–Malaysia FTA). The Korean data suggest an increase in the reasonable utilization level of the Korea–India FTA from

36.2 percent to 43.0 percent between 2012 and 2013. The Thai data also show an increase in the combined utilization rate of the Thailand–India FTA and the ASEAN–India FTA from 17.6 percent to 38.0 percent between 2005 and 2012. It is interesting that utilization of the India–Thailand FTA (70 percent in 2012) is more than double that of the ASEAN–India FTA (30 percent in 2012), which could indicate more attractive preference margins for the bilateral than the regional FTA. Likewise, the Malaysian data show a significant increase in utilization of the Pakistan-Malaysia FTA from 1.4 percent to 74.3 percent between 2006 and 2010. However, Vietnam data on the ASEAN–India FTA and Pakistan data on the Pakistan–Malaysia FTA indicate low utilization of such FTAs of well under 10 percent. Firm-level studies in Asia suggest that low FTA use can be attributed to factors such as a lack of awareness about FTAs, confusing tariff schedules and rules of origin, small preference margins, and delays and administrative costs (see Kawai and Wignaraja 2011; Tambunan and Chandra 2014).

Second, the comprehensiveness of the concluded South Asia–East Asia FTAs varies. Table 10.7 shows our evaluation of the comprehensiveness of key South Asia–East Asia FTAs according to criteria applied to liberalization in goods trade, services trade, and regulatory barriers.[15] The findings suggest that South Asia–East Asia FTAs come under two headings: (1) limited agreements tackling mainly barriers to goods trade, and (2) agreements that extend liberalization beyond goods

TABLE 10.6.

Use of Preferences in South Asia–East Asia FTAs

Country	FTA		Preference Use (%)		Sources
Korea	India–Korea FTA		36.2 (end 2012)	43.0 (November 2013)	Cheong 2014
Thailand	India–Thailand FTA		74.6 (2011)	70.0 (2012)	Tambunan and Chandra 2014, Wignaraja 2014
	ASEAN–India FTA		27.9 (2011)	28.9 (2012)	
	Combined	17.6 (2005)	36.6 (2011)	38.0 (2012)	
Vietnam	ASEAN–India FTA		7.4 (2011)		Wignaraja 2014
Malaysia	Malaysia–Pakistan FTA	1.4 (2006)	74.3 (2010)		Wignaraja 2014
Pakistan	Malaysia–Pakistan FTA	3.4 (2008–09)	1.9 (2009–10)	3.3 (2010–11)	Paracha and Manzoor 2011

Sources: Various sources as shown in column 6.
Note: FTA = free trade agreement.

[15] Goods liberalization evaluates the speed and coverage of tariff liberalization based on the criteria for FTAs in the WTO General Agreement on Tariffs and Trade. Services liberalization evaluates the number of services sectors covered based on the WTO General Agreement on Trade in Services. Coverage and liberalization in intellectual property, investment, government procurement, trade facilitation, and competition were based using criteria for individual issues such as adherence to international agreements such as the WTO Agreement on Trade-Related Aspects of Intellectual Property Rights and the Government Procurement Agreement.

TABLE 10.7.

Assessing South Asia–East Asia FTAs

Name of Agreement	Date Concluded	Goods Liberalization	Services Coverage	Deep Integration
Asia–Pacific Trade Agreement	1976	Limited	Excluded	Shallow
India–Singapore FTA	2005	Relatively fast	Comprehensive	Limited
Pakistan–China FTA	2007	Gradual	Some	Limited
Pakistan–Malaysia FTA	2008	Limited	Some	Limited
ASEAN–India FTA	2010	Gradual	Excluded	Shallow
India–Korea FTA	2010	Gradual	Comprehensive	Moderate
India–Japan FTA	2011	Relatively fast	Some	Deep
India–Malaysia FTA	2011	Relatively fast	Some	Moderate
Indonesia–Pakistan FTA	2013	Limited	Excluded	Excluded
Singapore–Sri Lanka FTA	2018	Relatively fast	Comprehensive	Deep

Source: Author's assessment based on the methodology outlined in Wignaraja, Ramizo, and Burmeister (2013).
Note ASEAN = Association of Southeast Asian Nations; FTA = free trade agreement.

trade to services trade and regulatory barriers. The APTA, the China-Pakistan FTA, the Pakistan–Malaysia FTA, and the Indonesia–Pakistan FTA are mainly agreements limited to goods trade. The other FTAs are somewhat more comprehensive. The ASEAN–India FTA initially covered goods liberalization but has recently expanded to cover services and investment. The India–Singapore FTA excludes agriculture and transit but has reasonable coverage of services and cooperation enhancement provisions. The India–Korea FTA also has reasonable coverage of services and moderate coverage of regulatory barriers while the India-Japan FTA covers some services and has wider coverage of regulatory barriers. However, the more recent Singapore–Sri Lanka FTA has much wider coverage than others. It represents a modern 21st century FTA that includes traditional trade issues but WTO plus issues such as competition, investment, intellectual property, and government procurement.[16]

The challenges in South Asia–East Asia FTAs should be addressed. Governments should adopt carefully designed FTA strategies to encourage business to make better use of existing and future FTAs. Korea—with an impressive experience of achieving high FTA utilization rates of averaging around 70 percent across its multiple FTAs—is held up as an example of a well-crafted FTA strategy (Cheong 2014). The core components of such FTA strategies are as follows:

(1) Focusing on concluding FTAs with major trading partners for economic reasons rather than peripheral trading partners for political reasons.

(2) Ensuring FTAs are comprehensive in the sense of being consistent with WTO rules (for example, the General Agreement on Tariffs and Trade Article XXIV and General Agreement on Trade in Services) and cover WTO plus issues.

---

[16] The contents of the Singapore–Sri Lanka FTA can be found at https://www.chamber.lk/index.php/news/179-insights-and-findings-on-the-sri-lanka-singapore-free-trade-agreement. For a commentary, see Wignaraja and Palit 2018.

(3) Encouraging the rationalization and flexibility of rules of origin and upgrading origin administration.

(4) Providing good business support including offering greater opportunities for business participation in FTA consultations, conducting FTA awareness and training programs and strengthening institutional support systems for small and medium enterprises.

(5) Publishing official FTA use statistics by FTA, industry, and firm size to facilitate monitoring and evaluation of FTAs as well as mid-course policy corrections as needed.

Regionally, in the medium term, South Asian and East Asian economies should continue with efforts to form a mega-FTA as a means to consolidate the growing numbers of bilateral and subregional agreements and to address the risk of a "spaghetti bowl" problem. Such a mega FTA can also promote continuing liberalization, induce structural reforms, and widen market access. An important mega-FTA is the Regional Comprehensive Economic Partnership (RCEP). The original parties including the 10 ASEAN members and their FTA partners (including India, Japan, China, Korea, Australia, and New Zealand) began negotiation in 2013 to create the world's largest trading bloc covering one third of world GDP and 40 percent of world trade. India had hoped that the RCEP would enable Indian business to increase exports to East Asia, to integrate into regional value chains and to invest in information technology services sectors in East Asia.

On November 15, 2020, after nearly seven years of intense talks and 31 rounds of negotiations, 15 countries signed the RCEP Agreement and said that they hoped to ratify it during 2021.[17] However, RCEP ratification could be delayed until 2022. To enter into force, the deal required six ASEAN signatories and three ASEAN dialogue partners to ratify the agreement domestically. The surge in COVID-19 cases in 2021 has complicated national efforts to ratify the agreement. On January 2022, nearly one year after it was signed, RCEP went into effect for 10 original partners. By September 2022, 13 countries had ratified the RCEP with only the Philippines and Myanmar yet to do so.

Furthermore, India did not sign the agreement, indicating several issues that prevented it from doing so. Previously cited issues include India's growing trade deficit with China and several other RCEP members, the risk of import surges from an RCEP deal that would hurt domestic farmers and business, and that service liberalization offers from ASEAN under RCEP were inadequate (particularly for cross-border movement of information technology professionals). Model-based assessments suggest that India sees Losses by not being a party to the RCEP agreement.[18] Moreover, without India's participation, the RCEP would be East

---

[17] See Regional Comprehensive Economic Partnership Agreement at https://www.dfat.gov.au/trade/agreements/not-yet-in-force/rcep.

[18] Using a CGE model, Petri and Plummer (2020) showed that the RCEP agreement without India will raise global national incomes in 2030 by an annual $186 billion. It will yield significant benefits for China, Japan, and Korea and losses for India.

Asia–centric and smaller in coverage of world GDP and trade. Nonetheless, RCEP with 15 members will still be the world's largest FTA.[19] The RCEP signatories said that the door was open for India to join the RCEP in the future when it is ready.

Now that India is out, it has an opportunity to identify core areas of comparative advantage in goods and services trade as well as undertake important structural reforms that would improve competitiveness of its business and ensure greater regulatory coherence with East Asia.[20] Furthermore, India can renew its existing FTAs with ASEAN, Japan, and Korea to reap more benefits and revamp the core components of its overall FTA strategy along the lines mentioned earlier. The RCEP principles contain an open accession clause permitting new members to join. The rest of South Asia has shown little interest in the RCEP, but this could change if they become concerned about being left out of an eventual mega-FTA between India and East Asia. South Asian economies should also closely follow the progress of the Comprehensive and Progressive Agreement for Trans-Pacific Partnership as outsider countries such as the United Kingdom are seeking membership.

Institution-Lite Regionalism

There is increasing recognition of the role played by regional institutions in promoting regional cooperation and integration in Asia (ADB 2010). Regional institutions can foster regional cooperation and integration among diverse economies with differing interests by using tools such as trust building, financing, and expertise. Their role is particularly important as a supporter of regional trade integration by providing a forum for ministerial discussions on deepening regional trade integration, setting regional trade rules, promoting informal exchanges on best practices trade policies among officials and think tanks, and conducting strategic studies on trade issues.

Much of the policy discussion in South Asia has centered on the effectiveness of the South Asian Association for Regional Cooperation (SAARC) versus the Bay of Bengal Initiative for Multi-Sectoral Technical and Economic Cooperation (BIMSTEC) as promoters of regional trade integration.

SAARC, the older of two regional institutions, was established in 1985 and has eight members (Afghanistan, Bangladesh, Bhutan, India, Maldives, Nepal, Pakistan, and Sri Lanka). The SAARC Secretariat was set up in Kathmandu in January 1987. The SAARC Charter has an ambitious set of objectives including promoting the welfare of the people; accelerating economic growth, social progress, and culture development; strengthening collective self-reliance; and to cooperate with international and regional organizations.

---

[19] The 15 RCEP member still comprise 30 percent of the world's population and around 30 percent of the world's GDP. https://www.mfat.govt.nz/en/trade/free-trade-agreements/free-trade-agreements-concluded-but-not-in-force/regional-comprehensive-economic-partnership-rcep/rcep-overview

[20] The implications of RCEP membership for India are discussed in Wignaraja (2019) and Sarma (2020).

However, SAARC has seen few tangible achievements in trade integration within South Asia. This may be explained by high levels of protection in the region (see Table 10.4), mistrust and restrictions on India-Pakistan trade, fears of domestic industries in smaller South Asian economies being swamped by cheap Indian imports, bureaucratic inertia, and security concerns (Sharma 2011; Khan 2012; Kathuria 2018). While a limited South Asia Free Trade Area (SAFTA) came into effect in 2006, there is little end in sight for prolonged discussions on Phase III of the SAFTA to fast-track sensitive lists. Moreover, The SAARC Motor Vehicle Agreement, critical for enhancing connectivity, remains unsigned. Senior officials from members have met over the years, but there is little discussion of deepening South Asia–East Asia rules-based trade engagement though a SAARC–ASEAN FTA. The hope that the creation of the SAARC COVID-19 Emergency Fund in March 2020 may advance trade cooperation in South Asia has faded with little thaw in India–Pakistan relations. Thus, intra-regional trade in South Asia (stuck at around 5 percent for decades) is among the lowest in the world (ADB 2010).

BIMSTEC was established in 1997 to explicitly focus on regional economic and technical cooperation between members in South Asia and Southeast Asia. It presently has five South Asian members (Bangladesh, Bhutan, India, Nepal, and Sri Lanka) and two Southeast Asian members (Thailand and Myanmar). Inactivity in SAARC has led to India giving recent priority to BIMSTEC as it fits neatly with three important policy initiatives guiding India's approach to regional cooperation—the Act East policy, the Indo-Pacific construct and the Neighborhood First policy (De 2020). In March 2022, the 5th BIMSTEC landmark summit saw thet adoption of the BIMSTEC Charter, which formalizes the grouping into an organization of member states and the BIMSTEC Master Plan for Transport Connectivity. Now BIMSTEC is in the spotlight, several improvements are needed for the institution to foster regional trade integration.

First, it is imperative that BIMSTEC reinvents itself as a regional institution focusing on enhancing regional trade integration in a broad sense for its members. This means significantly rebalancing its scope and trimming down its seven sectors of operation down to a handful of trade-related sectors, particularly trade and investment, connectivity, energy, the Blue Economy, technology, and people to people exchanges. Such a strong trade focus would help to avert protectionism and lay the foundation for a recovery in regional trade.

Second, it should adequately resource its Secretariat (set up in Dhaka in 1987) and develop technical and advisory competencies in these core trade-related sectors. This would require significant financial and technical support from major regional economies such as India and Thailand. A recent study suggested that the BIMSTEC Secretariat was severely underresourced for this task with a budget of about $0.2 million and less than 10 staff including the Secretary-General and some Directors (Xavier 2018). It is suggested that the budget for the BIMSTEC Secretariat be increased to $9 million by 2025 (with India and Thailand contributing $2 million each and the rest $1 million each). Another suggestion is a secondment scheme to the BIMSTEC Secretariat for specialists in trade and connectivity from members ministries of trade and think tanks.

Third, a renewed push should be made to conclude the 16-year negotiations for a BIMSTEC FTA which has had more than 20 rounds of negotiations since 2004. To maximize the economic benefits among members, the aim should be to achieve a modern and comprehensive FTA in terms of its coverage of issues and countries. This means going beyond the negotiation remit for a narrow BIMSTEC FTA with tariff concessions in goods trade, customs cooperation, investment cooperation, and dispute settlement (Didar Singh 2018). This can be achieved by the talks adding a built-in agenda to look at WTO plus issues such as government procurement, competition, and intellectual property, which are essential to the spread of GVCs between South Asia and Southeast Asia. The talks should also discuss provisions on technical cooperation. In parallel, India and Thailand could provide aid for trade to small economies (including grants and concessional loans) to soften the transitionary adjustment effects of trade opening on losing sectors and workers. Significant trade policy capacity needs to be built in small economies before they embark on trade talks and technical assistance provided to improve business use of FTAs in effect. An open accession clause for new members is needed whereby the agreement is open to accession on terms to be agreed by the parties.

South Asia is often described as a region having institution-lite regionalism (see ADB 2010). The future cycles of BIMTEC senior officials, ministerial meetings and leaders' summits offers an opportunity for undertaking a stock taking of BIMSTEC's achievements and providing a vision for the way forward, particularly to support regional trade integration.

QUANTIFYING THE BENEFITS OF TRADE INTEGRATION BETWEEN SOUTH ASIA AND EAST ASIA

Model-based studies are a useful tool to quantitatively assess the impact of various policy scenarios for regional trade integration between South and East Asian economies. Multicountry computable general equilibrium (CGE) models provide a rigorous and theoretically consistent framework to evaluate gains to South Asian economies from alternative policy scenarios for trade integration with East Asia. A CGE modeling approach incorporates the complex relations between prices, markets, and income. A multicountry CGE model permits taking account of the effects of a changing world economic environment as well as feedback linked to bilateral trade liberalization and reductions in trade costs resulting from better physical connectivity.

There are a handful of CGE studies on South and East Asian economies because of the recent origin of South Asia–East Asia integration schemes and limited CGE modeling capacity in South Asia. Although these studies vary in their modeling assumptions made, unit of analysis used and policy scenarios considered, the results are broadly consistent. Annex 1 contains a literature review.

The results of a CGE exercise by Wignaraja, Morgan, Plummer, and Zhai (2015, 2016) involving South and Southeast Asian economies are reported here.

The study uses an advanced CGE model featuring recent innovations in heterogeneous firms trade theory into the CGE framework. Policy scenarios are included featuring full liberalization of tariff barriers, a 50 percent reduction in nontariff barriers (NTBs), and improvements in infrastructure (both hard physical infrastructure and software such as trade and transport facilitation) manifest in reductions in trade costs. A long-term time framework for ambitious deepening liberalization is assumed. Liberalization of these barriers is assumed over the period 2016–25 and is compared relative to the baseline forecasts, with projections finishing in 2030.

Table 10.8 reports broad welfare effects for three policy scenarios from the study:

1. South Asia–Southeast Asia Policy Scenario 1: removal of all tariffs associated with South Asia–Southeast Asia trade but no changes in NTBs and other trade costs.

2. South Asia–Southeast Asia Policy Scenario 2: Scenario 1 plus a 50 percent cut in NTBs.

3. South Asia-Southeast Asia Policy Scenario 3: Scenario 2 plus a 15 percent cut in trade costs pertaining to South Asia-Southeast Asia trade. This ambitious scenario represents the deepest integration efforts among the three scenarios.

It is striking that, deeper South Asia-Southeast Asian economic integration efforts result in large and notable gains for the two subregions in all scenarios. Under Scenario 1, South Asia's GDP increases by 2.2 percent and Southeast Asia's GDP by 1.9 percent relative to the baseline, indicating that tariffs continue to hamper gains from trade between the subregions. All South Asian economies gain. The smallest South Asia economies—Nepal and other South Asian economies—exhibit the largest gains (more than 5 percent of GDP). India comes next (more than 2 percent of GDP). Sri Lanka, Pakistan, and Bangladesh experience smaller gains than others.

Even bigger gains, however, occur when NTBs and trade costs related to improvements in infrastructure fall. Scenario 3 shows a four-fold increase in GDP for South Asia (8.9 percent) relative to the baseline and a three-fold increase in GDP for Southeast Asia (6.4 percent). All economies within South Asia gain with Nepal and other South Asian economies witnessing the largest gains. Notable gains are also visible for India (8.7 percent), Sri Lanka, Pakistan, and Bangladesh.

The outcome of these policy scenarios implicitly assumes that South Asia is internally quite well integrated. However, as previously mentioned, the South Asia Free Trade Area (SAFTA) process involving the eight South Asian Association for Regional Cooperation members has lost momentum and that South Asia remains one of the least integrated regions globally. Furthermore, it is recognized that smaller, poorer and less diversified economies in South Asia facing significant challenges in realizing that potential of South Asia-Southeast Asia integration. For example, landlocked Bhutan and Nepal and Afghanistan facing political turbulence could find it difficult to attract foreign investment into SEZs. These economies may also

TABLE 10.8.

Effects of South Asia/Southeast Asia Trade Initiatives in 2030, Income on South Asia and Southeast Asia, Relative to Baseline
(Equivalent variation as percent of GDP)

Country	SA/SEA1	SA/SEA2	SA/SEA3
Total South Asia	**2.2**	**3.2**	**8.9**
India	2.3	3.3	8.7
Pakistan	0.8	1.8	7.0
Bangladesh	0.4	1.2	6.9
Sri Lanka	1.3	2.9	14.1
Nepal	5.4	9.0	30.0
Other South Asia[1]	5.2	8.3	31.7
Total Southeast Asia	**1.9**	**2.5**	**6.4**
Indonesia	2.3	2.4	5.0
Malaysia	2.8	3.6	9.7
Philippines	0.2	0.6	1.9
Singapore	3.1	4.8	14.4
Thailand	1.7	2.3	6.1
Vietnam	0.6	2.0	7.0
Cambodia	−0.3	−0.1	0.6
Lao P.D.R.	−0.1	−0.1	−0.1
Other ASEAN[2]	0.1	0.5	2.3

Sources: Wignaraja, Morgan, Plummer, and Zhai 2015, 2016.
Note: SA = South Asia; SEA = Southeast Asia; SA/SEAFTA1 = removal of all tariffs across SA and SEA over 2016–25; SA/SEAFTA2 = SA/SEA1 + 50 percent cut in nontariff barriers; SA/SEAFTA3 = SA/SEAFTA2 + 15 percent reduction in trade costs relevant to South Asian–Southeast Asian trade.
[1]"Other South Asia" includes Afghanistan, Bhutan, and Maldives.
[2]"Other ASEAN" includes Brunei Darussalam and Myanmar.

be constrained by a narrow commodity dependent export base as well as limited capacity to negotiate FTAs and to participate in regional organizations.

Nonetheless, to illustrate potential benefits of South Asian integration, Wignaraja, Morgan, Plummer, and Zhai (2015, 2016) also report the outcome of a deep integration South Asian policy scenario. This scenario seems useful as SAFTA has had a goods agreement in effect for some years and a services agreement took effect in 2012 as an expansion of SAFTA. Efforts are also being made to improve cross-border roads to link India's Northeast with neighboring economies. A deep integration South Asian policy scenario (with removal of all tariffs, a 50 percent cut in NTBs and a 15 percent reduction in trade costs) increases South Asia's GDP by 2.1 percent relative to the baseline. This figure compares with a 0.4 percent rise in South Asia's GDP for a policy scenario of only tariff removal. Earlier studies, largely concerned with removal of all tariffs, suggest smaller gains for South Asia from SAFTA.[21]

---

[21] Accordingly, Bandara and Yu (2003) reported gains for South Asia of $771.4 million, ADB and UNCTAD (2008) of $858.3 million, Raihan and Razzaque (2014) of $3.3 billion, and Siriwardana (2003) of $4 billion.

CONCLUSIONS

This chapter examined South Asia and East Asia trade integration in COVID times, focusing on the implications for South Asia. After decades of inactivity, South Asia–East Asia trade integration has accelerated since the 1990s. This trend is linked to factors such as the adoption of outward-oriented development strategies in South Asia, India's Look and Act East Policies, economic restructuring in East Asia, the spread of GVCs to South Asia, and China's BRI.

Trade flows between South Asia and East Asia grew rapidly from a small base driven by the larger economies from each region. Underlying South Asia's tilt toward trade with East Asia is a significant realignment of India's exports and imports toward East Asia. However, South Asia's other major economies and small states have typically seen falling shares of their global trade destined to East Asia, an increasing reliance on East Asian imports and limited exports to East Asia. Furthermore, a stylized North–South trade pattern is typically observed, whereby less developed South Asian economies export natural resource and labor-intensive products in exchange for capital and technology-intensive imports from more developed East Asian economies. Increased market-led regional trade integration has encouraged policy-led regional integration through the spread of a few South Asia–East Asia FTAs.

The COVID-19 economic shock has disrupted Asia's global trade and trade across Asia. Nonetheless, an Asian trade recovery is expected from the pandemic. Our projections also suggest a recovery in South Asia–East Asia trade in 2021–23 underpinned by various assumptions. Much economic realignment appears to be occurring and new trading opportunities are emerging. The trajectory of India-East Asia trade is critical in this scenario. As more value chain activity gravitates toward India, it could catalyze the development of regional value chains and services trade involving the rest of South Asia. It would also stimulate commodity between South Asia and East Asia. However, the reality could be different to the forecast as a high level of uncertainty exits.

Several national and regional policies are needed to support regional trade integration across Asia. South Asian economies have scope to streamline protection and gradually reduce trade barriers affecting goods and services trade. This will help them to integrate with East Asia as well as the global economy. Trade opening in South Asia should be supported with adjustment financing and technical assistance to losing sectors and economies, particularly in small economies.

Another priority is improving the performance of existing SEZs and investing in services SEZs to facilitate industrial clustering and exports. This requires good practice regulatory policies, competitive fiscal incentives and ensuring political stability. The feasibility of SEZs in small economies in South Asia should be carefully studied and policy lessons drawn.

Pursuing comprehensive FTAs eventually leading to RCEP can provide a framework of regional rules-based trade to help insure against rising protectionist tendencies. Although India is not a party to the RCEP agreement, it can prepare for future membership by undertaking structural reforms to improve business competitiveness and greater regulatory coherence with East Asia. If India joins, the rest of South Asia might be incentivized to seek RCEP membership.

A reinvented and bolder BIMSTEC focused on trade integration can be an important vehicle to South Asia–East Asia policy-led integration and support the interest of small economies. Better resourcing of the BIMSTEC Secretariat and pushing to conclude a comprehensive BIMSTEC FTA are key agenda items. Significant trade policy capacity should be built in small economies in South Asia before they embark on trade talks and technical assistance is needed to improve business use of FTAs in effect. An open accession clause for new members is also needed whereby a BIMSTEC agreement is open to accession on terms to be agreed by the parties.

The findings from CGE studies indicate that South Asian economies can gain in terms of economic welfare by integrating with East Asia. A deep integration policy scenario involving tariffs cuts, reductions in NTMs and falling trade costs through infrastructure investments brings more significant gains than a scenario involving tariff cuts. Although India, Pakistan, and Bangladesh see some gains under deep integration, smaller South Asian economies (Afghanistan, Bhutan, Nepal, Maldives, and Sri Lanka) experience significant gains. While broad South Asia–East Asia integration may be desirable, geopolitics might rule it out for some time. Accordingly, a narrower geographical coverage (for example, between South Asian and Southeast Asian economies) could act as a building block for eventual integration across Asia.

To avoid a potential backlash against regionalization, attention should be paid to ensuring actual gains from trade for South Asia's smaller and poorer economies. The findings suggested that smaller South Asian economies trade relatively little with East Asia partly linked to their dependence on a narrow range of commodity exports. They also lack the capacity to negotiate in FTAs and participate effectively in regional institutions. Further research is needed to better understand the special circumstance facing smaller South Asian economies and the obstacles they experience in realizing the gains from Asian regionalism.

Annex 10.1. CGE Studies of South Asia–East Asia Trade Integration

There are a handful of CGE studies on South and East Asian economies because of the recent origin of South Asia–East Asia integration schemes and limited CGE modeling capacity in South Asia. These studies vary in their modeling assumptions made, unit of analysis used, and policy scenarios considered. An early study by Bandara and Yu (2003) used a global computable general equilibrium (CGE) model to evaluate the effects of tariff elimination under a South Asia–ASEAN free trade area (FTA). They pessimistically report that all South Asian countries, including India, would incur welfare losses from such an FTA, while ASEAN as a whole would see modest gains. However, more recent and comprehensive simulation studies report different results.

As part of the work related to the Comprehensive Asia Development Plan prepared by the Economic Research Institute for ASEAN and East Asia (ERIA) for the East Asian Summit, Kumagai and others (2013) used the IDE/ERIA Geographical Simulation Model, a detailed regional model, to estimate the impacts on the cumulative increase of GDP of countries in the two regions from 2010 to 2030 relative to the base case for a number of connectivity projects, including the Mekong–India Economic Corridor, the Dawei and Kyaukphyu deep-sea ports in Myanmar, and the India–Myanmar–Thailand Trilateral Highway. For the Mekong–India Economic Corridor alone, they found cumulative impacts of more than 5 percent for Cambodia, Myanmar, Thailand, and Vietnam, and more than 2.5 percent for India.

Regarding trade integration, a CGE study by Mohanty and Phohit (2008) shows welfare gains for members of the ASEAN+3–India FTA ranging from $52 billion for a simple FTA (involving only liberalization of tariffs) to $114 billion for a more comprehensive FTA (involving liberalization of tariffs as well as reduction in barriers to investment and services).

Using a slightly different regional unit of analysis (ASEAN+3 economies and South Asia), Francois and Wignaraja (2008, 2009) estimates large gains of about $260 billion, or 2 percent of GDP, from an East and South Asian FTA, under conservative assumptions. Countries obtaining relatively large positive income impacts (more than 2 percent) include Korea, Indonesia, Malaysia, Philippines, Singapore, Thailand, Vietnam, India, and Sri Lanka. In addition, India sees somewhat larger gains from an ASEAN+3 and South Asia policy scenario than an ASEAN+3 and India policy scenario. This result indicates that India has an incentive to include the rest of South Asia in a regional integration scheme with East Asia, rather than going it alone with East Asia.

While a broad ASEAN+3 and South Asia policy scenario is desirable from an economic welfare point of view, current political events in Asia may rule it out for some time. Japan–China tensions persist over disputed islands, which make it difficult for early conclusion of regional integration arrangements involving Asia's two largest economies. Uncertainties also exist over the state of India–China political relations, given growing competition between these rising powers in Asia and the recent skirmish on the disputed Himalayan border. Accordingly, geopolitical considerations suggest that it would be useful to explore policy scenarios with a narrower geographical coverage (for example, between South Asian and Southeast Asian economies), which act as a building block for eventual integration across Asia. It is also useful to consider policy scenarios with varying degrees of deep integration efforts.

ANNEX TABLE 10.1.

Legal Status of FTAs between South Asia and East Asia

FTA Status	FTA Name	Relevant Date
Signed and in effect[1]		
1	Asia–Pacific Trade Agreement	6-17-1976
2	India–Singapore Comprehensive Economic Cooperation Agreement	8-01-2005
3	Pakistan–People's Republic of China Free Trade Agreement	7-01-2007
4	Malaysia–Pakistan Closer Economic Partnership Agreement	1-01-2008
5	ASEAN–India Comprehensive Economic Cooperation Agreement	1-01-2010
6	India–Korea Comprehensive Economic Partnership Agreement (FTA upgrade negotiations launched in November 2019)	1-01-2010
7	India–Malaysia Comprehensive Economic Cooperation Agreement	7-01-2011
8	India–Japan Comprehensive Economic Partnership Agreement	8-01-2011
9	Indonesia–Pakistan Free Trade Agreement	9-13-2013
10	Sri Lanka–Singapore Free Trade Agreement	5-01-2018
Signed and not in effect[2]		
1	China–Maldives Free Trade Agreement	12-07-2017
Negotiations launched[3]		
1	Pakistan–Singapore Free Trade Agreement	8-24-2005
2	India–Indonesia Comprehensive Economic Cooperation Arrangement	10-04-2011
3	Regional Comprehensive Economic Partnership (negotiations concluded in November 2019)	5-09-2013
4	India–Thailand Free Trade Area	1-2014
5	People's Republic of China–Sri Lanka Free Trade Agreement	9-23-2014
6	Pakistan–Thailand Free Trade Agreement	9-27-2015
7	Sri Lanka–Thailand Free Trade Agreement	7-2018
Proposed/under consultation and study[4]		
1	India–People's Republic of China Regional Trading Agreement	6-23-2003
2	Pakistan–Philippines Free Trade Agreement	4-01-2004
3	Comprehensive Economic Partnership for East Asia (CEPEA/ASEAN+6)	12-14-2005
4	Brunei Darussalam–Pakistan Free Trade Agreement	8-2007
5	ASEAN–Pakistan Free Trade Agreement	8-13-2009
6	Malaysia–Sri Lanka Free Trade Agreement	10-2013
7	Republic of Korea–Pakistan Free Trade Agreement	6-18-2013
8	Japan–Sri Lanka Free Trade Agreement	1-01-2015
9	Pakistan–Vietnam Free Trade Agreement	12-09-2015
10	Nepal–People's Republic of China Free Trade Agreement	3-21-2016
11	Bangladesh–People's Republic of China Free Trade Agreement	2016
12	Japan–Pakistan FTA	2017
13	Indonesia–Sri Lanka Free Trade Agreement	2018
14	Bangladesh–Thailand Free Trade Agreement	2020
15	Bangladesh–Malaysia Free Trade Agreement	2021

Source: Asian Development Bank 2021.
Note: ASEAN+6 = ASEAN (Brunei Darussalam, Burma, Cambodia, Indonesia, Philippines, Malaysia, Laos, Singapore, Thailand, and Vietnam) plus six countries outside ASEAN (Australia, China, India, Japan, Korea, and New Zealand); FTA = free trade agreement.
[1] Date the FTA was signed and entered into effect.
[2] Date the FTA was signed (but not yet in effect).
[3] Date the FTA negotiations were launched.
[4] Date the FTA was proposed/under consultation and study.

REFERENCES

Arif, Umaima, Muhammad Javid, and Farzana Naheed Khan. 2021. "Productivity Impacts of Infrastructure Development in Asia." *Economic Systems* 45 (1): 100851.

Arnold, John. 2009. "The Role of Transport Infrastructure, Logistics, and Trade Facilitation in Asian Trade." In *Pan-Asian Integration: Linking East and South Asia*, edited by Joseph Francois, Pradumna B. Rana, and Ganeshan Wignaraja, 351–438. Basingstoke, UK: Palgrave Macmillan.

Asian Development Bank (ADB). 2008. *Emerging Asian Regionalism: A Partnership for Shared Prosperity.* Manila, Philippines: Asian Development Bank.

Asian Development Bank (ADB). 2010. *Institutions for Regional Integration: Toward an Asian Economic Community.* Manila, Philippines: Asian Development Bank.

Asian Development Bank (ADB). 2015. *Asian Economic Integration Report 2015: How Can Special Economic Zones Catalyze Economic Development?* Manila, Philippines: Asian Development Bank.

Asian Development Bank (ADB). 2021. *Asia Regional Integration Center.* Manila, Philippines: Asian Development Bank. https://aric.adb.org/.

Asian Development Bank (ADB) and Asian Development Bank Institute (ADBI). 2015. *Connecting South Asia and Southeast Asia.* Manila, Philippines, and Tokyo, Japan: ADB and ADBI.

Asian Development Bank (ADB) and United Nations Conference on Trade and Development (UNCTAD). 2008. *Quantification of Benefits from Economic Cooperation in South Asia.* New Delhi, India: Macmillan India.

Bandara, Jayatilleke, and Wusheng Yu. 2003. "How Desirable is the South Asian Free Trade Area?" *The World Economy* 26 (9): 1293–323.

Banik, Arindam, and Pradip K. Bhaumik. 2014. "Assessing the Barriers to Trade in Services in South Asia." *Global Business Review* 15 (4): 795–814.

Bhagwati, Jagdish N. 1995. "US Trade Policy: The Infatuation with FTAs." Columbia University Discussion Paper Series 726, Columbia University, New York, NY.

Bhagwati, Jagdish N. 2008. "Termites in the Trading System: How Preferential Agreements Undermine Free Trade." Oxford, UK: Oxford University Press.

Board of Investment Pakistan. 2021. "Special Economic Zone Framework in Pakistan." Board of Investment Pakistan. https://invest.gov.pk/index.php/sez.

Board of Investment Sri Lanka. 2017. *Annual Report 2017.* Colombo Board of Investment Sri Lanka. https://www.parliament.lk/uploads/documents/paperspresented/annual-report -board-of-investment-2017.pdf.

Castañeda-Navarrete, Jennifer, Jostein Hauge, and Carlos López-Gómez. 2021. "COVID-19's Impacts on Global Value Chains, As Seen in the Apparel Industry." *Development Policy Review* 39: 953–70.

Cheong, Inkyo. 2014. "Implications of the Republic of Korea's Package for Enhancing FTA Utilization." United Nations Economic and Social Commission for Asia and the Pacific (UNESCAP) ARTNet Policy Brief 42 (December). Bangkok: UNESCAP.

Dasgupta, Dipak, Nihal Pitigala, and Julien Gourdon. 2012. "South Asia's Economic Prospects from Global Rebalancing and Integration." In *Economic Reform Processes in South Asia: Toward Policy Efficiency*, edited by Philippa Dee, 23–42. Abingdon, UK: Routledge.

De, Prabir. 2020. *Act East to Act Indo-Pacific: India's Expanding Neighbourhood.* New Delhi, India: KW Publishers.

Dee, Philippa, ed. 2012. *Economic Reform Processes in South Asia: Toward Policy Efficiency.* Abingdon, UK: Routledge.

Didar Singh, A. 2018. "Rationale for a BIMSTEC Free Trade Agreement." DPG Regional Brief III (15). New Delhi: Delhi Policy Group.

Export Development Board Sri Lanka. "2021 Sri Lanka Export Development Board." Colombo, Sri Lanka: Export Development Board Sri Lanka. https://www.srilankabusiness.com/.

Francois, Joseph F., and Ganeshan Wignaraja. 2008. "Economic Implications of Asian Integration." *Global Economy Journal* 8 (3): 1–46.

Francois, Joseph F., and Ganeshan Wignaraja. 2009. "Pan-Asian Integration: Economic Implications of Integration Scenarios." In *Pan-Asian Integration: Linking East and South Asia*, edited by Joseph Francois, Pradumna B. Rana, and Ganeshan Wignaraja, 487–536. Basingstoke, UK: Palgrave Macmillan.

Francois, Joseph, Pradumna B. Rana, and Ganeshan Wignaraja, eds. 2009. *Pan-Asian Integration: Linking East and South Asia*. Basingstoke, UK: Palgrave Macmillan.

Gupta, Sanjay, and Sumit Ganguly. 2020. "Why India Refused to Join the World's Biggest Trading Bloc." *Foreign Policy* 23 (November). https://foreignpolicy.com/2020/11/23/why -india-refused-to-join-rcep-worlds-biggest-trading-bloc/.

International Monetary Fund (IMF). 2021. "IMF Direction of Trade Statistics Database." Washington, DC: IMF. https://data.imf.org/? sk=9d6028d4-f14a-464c-a2f2-59b2cd424b85.

Jain, Rajeev, and J. B. Singh. 2009. "Trade Patterns in SAARC Countries: Emerging Trends and Issues." Reserve Bank of India Occasional Papers 30 (3): 73–117.

Kathuria, Sanjay, ed. 2018. *A Glass Half Full: The Promise of Regional Trade in South Asia*. South Asia Development Forum. Washington, DC: World Bank.

Kaur, Sandeep, Sangeeta Khorana, and Manpreet Kaur. 2020. "Is There Any Potential for Services Trade of South Asia." *Foreign Trade Review* 55 (3): 402–17.

Kawai, Masahiro, and Ganeshan Wignaraja. 2011. "Introduction." In *Asia's Free Trade Agreements: How is Business Responding?*, edited by Kawai and Wignaraja. Cheltenham, UK: Edward Elgar.

Kawai, Masahiro, and Ganeshan Wignaraja. 2013. "Patterns of Free Trade Areas in Asia." Policy Studies No. 65, East-West Center, Honolulu, Hawaii.

Kelegama, S. 2009. "Introduction: Opportunities and Risks of Liberalizing Trade in Services", in Trade in Services in South Asia: Opportunities and Risks of Liberalization, edited by S. Kelegama. New Delhi: Sage Publications.

Khan, Mohsin S. 2012. "India–Pakistan Trade: A Roadmap for Enhancing Economic Relations." In *Economic Reform Processes in South Asia: Toward Policy Efficiency*, edited by Philippa Dee. Abingdon, UK: Routledge.

Kumagai, Satoru, Kazunobu Hayakawa, Ikumo Isono, Souknilanh Keola, and Kenmei Tsubota. 2013. "Geographical Simulation Analysis for Logistics Enhancement in Asia." *Economic Modelling* 34 (C): 145–53.

McKinsey Global Institute. 2019. "Globalization in Transition: The Future of Trade and Value Chains." McKinsey Global Institute.

Ministry of Commerce, People's Republic of China. 2017. "China and Maldives Sign the Free Trade Agreement." Ministry of Commerce, People's Republic of China.

Moberg, Lotta. 2017. *The Political Economy of Special Economic Zones: Concentrating Economic Development*. London, UK: Routledge.

Mohanty, S. K., and Sanjib Pohit. 2008. "Welfare Gains from Regional Economic Integration in Asia: ASEAN+3 or EAS." In *Asia's New Regionalism and Global Role: Agenda for the East Asia Summit*, edited by Nagesh Kumar, K. Kesavapany, and Yao Chaocheng. New Delhi and Singapore: Research and Information System for Developing Countries and Institute of Southeast Asian Studies.

Pant, Harsh V., and Premesha Saha, eds. 2021. *Mapping the Belt and Road Initiative: Reach, Implications, Consequences.* New Delhi: Observer Research Foundation.

Paracha, Sohail A., and M. R. Manzoor. 2011. "Economic Evaluation of Pak-Malaysia Free Trade Agreement, Report of the Pakistan Institute of Trade and Development (PITD)." Pakistan Institute of Trade and Development, Islamabad.

Petri, Peter A., and Michael G. Plummer. 2020. "East Asia Decouples from the United States: Trade War, COVID-19, and East Asia's New Trade Blocs." Peterson Institute for International Economics Working Paper Series 20-9, Peterson Institute for International Economics, Washington, DC.

Plummer, M. G., P. Morgan, and G. Wignaraja, eds. 2016. *Connecting Asia: Infrastructure for Integrating South and Southeast Asia*. Cheltenham, UK: Edward Elgar.

Prasain, Krishana. 2020. "Six Years On, Nepal's First Economic Zone Struggles to Find Investors." *The Kathmandu Post*. https://tkpo.st/2R4ks3vhttps://kathmandupost.com/money/2020/01/09/six-years-on-nepal-s-first-economic-zone-struggles-to-find-investors.

Raihan, Selim, and Mohammad A. Razzaque. 2014. "Assessing Gains from SAFTA." In *Regional Integration in South Asia: Trends, Challenges and Prospects*, edited by Mohammad A. Razzaque and Yurendra Bassnett. London, UK: Commonwealth Secretariat.

Rana, Pradumna Bickram, and John Malcolm Dowling. 2009. *South Asia: Rising to the Challenge of Globalization*. Singapore: World Scientific Press.

Rana, Pradumna Bickram, and Wa-Mun Chia. 2015. "Economic Policy Reforms in South Asia: An Overview and the Remaining Agenda." RSIS Working Paper No. 289, S. Rajaratnam School of International Studies, Nanyang Technological University, Singapore.

Sarma, Nandini. 2020. "Free Trade After RCEP: What Next for India?" ORF Brief 353 (April), Observer Research Foundation, New Delhi, India.

Scollay, Robert, and Annette Pelkmans-Balaoing. 2009. "Current Patterns of Trade and Investment." In *Pan-Asian Integration: Linking East and South Asia*, edited by Joseph Francois, Pradumna B. Rana, and Ganeshan Wignaraja, 63–162. Basingstoke, UK: Palgrave Macmillan.

Sharma, Sheel Kant. 2011. "South Asian Regionalism: Prospects and Challenges." *Indian Foreign Affairs Journal* 6 (3): 305–14.

Siriwardana, Mahinda. 2003. "Trade Liberalisation in South Asia: Free Trade Area or Customs Union." *Journal of South Asian Studies* XXVI (3): 309–29.

Suominen, Kati. 2019. "Regional Trade Agreements: Myths and Misconceptions." In *Handbook of International Trade Agreements: Country, Regional and Global Approaches*, edited by R. E. Looney. London, UK: Routledge.

Tambunan, Tulus, and Alexander C. Chandra. 2014. "Utilisation Rate of Free Trade Agreements by Local Micro, Small and Medium Enterprises: A Story of ASEAN." *Journal of International Business and Economics* 2 (2): 133–63.

United Nations Comtrade. 2021. "International Trade Statistics Database." New York, NY: United Nations. Available at: https://comtrade.un.org/.

United Nations Conference on Trade and Development (UNCTAD). 2019. "World Investment Report 2019: Special Economic Zones." Geneva, Switzerland: United Nations Conference on Trade and Development.

United Nations Conference on Trade and Development (UNCTAD). 2021. "UNCTAD Statistics." Geneva, Switzerland: United Nations Conference on Trade and Development. https://unctad.org/statistics.

Wignaraja, Ganeshan. 2014. "Will South Asia Benefit from Pan-Asian Integration?" *South Asia Economics Journal* 15 (2): 175–97.

Wignaraja. Ganeshan. 2019. "RCEP and Asian Economic Integration." In *Handbook of International Trade Agreements: Country, Regional and Global Approaches*, edited by R. E. Looney. London, UK: Routledge.

Wignaraja, Ganeshan, Dorothea. Ramizo, and Luca Burmeister. 2013. "Assessing Liberalization and Deep Integration in FTAs: A Study of Asia-Latin America FTAs." *Journal of East Asian Economic Integration* 17 (4): 385–416.

Wignaraja, Ganeshan, Peter J. Morgan, Michael G. Plummer, and Fan Zhai. 2015. "Economic Implications of Deeper South Asian-Southeast Asian Integration: A CGE Approach." *Asian Economic Papers* 14 (3): 63–81.

Wignaraja, Ganeshan, Peter J. Morgan, Michael G. Plummer, and Fan Zhai. 2016. "Economic Implications of Deeper South Asian-Southeast Asian Integration: A CGE Approach." In *Connecting Asia: Infrastructure for Integrating South and Southeast Asia*, edited by Michael G. Plummer, Peter J. Morgan, and Ganeshan Wignaraja. Cheltenham, UK: Edward Elgar.

Wignaraja, Ganeshan, and Amitendu Palit. 2018. "Sri Lanka Singapore Free Trade Agreement: Towards a Shared Economic Future." Institute of South Asian Studies (ISAS) Brief 26, No. 591 (July), National University of Singapore.

Wignaraja, Ganeshan, Dinusha Panditaratne, Pabasara Kannagara, and Divya Hundlani. 2020. "Chinese Investment and the BRI in Sri Lanka." Chatham House Research Paper (March), Asia-Pacific Programme, London, UK.

World Bank. 1993. *The East Asian Miracle, Economic Growth and Public Policy*. Washington DC: World Bank.

World Bank. 2012. "Services Trade Restrictiveness Database." Washington, DC: World Bank. https://www.worldbank.org/en/research/brief/services-trade-restrictions-database.

World Economic Forum. 2019. "Global Competitiveness Index 2019." Geneva, Switzerland: World Economic Forum.

World Trade Organization (WTO). 2009 and 2020. World Tariff Profiles 2009 and 2020. Geneva: World Trade Organization. https://www.wto.org/english/res_e/statis_e/statis_e.htm.

World Trade Organization (WTO). 2011. *Trade Policy Review: India*. Geneva, Switzerland: WTO.

World Trade Organization (WTO). 2022. "Trade Growth to Slow Sharply in 2023 as Global Economy Faces Strong Headwinds." WTO Press Release 909. Geneva, Switzerland: World Trade Organization, October 5.

Xavier, Constantino. 2018. "Bridging the Bay of Bengal: Toward a Stronger BIMSTEC." Carnegie India Research Paper, Carnegie India, New Delhi, India.

.

CHAPTER 11

Scaling Up Quality Infrastructure Investment in South Asia

Olivier Bizimana, Laura Jaramillo, Saji Thomas, and Jiae Yoo

South Asia needs large infrastructure investments to achieve its development goals, and public investment can also support the COVID-19 recovery. Regression estimates that account for the quantity and quality of investment suggest that public infrastructure was a key driver of productivity growth in South Asia. Going forward, higher public infrastructure spending can raise growth, but its benefits depend on how it is financed and managed. Model simulations show that tax financing, concessional lending, or private sector financing through public-private partnerships are more advantageous than government borrowing through financial markets because they support growth while containing the impact on public debt. However, the optimal choice also depends on available fiscal space, taxation capacity, implementation risks, and public investment efficiency. To reap the most benefits from higher infrastructure investment, South Asian countries need to manage fiscal risks carefully, including from public-private partnerships and state-owned enterprises, and improve public investment efficiency.

INTRODUCTION

South Asia needs large infrastructure investments to achieve its development goals, and public investment can support the COVID-19 recovery. Public investment projects can be an important tool to promote employment and economic activity in the near term to support the recovery. Over the medium term, public investment is essential to raise productivity, achieve the Sustainable Development Goals (SDGs), and build a resilient economy.

The authors are grateful to Ha Vu, Rui Monteiro, Ranil Salgado, Sandeep Saxena, Eivind Tandberg, and the participants of the Regional Forum on Fostering Growth in South Asia (2020, New Delhi) for comments and to Shihui Liu and Kevin Rivas for help with the figures and text formatting.

South Asia needs to scale up and improve the quality of its public infrastructure investment. Countries in the region have made important progress expanding their infrastructure network, including utilities, transportation, telecommunications, and health. However, the quantity and quality of infrastructure remains below that of emerging market peers in Asia. Panel regression estimates suggest that infrastructure development has been a key driver of productivity growth in South Asia over recent decades. Going forward, growth could significantly increase by upgrading both the quantity and quality of infrastructure.

Higher government spending on infrastructure can raise growth, but its benefits depend on how it is financed and managed. COVID-19 has exacerbated previous challenges to the financing of an infrastructure push as countries in the region are now facing higher debt to GDP, tax revenue shortfalls, and in some cases, higher sovereign spreads. At the same time, there may be limits on the availability of concessional financing given the increased demand for resources worldwide because of COVID-19. Countries therefore need to look at the trade-offs and risks involved in the different financing options: raising taxes, raising debt, or expanding reliance on private sector financing through public-private partnerships (PPPs). Model simulations using the IMF's Flexible System of Global Models (FSGM) applied to selected countries in the region show that tax financing, concessional lending, or PPP financing are more advantageous than government borrowing through financial markets because they support growth while containing the impact on public debt. While PPPs might seem more appealing than the other forms of financing infrastructure investment, implementation may entail additional costs and growth payoffs are feasible only if projects are well-designed and well-implemented to be highly efficient. Moreover, PPPs pose important fiscal risks. The simulation results also show that the optimal financing choice is country specific and depends on available fiscal space, taxation capacity, and the efficiency of the public sector investment.

To reap the most benefits from higher infrastructure investment, South Asian countries will need to manage fiscal risks carefully and improve public investment efficiency. A larger share of infrastructure projects in South Asia are implemented by state-owned enterprises (SOEs) than by general government entities, while PPPs remain limited. Although PPPs or SOEs can provide significant benefits, including greater efficiency of spending, they also entail significant risks that need to be addressed. In particular, countries need to take steps to accurately estimate and monitor associated fiscal costs and ensure transparency and accountability of PPP and SOE investment. In addition, countries in South Asia need to take action to increase the efficiency of public investment to get greater growth payoffs from additional public infrastructure spending. Improvements are needed in public investment management, particularly in the practices of project appraisal and selection, maintenance funding, and multiyear budgeting.

This chapter is organized as follows. The first section takes stock of infrastructure needs in South Asia, looking at both quantity and quality. The second section analyzes the trade-offs involved with different financing options. The third section looks at the role of PPPs and SOEs in implementing infrastructure spending in South Asia, outlining measures to mitigate related risks. The fourth section underscores the role of public investment management in raising public investment efficiency, drawing on lessons from public investment management assessments (PIMAs) carried out in the region. The fifth section concludes.

INFRASTRUCTURE NEEDS IN SOUTH ASIA

Infrastructure plays a vital role for sustained economic growth. Several studies have found significant total factor productivity effects of infrastructure in Asian economies (Nishimizu and Hulten 1978; Hsieh 1999; Hulten and others 2006). In the current context of the COVID-19 shock, public investment projects can be an important tool to support near-term employment and economic activity (IMF 2020a; IMF 2020d). Public investment has been found to have a higher fiscal multiplier than other spending, implying a stronger boost to aggregate demand (Abiad and others 2016).

Countries in South Asia need more and higher-quality infrastructure to achieve their development goals. Accelerating sustainable infrastructure development is key to achieving the Sustainable Developmental Goals, as countries in South Asia often lag in terms of basic infrastructure (UNESCAP 2017). Closing existing gaps in infrastructure has the potential to boost growth and alleviate poverty in the region (Andrés and others 2013).

Countries in South Asia have made important progress expanding their infrastructure network, but have not yet matched peers in the rest of Asia in terms of both quantity and quality (Figure 11.1).

- *Electricity:* Despite the increase in the past two decades, electricity generation capacity in most South Asian countries remains low compared with regional peers, except for Bhutan where electricity is its main export. Supply of electricity is often unreliable because of chronic shortages (Singh and others 2015), and this is considered as one of main constraints to potential growth (World Bank 2018). The quality of electricity provision services, as proxied by the efficiency in transmission and distribution, is also somewhat lower in South Asian countries than Asian emerging markets.

- *Transportation:* Road connectivity, measured by the length of road per area, is poor in most South Asian countries, with the exception of India (which has one of the largest road networks in the world). The quality of roads, as measured by the share of paved roads, is relatively low and has deteriorated in some countries.

- *Telecommunication:* The penetration of telecommunication has been dramatic in the last two decades. Even with such an increase, however, internet access and data capacity in most South Asian countries are still low compared with regional peers.

Figure 11.1. Infrastructure Quantity and Quality in South Asia, 1990–2017

1. Electricity Generating Capacity
(Megawatts per 1000 workers)

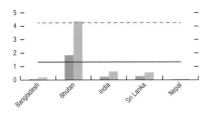

2. Electricity Transmitted and Distributed to Consumers
(Percent of total production)

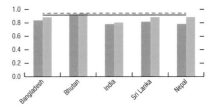

3. Road Length
(Kilometer per square kilometer of land area)

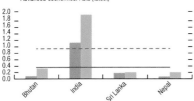

4. Road Quality
(Share of paved road to toal road length)

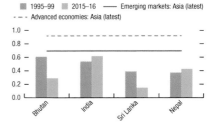

5. Internet Access
(Percent of households with internet access)

6. Internet Service Quality
(International Internet bandwidth per user, bit/s, rescaled to 0–1)

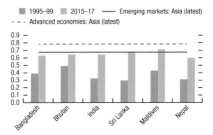

7. Access to Water, At Least Basic
(Percent of population)

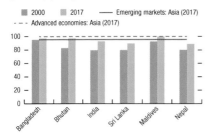

8. Access to Safely Managed Water
(Percent of population using improved water supplies)

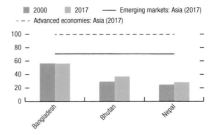

Sources: UN Energy Statistics; World Bank; International Road Federation; International Telecommunication Union; Nepal Electricity Authority; WHI and UNICEF Joint Monitoring Programme for Water Supply, Sanitation, and Hygiene; and authors' calculations.

- *Health:* Access to water, especially safely managed water, is not universal in several countries in South Asia. Even in countries that provide greater access to basic water, a much smaller share of the population has access to safely managed water that is free of pathogens and elevated levels of toxic substances.

The cross-country empirical analysis shows that both quantity and quality of infrastructure matter for growth. Using a panel of 80 countries for the period 1990–2017, an aggregate production function augmented with physical infrastructure variables is estimated.[1] The analysis applies the approach by Calderon and Servén (2004 and 2008), extended to take into account the quality aspect of infrastructure (see Bizimana and others 2021 and IMF 2020c for details on the methodology).[2] The results confirm that infrastructure expansion in quantity makes a significant contribution to productivity growth (Table 2.1, columns 1 to 4). Moreover, for any given quantity, improving quality would also yield a significant additional boost to growth (Table 11.1, columns 5 to 8).

The regression analysis suggests that infrastructure development has been a driver of productivity growth in South Asia over the last decades. Based on the regression estimates in Table 11.1, productivity growth can be decomposed into its contributing factors to quantify the contribution of infrastructure expansion and quality improvement.[3] The decomposition shows that about one-third of productivity growth in the last two decades can be attributed to infrastructure development (Figure 11.2). The expansion in the quantity of infrastructure has been an important driver, especially the explosive penetration of the internet. Quality improvement also explains some of the productivity growth, in particular internet data capacity and the efficiency in electricity service provision.

Upgrading infrastructure quantity and quality to bolster potential growth would entail a large ramp up in spending and improvement in spending efficiency. Studies have found that the South Asia region would need to invest between 5 and

---

[1] The empirical analysis uses physical measures of infrastructure rather than monetary ones such as public expenditure. Public expenditure tends to be less accurate as it is affected by efficiency and government procurement practices and does not reflect the increasing private sector participation in infrastructure development. Furthermore, the analysis focuses on power, transportation, and telecommunications as these factors have been found to be among the most important for growth, and their data are more widely available. Health indicators are not included in the empirical analysis because of lack of adequate data availability.

[2] To capture the quantity and quality of infrastructure, aggregate synthetic indices are used rather than including individual measures of different types of infrastructure. Various estimation methods are considered, including the generalized method of moments (GMM) estimation developed by Arellano and Bond (1991) to alleviate the endogeneity issue and bias stemming from the correlation between the lagged dependent variable and fixed effects in the error term.

[3] Note that better infrastructure would also enable faster industrialization, which the regression analysis revealed as another important contributing factor enabling a growth leap among lower-middle income economies.

TABLE 11.1.

Infrastructure and Growth

Dependent Variable: GDP per Worker (Log Difference)	(1) Pooled OLS	(2) Panel with Time Effect	(3) Within Estimator	(4) Difference GMM	(5) Pooled OLS	(6) Panel with Time Effect	(7) Within Estimator	(8) Difference GMM
Lag. output	−0.061***	−0.106***	−0.377***	−0.379***	−0.103***	−0.116***	−0.385***	−0.372***
	(0.010)	(0.015)	(0.033)	(0.077)	(0.012)	(0.016)	(0.051)	(0.122)
Education	0.043***	0.025	−0.023	−0.064	0.048***	0.046***	0.008	0.000
	(0.012)	(0.018)	(0.028)	(0.081)	(0.013)	(0.017)	(0.031)	(0.070)
Financial development	0.001	−0.013	−0.002	0.001	−0.000	−0.008	0.002	0.001
	(0.008)	(0.009)	(0.010)	(0.011)	(0.008)	(0.008)	(0.010)	(0.010)
Government burden	−0.024	−0.013	−0.054	0.007	−0.016	−0.013	−0.088*	−0.055
	(0.017)	(0.023)	(0.033)	(0.072)	(0.018)	(0.023)	(0.050)	(0.086)
Trade openness	−0.001	−0.009	−0.005	−0.017	−0.002	0.001	0.036	0.091
	(0.010)	(0.015)	(0.024)	(0.053)	(0.010)	(0.014)	(0.033)	(0.066)
Institutional quality	0.021	0.044	0.065	0.094	0.016	−0.037	−0.014	−0.061
	(0.046)	(0.055)	(0.069)	(0.165)	(0.056)	(0.064)	(0.093)	(0.196)
Inflation	0.003	−0.003	−0.007	−0.011	0.015	0.007	−0.000	0.025
	(0.008)	(0.008)	(0.009)	(0.019)	(0.009)	(0.010)	(0.012)	(0.020)
Modern sector share	−0.081	0.001	0.611***	0.271	0.389***	0.457***	0.696***	1.010**
	(0.067)	(0.083)	(0.181)	(0.522)	(0.100)	(0.125)	(0.223)	(0.446)
Terms of trade	0.013	0.010	−0.061***	−0.120**	0.005	0.015	−0.038	−0.048
	(0.022)	(0.021)	(0.022)	(0.051)	(0.027)	(0.023)	(0.026)	(0.046)
Terms of trade shocks	0.010	0.042	0.142*	0.190*	0.080	0.134	0.137	0.099
	(0.120)	(0.087)	(0.080)	(0.099)	(0.135)	(0.101)	(0.100)	(0.092)
Infrastructure quantity	0.034***	0.068***	0.151***	0.216***	0.023**	0.042***	0.141***	0.155**
	(0.009)	(0.013)	(0.025)	(0.052)	(0.010)	(0.012)	(0.031)	(0.062)
Infrastructure quality					0.023***	0.020**	0.031**	0.055**
					(0.007)	(0.008)	(0.013)	(0.025)
No. of observations	367	367	367	270	249	249	249	161
No. of countries		97	97	92		88	88	78
No. of instruments				54				47
Arellano-Bond test for AR(2)				0.10				0.27
Hansen test				0.24				0.42

Sources: UN Energy Statistics; International Road Federation and International Telecommunication Union; World Bank; Barro and Lee 2013; International Country Risk Guide dataset; and IMF staff estimates.

Note: Robust standard errors are in parentheses. Country and period dummies and constants are not reported for brevity. Following the approach in Calderon and Serven (2004), infrastructure quantity and quality refer to the synthesized aggregate indices constructed as the first principal component of the underlying physical measures of infrastructure quantity and quality of three types of utilities: electricity (generation capacity in megawatt per 1000 workers and the share of electricity losses in transmission and distribution), road connectivity (length in kilometers per area and the share of paved roads), and telecommunication (share of households with Internet access and international Internet bandwidth per user). GMM = generalized method of moments; OLS = ordinary least squares.
***$p < 0.01$, **$p < 0.05$, and *$p < 0.1$.

Figure 11.2. Contribution of Infrastructure Development to Productivity Growth
(Annualized average in percentage points)

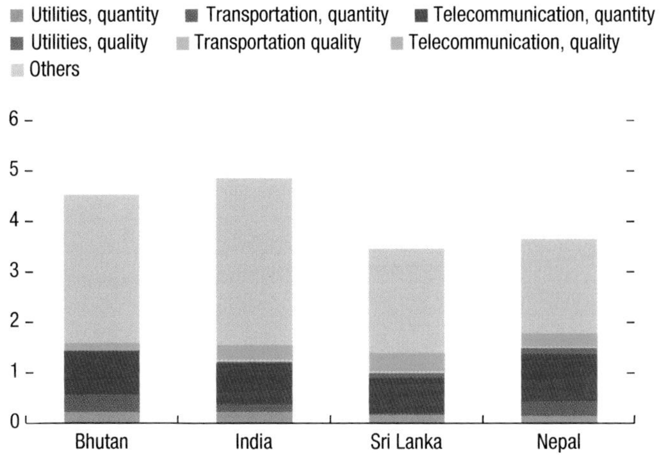

Source: Authors' estimates.
Note: Data are for between 1995–2000 and 2015 to latest. Calculation is based on the generalized method of moments regression estimates of productivity growth on infrastructure indices (Table 11.1, column 8). The contribution of infrastructure quantity and quality indices is decomposed into three underlying infrastructure types based on their respective weights in constructing their first principal component.

10 percent of GDP per year to reach the infrastructure level required to meet increasing demand and deliver healthy growth (Andrés and others 2014; Asian Development Bank Institute 2017; Vu and others 2020).[4] Given the large costs and its lumpy nature, the growth benefits will depend crucially on how additional infrastructure spending is financed and how it is managed.

TRADE-OFFS INVOLVED WITH DIFFERENT FINANCING OPTIONS

A big question is how to finance a ramp-up in public infrastructure spending. South Asian countries must decide between financing investment through increased taxation or debt, taking into consideration their macroeconomic effects. Given limited fiscal space to increase borrowing in many countries—which has been further eroded by the COVID-19 pandemic—as well as difficulties to

---

[4] In the past, Andrés and others (2014) estimated the investment needs between 6.6 and 9.9 percent of GDP per year for the period of 2011-20. More recently, ADBI (2017) estimated infrastructure investment needs for South Asia at 7.6 percent of GDP for the period of 2016–30 as a baseline, and up to 8.8 percent once accounting for climate mitigation and adaptation. Vu and others (2020) found that the Asia-Pacific region needs to invest about 5 percent of GDP to achieve SDGs, with large needs especially in road infrastructure.

mobilize revenues, consideration may also be given to greater use of private sector financing through PPPs.

Each of these financing options entails different trade-offs. In particular, countries need to ensure that the infrastructure investment push does not compromise fiscal sustainability that would jeopardize growth over the medium term. This section analyzes the growth–debt trade-offs faced by South Asian countries using macro-model simulations for selected economies.

How to Finance Infrastructure Investment

The macroeconomic effects of increasing public infrastructure investment are evaluated using the IMF's FSGM.[5] The FSGM is an annual, multiregion, general equilibrium model of the global economy combining both micro-founded and reduced formulations of various economic sectors. In the model, total consumption consists of spending from households that can save and from those who can only consume out of current income (liquidity-constrained consumers). Firms produce goods and services using labor and their holdings of private capital. The government purchases final goods directly, including consumption and investment goods, and makes transfers to households, funded with various tax instruments.

The FSGM is well suited to analyze the macroeconomic effects of a government infrastructure push. In addition to affecting aggregate demand directly, government investment also cumulates into a public capital stock, raising the economy wide level of productivity. The accumulation of public investment into public capital varies from country to country, depending on the efficiency of public investment management. Moreover, the non-Ricardian dynamics of the model imply significant macroeconomic responses from fiscal policy both in the short and long terms. The simulations are undertaken for four selected South Asian economies: India, Sri Lanka, Bangladesh, and Maldives.[6]

The simulations assume a permanent increase in public investment of 1 percent of GDP phased in more than five years, with varying financing options. Although the region has larger infrastructure needs (as indicated earlier), a 1 percent of GDP increase in public investment spending is used for simplicity and comparison across countries. Hence, the simulations show a conservative estimate of potential output gains.

The simulations explore four financing options:[7]

1. *Option 1: Tax financing through a higher consumption tax.* The increase in public investment spending is budget-neutral, accommodated by an equivalent

---

[5] FSGM's theoretical structure and simulation properties are laid out in Andrle and others (2015).

[6] This analysis uses the Asia and Pacific Department Model (APDMOD), a module of the FSGM that contains individual blocks for 15 Asian countries and 9 additional regions that represent the rest of the world.

[7] For simplicity, it is assumed that project costs are the same under the different options. Financing of infrastructure through SOEs is not modeled in this section because of inadequate cross-country data regarding SOE financial positions and efficiency levels.

increase in indirect tax revenue.[8] For this set of countries, a 1 percent of GDP increase in consumption tax would imply tax rate hike of 1.4 to 1.7 percentage points.

2. *Option 2: Debt financing through financial markets.* Higher public investment spending is fully financed by market borrowing, with an impact on borrowing costs.[9] The simulations assume a rise in the risk premium by 3 basis points per unit increase in the ratio of public debt to GDP. While, for simplicity, the change in the risk premium in relation to debt increases is assumed to be the same for all countries, the impact on interest costs is larger for countries with an initial higher debt level.[10]

3. *Option 3: Debt financing through concessional loans.* The rise in public investment spending is fully financed by concessional borrowing. The simulations assume that the concessional loans are granted with below-market interest rates.[11]

4. *Option 4: Private sector financing through PPPs.* The government and the private sector partner to build and operate public infrastructure. Private concessionaires build the infrastructure using private finance, and then operate the facilities, recouping their expenses through future income stream from concession (for example, toll revenue or other user charges).[12] The simulations assume user-funded PPPs—where the users pay fees for using the infrastructure—that allow   the   private   concessionaire   to   fully   recover   costs   and   the

---

[8] Given the potential scarring effects of the COVID-19 crisis, a consumption tax increase is preferred over direct taxes (both personal income tax and corporate income tax), because it has the least distortionary effects on capital and labor supply in the long term (see IMF 2013; and the analysis for emerging Asia in Vu and others 2020). Model simulations, not presented in this chapter for brevity, show that an increase in direct taxes (personal income tax and corporate income tax) results in much smaller output gains than a VAT hike.

[9] In the FSGM, option 2 is implemented by adjusting the fiscal deficit target to the additional discretionary spending. In options 2 and 3, the fiscal balance is affected by the cycle, reflecting automatic stabilizers, while general lumpsum transfers adjust to cover the increased debt-service costs associated with a permanently higher deficit. In principle, any fiscal instrument in FSGM can be used for automatic adjustment toward the deficit target. General lumpsum transfers are used because they have the least distortionary effects.

[10] The risk premium is exogenous in the FSGM and calibrated based on the increase in the debt-to-GDP ratio to better reflect the crowding-out effect of government debt. The assumption of 3 basis points (the same for all countries in the sample) is based on Kumar and Baldacci (2010), who find risk premium elasticities in the range of 3–5 basis points for a panel of advanced and emerging market economies. The value of 3 basis points is somewhat conservative in light of the relatively high initial debt-to-GDP in most of the selected economies. The model does not account for possible differences in risk premiums across countries arising from initial debt levels and market access. However, if countries with high initial debt stock were assumed to face a larger change in risk premium, the results would be qualitatively the same.

[11] In option 3, the FSGM simulations are conducted under the assumption that the risk premium does not respond to the rise in the debt-to-GDP ratio.

[12] User fees, which do not explicitly appear in the model, are accounted for as a reduction in targeted transfers to households, which are associated with lower multipliers than taxes.

government has no direct payment obligations.[13] The simplifying assumption in the model is that PPPs have similar costs to traditional public investment and that users are willing to pay the fees to cover these costs. However, experience in this regard has varied from country to country and project to project. Larger growth payoffs under PPP financing are feasible only if projects are well-designed and well-implemented to be significantly more efficient than traditional public investment (option 4a). Inefficiencies in implementation of PPPs can result in higher costs, dampening the positive growth impact (option 4b).[14]

How Scaling Up Infrastructure Investment Bolsters Output

Higher public investment lifts real GDP in the short and long terms in all selected countries across the four financing options. The magnitude of the output gains varies, however, depending on the financing options as well as each country's initial conditions, especially the level of government investment efficiency.[15] Figure 11.3 shows the simulation results of the effects of a ramp up in infrastructure spending on real GDP after 10 years.[16]

- *Option 1.* Under the consumption tax-financed option, the public investment push leads to significant output gains in the long term. Higher public investment raises the public capital stock, which boosts the general productivity of the economy. The resulting rise in the marginal productivity of capital and labor stimulates private investment and raises labor demand. This lifts private consumption in the long term. In the short term, however, the increase in taxes discourages private consumption, partially offsetting the stimulative impact of higher public investment spending. All in all, the rise in public investment financed with consumption taxes results in cumulative increases in real GDP between 1.6 percent and 2.7 percent in the long term.

- *Option 2.* The long-term effect on real GDP of the market-financed increase in public investment is more muted. The adverse effects on output become apparent over time, as the rise in government's borrowing costs associated with higher public debt-to-GDP crowds out private investment and depresses the private capital stock. However, private consumption is higher.

---

[13] Rather than relying on user fees, the government could alternatively compensate the private concessionaire through availability payments (where the government pays for the services through predetermined payments over the term of the contract). In the model, availability payments would need to be financed with taxation or debt, and therefore the model results would be similar to options 1 or 2.

[14] For option 4b, the simulations assume that the calibrated value for public investment efficiency is lower by 10 percent.

[15] In the FSGM, the calibration of the parameter of public investment efficiency is based on the combination of long-term output elasticity of government investment (Ligthart and Suárez 2005) and the IMF's survey-based measures of infrastructure quality (IMF 2015).

[16] The output gains after 20 years are larger, with the levels of GDP higher by about 3.5 percent to 5.2 percent (option 1), 3.2 percent to 5.0 percent (option 2), 3.9 percent to 5.6 percent (option 3), and 3.8 percent to 5.4 percent (option 4).

Figure 11.3. Impact of 1 Percent of GDP Higher Public Investment on Real GDP, Year 10
(Percent deviation from control)

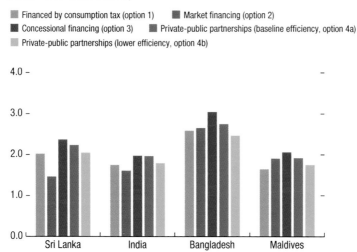

Source: Authors' estimates.

Labor supply expands by more than in the tax-financed variant, as households need to work more to offset lower transfers that are required to stabilize public debt in the long term. Overall, real GDP gains from higher public investment in the market-financing option are comprised between 1.5 percent and 2.6 percent in the long term.

- *Option 3.* With concessional financing, the public investment push generates sustained output gains. The rising government debt-to-GDP ratio no longer crowds out significantly private investment, reflecting the absence of risk premia. Private consumption increases substantially in the short- to medium-terms, as households need to work more to offset lower transfers that are required to stabilize public debt in the long term. Overall, real GDP is 2 percent to around 3 percent higher in the long term.

- *Option 4.* When implemented efficiently, PPPs generate substantial GDP gains in the short and long terms (option 4a). As in the other financing options, in the short term, higher aggregate demand lifts output through multiplier effects. Private consumption is, however, initially somewhat dampened by lower targeted transfers (user fees). Similar to the other options, private investment as well as labor demand—and hence wages—rise sharply reflecting the permanent increase in the level of productivity. This bolsters private consumption over the medium to long term. Overall, the level of GDP is between 1.9 percent and 2.7 percent higher in the long term. In contrast, lower public investment efficiency of PPPs (option 4b) would dampen the positive effect on GDP, with an increase of about 1.7 to 2.4 percent in the long term.

It is important to note that across all options, countries with relatively lower initial public debt ratio and higher initial levels of government investment efficiency record the largest cumulative increase in real GDP in the long term. Bangladesh, which has a higher calibrated value for efficiency and a lower initial ratio of public debt to GDP, displays the biggest output gains in the long term under all four financing options.

Beware the Growth–Debt Trade-Offs

The macroeconomic benefits of additional infrastructure investment need to be balanced with the fiscal costs. This is especially crucial for countries such as India, Sri Lanka, and Maldives, where government debt-to-GDP ratios are running high by historical standard, and hence have more limited fiscal room (IMF 2020d). Moreover, the COVID-19 crisis has exacerbated the fiscal challenges that these countries face to finance an infrastructure push. Most countries are expected to face larger debt-to-GDP ratios, pressure on borrowing costs, weaker tax collection, and possible limits on the availability of concessional financing given the increased demand for resources worldwide.

The simulation results displayed in Figure 11.4 quantify the trade-off between growth and debt that each country faces. The set of figures plot the simulation results of the effects of an increase in government investment on real GDP and debt-to-GDP ratio in the short to medium term (three years) and in the long term (10 years), relative to a control scenario without a scale-up in infrastructure investment. The main findings are as follows:

- Under the consumption tax-financed scenario (option 1), by construction, the general government balance is unchanged, as the increase in public investment spending is financed with higher consumption taxes. The debt-to-GDP ratios improve slightly in the short to medium term, reflecting the impact of higher output, and converge to steady state in the long term.
- Under both debt financing options—market (option 2) and concessional borrowing (option 3)—the government debt-to-GDP ratios increase markedly. Under the market financing scenario (option 2), higher public debt raises the government's risk premium, and the debt-to-GDP ratios increase by about 7–8 percentage points in most of the selected economies in the long term. The rise in the public debt ratios is slightly more contained in option 3 (6–7 percentage points).
- Under the PPPs option (option 4), the government balance remains unchanged, as the infrastructure investment is financed by the private sector that recoups its expenses through user charges. The debt-to-GDP ratios decline slightly in the short to medium term, reflecting higher output, and converge to steady state in the long term.

What Is the Optimal Financing Option?

The simulation results show that tax financing, concessional lending, or PPP financing are more advantageous than market financing in addressing the long

Figure 11.4. Growth–Debt Trade-Off from Higher Public Investment

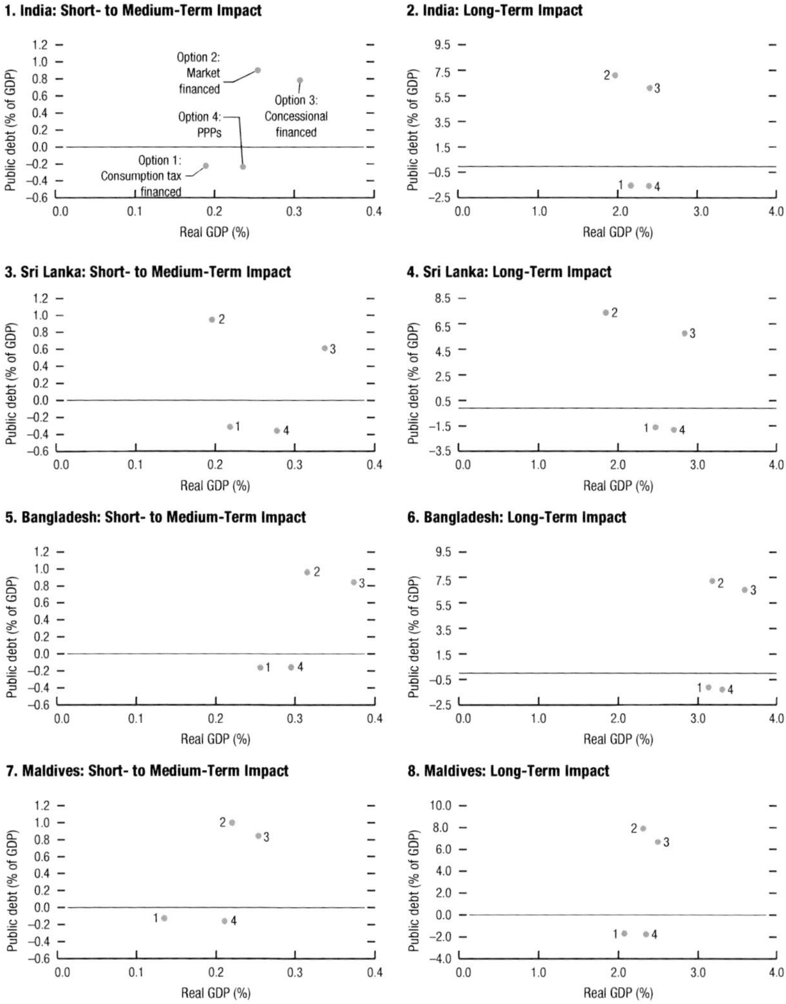

Source: Authors' calculations from Flexible System of Global Model simulations.
Note: PPPs = public-private partnerships.

term growth-debt trade-off. Overall, the optimal financing choice is country specific and depends on the level of government debt-to-GDP ratio, taxation capacity, implementation risks for PPPs, and the efficiency of the public sector.

- *In the short to medium term,* a ramp-up in public infrastructure investment financed with concessional resources (option 3) yields higher output gains than market-funding (option 2), as the borrowing costs remain contained under the former option. Concessional borrowing generates also slightly higher output than the consumption tax-financing (option 1) and the PPPs scheme (option 4). However, option 3 also results in higher public debt that can increase fiscal vulnerability. Moreover, in the wake of the pandemic crisis, countries may not be eligible for concessional financing, or may face challenges in accessing sufficient amounts of concessional financing, in view of the increased demand for resources from countries around the world and uncertainty as to whether donor countries will be scaling up support.[17] Hence, the concessional financing (option 3) may still not be preferred (or feasible) compared with consumption tax-financing (option 1) or PPPs arrangement (option 4).

- *In the long term*, however, the relative advantage of concessional financing (option 3) over PPPs financing (option 4) diminishes. Although output gains under option 3 are broadly the same as in option 4, debt in option 3 is considerably higher as option 4 has no increase in debt to GDP. PPPs arrangement appears better suited than VAT financing in addressing the growth-debt trade-off in the long term, especially in a post–COVID-19 crisis environment where raising taxes might be politically challenging. However, although PPPs might seem more appealing than the other forms of financing infrastructure investment, PPPs can also entail higher costs and implementation risks that can diminish their growth payoffs, as illustrated by option 4b in Figure 11.3. PPPs overperform only if their design and implementation is highly efficient. It is important to note that, PPPs pose challenges for fiscal management and entail fiscal risks.

INFRASTRUCTURE INVESTMENT THROUGH PPPS AND SOES

Public and Private Contributions to Infrastructure Investment

A larger share of infrastructure projects in South Asia are implemented by SOEs than by general government entities, while private involvement remains relatively limited.[18] SOEs carry out 44 percent of infrastructure investment, compared with 40 percent by the general government and 15 percent through private participation in infrastructure (Figure 11.5). While annual general government spending on public investment averaged 8 percent of GDP in 2017 across countries in South Asia, yearly PPP investments remained relatively small at 1 percent of GDP (IMF 2019). SOEs and private participation in infrastructure have been prominent in the transport and energy sectors, more so than in other regions, with SOEs also investing in water infrastructure.[19]

---

[17] Some countries may not be eligible for concessional financing because of their income level or scale of projects.

[18] OECD (2015) classifies the modes of infrastructure delivery as (1) direct (public) provision; (2) traditional public procurement; (3) state-owned enterprises (in full or in part); (4) public-private partnerships and concessions; and (5) privatization with regulation.

[19] Some countries have also pursued public investments through the Belt and Road Initiative, but reliable data are not readily available for these investments.

Figure 11.5. Public Entity, State-Owned Enterprise, and Private Participation in Investment, by Region and Sector, 2017

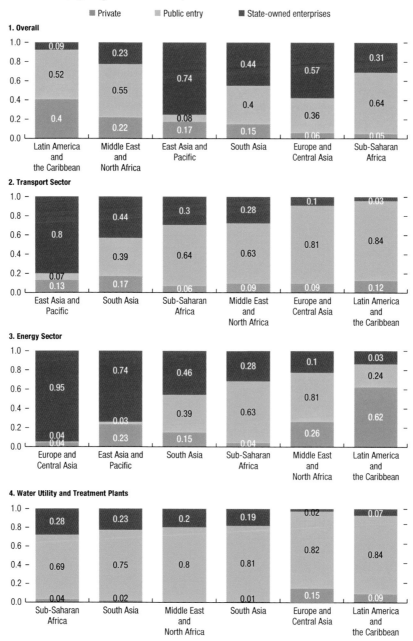

Source: World Bank 2017.

Note: Private refers to private participation in infrastructure, which includes public-private partnerships as well as other forms of private involvement in the delivery and/or management of public infrastructure.

Public-Private Partnerships

When used effectively, PPPs can deliver substantial benefits. Governments typically enter into PPPs for infrastructure to GML (1) attract private capital investment that can supplement public resources; (2) increase efficiency of investment and use available resources more effectively; and (3) reform sectors through a reallocation of roles, incentives, and accountability (Asian Development Bank 2008). By involving private sector management and innovation, PPPs may deliver better quality and lower cost services than traditional public procurement of assets and services.

However, PPPs can also entail additional costs. In some cases, a well-structured, well-implemented PPP will have lower life-cycle costs than traditional public investment (Dokko, Kearney, and Stollerman 2016). However, other studies suggest that PPPs have tended to be more expensive than traditional public investment (United Nations 2016). Private borrowing costs often tend to be higher than those of the public sector. PPPs often involve higher transaction costs, as they are very complex to negotiate, implement, and are also frequently renegotiated.[20] PPPs are also associated with contingent fiscal liabilities that add to these costs (Irwin, Mazraani, and Saxena 2018). These additional costs suggest that PPPs user fees would need to be higher than taxes collected to finance traditional government investment. In addition, users' willingness to pay may vary widely from project to project and charging cost-based fees may not always be politically feasible. PPP contracts therefore may involve some element of government contribution. This can be explicit (for example, availability payments) or implicit (for example, minimum revenue payments or other forms of guarantees).

Fiscal risks associated with PPPs can have a significant impact on the government's finances through direct and contingent liabilities.[21] Such liabilities include capital subsidies, volume-based payments for services, tax incentives, and payments related to guarantees on revenue, exchange-rate, interest-rate, or debt (Irwin, Mazraani, and Saxena 2018). Implicit liabilities, created by ineffective contract management or poorly managed renegotiation, generate additional fiscal risks. Moreover, if public investment through PPP projects are not adequately disclosed, it could threaten the integrity of the budget and complicate fiscal discipline and good governance (IMF 2004; Akitoby and others 2007).

The benefits from PPPs can only be reaped if associated fiscal risks are managed adequately, based on a strong legal and fiscal institutional framework. The following are several important steps to address fiscal risks related to PPPs include:[22]

---

[20] For example, infrastructure projects entail risks related to land acquisition, environmental, and other clearances. Complexities arise as PPP contracts allocate these risks between the government and private sector.

[21] In contrast to traditional investment projects fully financed by the government that can be rolled back if needed, PPPs create long-term binding commitments that cannot be scaled down once entered into.

[22] See Irwin, Mazraani, and Saxena 2018.

- *Sound PPP framework.* Establish policies, procedures, and institutions that define how PPPs will be identified, planned, assessed, selected, budgeted, procured, monitored, and accounted (Asian Development Bank 2008; World Bank 2014b).

- *Controlling costs.* Establish a gateway process managed by the ministry of finance; develop a risk sharing framework, where the government bears only those risks that it strongly influences; establish clear lines of accountability, with central review of major commitments and decentralization of smaller decisions and contract monitoring; and impose limits on the total sum of commitments on PPPs (Irwin, Mazraani, and Saxena 2018).

- *Disclosure of costs and risks.* An inventory of all PPP projects should be maintained with proper fiscal accounting of their full lifetime costs. Governments should aim at full disclosure in the budget documents of current government commitments (including guarantees) and expected budgetary costs of existing PPP contracts. New PPPs should be assessed within the medium-term fiscal framework to check for fiscal affordability. PPPs risks should be disclosed in fiscal risk statements (IMF 2014, 2018a).

State-Owned Enterprises

Government infrastructure investment through SOEs is often justified to correct market failures. One example of market failure is a natural monopoly, wherein the initial cost of building the infrastructure is so large that private firms are reluctant to enter the market (IMF 2020b). SOEs have been therefore typically involved in network industries, such as energy, transportation, and water and sewer systems. Governments have also relied on SOEs when the latter are able to raise financing independently, or also to keep the investment off the government's balance sheet.

However, weak governance affects SOEs' financial performance and their ability to provide quality infrastructure investment. Profits and productivity have been lower in SOEs than in private firms (IMF 2020b), partly attributed to weak governance and unfunded mandates (for example, providing services at below-cost recovery levels or promoting employment beyond what is efficient for the firm).[23] Moreover, SOEs that are inefficient and cash-strapped are not able to invest to adequately maintain or expand infrastructure networks. They also suffer from lack of transparency and accountability.

Improvements in the governance and productivity of SOEs are paramount to improve profitability and minimize fiscal risks. Countries should improve the financial oversight of SOEs, including through periodic monitoring of SOE financial performance, costing the delivery of quasi-fiscal activities in the annual budget, and disclosing them in financial reports (IMF 2014; Allen and Alves 2016). By reducing internal inefficiencies, SOEs can provide better results for

---

[23] Inefficient SOEs impose substantial fiscal costs on public finances in the form of government guarantees, subsidies, soft loans, or capital injections. IMF (2020b) found that maximum annual support to nonfinancial SOEs reached 16 percent of GDP.

infrastructure spending. In addition, countries should take steps to promote objective pricing of infrastructure assets and services, and implement effective supervision of public enterprises' investment plans.

IMPROVING PUBLIC INVESTMENT EFFICIENCY

Increasing the efficiency of public investment will give countries greater growth payoffs from public infrastructure spending. Public Investment Management Assessment (PIMA) results for a sample countries in the region suggest that South Asia has significant room to enhance the efficiency of public investment.[24] The estimated efficiency score—which estimates the relationship between the public capital stock and indicators of access to and the quality of infrastructure assets—for South Asia is only around 50 percent of the best performing peer countries, and is below other emerging market and developing countries in Asia.[25] Reducing the public investment efficiency gap could increase long-term growth, as highlighted in the previous section using model-based simulations and also in IMF (2015).

Strengthening infrastructure governance can help countries improve public investment efficiency. The results of PIMA for a sample of countries in South Asia show that most public investment management practices have good institutional strength but effectiveness in the implementation of public investment management institutions is generally weak (Figure 11.6):

- *Project appraisal.* All the countries have weak mechanisms to effectively appraise investment project proposals before they are selected. The lack of a standard appraisal methodology makes it difficult to ensure the quality of projects. This causes delays in project implementation and raises the risk that less worthy projects are selected.

- *Project selection.* A major weakness is the lack of consistent criteria to identify and select investment projects and quantify their costs. None of the countries in the sample have an effective review of major projects by a central ministry before being included in the budget. These weaknesses not only make it difficult to ensure that the best projects are selected, but also undermine the ability to choose the most appropriate delivery modes. To improve the transparency of project selection, countries should create a pipeline of appraised, adequately costed, projects for subsequent budget consideration.

---

[24] PIMA assesses the public investment decision-making process at three key stages: (1) planning sustainable levels of investment across the public sector; (2) allocating investment to the right sectors and projects; and (3) implementing projects on time and on budget. See IMF (2015) and IMF (2018b). By mid-2020, the IMF had conducted PIMAs for three countries in South Asia: Maldives, Sri Lanka, and Bangladesh.

[25] A country's performance is assessed based on the Public Investment Efficiency Index that compares the country's levels of infrastructure coverage and quality (outputs) to its levels of public capital stock and income per capita (inputs). A "frontier," consisting of the countries achieving the highest output per unit of input, is drawn. The performance of a total of 128 countries is compared with the frontier (see IMF 2015).

Figure 11.6. PIMA Scores, by Dimension

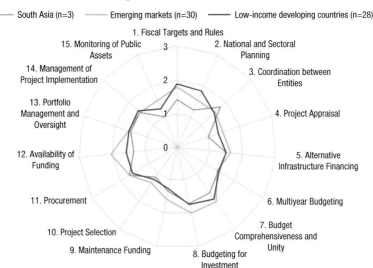

Sources: PIMA and IMF staff estimates.
Note: PIMA = Public Investment Management Assessment.

Clear and transparent criteria for project prioritization also need to be defined.

- *Maintenance funding.* Mechanisms for maintenance funding are not very effective and budgeted maintenance levels are low compared with the capital stock. Most countries do not have a standard methodology or sufficiently disaggregated data to estimate the costs of routine maintenance and major capital maintenance needs.

- *Multiyear budgeting.* Most countries do not have a medium-term framework for capital spending to guide multiyear investment planning. Countries do not publish the projections of overall or disaggregated capital spending by ministry or sector over the medium term. Moreover, the financing of project outlays is frequently subject to budget cuts and cash rationing, leading to arrears and implementation delays.

CONCLUSIONS

In South Asia, greater infrastructure spending can support the COVID-19 recovery and raise growth over the medium term, but its benefits will depend on how it is financed and how it is managed. Countries in South Asia need to both extend infrastructure networks and improve their quality. However, the strategy to finance the boost in infrastructure spending—whether through taxes, debt, or PPPs—will affect the outcome. The optimal financing choice is country-specific and will be a function of available fiscal space, taxation capacity, as well as efficiency of the public sector. The economic gains of higher infrastructure spending will also hinge on how it is managed. Countries in South Asia rely on SOEs, while PPPs remain limited. While these alternatives can have advantages in terms of efficiency, the associated implementation and fiscal risks need to be carefully monitored, managed, and disclosed. South Asia will also need to implement reforms to strengthen public investment management to improve the efficiency of additional spending.

REFERENCES

Abiad, Abdul, Davide Furceri, and Petia Topalova. 2016. "The Macroeconomic Effects of Public Investment: Evidence from Advanced Economies." *Journal of Macroeconomics* 50: 224–40.

Akitoby, Bernardin, Richard Hemming, and Gerd Schwartz. 2007. "Public Investment and Public-Private Partnerships." IMF Economic Issues 2007/002, International Monetary Fund, Washington, DC.

Allen, Richard, and Miguel Alves. 2016. "How to Improve the Financial Oversight of Public Corporations." IMF How To Notes, International Monetary Fund, Washington, DC.

Andrés, Luis, Dan Biller, and Matias Herrera Dappe. 2013. "Reducing Poverty by Closing South Asia's Infrastructure Gap." World Bank Working Paper, World Bank, Washington, DC.

Andrés, Luis, Dan Biller, and Matias Herrera Dappe. 2014. "Infrastructure Gap in South Asia, Infrastructure Needs, Prioritization, and Financing." World Bank Policy Research Working Paper 7032, World Bank, Washington, DC.

Andrle, Michal, Patrick Blagrave, Pedro Espaillat, Keiko Honjo, Benjamin L. Hunt, Mika Kortelainen, René Lalonde, Douglas Laxton, Eleonara Mavroeidi, Dirk V. Muir, Susanna Mursula, and Stephen Snudden. 2015. "The Flexible System of Global Models—FSGM." IMF Working Paper 2015/64, International Monetary Fund, Washington, DC.

Arellano, Manuel, and Stephen Bond. 1991. "Some Tests of Specification for Panel Data: Monte Carlo Evidence and an Application to Employment Equations." *Review of Economic Studies* 58 (2): 277–97.

Asian Development Bank. 2008. *Public–Private Partnership Handbook.* Manila, Philippines: Asian Development Bank.

Asian Development Bank Institute. 2017. "Meeting Asia's Infrastructure Needs," Working Paper 11711 Asian Development Bank, Manila, Philippines.

Barro, Robert J., and Jong-Wha Lee. 2013. "A New Data Set of Educational Attainment in the World, 1950–2010." *Journal of Development Economics* 104 (C): 184–198.

Bizimana, Olivier, Laura Jaramillo, Saji Thomas, and Jiae Yoo. 2021. "Scaling Up Quality Infrastructure Investment in South Asia." IMF Working Paper 2021/117, International Monetary Fund, Washington, DC.

Calderon, Cesar A., and Luis Servén. 2004. "The Effects of Infrastructure Development on Growth and Income Distribution." World Bank Policy Research Working Paper 3400, World Bank, Washington, DC.

Calderon, Cesar A., and Luis Servén. 2008. "Infrastructure and Economic Development in Sub-Saharan Africa." World Bank Policy Research Working Paper 4712, World Bank, Washington, DC.

Dokko, Jane, Owen Kearney, and Neal Stollerman. 2016. "An Economic Framework for Comparing Public-Private Partnerships and Conventional Procurement." US Department of the Treasury Office of Economic Policy, Washington, DC.

Hsieh, Chang-Tai. 1999. "Productivity and Factor Prices in East Asia." *American Economic Review* 89 (2): 133–8.

Hulten, Charles R., Esra Bennathan, and Sylaja Srinivasan. 2006. "Infrastructure, Externalities, and Economic Development: A Study of the Indian Manufacturing Industry." *World Bank Economic Review* 20 (2): 291–308.

International Monetary Fund (IMF). 2004. "Public-Private Partnerships." IMF Policy Paper, Washington, DC.

International Monetary Fund (IMF). 2013. *Fiscal Monitor: Taxing Times.* Washington, DC, October.

International Monetary Fund (IMF). 2014. *Fiscal Transparency Code.* Washington DC.

International Monetary Fund (IMF). 2015. "Making Public Investment More Efficient." IMF Policy Paper, Washington, DC.

International Monetary Fund (IMF). 2018b. "Public Investment Management Assessment - Review and Update." IMF Policy Paper, Washington, DC.

International Monetary Fund (IMF). 2018a. "Fiscal Transparency Handbook." IMF, Washington, DC.

International Monetary Fund (IMF). 2019. Investment and Capital Stock Dataset (ICSD), Fiscal Affairs Department. http://workspaces.imf.org/departments/FAD/FAST/main/data.html?search=1.

International Monetary Fund (IMF). 2020a. *Fiscal Monitor: Policies for the Recovery.* Washington, DC, October.

International Monetary Fund (IMF). 2020b. *Fiscal Monitor: State-Owned Enterprises: The Other Government.* Washington, DC, April.

International Monetary Fund (IMF). 2020c. "Nepal, Selected Issues: Infrastructure Development and Growth," IMF Country Report 20/97, Washington DC.

International Monetary Fund (IMF). 2020d. *World Economic Outlook Update: A Crisis Like No Other, An Uncertain Recovery.* Washington, DC, June.

Irwin, Timothy C., Samah Mazraani, and Sandeep Saxena. 2018. "How to Control the Fiscal Costs of Public-Private Partnerships." IMF How To Notes, Washington, DC.

Kumar, Manmohan S., and Emanuele Baldacci. 2010. "Fiscal Deficits, Public Debt, and Sovereign Bond Yields." IMF Working Paper 2010/184, International Monetary Fund, Washington, DC.

Ligthart, Jenny E., and Rosa M. Martin Suárez. 2005. "The Productivity of Public Capital: A Meta Analysis." Working Paper, Tilburg University The Netherlands.

Nishimizu, Mieko, and Charles Hulten. 1978. "The Sources of Japanese Economic Growth, 1955–71." *Review of Economics and Statistics* 60 (3): 351–61.

Organisation for Economic Co-operation and Development (OECD). 2015. *Towards a Framework for the Governance of Infrastructure.* Paris: OECD.

Singh, Anoop, Tooraj Jamasb, Rabindra Nepal, and Michael Toman. 2015. "Cross-Border Electricity Cooperation in South Asia." World Bank Policy Research Working Paper 7328, Washington, DC.

United Nations. 2016. "Public-Private Partnerships and the 2030 Agenda for Sustainable Development: Fit for Purpose?" DESA Working Paper 148 Department of Economic & Social Affairs, United Nations, New York, NY.

United Nations Economic and Social Commission for Asia and the Pacific (UNESCAP). 2017. "Achieving the Sustainable Development Goals in South Asia: Key Policy Priorities and Implementation Challenges." UNESCAP, Bangkok, Thailand.

Vu, Ha, Olivier Bizimana, and Masahiro Nozaki Nozaki. 2020. "Boosting Infrastructure in Emerging Asia. In *Well Spent: How Strong Infrastructure Governance Can End Waste in Public Investment,* edited by Gerd Schwartz, Manal Fouad, Torben S. Hansen, and Genevieve Verdier. Washington DC: International Monetary Fund.

World Bank. 2014a. "Corporate Governance of State-Owned Enterprises: A Toolkit." Washington, DC: World Bank.

World Bank. 2014b. "Public-Private Partnerships Reference Guide. Version 2.0." Washington, DC: World Bank.

World Bank. 2014b. "Public-Private Partnerships Reference Guide. Version 2.0." Washington, DC: World Bank.

World Bank. 2017. *Who Sponsors Infrastructure Projects? Disentangling Public and Private Contributions.* Washington, DC: World Bank.

World Bank. 2018. "Nepal: Systematic Country Diagnostic." Washington, DC: World Bank.

World Health Organization and United Nations International Children's Fund. 2019. "Joint Monitoring Programme for Water Supply, Sanitation, and Hygiene: Estimates on the Use of Water, Sanitation and Hygiene by Country (2000–17)."

CHAPTER 12

On Modernizing Monetary Policy Frameworks in South Asia

Chetan Ghate and Faisal Ahmed

South Asia, a region with diverse economies, has significant variation in its mone-tary policy frameworks, ranging from monetary targeting to flexible inflation tar-geting. This chapter provides an overview of the monetary policy frameworks in South Asia, including the flexible inflation targeting regime in India and Sri Lanka and the ongoing upgrades in frameworks in other South Asian economies, with implications for monetary policy credibility that can help the economies better cope with various shocks. As observed before and during the COVID-19 pandemic in advanced and developing economies, monetary policy plays a critical role in macro-economic management. The chapter highlights the intra-regional lessons and important considerations going forward, building on the lessons from the flexible inflation targeting adoption in India, as other South Asian economies continue modernizing their monetary policy frameworks.

INTRODUCTION

A broad consensus exists that the primary goal of monetary policy is to maintain price stability, with annual inflation in the low and single digits.[1] In practical terms, central banks implement price stability through one of three operational frameworks: inflation targeting, monetary targeting, and exchange rate targeting. Of these three, inflation targeting has seen increasing adoption around the world, first in New Zealand in 1989, then in a growing number of advanced and emerg-ing economies. Several key attributes of inflation targeting—policy indepen-dence, an explicit target for inflation, transparency, and accountability—can help boost monetary policy credibility and have been widely recognized for their contribution to price stability (Schmidt-Hebel and Carrasco 2016; Walsh 2015; Kamber, Karagedikli, and Smith 2015).

South Asia's monetary policy frameworks are diverse, ranging from exchange rate targeting (Nepal, Bhutan, and Maldives) and broad monetary targeting

Contributions from Stephan Ide, Md. Hossain Imam, and Nimarjit Singh are gratefully acknowledged.

[1] For related literature, see Bernanke and others 1999; Mishkin and Schmidt-Hebbel 2001; Batini 2004; and Batini and Laxton 2006.

(Bangladesh) to flexible inflation targeting in India and Sri Lanka. The monetary policy anchor both in Bhutan and Nepal is the peg with the Indian Rupee. Although both India and Sri Lanka have implemented flexible inflation targeting (FIT), India's experience has been longer and can serve as an example of a formal adoption of FIT with some intra-regional lessons, especially for the larger economies in the region as they are going through middle-income transitions.[2]

Although widely adopted, inflation targeting has not won universal acceptance, especially in the context of emerging market and developing economies (EMDEs). In addition to their mandate of price stability, central banks are often held responsible for a range of outcomes, varying from unemployment, financial stability, exchange rates, current account deficits, and more recently, income inequality, making them policy makers of last resort (Davig and Gurkayanak 2015). In EMDEs that are at early stages of development, the preference for policies that generate high growth might perceive the adoption of inflation targeting as a constraint on supporting employment and growth.[3]

Exchange rate flexibility under inflation targeting is an additional policy consideration for EMDEs since imported inflation can affect monetary policy outcomes. For EMDEs, large volatility of capital flows amid rising financial integration can amplify risks and vulnerability to crises. Many EMDE central banks therefore build up foreign exchange reserves to serve as external buffers. That said, the policy challenge to EMDE central banks remains in the context of determining the degree and timing of any foreign exchange intervention to smooth out excessive volatilities. Risk-off capital outflows can result in sharp nominal and real depreciation amid sticky prices, which, in turn, can have undesirable effects, including on inflation. This highlights the challenges many EMDEs face in protecting domestic policy independence, with implications for capital flows and macroeconomic management.

This chapter takes stock of the monetary policy frameworks in South Asia, with a special focus on the Indian experience with flexible inflation targeting (FIT) since the adoption of the Monetary Policy Framework in March 2015. In the runup to the adoption of FIT, inflation in India was high (above 6 percent for more than 40 months through mid-2014), accompanied by large current account deficits (4.8 percent in FY2012/13) and exchange rate pressures, with market analysts' focus on reserve adequacy amid macro stability concerns from high inflation and current account pressures. During the July–September Taper Tantrum of 2013, the Indian Rupee depreciated by around 20 percent and economic growth moderated.

Amid a growing recognition that the multiple indicator approach to monetary policy in India had certain limitations and drawing upon the recommendations of an expert committee (RBI 2014), the Reserve Bank of India (RBI) implemented a systems-change in the conduct of monetary policy to deal with high and persistent

---

[2] Flexible inflation targeting means monetary policy aims at stabilizing both inflation around the inflation target and the real economy, whereas strict inflation targeting focuses on stabilizing inflation only.

[3] Furthermore, Schmidt-Hebbel and Carrasco (2016) showed that, based on a sample of advanced economies and EMDEs, there has not been significant change in macroeconomic performance, as measured by the first and second moments in output and inflation.

inflation. The RBI became a flexible inflation targeter with the headline consumer price index as the nominal anchor for the economy.[4] The full institutional architecture was laid out in a Monetary Policy Framework Agreement between the RBI and the Government of India in 2015 that set a medium-term inflation target of 4±2 percent, with the mid-point of the band to be achieved by the end of FY2017/18, as it was.

Aided by the flexible inflation targeting regime, during 2015–19, consumer price index headline inflation in India averaged 4.2 precent, but a food price shock in late 2019 and the supply disruptions during the pandemic led to higher food and overall inflation in 2020 and 2021. Inflation pressures have remained persistent with rising core inflation from supply disruptions and higher input costs in recent months (August 2021). Taking a longer view, recent RBI and IMF research have found that the adoption of FIT has been accompanied by better anchoring of inflation expectations (Blagrave and Lian 2020; Asnani and others 2021; RBI 2021).

Some of the lessons from the implementation of FIT in India are relevant for the larger South Asian economies such as Bangladesh and Sri Lanka that are working on upgrading their monetary policy frameworks. Some of the challenges associated with monetary policy implementation and transmission stem from the depth and soundness of the financial system (for example, the level of nonperforming assets in the banking system, liquidity forecasting and management, and bond market development) and have broader resonance among the economies in the region.

COSTS AND BENEFITS OF INFLATION TARGETING

Inflation targeting is a monetary policy framework with price stability as its main goal. This goal is reflected in a unique numerical target in the form of a level or range for annual inflation. While the main goal of inflation targeting is price stability, output and (possibly) financial stability are often included as part of the mandate.[5] The inflation forecast serves as the intermediate target of policy (Svensson 1997). Under inflation targeting, the inflation target is pursued by a monetary authority endowed with operational and instrumental independence. According to a 2019 Bank for International Settlements study, there were 36 countries that were operating a full-fledged inflation targeting regime (Agénor and Silva 2019).

There is a voluminous literature on the benefits and costs of inflation targeting.[6] In terms of the benefits, inflation targeting can help build central bank credibility

---

[4] Most emerging market countries use headline inflation as the target, reflecting the role food and fuel inflation play in the formation of inflation expectations, and the ease of communication.

[5] Two early EMDE adopters of inflation targeting where Thailand and Chile. The Bank of Thailand adopted inflation targeting in 2000, and originally had an explicit legal objective of financial stability. Chile adopted inflation targeting in 1999.

[6] See Batini and Laxton (2006) and Schmidt-Hebel and Carrasco (2016) for a detailed discussion of the costs and benefits of inflation targeting in advanced economies and EMDEs.

as the target provides transparency and commitment about the central bank's policy objective. This makes a central bank time consistent and allows economic agents to better understand and evaluate the performance of the central bank leading to a more durable anchoring of inflationary expectations. To achieve the goal, the central bank must make consistent efforts in attaining the inflation target to establish a reputational equilibrium between the central bank and agents in the economy.

Inflation targeting can also provide some flexibility by targeting inflation over the medium term. Deviations from the target don't necessarily imply a loss in credibility if inflationary expectations are anchored around the target.[7] Schmidt-Hebbel and Carrasco (2016) showed that inflation targeting has led to a better anchoring of inflationary expectations in EMDEs. They also suggested that inflation targeting, by lowering output costs, leads to better inflation-output trade-offs compared with alternative frameworks. Using the framework of Cecchetti and Ehrmann (1999), they showed that monetary policy efficiency, defined as the inflation-output variability frontier, has significantly improved (that is, shifted inwards) after the adoption of inflation targeting. They also showed that inflation targeting has significantly reduced long-term inflation rates both relative to their own non-inflation targeting history, as well as to non–inflation targeting EMDEs.

In terms of costs, inflation targeting is seen as offering limited discretion which can constrain growth. Countries in South Asia that are at the early stages of development might have a preference for high growth and thus view the adoption of inflation targeting as a constraint.[8] Batini and Laxton (2006) listed four broad categories for the successful implementation of inflation targeting: central bank institutional independence, central bank technical infrastructure, economic structure, and financial system development and health. They show, however, that for several adopting EMEs, the previously mentioned preconditions were satisfied in part or to a limited degree. IMF (2006) also noted that the importance of these pre conditions is often over-stated. Schmidt-Hebbel and Carrasco (2016) suggested that many countries—especially EMDEs—have adopted inflation targeting at an early stage in their development. Some adopted partial inflation targeting without giving up their exchange rate anchor (for example, Chile, Columbia, and Israel) and for several years had both exchange rate bands and inflation targets in place.

FLEXIBLE INFLATION TARGETING: THE INDIAN EXPERIENCE

Drawing upon the recommendations of the Report of the Expert Committee to Revise and Strengthen the Monetary Policy Framework (RBI 2014), the RBI implemented a systems-change in the conduct of monetary policy to deal

---

[7] In operational terms, it is often challenging to identify whether private agents view deviations as temporary errors, or as a change in how policy will be set in the future.

[8] This view remains relatively popular in some of the South Asian countries. When growth falls, the dominant consensus is that the central bank can take a risk on inflation and should not be an inflation targeter during a low growth period.

with high and persistent inflation. The RBI became a flexible inflation targeter with the headline consumer price index as the nominal anchor for the economy.

Several institutional changes were implemented for the FIT framework. Starting in 2014, a bimonthly policy review cycle was implemented with biannual (October and April) monetary policy reports (MPRs) from September 2014. The Monetary Policy Framework Agreement signed between the RBI and the government of India in March 2015 required the RBI to set out in the public domain the operating procedure of monetary policy which was fulfilled in the April 2015 monetary policy report (Patra and others 2016).[9] A glide path of two years was adopted, considering a lag in the monetary transmission mechanism of around 6–8 quarters. Aided by the adoption of the FIT and disinflationary shocks to fuel and food prices, inflation moderated, with average headline inflation in 2014–15 declining to 5.8 percent (down from, on average, 10 percent during 2012–13 and 9.4 percent during 2013–14) and remaining within the RBI's target band of 2–6 percent till January 2020 (Figures 12.1 and 12.2), when the food price shock in late 2019 and the COVID-19–related supply disruptions during 2020 and 2021 led to elevated inflationary pressures. It should be noted that since the signing of the Monetary Policy Framework Agreement until January 2020, inflation crossed 6 percent on only a handful of occasions.

Figure 12.1. Inflation and Real Repo Rate in India
(Percent change, year on year, annual average)

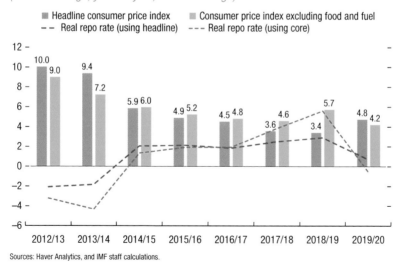

Sources: Haver Analytics, and IMF staff calculations.

---

[9] While high inflation amid low growth had created a disquiet, politically, the adoption of inflation targeting in India was helped by the fact that the aversion to inflation laid the foundation for a broad-based policy commitment in terms of lower inflation.

Figure 12.2. Inflation and Real Repo Rate in India
(Percent change, year on year, monthly)

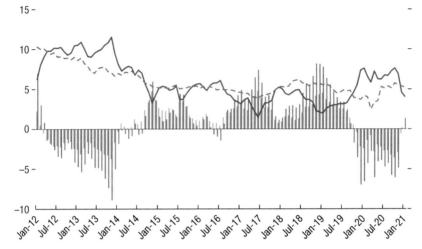

Sources: Haver Analytics; and IMF staff calculations.

Looking back, it is instructive to understand the reasons behind the persistent high inflation after the global financial crisis of 2007–09 and constraints to monetary policy implementation.

First, sizeable fiscal deficits contributed to demand pressures, which might have supported growth but also led to some overheating. The center's fiscal deficit continued to remain large even after the global financial crisis shock, with the overall (state plus central) fiscal deficit at around 7 percent of GDP in 2013–14, an increase from around 4 percent during 2007–08. Part of the increase in the deficit reflected public sector salary increases associated with the 6th Pay Commission in 2005 and higher food subsidies.

Second, the Government of India's price support program with a minimum support price (MSP) of key agricultural commodities and a large open-ended procurement of agricultural commodities contributed to inflationary pressures. As noted by Ghate and Kletzer (2016) and Ghate, Gupta, and Mallick (2018), government policies and food procurement shocks had effectively placed a rising floor on food and wages leading to food inflation and a wage-price spiral with rising wage expectations as rural wages are effectively indexed to food inflation.[10] During 2007–13, rural agriculture and nonagricultural wages in India rose by 17

---

[10] There are years, however, when amid a marginal increase in MSP, favorable production from a good monsoon and a decline in global commodity prices, food inflation moderated as in 2017.

and 10 percent, respectively. The transmission of food inflation into nominal wages was almost immediate.[11]

Third, on the monetary policy front, the real policy rate was below the neutral rate for several years in the aftermath of the global financial crisis, amid rising inflation (Rajan 2016). Both short- and long-term inflation expectations increased sharply amid strong aggregate demand.[12] A further complicating factor was that before the implementation of inflation targeting in India, monetary policy was guided by a multiple indicator approach with no clearly defined nominal anchor. Instead, growth, price stability, and financial stability were targeted with relative weights depending on prevailing economic conditions (Cristadoro and Veronese 2011). As pointed out by Mohan (2009), price stability was an important but not an exclusive goal of monetary policy in India. As noted by the expert committee (RBI 2014), a loss of credibility arises from high inflation especially in a framework with a multiple indicator approach.[13] The lack of a clearly defined nominal anchor foments time inconsistency in policy implementation.

Fourth, financial repression accompanied by fiscal dominance had accompanied Indian monetary policy for decades. Despite the phasing out of the RBI's participation in the primary issuance of government securities, open market operations were continually employed to manage yields in the face of large government borrowings.[14] Despite some moderation during 2014–18, the overall fiscal balance remained elevated at more than 6 percent of GDP, before gradually increasing to more than 7 percent of GDP in 2019 and crossing 11 percent of GDP, amid the pandemic shock. As in many other countries, the postpandemic increase in fiscal deficits and debt raises the risks of financial repression, especially if growth remains tepid.

Fifth, monetary transmission, especially through the bank lending channel, remained limited, reflecting the level of nonperforming assets and the impact of small savings on the deposit rates and thus the lending rates.[15] The Expert Committee (RBI 2014) highlighted several other structural factors that hinder monetary transmission in India such as the presence of a large informal sector, and

---

[11] It should also be noted that in India, typically, there is a sharp increase in inflation in the summer months, followed by a moderation around November. Given the large weight (45.9 percent) of food in headline inflation, large swings in specific components of the food basket leads to forecast errors.

[12] See Cristadoro and Veronese (2011) for an excellent discussion of Indian monetary policy before the implementation of FIT.

[13] The multiple indicator approach contradicts the classic Tinbergen principle, that is, that central banks should have an equal number of instruments under their control to effectively direct policy toward each target.

[14] While RBI has stopped subscribing in the primary market, the monetary implications of subscribing in the secondary market are equivalent. That said, direct monetization of deficit could potentially raise concerns about the central bank independence.

[15] In recent years, the small savings rate (national savings certificates, provident funds, and so on) have reflected some adjustments in line with the movements in the government securities' yields.

financial repression through a statutory liquidity ratio (SLR).[16] The SLR was viewed as distorting the term structure of the interest rate for the benefit of the government, constituting a form of financial repression. Before inflation targeting in India, banks often held excess SLR because of "lazy banking," where banks park liquidity in risk-free assets. If a bank had excess SLR, then the RBI had to provide banks with liquidity leading to unlimited accommodation. The liquidity adjustment facility had become a permanent monetary injection and had created a disjunction between interest rates and monetary aggregates.

EVOLUTION OF MONETARY POLICY FRAMEWORKS IN SOUTH ASIA

The diversity in monetary policy frameworks in South Asia is large: three countries (Nepal, Bhutan, and Maldives) follow exchange rate targeting; Bangladesh follows broad monetary targeting; and India formally adopted FIT in 2015 with Sri Lanka following in 2020 (Table 12.1).[17] Given South Asia's level of economic and financial sector development, central banks in the region have focused on the necessary upgrades to increase monetary policy effectiveness in line with their framework as the diverse economies (Figures 12.3 and 12.4) and financial sectors in the region undergo structural changes.

TABLE 12.1.

Monetary Policy Frameworks in South Asia		
Country	**Monetary Policy Regime**	**De Facto Exchange Rate Regime**
Bangladesh	Monetary targeting	Stabilized arrangement
Bhutan	Exchange rate targeting	Conventional peg
India	Flexible inflation targeting	Flexible
Maldives	Exchange rate targeting	Stabilized arrangement
Nepal	Exchange rate targeting	conventional peg
Sri Lanka	Flexible inflation targeting	Floating

IMF (2015) identified key building blocks for lower and middle-income countries to establish effective monetary policy frameworks. A central bank should have a clear mandate in terms of its goals with price stability as the primary or overriding objective of monetary policy over the medium term. Important first steps are developing forward-looking and interest-rate-focused frameworks aligned with the central bank's capacities and the country's macro-financial

[16] Recent RBI reforms including external benchmarking amid ample systemic liquidity during the recent easing cycle have improved transmission through the bank-lending channel.

[17] One challenge with money and exchange rate targets is that money targets are hard to control because of shifts in money demand and the multiplier, which require periodic resets. Furthermore, central bank control over the exchange rate may be limited because the level of the exchange rate is determined by the international demand and supply of domestic currency versus the anchor currency. Shifts in sentiment about the domestic currency can trigger abrupt changes in relative values that cannot be offset by central bank actions. See IMF (2005, WEO).

Figure 12.3. Growth, Money, and Inflation in South Asia

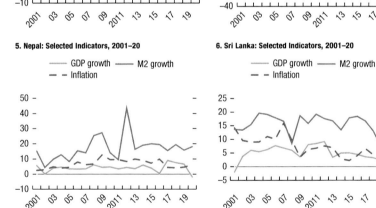

Sources: Haver Analytics; and IMF staff calculations.
Note: M2 = broad money.

development.[18] This will allow transmission of the announced central bank policy stance to bank financing and financial market conditions. Across the region, it will be key to reduce fiscal dominance, especially in the context of higher debt during the postpandemic recovery, increase central bank operational independence, and create greater reliance on market-based procedures.

---

[18] See Laurens and others (2015). See also Banerjee and others (2020) for a dynamic stochastic general equilibrium model with banking sector frictions calibrated to India.

Figure 12.4. Inflation, Policy Rate, and Fiscal Balances in South Asia

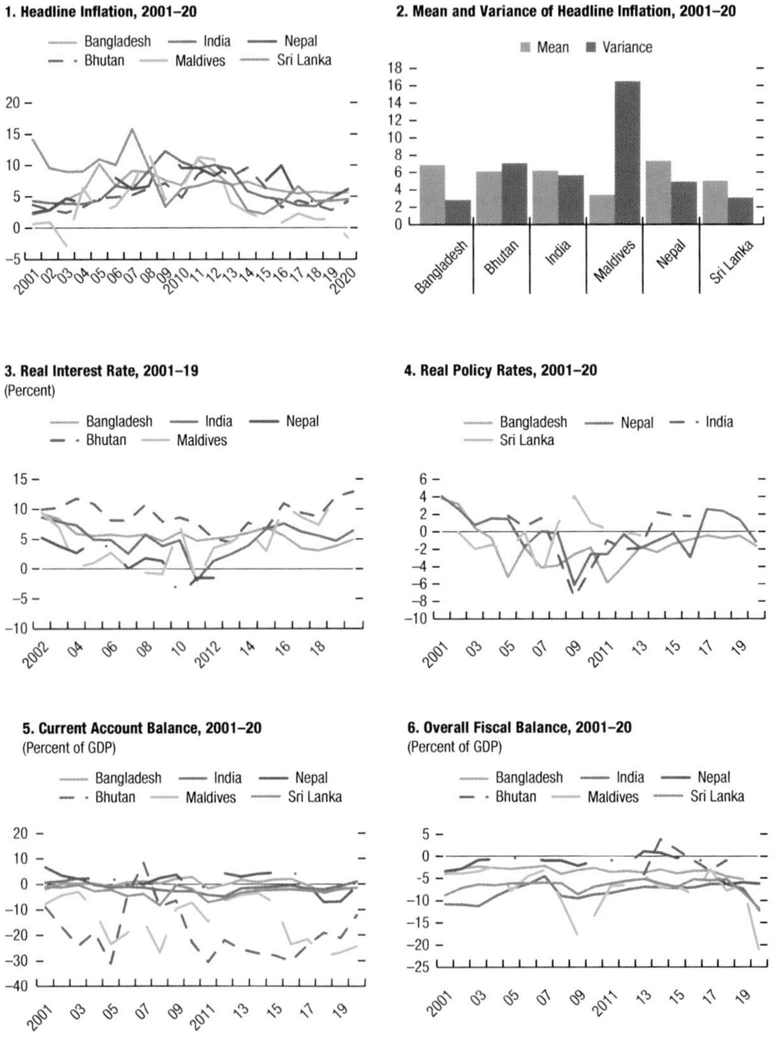

1. Headline Inflation, 2001–20

2. Mean and Variance of Headline Inflation, 2001–20

3. Real Interest Rate, 2001–19
(Percent)

4. Real Policy Rates, 2001–20

5. Current Account Balance, 2001–20
(Percent of GDP)

6. Overall Fiscal Balance, 2001–20
(Percent of GDP)

Sources: Haver Analytics; and IMF staff calculations.

BANGLADESH

Monetary policy in Bangladesh aims at maintaining price stability and ensuring growth. The dual mandate responds to the challenge in a developing country to expand output through productivity growth, in a context where low inflation alone may not suffice to reach poverty and output growth targets. Bangladesh Bank formulates its monetary program in the context of a monetary targeting regime. Bangladesh Bank actions aim at steering M2 growth while it uses judgment when deciding on the policy stance. While the de jure exchange rate arrangement is classified as floating, the de-facto exchange rate arrangement is classified as stabilized, effective February 2020, with interventions in the spot markets to limit volatility of the exchange rate against the US dollar.

As Bangladesh's deepening trade and financial integration continues, the current monetary targeting regime with a reserve monetary operational target to ensure price stability needs to be recalibrated. As noted in the monetary policy statements before the pandemic, the Bangladesh Bank expressed its interest in moving toward introducing an interest rate operational target within a flexible monetary targeting regime. In this framework, monetary aggregates remain an important input in the forward-looking decision-making process to determine the appropriate policy stance as they continue to contain useful information on current economic conditions, the nature of the shocks, and forward-looking information about future inflation.

The increasing focus on the interest rate as the operational target of the monetary policy framework would benefit from the removal of the existing impediments to the monetary transmission mechanism stemming from the pricing of the National Savings Certificates, the recent introduction of bank lending and deposit interest rate caps, and the already-elevated nonperforming loans, even before the pandemic. The distortions from the National Savings Certificates need to be moderated to deepen further the government bond market and improve monetary transmission.

BHUTAN

The monetary policy anchor in Bhutan is the exchange rate in relation to the Indian rupee. Since its introduction in 1974, the ngultrum has been pegged to the Indian rupee at par. Given close economic ties with India, the exchange rate peg to the Indian rupee has served Bhutan well as a nominal anchor. For liquidity management, the Royal Monetary Authority (RMA) currently relies on administrative tools to implement monetary policy, such as the cash reserve ratio and the daily sweeping of government-related accounts (account of the government and hydro-projects related accounts) held in the commercial banks to the RMA.

For the peg to the India Rupee to be sustainable and credible, trend inflation in Bhutan cannot deviate significantly from trend inflation in India once differences in trend productivity growth are taken into account. Recent IMF research has found strong co-movement in headline inflation between India and countries in South Asia because of food-price inflation, but co-movement in core inflation much weaker (Blagrave 2019). This suggests that domestic factors largely shape core inflation in Bhutan. Given the degree of capital flows, the RMA has some policy space to deviate from the RBI's policy rate. The RMA in recent years has placed strong emphasis on liquidity management to support the peg regime as it can help steer short-term interest rates close to the desired policy stance. Bhutan has also focused on developing the government bond market, with the recent issuances of longer-term bonds.

MALDIVES

The monetary policy anchor in Maldives is a peg in relation to the US dollar with an open capital account. Fiscal dominance poses challenges for monetary policy credibility and the exchange rate regime, as previously reflected by the emergence of a parallel foreign exchange market, with a spread to the official market exchange rate and a related multiple currency practice, as the authorities have rationed foreign exchange supply because of low international reserves. The high level of dollarization has complicated monetary policy and financial intermediation in local currency.

The authorities' plan of implementing a broad range of reforms to monetary and exchange rate policies based on their Strategic Plan was delayed with the outbreak of the COVID-19 pandemic and the consequent central bank financing of fiscal deficit. The Strategic Plan aims to (1) strengthen the monetary policy and operational framework, including defining an interest rate corridor and directing short-term interbank interest rates inside it; (2) develop two-sided functioning foreign exchange markets; and (3) review the current exchange rate regime to maintain exchange rate stability and implement a strategy for partial and gradual de-dollarization and foreign exchange reserve accumulation. For an open economy as Maldives with a diversified set of trading partners, shifting the exchange rate target to a composite basket peg from the current peg to the US dollar is currently being considered.

NEPAL

The exchange rate peg to the Indian rupee (one Indian rupee to per 1.6 Nepalese rupee) has served as a transparent nominal anchor for monetary policy. The peg continues to benefit Nepal in view of its close economic relationship with India and the need to build policy implementation capacity. The Nepal Rastra Bank (NRB) Act 2002 does not assign price stability as the primary goal of monetary policy. From that perspective, the monetary policy framework does not provide explicit guidance on how to prioritize policy actions in the event of a conflict among policy objectives (price stability, external sector stability, and output growth). In pursuing these objectives, the NRB uses monetary and credit aggregates as information variables, and banks' excess reserves as an operating target. To curb risk-taking behavior caused by the low real interest rates, the NRB in the past relied on macroprudential measures.

Given the close trade integration (with around 70 percent of Nepalese imports coming from India) and the exchange rate regime, co-movements of headline inflation in India and Nepal remain high (around 0.70). The RBI's inflation target (4 ± 2 percent) has implications for the NRB's monetary policy conduct. In presence of the exchange rate regime, the medium-term inflation objective needs some alignment with India's. A wider target band than in India can afford monetary policy the flexibility to deal with shocks, particularly during the transition to a fully market-based liquidity management framework.

In late 2017, the NRB introduced an interest rate corridor for guiding short-term interbank rates. Standing liquidity facility rate and one-week deposit collection rate serve as the upper and lower limits of the corridors. The effectiveness of the interest rate corridor in stabilizing short-term money market rates is dependent on effective NRB liquidity forecasting and a commitment to stabilize liquidity conditions, with overnight repo rate as the main policy rate. This commitment needs to be underpinned by sufficient operational independence since attempts to save costs by only periodically draining excess liquidity are damaging to the economy and central bank credibility.

SRI LANKA

Among the South Asia countries, Sri Lanka also committed to modernizing its monetary policy framework. The Central Bank of Sri Lanka has communicated that its monetary policy framework follows FIT, aimed at stabilizing inflation at mid single-digit levels over the medium-term while supporting economic growth to reach its potential. The key elements of the framework include price stability as a mandate of the central bank (along with the mandates of economic stability and financial system stability), a market-oriented approach toward the exchange rate policy, and strengthening the autonomy, governance, and accountability frameworks of the Central Bank of Sri Lanka.

Following several decades of high inflation and exchange rate volatility (from the 1970s through 2000s), inflation has been in single digits for over a decade now, with inflation expectations aided by the central bank's commitment and communication. Sri Lanka could further consolidate its progress made toward the FIT by allowing greater exchange rate flexibility, supporting domestic debt market developments, and safeguarding the central bank's operational autonomy.

At present, the central bank conducts monetary policy under the FIT. Under the FIT framework, the central bank expects to rely mostly on market-based instruments, policy interest rates, and open market operations to guide the average weighted call money rate, which is considered as the operating target, as it was previously under the enhanced monetary policy framework before the adoption of the FIT. To support the forward-looking nature of the framework, macroeconomic projections, including inflation projections, are being strengthened, as reflected in the publication of the inflation fan charts since 2020.[19] The central bank has also prioritized improving its communications strategy, in support of the current FIT framework, including by communicating the overall monetary policy direction for the forthcoming year announced at the Road Map during the first week of each year, followed by eight monetary policy announcements that take place throughout the year.

SOME CONSIDERATIONS FOR MONETARY POLICY FRAMEWORK UPGRADES

As mentioned in the introduction, Batini and Laxton (2006) list four broad categories for the successful implementation of inflation targeting: central bank institutional independence, central bank technical infrastructure, economic

---

[19] This effort has involved developing a structural model-based Forecasting and Policy Analysis System, including with IMF technical assistance, to strengthen the monetary policy decision making process and to support Sri Lanka's transition to FIT.

structure, and financial system development and health. These preconditions are also supportive of the evolutions of monetary policy frameworks in select South Asian economies, as they upgrade their frameworks (for example, Bangladesh, Sri Lanka) and the increased effectiveness of monetary policy implementation under the current regimes.

Financial markets in South Asia (excluding India) are at early stages of development and face various forms of market development constraints (Figure 12.5). For

Figure 12.5. Financial Development in South Asia

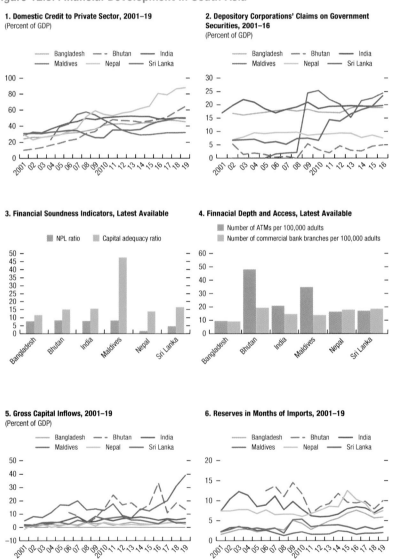

Source: Haver analytics; and IMF staff calculations.

example, Bhutan had its first issuance of a government bond in 2020. Bond markets remain relatively small in Bangladesh, constrained by the higher risk-free interest in national savings certificates. Given the level of national savings, there is significant scope for market development in these economies, if accompanied by market-based pricing of government securities and continued liberalization (for example, the removal of cap on interest and deposit rates in Bangladesh).

The experience of India, with its relatively larger and more development financial system and a longer track reform of FIT, is instructive for other countries with regards to the increasing degrees of liberalization that supported market development. In the 1970s and 1980s, the focus of financial sector reform in India was on directed credit and to widen the spread of the financial sector. In the 1990s, there was a recognition that the gains from liberalization in the real sector depended on reforms in the financial sector. This led to the dismantling of administered/structured interest rates, the introduction of new prudential norms (such as capital adequacy norms), and the recapitalization of public sector banks. After 2008, reforms have assumed a new connotation with a greater emphasis on regulation.

What would be some lessons from India and recommendations for countries in South Asia who want to upgrade their monetary policy frameworks, including by adopting inflation targeting?

First, there needs to be broad-based recognition and commitment that inflation adversely impacts the economy and the well-being of many. Bringing inflation down in a significant and durable manner requires a rule-based monetary policy that can improve transparency and predictability, while minimizing discretion and time inconsistency.[20] Equally important is the process of monetary policy design and implementation that takes into consideration the latest economic activity and capacity, as done under FIT. At present, all RBI Monetary Policy Committee deliberations feature data from a variety of surveys conducted by the RBI on the Indian economy, which are incorporated in the projections of growth and inflation by the RBI.[21] One challenge that many central banks—both in advanced and developing countries—face is the estimation of variables such as the output gap, highlighting the need for improving macroeconomic data.

Second, there needs to be a common understanding and acceptance about the nominal anchor. During the multiple indicator approach in India, there was lack of clarity on the inflation measure that was being targeted or the degree of

---

[20] After the high inflation episode in India from 2010 to 2013, the RBI maintained a positive real policy interest rate, which signaled a commitment to reducing inflation.

[21] Results from the following surveys in Monetary Policy Committee deliberations are routinely included: Outlook of the Private Corporate Sector, Enterprise Surveys, a Consumer Confidence Survey, Inflation Expectations Surveys of Households, Survey of Professional Forecasters, Developments in the Housing Sector, Global Macroeconomic Developments, Developments in India's External Sector, and Monetary Policy Transmission. The inflation and growth projections are done by Department of Statistics Information and Management, the Department of Economic Policy Research, and the Monetary Policy Department, with contributions from the Strategic Research Unit. A Forecasting and Policy Analysis System model is estimated and calibrated to generate the balance of risks.

commitment by the central bank. Elevated inflation expectations became entrenched among households and businesses.

Third, inflation targeting requires strong monetary-fiscal coordination. As noted by Chari and Kehoe (1990), economic policy setting means that policy makers need to think of policy as choosing a strategy or a contingent policy rule that tells the policy maker how to respond to shocks. In fiscal and monetary policy, expectations—that is, the future course of policy—matter. This makes policy setting inherently "now" versus "then" decisions. For example, the burst of fiscal expansion in India after the global financial crisis was slow to unwind, and there were some unintended consequences of the stimulus. This implies that monetary policy rules need to be backed up by fiscal rules. Looking ahead, as South Asian economies prepare for the postpandemic recovery, especially amid large fiscal deficits and higher public debt, stronger commitment to and clarity regarding medium-term fiscal consolidation plans would be important for upgrading the monetary policy frameworks and their effectiveness.

Fourth, central banks need to further improve their liquidity forecasting as they upgrade their monetary policy frameworks. Liquidity management and monetary policy cannot be moving in separate directions. The movements in government cash balances complicate liquidity forecasting. Furthermore, central banks need to widen their instruments to smooth out the volatility in call money markets.

Fifth, monetary policy framework upgrades require a well-functioning and liquid market in government securities. This helps minimize counterparty and liquidity risk in the banking system, and fosters an interbank repo market and a reliable yield curve.[22] Further development of government securities markets in South Asia would benefit from a more market-based pricing of government bonds and National Savings Certificates.

Sixth, developing an inter-bank market where banks lend to each other is important for improving monetary transmission. In this context, two-way open market operations can help, as shown by the Indian experience. Before inflation targeting, the open market operations conducted by the RBIs were generally one sided (purchases).

Seventh, one lesson from India for the region is the recognition that central banks cannot address all the inefficiencies in the economy, and if other policy makers (fiscal, financial) do not internalize the consequences of their actions, more inefficiencies can occur in the presence of diffuse and uncoordinated policy making amongst several policy makers (Davig and Gurkayanak 2015). Successful monetary policy requires a clearly defined mandate emphasizing price stability as well as a clear nominal anchor.

---

[22] There might also be some additional institutional constraints in South Asia when central banks are also debt managers.

Finally, as some of the larger South Asian economies (for example, Sri Lanka, Bangladesh) upgrade their monetary policy frameworks (for example, Bangladesh moving from a quantity-based (monetary) targeting framework to a price-based (interest) targeting framework), allowing greater exchange rate flexibility can support monetary transmission. In that context, adequate reserve coverage could help avoid excessive volatilities, given limited foreign exchange market development.

REFERENCES

Agénor, P., and L. Silva. 2019. *Integrated Inflation Targeting: Another Perspective from the Developing World*. Bank for International Settlements.

Asnani, S., P. Kumar, J. Surti, and S. Toma. 2021. "Does Inflation Targeting Anchor Inflation Expectations? Evidence from India." Manuscript.

Banerjee, S., P. Basu, and C. Ghate. 2020. "A Monetary Business Cycle Model for India." *Economic Inquiry* 58(3): 1362–86.

Batini, N., 2004. "Achieving and Maintaining Price Stability in Nigeria." IMF Working Paper 04/97, International Monetary Fund, Washington, DC.

Batini, N., and D. Laxton. 2006. "Under What Conditions Can Inflation Targeting be Adopted? The Experience of Emerging Markets." Working Paper 406, Central Bank of Chile.

Bernanke, B.S., T. Laubach, F.S. Mishkin, and A.S. Posen. 1999. *Inflation Targeting: Lessons from the International Experience*. Princeton, N.J.: Princeton University Press.

Blagrave, P. 2019. "Inflation Co-Movement in Emerging and Developing Asia: The Monsoon Effect," IMF Working Paper 19/147, International Monetary Fund, Washington, DC.

Blagrave, P., and W. Lian. 2020. "India's Inflation Process Before and After Flexible Inflation Targeting," IMF Working Paper 2020/251, International Monetary Fund, Washington, DC.

Cecchetti, S., and M. Ehrmann. 1999. "Does Inflation Targeting Increase Output Volatility? An International Comparison of Policymakers' Preferences and Outcomes." NBER Working Paper, National Bureau of Economic Research.

Chari, V.V., and P. Kehoe. 1990. "Sustainable Plans," *Journal of Political Economy* 98 (4): 783–802.

Cristadoro, R., and G. Veronese. 2011. "Monetary Policy in India: Is Something Amiss?" *Indian Growth and Development Review*, Emerald Group Publishing, 4(2): 166–92.

Davig, T., and R. Gurkayanak. 2015. "Is Optimal Monetary Policy Always Optimal?" CESifo Working Paper Series 5473, Center for Economic Studies, Munich, Germany.

Ghate, C., and K. Kletzer. 2016. "Introduction" in *Monetary Policy in India*, edited by C. Ghate and K. Kletzer. New Delhi: Springer.

Ghate, C., S. Gupta, and D. Mallick. 2018. "Terms of Trade Shocks and Monetary Policy in India," *Computational Economics* 51(1): 75–121.

International Monetary Fund (IMF). 2006. "Has Globalization Affected Inflation," Chapter III, *World Economic Outlook*, Spring. International Monetary Fund, Washington, DC.

International Monetary Fund (IMF). 2015. "Evolving Monetary Policy Frameworks in Low-Income and Other Developing Countries," IMF Policy Paper, International Monetary Fund, Washington, DC.

Kamber, G., O. Karagedikli, and C. Smith. 2015. "Applying an Inflation-Targeting Lens to Macroprudential Policy Institutions," *International Journal of Central Banking* 11(4): 395–429.

Laurens, B.J., K. Eckhold, D. King, N. Maele, A. Nasser, and A. Durre. 2015. "The Journey to Inflation Targeting: Easier Said than Done." IMF Working Paper 15/136, International Monetary Fund, Washington, DC.

Mishkin, F., and K. Schmidt-Hebbel. 2001. "One Decade of Inflation Targeting in the World: What Do We Know and What Do We Need to Know?" NBER Working Paper 8397, National Bureau of Economic Research, Cambridge, MA.

Mohan, R. 2009. "Global Financial Crisis—Causes, Impact, Policy Responses and Lessons," Bank for International Settlements Review 54/2009.

Patra M., M. Kapur, R. Kavediya, and S. M. Lokare. 2016. "Liquidity Management and Monetary Policy: From Corridor Play to Marksmanship," in *Monetary Policy in India*, edited by C. Ghate and K. Kletzer. New Delhi: Springer.

Rajan, R. 2016. "The Fight against Inflation—A Measure of Our Institutional Development," Foundation Day Lecture Tata Institute of Fundamental Research, Mumbai, 20 June 2016.

Reserve Bank of India (RBI). 2014. "Report of the Expert Committee to Revise and Strengthen the Monetary Policy Framework." Reserve Bank of India, Mumbai.

Reserve Bank of India (RBI). 2021. "Report on Currency and Finance." Reserve Bank of India, Mumbai.

Schmidt-Hebbel, K., and Carrasco, M. 2016. "The Past and Future of Inflation Targeting: Implications for Emerging Market and Developing Economies," in *Monetary Policy in India*, edited by C. Ghate and K. Kletzer. New Delhi: Springer.

Svensson, L. 1997. "Inflation Forecast Targeting: Implementing and Monitoring Inflation Targets." *European Economic Review* 41(6): 1111–46.

Walsh, C. 2015. "Goals and Rules in Central Bank Design," CESifo Working Paper Series 5293. Center for Economic Studies, Munich, Germany.

CHAPTER 13

Advancing Financial Development and Inclusion in South Asia

Gerard J. Almekinders, Faisal Ahmed, and Sumiko Ogawa

South Asia would benefit from further increasing the dynamism in its financial system as countries in the region undergo middle-income transitions. As a largely bank-based system, upgrading the efficiency of financial intermediation through the banking system remains imperative. The analysis in this chapter shows that, more so than in other regions, public sector banks (PSBs) account for a significant share of South Asia's banking sector. Even before the pandemic, the efficiency of the PSBs declined in relation to their peers. For a sustained postpandemic recovery, the urgency of implementing long-standing reforms in the PSBs has increased further. Improved governance is critical for the efficiency of both public and private commercial banks. Going beyond the volume of credit intermediation, the financial inclusion agenda prioritized by the South Asian countries can improve the quality of growth. In this respect, digitization can help democratize financial access.

A well-developed, efficient and stable financial system is a key requirement to support sustainable and inclusive growth. Other chapters in this book highlight that South Asia was among the fastest growing regions in the world in the years immediately preceding the onset of the COVID-19 pandemic. They also discuss some of the key challenges that need to be overcome to reinvigorate the region's growth to catch up with emerging market peers. This chapter focuses on financial sector policies that can help boost investment and financial inclusion to further support growth and raise the living standards of the region's young and rapidly expanding population. In particular, given the dominant role banks play in the region's financial system, the chapter provides an overview of South Asia's banking system and analyzes the efficiency of South Asian banks relative to each other and compared with those in peer countries. More so than in other regions, public sector banks (PSBs) account for a significant share of South Asia's banking sector. At times, PSBs have suffered from high nonperforming assets, most recently in Bangladesh and India and until a few years ago also in Nepal and Sri Lanka. The analysis in the chapter indicates that the efficiency of PSBs declined over the decade preceding the pandemic. On average, it was also lower than that of private sector banks (PVBs) in recent years. A cross-country comparison further suggests that the efficiency of banks in South Asia, particularly PSBs, has remained relatively low in relation to their peers in recent years. PSBs can play an important role in supporting the region's governments' policies, including with regard to promoting financial inclusion. However, strengthening their risk management and governance and reducing the large presence of the government in the banking system could help improve the efficiency of South Asia's banking sector. The resulting better-allocated credit can support investment and growth. At the same time, important gains can be expected from South Asian countries embracing the opportunities offered by fintech to boost growth and inclusion, while balancing risks to stability and integrity. All South Asian countries have adopted their own inclusion strategies. For example, Sri Lanka called 2020 the "Year of Digital Transactions." Steadfast implementation will improve access to financial services with important implications for economic efficiency and growth.

INTRODUCTION: GROWTH, FINANCIAL DEVELOPMENT, AND INCLUSION IN SOUTH ASIA

Before the onset of the COVID-19 pandemic, South Asia was one of the global growth leaders, and growth compared favorably with G20 emerging market economies. However, South Asia's income per capita remained relatively low, and income disparities were widening. Moreover, investment growth had been comparatively modest (Figure 13.1). While investment growth also disappointed in several G20 emerging market economies in the run-up to the pandemic, strong investment growth is particularly important if South Asia is to recover swiftly from the current crisis, catch up with emerging market economies, and create jobs for a young and growing population and restore and sustain inclusive growth.[1] The need for greater investment, especially private investment and investment in infrastructure, is highlighted also elsewhere in the book.

Financial development and inclusion in South Asia remain lower than in peers. The IMF Financial Development Index captures the depth, access, and efficiency of financial institutions and markets (Svirydzenka 2016). Measured by the mean and median of the IMF Financial Development Index, South Asia ranked lower than G20 peers (Argentina, Brazil, China, Indonesia, Mexico, Russia, South Africa, and Turkey) and ASEAN-8 peers (Brunei, Cambodia, Lao P.D.R., Malaysia, Myanmar, Philippines, Thailand, and Vietnam) in 2017 (Figure 13.2). Going by the index, India's financial development, which is the highest in South Asia, is also lower than the mean and median value for G20 peers.

Relative to other emerging market economies and countries in Asia and the Pacific, India's financial markets efficiency and financial markets depth stands

---

[1] Das and Tulin (2017) study private investment in India against the backdrop of a significant investment decline over the past decade. They find that financial frictions have played a role in the investment slowdown. Firms with higher financial leverage invest less, as do firms with lower earnings relative to their interest expenses. Consistent with the notion of credit constraints leading to pro-cyclical investment, they also find that firms with higher leverage are (1) less likely to undertake new investment projects, (2) less likely to complete investment projects once begun, and (3) undertake shorter-term investment projects.

Figure 13.1. Growth and Investment in South Asia and G20 Peers

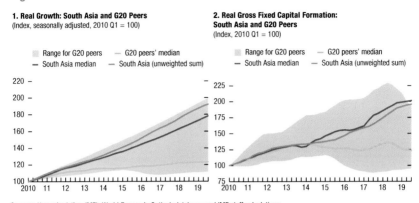

1. Real Growth: South Asia and G20 Peers
(Index, seasonally adjusted, 2010 Q1 = 100)

2. Real Gross Fixed Capital Formation: South Asia and G20 Peers
(Index, 2010 Q1 = 100)

Sources: Haver Analytics; IMF's World Economic Outlook database; and IMF staff calculations.
Note: G20 peers = Argentina, Brazil, China, Indonesia, Mexico, Russia, South Africa, and Turkey.

Figure 13.2. Financial Development Index

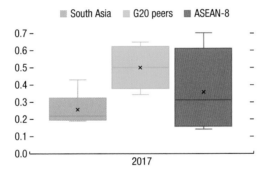

Sources: IMF's Financial Development Index Database; and IMF staff calculations.
Note: The boxes encompass the first quartile, the median (line), the mean (×), and the third quartile of the data. The whiskers indicate the minimum and maximum values. ASEAN-8 = Brunei, Cambodia, Lao P.D.R., Malaysia, Myanmar, Philippines, Thailand, and Vietnam; G20 peers = Argentina, Brazil, China, Indonesia, Mexico, Russia, South Africa, and Turkey.

out. However, the IMF Financial Development Index suggests that India trailed peers regarding the efficiency of and access to financial institutions in 2017 (Figure 13.3). The other South Asian countries considerably lagged their peers in financial markets development as well as access to financial institutions. According to the World Bank Global Financial Inclusion (Findex) database, only 11 percent of adults in South Asia were borrowing from and saving with a financial institution in 2021.[2] While a considerable share of adults reported having borrowed in the preceding year (44 percent), they mostly did not access financial institutions and instead turned to other sources of funds, including family and friends. In addition, 32 percent of South Asian adults with accounts at a financial institution reported the account being inactive—for example, not making any

---

[2] These numbers are importantly driven by Bangladesh and India's large populations. For example, bank penetration is higher in Sri Lanka.

Figure 13.3. Financial Development Subindices, 2017

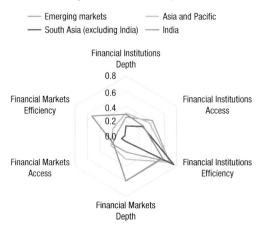

Sources: IMF's Financial Development Index Database; and IMF staff calculations.

deposits or withdrawals—suggesting limited use of financial services as well as ample scope for policies to encourage more intensive use of the no-frills accounts, which have been launched successfully in South Asian countries.

OVERVIEW OF SOUTH ASIA'S BANKING SECTOR

South Asia experienced considerable financial deepening over the past two decades. Bangladesh, Bhutan, and Nepal all saw very rapid increases in the credit to GDP ratio (Figure 13.4). Sri Lanka experienced an acceleration of credit growth after the end of the civil war in 2009. In India, after a considerable rise in

Figure 13.4. Bank Credit to the Private Sector
(Percent of GDP)

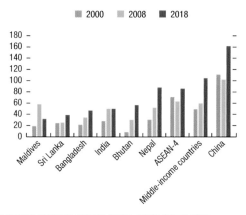

Sources: World Bank's World Development Indicators; national authorities; and IMF staff calculations.
Note: ASEAN-4 = Indonesia, Malaysia, Philippines, and Thailand.

the credit to GDP ratio between 2000 and 2008, the ratio stagnated during the next 10 years owing to stresses in PSBs even as the economy expanded rapidly. The strong growth of remittances appears to have lent strong support to financial deepening. By providing a stable flow of interest-insensitive funding, remittances tend to expand bank balance sheets and encourage intermediation (Barajas and others 2016). The inflow of remittances amounted to US $110 billion in 2018, equivalent to 3.5 percent of the region's GDP (Figure 13.5). This exceeds the comparatively low remittances in China and ASEAN-4 (Indonesia, Malaysia, Philippines, and Thailand) countries, except the Philippines.

Nevertheless, South Asia's financial sector remains relatively shallow in relation to regional comparators and is largely bank based. Except for India, equity and bond markets remain relatively underdeveloped (Figure 13.6). Further development of the sector is needed along with deepening of capital markets to spur private entrepreneurship and effectively mobilize long-term capital, which is especially important for infrastructure investment. The importance of reinvigorating efforts to advance financial development once the pandemic has been overcome is highlighted by the deceleration of credit growth in the region's four largest economies: the median private sector credit growth fell to 7.4 percent in December 2020, the lowest level in at least 14 years (Figure 13.7). With average inflation in the region's four largest economies in a range of 5–6½ percent, the region's median real private sector credit growth averaged less than 2 percent in 2020. The slowdown of credit growth in the region is caused by a confluence of factors. Underlying structural weaknesses affecting the region's banking systems have been playing out against the backdrop of a cyclical downturn in the region's economies, which has been exacerbated by the crisis caused by the COVID-19 pandemic.

One of the structural weaknesses pertains to PSBs' significant share of South Asia's banking sector. State-owned banks play an important role in financing private and public investment in South Asia, also compared with

Figure 13.5. Remittance Inflows
(Percent of GDP)

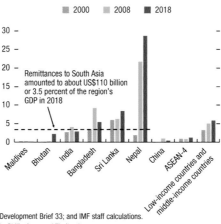

Sources: World Bank Migration and Development Brief 33; and IMF staff calculations.
Note: ASEAN-4 = Indonesia, Malaysia, Philippines, and Thailand.

Figure 13.6. South Asia: Financial Depth
(Percent of GDP, 2018 or latest)

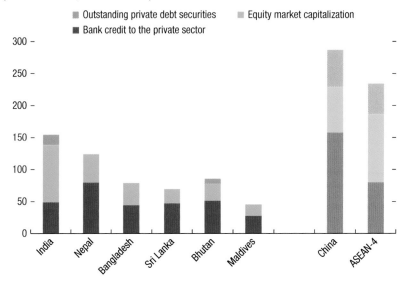

Sources: IMF's International Financial Statistics; and FinStats.
Note: ASEAN-4 = Indonesia, Malaysia, Philippines, and Thailand.

Figure 13.7. Private Sector Credit Growth in South Asia,
Excluding Bhutan and Maldives
(Percent)

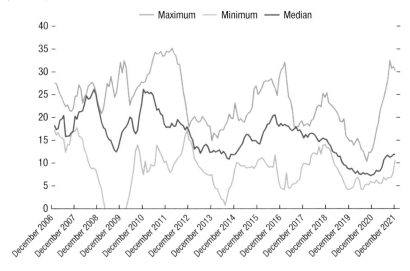

Sources: Central banks of Bangladesh, India, Nepal, and Sri Lanka.

peers (Figures 13.8 and 13.9). Empirical studies discussed in more detail in the next section suggests that high reliance on state banks' lending is often associated with a deterioration in the quality and efficiency of financial intermediation and resource allocation (World Bank 2013), higher credit to the public sector, and weaker fiscal discipline (Gonzalez-Garcia and Grigoli 2013). State-owned banks also tend to have weaker performance compared with private and foreign banks (Cull and others 2017). Some of these dynamics seem to be at play in South Asia, notably in Bangladesh and India, where nonperforming loans have tended to be significantly higher, and capitalization levels and profitability significantly lower in state-owned banks relative to private financial institutions (Figure 13.10).[3] This has, in turn, affected credit provision to the economy, leading to increasing reliance on nonbank financial

Figure 13.8. Share of Public Sector Bank Assets
(Percent of total bank assets)

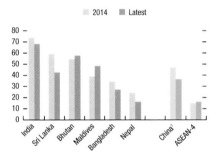

Sources: Banking Regulation and Supervision Survey; India 2017 Financial Sector Assessment Program report; Bangladesh Bank; Nepal Rastra Bank; and Royal Monetary Authority of Bhutan.
Note: ASEAN-4 = Indonesia, Malaysia, Philippines, and Thailand.
[1] The share of the large four state-owned banks.

Figure 13.9. Composition of Credit, 2017
(Percent)

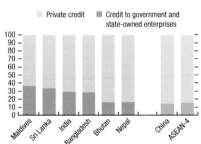

Sources: IMF's World Economic Outlook database; International Financial Statistics; and FinStat.
Note: ASEAN-4 = Indonesia, Malaysia, Philippines, and Thailand.

---

[3] Financial soundness indicators may not be comparable across countries because of differences in national accounting standards. Furthermore, weaknesses in asset classification definitions and provisioning requirements may overstate banks' capitalization and understate asset quality issues.

Figure 13.10. Financial Soundness Indicators by Bank Ownership in South Asia

Nonperforming loans in public sector banks considerably exceeded those in private banks in Bangladesh and India in 2018. In Nepal, an earlier large gap had all but disappeared by 2018.

1. Nonperforming Loan Ratio
(Percent, weighted average)

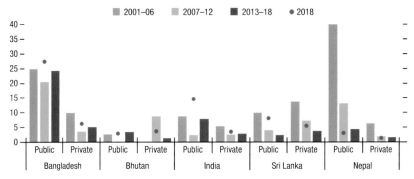

Private banks consistently topped public banks on capital adequacy ratios. Nepal's public banks have come a long way. Bangladesh's public banks' capital adequacy ratio was still in the single digits in 2018.

2. Capital Adequacy Ratio
(Percent, weighted average)

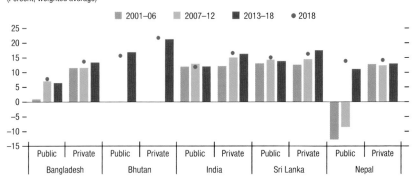

Private banks typically reported higher returns on assets. In 2018, recognition of nonperforming loans caused India's public banks to report losses. Bangladesh public banks also did poorly.

3. Return on Assets
(In percent, weighted average)

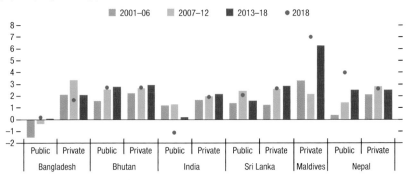

Sources: Fitch Connect and authors' calculations.
Note: Reflecting data availability, this includes 52 banks for Bangladesh, 2 for Bhutan, 57 for India, 24 for Sri Lanka, and 28 for Nepal.

institutions, with new regulatory and supervisory challenges. The pandemic will likely exacerbate the preexisting vulnerabilities with important implications for the postpandemic recovery, highlighting the need to make progress with the long-standing financial sector reforms.[4]

As discussed in the next section of this chapter, cross-country studies indicate that foreign banks have tended to achieve higher capitalization and profitability and lower nonperforming loans than domestic banks. However, the footprint of foreign banks remains small in South Asia. They typically focus on large corporate and retail clients and capital market transactions, obviating the need for large branch networks. Cross-country data in Claessens and Van Horen (2012) indicates that foreign banks in South Asia play a considerably smaller role than in other emerging market economies and developing countries. If anything, the market share of foreign banks has been on a declining trend in recent years, falling to 5.8 percent of total bank assets in India in 2016–17, down by 1 percentage point from 2010–11, and to 4.6 percent of total bank assets in Bangladesh in 2017, down by 3.4 percentage points from 2008.

The continued relatively limited presence of foreign banks in South Asia is consistent with the region's relatively limited financial openness. South Asian countries' frameworks for capital flow management measures are moving in the general direction of capital account liberalization. However, reforms have been taking place at a measured pace. In a cross-country sample of 100 countries, based on information provided in the IMF's Annual Report on Exchange Arrangements and Exchange Restrictions, the three South Asia countries for which data is available (Bangladesh, India, and Sri Lanka) stand out for the relatively restrictive de jure regime for capital inflows (Figure 13.11). South Asia's relatively restrictive regime for capital inflows is associated with smaller capital inflows resulting in a lower stock of portfolio and foreign direct investment (FDI) liabilities than in peers relative to the size of the economy (low de facto financial openness).

With India's dominant PSBs held back by balance sheet weaknesses, PVBs and, importantly, nonbank financial institutions (NBFIs) expanded rapidly to satisfy India's demand for credit in recent years through 2020–21. Meanwhile, the structure of credit provision in the other South Asian countries remained broadly unchanged:

- In India, amid rapid economic growth, PSBs' share of total loans and advances declined by 22 percentage points over a period of 10 years, to 42.9 percent by March 2021 (Table 13.1). This resulted in large part from

---

[4] In response to the pandemic, South Asian countries eased monetary policy significantly, provided substantial liquidity support, and implemented a range of financial sector measures, including debt service moratoria, emergency or subsidized lending to firms (for example, working capital loans, micro loans, or loans targeted to specific industries). To support liquidity, central banks also made refinancing schemes available. For more details, see Hodge and Moussa 2021. As some of the measures are withdrawn, a significant impact on the financial systems is expected to emerge, subject to the pace of the recovery and the extent of spillovers from corporate and micro-, small-, and medium-size enterprise insolvencies.

Figure 13.11. Relatively Low De Jure and De Facto Financial Openness Compared with Peers in South Asia

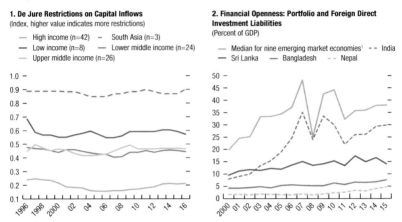

1. De Jure Restrictions on Capital Inflows
(Index, higher value indicates more restrictions)

— High income (n=42)   — South Asia (n=3)
— Low income (n=8)   — Lower middle income (n=24)
— Upper middle income (n=26)

2. Financial Openness: Portfolio and Foreign Direct Investment Liabilities
(Percent of GDP)

— Median for nine emerging market economies[1]   -- India
— Sri Lanka   — Bangladesh   -- Nepal

Sources: Fernández and others 2016; Lane and Milesi-Ferretti 2006; and External Wealth of Nations database.
[1]Brazil, China, Indonesia, Israel, Philippines, Russia, Thailand, Turkey, and Vietnam.

difficulties and stresses afflicting PSBs, including rising nonperforming loans. During this period, PVBs' share of total loans and advances increased by almost 11 percentage points to 26.6 percent. More than half of PSBs' lost market share was gained by India's two main groups of NBFIs: nonbank financial companies (NBFCs) and housing finance companies (HFCs). Their combined share of total loans and advances in India reached almost 27 percent in March 2021, up from less than 16 percent in 2011. By March 2021, the combined assets of NBFIs were more than a quarter the size of commercial banks' assets, up from a sixth in March 2011.

• In Sri Lanka and Bangladesh, following a rapid expansion of finance and leasing companies during 2013–17, commercial banks increased their market share of loans and advances to 90 and 94 percent, respectively, in 2021 amid sustained rapid overall credit growth (Tables 13.2 and 13.3). In Sri Lanka, finance and leasing companies expanded their loan books rapidly between 2013 and 2017. However, loan quality issues curtailed their growth during 2018–21. In Nepal, commercial banks increased their market share amid rapid growth of bank credit and notwithstanding the sustained rapid growth of microfinance institutions (Table 13.4). The central bank of Nepal's requirement for banks to hold higher paid-up capital contributed to a consolidation of the number of banks and financial institutions as mergers were associated with a reduction in the number of development banks and finance companies.

The rapid expansion of India's PVBs and NBFIs at a time when the economy was growing rapidly but PSBs were held back by poorly performing loans on their balance sheets highlights the importance of robust and efficiently allocated bank credit to sustain rapid economic growth. This is also implied by the broad

TABLE 13.1.

Loans and Advances from Banks and Nonbank Financial Institutions in India

	Percent of Total Assets					Compound Annual Growth Rate (Percent)	Year-on-Year Change in Assets (Percent)			
	2010/11	2016/17	2018/19	2019/20	2020/21	2010/11 to 2016/17	2017/18	2018/19	2019/20	2020/21
Total assets	100.0	100.0	100.0	100.0	100.0	12.5	10.9	10.5	8.4	9.2
Scheduled commercial banks	86.0	83.7	80.0	80.1	79.8	12.0	7.6	8.8	8.5	8.8
Public sector banks	63.4	57.5	49.0	47.9	47.8	10.7	3.0	1.3	6.1	8.8
Private sector banks	16.8	21.3	25.5	25.9	26.2	17.1	19.4	23.2	10.1	10.3
Foreign banks	5.9	4.9	5.1	5.6	5.2	9.0	5.5	21.5	19.7	0.0
Nonbank financial companies	10.4	10.9	13.6	13.7	14.2	13.4	27.6	20.0	9.1	12.8
Housing finance companies	3.6	5.4	6.4	6.2	6.0	20.5	27.6	13.7	5.6	6.4

	Percent of Total Loans and Advances					Compound Annual Growth Rate (Percent)	Year-on-Year in Loans and Advances (Percent)			
	2010/11	2016/17	2018/19	2019/20	2020/21	2010/11 to 2016/17	2017/18	2018/19	2019/20	2020/21
Total loans and advances	100.0	100.0	100.0	100.0	100.0	12.5	12.8	12.5	6.3	6.1
Scheduled commercial banks	84.4	78.5	73.8	73.9	73.1	11.2	7.8	10.6	6.5	5.0
Public sector banks	64.9	53.8	44.9	44.2	42.9	9.0	2.5	3.4	4.5	3.1
Private sector banks	15.7	21.5	25.4	26.0	26.6	18.6	20.0	24.9	9.0	8.7
Foreign banks	3.8	3.2	3.0	3.1	2.9	9.2	6.4	13.1	7.8	-1.2
Nonbank financial companies	10.8	14.3	17.4	17.6	18.2	18.0	32.6	16.0	8.1	9.7
Housing finance companies	4.9	7.1	8.9	8.5	8.6	19.9	28.2	23.1	1.8	8.0

Sources: Reserve Bank of India; and authors' calculations.

TABLE 13.2.

Loans and Advances from Banks and Nonbank Financial Companies in Sri Lanka

	Percent of Loans and Advances			Compound Annual Growth Rate of Loans and Advances (Percent)	
	2013	2017	2021	2013–17	2017–21
Total loans and advances	100.0	100.0	100.0	17.4	11.6
Commercial and specialized banks	86.8	85.9	90.2	17.0	13.0
Finance and leasing companies	13.2	14.1	9.8	19.3	2.0

Sources: Central Bank of Sri Lanka; and IMF staff calculations.

TABLE 13.3.

Loans and Advances from Banks and Nonbank Financial Companies in Bangladesh

	Percent of Total Assets			Compound Annual Growth Rate of Assets (Percent)	
	2013	2017	2021	2013–17	2017–21
Total assets	100.0	100.0	100.0	15.6	11.5
Commercial and specialized banks	94.9	93.6	95.5	15.2	12.1
Finance and leasing companies	5.1	6.4	4.5	22.1	2.1
	Percent of Loans and Advances			Compound Annual Growth Rate of Loans and Advances (Percent)	
	2013	2017	2021	2013–17	2017–21
Total loans and advances	100.0	100.0	100.0	13.4	11.5
Commercial and specialized banks	94.2	92.6	94.4	12.9	12.1
Finance and leasing companies	5.8	7.4	5.6	20.7	3.7

Sources: Bangladesh Bank; and IMF staff estimates.

TABLE 13.4.

Assets and Loans and Advances from Banks and Microfinance Companies in Nepal

	Percent of Total Assets			Compound Annual Growth Rate of Assets (Percent)	
	2012/13	2016/17	2020/21	2012/13 to 2016/17	2016/17 to 2020/21
Total assets	100.0	100.0	100.0	18.0	19.8
Commercial banks	78.2	83.4	83.2	19.9	19.8
Development banks	13.1	9.7	8.0	9.6	14.2
Finance companies	6.6	2.6	1.9	−6.1	11.1
Microfinance institutions	2.2	4.3	6.9	39.1	35.1
	Percent of Loans and Advances			Compound Annual Growth Rate of Loans and Advances (Percent)	
	2012/13	2016/17	2020/21	2012/13 to 2016/17	2016/17 to 2020/21
Total loans and advances	100.0	100.0	100.0	21.1	21.3
Commercial banks	77.3	82.5	81.8	23.1	21.1
Development banks	13.5	10.1	8.4	12.4	15.8
Finance companies	6.8	2.4	1.7	−7.0	11.9
Microfinance institutions	2.4	5.1	8.1	46.1	36.1

Sources: Nepal Rastra Bank; and IMF staff calculations.
Note: Cooperatives are not included; their loans and advances were equivalent to 14 percent of total loans and advances of banks and microfinance companies in mid-2017.

Figure 13.12. Credit Intensity of Output in India

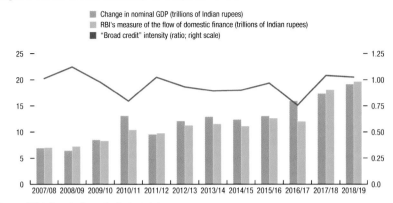

Sources: CEIC; Indian authorities; and authors' calculations.
Note: The ratio refers to the flow of new financing divided by the change in nominal GDP.

stability of India's credit intensity of output over the period between the global financial crisis and the onset of the COVID-19 pandemic: additional units of output require additional units of credit (Figure 13.12). If the existing dominant institutions (in the case of India, the PSBs) can't satisfy the additional demand for credit, then previously less prominent suppliers will spring up and/or new suppliers will emerge, provided the regulatory framework allows for this.[5] Sustained rapid credit expansion among new suppliers can lead to a buildup of risk.

As efforts are being made to strengthen governance and regulation of commercial banks, including PSBs, care should be taken to prevent migration of risks to less regulated financial institutions. In India, NBFCs and HFCs grew rapidly relying on short-term funding, while PSBs struggled with legacy nonperforming assets and their cleanup.[6] Following the stress in the NBFI sector in 2019, triggered by defaults of a large NBFC and an HFC, the Reserve Bank of India (RBI) strengthened regulation and supervision of NBFCs to be more in line with banks, and regulation of HFCs was brought under the RBI.

With the onset of COVID-19 and the prolonged economic fallout, risks to banks' asset quality have increased. Loan moratoriums put in place in many countries (for example, Bangladesh, India, Nepal, and Sri Lanka) provided temporary relief to borrowers. However, to the extent that the pandemic holds back economic activity for an extended period, firms and households may continue to

---

[5] The broad credit intensity of output is calculated based on the Reserve Bank of India's data on Flow of Funds to the Commercial Sector. The data in Figure 13.12 on the RBI's measure of the flow of domestic finance is based on the flow of funds from banks plus the flow of funds from domestic nonbanks, encompassing NBFCs and HFCs, among others (see, for example, Table IV.3 in the RBI's October 2019 Monetary Policy Report).

[6] The rapid growth of India's NBFIs can be seen in part as a result of regulatory arbitrage as the statutory liquidity ratio (SLR) and priority sector lending limits did not apply to NBFCs and HFCs.

experience repayment difficulties once the measures expire, potentially leading to increases in delinquencies. Furthermore, should the economic recovery be protracted and the "new normal" significantly change the viability of businesses in some industry, some borrowers that were previously viable may face solvency challenges. This could exacerbate asset quality problems and may require recapitalization and resolution of some institutions. A relaxation in loan classification requirements (for example, in Bangladesh) obscures bank supervisors' and the public's understanding of banks' asset quality and typically merely delays the materialization of loan quality problems.

EFFICIENCY OF BANKS IN SOUTH ASIA

The previous section highlighted the need for an efficient banking system to finance growth in South Asia. It also pointed out that despite high private sector credit growth over the past decade, South Asia's financial depth and capital market development continues to lag ASEAN-4 countries and China. With South Asia's stable and low credit intensity of output and with credit growth now decelerating across the region, it is clear that the efficiency of the allocation of financial resources needs to improve to support sustainable and inclusive growth.

Literature Review

The relationship between bank ownership (foreign versus domestic; state-owned versus private) and performance has received considerable academic attention. Cross-country evidence suggests that foreign-owned banks tend to be more efficient than domestic banks in developing countries. However, while the presence of foreign-owned banks promotes competition it can also transmit external shocks and might not always increase access to credit (Cull and others 2017). A number of studies has found that government-owned banks operating in developing countries tend to have a higher level of nonperforming loans than privately owned banks (IADB 2005; Iannotta and others 2007; Micco and others 2007; Berger and others 2009; Farazi and others 2013). That said, other studies have shown that PSB lending is less procyclical than PVB lending (Micco and Panizza 2006; Brei and Schclarek 2013; Önder and Özyıldırım 2013). The findings on the relationship between government bank ownership and the likelihood of banking crises are mixed. Caprio and Martinez Peira (2002) found a positive association, but La Porta and others (2002) does not find a significant correlation.

Cross-country and country-specific studies tend to show that government ownership of banks can lead to inefficiency in resource allocation and hold back innovation and thereby cause a drag on efficiency and growth. Government-owned banks tend to direct higher amounts of lending to politically strategic sectors or regions (Carvalho 2014; Sapienza 2004; Khwaja and Mian 2005), and/or target firms that have political ties to the detriment of other firms (Khwaja and Mian 2005; Carvalho 2014). Studies from the early 2000s provide some evidence that government ownership is negatively associated with domestic banking sector efficiency, as measured by net interest margins and overhead costs (Barth and others 2001; La Porta and others 2002). However, the results are less robust once cross-country differences in regulatory and supervisory characteristics are controlled for (Barth and others 2004). Cross-country analysis in Xiao and Zhao (2012) found that in countries with lower government ownership of banks, banking sector development significantly enhances firm innovation; while in countries with higher government ownership of banks, banking sector development has no significant or sometimes even significantly negative effects on firm innovation. In a study on data for Germany, Bian and others (2017) found that extensive government involvement in the allocation of credit comes at the cost of lower corporate innovation and therefore of economic development. Such negative effects are significantly stronger for smaller firms since their access to finance is more dependent on the local supply of lenders.

The role of PSBs in the Indian banking system has been closely studied. Acharya and others (2010) argued that state ownership—by implicitly conferring stronger guarantees on PSBs—distorts the playing field between various banking sector players and recommended a gradual exit of the state from the Indian banking sector. Gupta and others (2011), using bank-level data from 1991–2007, found that even after liberalization, public banks allocated a larger share of their assets to government securities than did private banks and that public banks were more responsive in allocating relatively more resources to finance the fiscal deficit even during periods when the requirement to hold government securities as a share of assets formally declined. Sensarma (2006) showed that the efficiency of Indian banks gradually improved during 1986–2000, reflecting the increase in competition during the period, including from the entry of new private banks and the establishment of new public banks. Using data envelopment analysis for 2005–18, Herwadkar and others (2019) found that labor cost efficiency of Indian banks for the period 2005–2018 had not improved, and large banks were found to be more efficient than small banks owing to economies of scale. Sanyal and Shankar (2011) analyzed the effect of ownership and competition on bank productivity, while controlling for size and structure of the bank, and showed that private banks dominate the public and foreign banks, both in terms of productivity levels and productivity growth.

Assessment of Bank Efficiency

This section presents an ownership-based analysis of efficiency of banks in South Asia in relation to peer countries using data envelopment analysis, which is a nonparametric linear programming method that can be applied to entities with common inputs and outputs, for example, deposits, interest and noninterest costs, profits, loans, and assets in the case of banks. The method allows estimation of technical efficiencies (assuming that all banks operate at the optimal scale, that is, at constant returns to scale) benchmarked against the efficiency frontiers of the sample entities. Technical efficiency can be broken down into pure technical efficiency (assuming that banks do not always operate at the optimal size, that is, variable return to scale) and scale efficiency. As the results are sensitive to the combination of inputs and outputs, several input/output combinations were considered based on existing studies, and simple averages of the estimated efficiency scores are presented in the following sections.[7]

The analysis covers the largest 20 banks in terms of assets for the six South Asian countries and five peer countries (Brazil, China, Indonesia, Russia, and Vietnam) over the period of 2001–18 (Figure 13.13).[8] PSBs have large footprints in the financial sector in these countries and tend to have weaker balance sheets especially in South Asia.

- PSBs account for more than half of the assets of the largest 20 banks, except for Nepal, and as high as around 80 and 70 percent for India and Sri Lanka, respectively. The fact that the number of PSBs in the sample is less than half for most South Asian countries implies that PSBs on average have larger assets than private banks.

- PSBs have higher nonperforming loan ratios than private banks in most of South Asia and some of the peer countries. PSBs' profitability tends to be lower than that of private banks, in part reflecting the higher provisioning burden from nonperforming loans.

- Capital adequacy ratios of South Asian PSBs are lower than their private peers, despite repeated recapitalization in several countries (as will be discussed later).

The data envelopment analysis results are consistent with the differential financial soundness indicators of PSBs and private banks (Figure 13.14).

- Technical efficiency scores[9] indicate that PSBs tended to have lower efficiency compared with their in-country private peers throughout the 2001–2018 period. The gap widened over time for Bangladesh, India, and Sri Lanka, whereas it narrowed rapidly in the most recent years in Nepal. Compared with banks in peer countries, both PSBs and private banks in South Asia had lower efficiency.

The efficiency gap with peer countries is more pronounced when looking at pure technical efficiency, where comparator banks experienced an improvement in the efficiency scores while those of South Asian banks stayed broadly unchanged. Private banks tended to have higher pure technical efficiency than PSBs in South Asia, whereas the reverse was the case for comparator countries.

Banking efficiency in South Asia has been held back by the large presence of PSBs and overall weak governance, in conjunction with weak legal and judicial systems. These factors have likely weakened risk assessments and distorted resource

---

[7] The analysis may not fully reflect the broader macro-environment and more in-depth analyses may be needed into each country's case to better interpret the results.

[8] Data on the financial performance of individual banks are taken from Fitch Connect. Because of the small number of banks with available data, results shown do not include Bhutan (which were included to some extent in the previous section) and Maldives.

[9] Technical efficiency scores are estimated based on constant returns to scale, that is, assuming all entities are operating at the optimal scale. On the other hand, with the variable returns to scale assumption, the overall efficiency is disaggregated into pure technical efficiency and scale efficiency.

Figure 13.13. Overview of Banks Included in the Data Envelopment Analysis

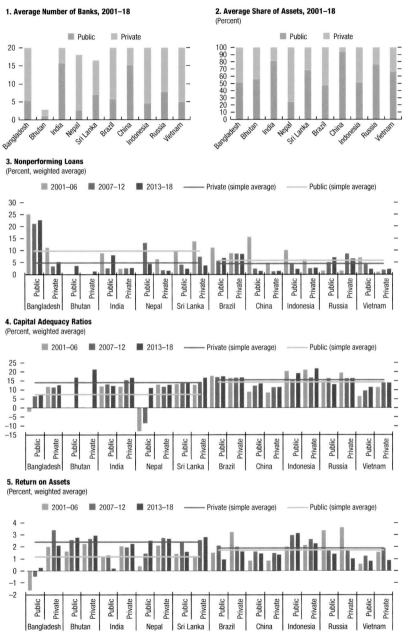

Sources: Fitch Connect; and authors' calculations.

Figure 13.14. Efficiency Scores, by Country and Ownership

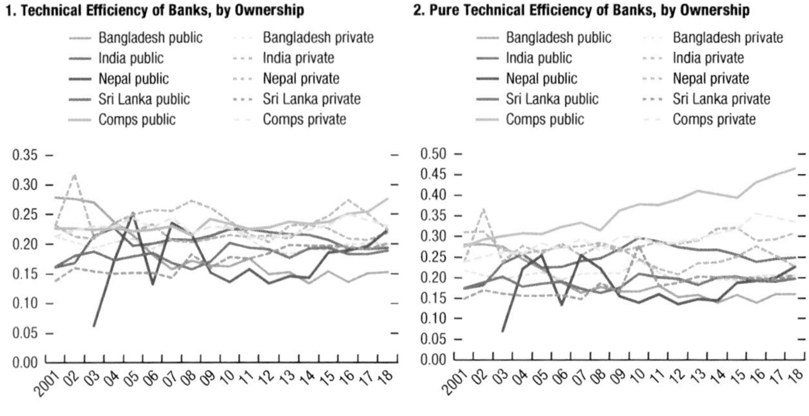

1. Technical Efficiency of Banks, by Ownership

- Bangladesh public
- India public
- Nepal public
- Sri Lanka public
- Comps public
- Bangladesh private
- India private
- Nepal private
- Sri Lanka private
- Comps private

2. Pure Technical Efficiency of Banks, by Ownership

- Bangladesh public
- India public
- Nepal public
- Sri Lanka public
- Comps public
- Bangladesh private
- India private
- Nepal private
- Sri Lanka private
- Comps private

Source: Authors' calculations.

allocation. Moreover, directed lending requirements were in place during much if not all of the 2001–18 sample period in Bangladesh, India, Nepal, and Sri Lanka.[10] Accordingly, commercial banks were required to allocate a certain minimum share of total credit to specified priority sectors such as agriculture, industry, and small- and medium-size companies. These requirements typically applied regardless of ownership and often complemented mandatory support to government policies in other ways. For example, the 2017 India Financial System Stability Assessment conducted in the context of the IMF's Financial Sector Assessment Program (IMF 2017) pointed out that all Indian banks were mandated to hold 20 percent of assets in government securities to satisfy the SLR and allocate 40 percent of net credit to "priority sector lending." The Financial Sector Assessment Program further noted that the buildup of high corporate leverage to support infrastructure investments in the 2000s was largely financed by PSBs. Deteriorating global and domestic conditions in 2013 and structural bottlenecks (for example, delays in environmental clearances and land acquisition permits) took a toll on firms' debt repayment capacity, particularly in metals, engineering, and transportation infrastructure, and led to a marked deterioration in PSBs' asset quality.

Inefficiency of PSBs poses fiscal contingency risks, which have repeatedly materialized in South Asia.

- In Bangladesh, nonperforming loans in PSBs range between 20 and 30 percent, implying significant efficiency costs and contingent liabilities, which have in part already materialized as seen by frequent recapitalizations in the past. For example, in the nine fiscal years through FY2017/18, Bangladesh's central government budget allocations for recapitalizations of state-owned banks averaged 0.12 percent of GDP per annum. In the absence of reforms,

[10] Directed lending requirements were introduced in Bhutan in 2018.

creating a public asset management corporation to deal with nonperforming loans in PSBs would pose significant fiscal risk going forward.

- In India, the government capital infusions in state-owned banks averaged 0.15 percent of GDP per annum in the seven fiscal years through FY 2016/17. Moreover, amid fiscal pressures and a high level of public debt, PSBs received capital injections from the government averaging 0.6 percent of GDP in 2017/18 and 2018/19.

- In Nepal, the three state-owned banks with negative capital have received significant recapitalizations from the budget, including in the context of financial sector reform programs financed by the Asian Development Bank and the World Bank.[11] Amid rapid credit growth and weak loan-classification standards, their nonperforming loan ratios have come down considerably, but inefficiencies and risks have not gone away.

Repeated recapitalizations from the government budget generate moral hazard and distort banks' risk management and lending practices further. There are efforts to address the governance issue. For example, the government of India launched a governance reform of PSBs in 2018 and published a progress report in 2019 (Boston Consulting Group and India Banks' Association 2019). More recently, the RBI circulated a discussion paper on governance in commercial banks, with the aim to align the regulatory framework to international practice (RBI 2020).

FINANCIAL INCLUSION IN SOUTH ASIA

Financial inclusion is a multidimensional concept, with implications for growth and financial and economic stability. Staff research has shown potentially significant growth benefits from financial inclusion, especially for low-income developing countries (LIDCs) in Asia-Pacific (IMF 2018). Financial inclusion appears to be positively correlated with per capita income growth.[12] Furthermore, greater financial inclusion is associated with significant poverty reduction.[13] In terms of channels through which inclusion affects growth in bank-based financial systems, greater access of firms and households to various banking services, as well as increasing women users of these services, leads to higher growth (Sahay and others 2015). Sectors dependent on external finance grow more rapidly in countries with greater financial inclusion.

South Asia has made significant strides in terms of financial inclusion. For example, account ownership in India and Sri Lanka is well above the levels expected of countries with similar income levels. That said, there remains

---

[11] Ozaki (2014) described how successive recapitalizations from the government budget were effected to turn the capital of Nepal's PSBs positive.

[12] For illustrative purposes, a 1 percent increase in the financial inclusion index level in LIDCs—which is equivalent to improving financial inclusion from the fourth to the third quartile—is associated with a cumulative 0.14 percentage point increase in per capita income growth over a five-year period (IMF 2018).

[13] As an illustration of this relationship, an increase in the financial inclusion index level of 1 percent, corresponding to moving from the fourth to third quartile, is estimated to lower the poverty level by 1.4 percent of the total population in Asia-Pacific for more than a five-year period (IMF 2018).

significant room for improving inclusion, including through increasing the share of active usage of accounts and reducing gender gaps in South Asia, which, at 18 percentage points, rank as one of the largest in Asia.[14] Transactions by both banked and unbanked continue to rely heavily on cash, though steady progress has been made in recent years. Digitizing such payments offers great potential and can spur an increase in account penetration and the use of accounts. Recent IMF studies (IMF 2018, 2019) show that South Asia can reap a growth dividend from improving financial inclusion: closing the financial inclusion gap of South Asian

Figure 13.15. Access to Finance and Impact of Financial Inclusion on Income Growth

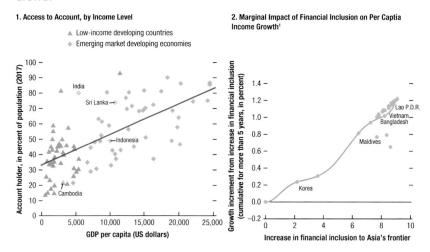

Source: IMF 2018.
[1]Based on country's level and closing gap versus Asia's financial inclusion frontier.

Figure 13.16. The Effect of Financial Inclusion on Growth
(Percent)

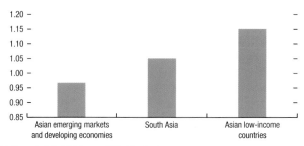

Sources: IMF's World Economic Outlook database; and IMF staff estimates.
Note: The figures show the effect of additional growth from closing the gap relative to the frontier.

---

[14] Despite recent progress, gender disparities have been significant, particularly in South Asia, where less than 40 percent of women have a bank account, compared with nearly 60 percent of men (Demirguc-Kunt and others 2018; IMF 2018).

countries in relation to the frontier is associated with a gain in growth by around 1 percentage point (Figures 13.15 and 13.16).

The steady progress in financial inclusion in South Asia in recent years has benefited from the priority the authorities in South Asian countries have placed on improving inclusion, including through financial inclusion strategies and innovation. For example, the launch of the Pradhan Mantri Jan Dhan Yojana program in India in 2014, one of the world's largest financial inclusion initiatives to date, is one prominent example of India's national-level commitment to advancing financial inclusion. PMJDY's objective is to ensure access to financial services such as basic savings accounts, credit, remittances, insurance, and pension products among individuals who are often excluded from the formal financial sector.

National financial inclusion strategies have been adopted or are in the process of being adopted in most of the South Asian countries. India launched the National Strategy for Financial Inclusion 2019–2024. Nepal adopted the Financial Inclusion Roadmap 2017–2022. Bhutan is implementing the National Financial Inclusion Strategy 2018–2023. Bangladesh prepared a National Financial Inclusion Strategy 2019–2024. The common elements among the national strategies include the focus on fintech or digital inclusion; micro-, small-, and medium-size enterprises and agriculture to improve inclusion; reduce poverty and inequality; and support job creation and growth. The urgency of and positive spillover from many of these priorities would increase further during the post–COVID-19 recovery.

South Asia has been the home of one of the pioneering innovations in financial inclusion—microfinance—that also helped reduce gender gaps in inclusion as it heavily focused on women borrowers. Microfinance initially and extensively spread in Bangladesh, before also catching on in other countries. South Asia accounts for more than 70 percent of the microfinance borrowers in the world. Leveraging technology (for example, with microfinance products) highlighted in the national financial inclusion strategies can extend the frontier of inclusion.

Fintech is playing a growing role in improving financial inclusion around the world, by reducing costs and providing economies of scale and facilitating access to

Figure 13.17. Made or Received Digital Payments in the Past Year, Age 15+ Years
(Percent)

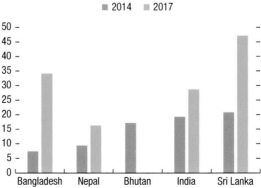

Source: Findex database.
Note: No data are available for Bhutan in 2017.

Box 13.1. Advances in Digital Financial Inclusion

Digital financial services offer potential for advancing financial inclusion. Taking advantage of the increasing availability of indicators of financial inclusion through digital means, Sahay and others (2020) developed a comprehensive measure of financial inclusion covering 52 emerging markets and developing economies, including three South Asian countries (Bangladesh, India, and Sri Lanka). It uses a three-stage principal component analysis to construct composite indices of access to and usage of digital and traditional (through financial institutions) payments services, which in turn are aggregated into a comprehensive financial inclusion index.

They found that digital finance has been the main driver of financial inclusion in recent years: digital financial inclusion, measured by the index, improved between 2014 and 2017 in all countries, even in cases where traditional financial inclusion retreated somewhat (Figure 13.1.1). African and Asian countries led the improvement in digital financial inclusion on average (panel 1), while there are considerable variations within regions.

Digital finance appears to be contributing to filling the gap left by traditional financial institutions in some cases (panel 2). Sahay and others (2020) looked into factors associated with digital financial inclusion, using its subindices on access to and usage of digital payments services. Various macroeconomic, financial, and socioeconomic indicators are examined, including (1) level of economic development, (2) financial sector efficiency, (3) level of competition in the financial sector, (4) financial stability, (5) government/institution quality, and (6) urban population. The indices of access to and usage of traditional financial services are also included to account for potential substitutability and complementarity between the two means of financial inclusion.

The analysis found the following:

- Usage tends to be higher where access to digital infrastructure is better, and where there is already a high usage of traditional financial services. This could reflect trust in the financial system and financial literacy.
- Supply of digital financial services tends to be higher where there is inefficiency in traditional financial institution and the quality of government/institution is higher. High bank concentration is negatively associated with the measure of access, pointing out the importance of the competitive environment.

Figure 13.1.1. Digital versus Traditional Financial Inclusion

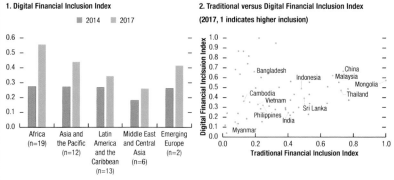

Source: Sahay and others 2020.

payment services and finance for previously excluded segments of the population. The usage of fintech in financial transactions increased significantly in South Asia between 2014 and 2017, particularly in Bangladesh and Sri Lanka (Figure 13.17).

Fintech eased the delivery of social safety net payments during the COVID-19 shock and helped mitigate the adverse impact of the shock. For example, in India, 200 million account holders of the Pradhan Mantri Jan Dhan Yojana program, a financial inclusion program, were able to receive account-based cash transfers as an immediate response to the COVID-19 pandemic. Digital cash transfer was also adopted in other South Asian countries. For example, Bangladesh has initiated digital transfer for wages and government-to-person cash transfers to beneficiaries during the pandemic. In India, the government is planning to launch a central bank digital currency to further support, inter alia, financial inclusion.

A recent IMF study (Sahay and others 2020) developed a new index of digital financial inclusion (see Box 13.1). This study showed that digital finance is increasing financial inclusion and is associated with higher GDP growth, suggesting digital financial inclusion could play an important role in mitigating the economic and social impact of the ongoing COVID-19 crisis, including by enabling contactless and cashless transactions. During the COVID-19 pandemic, technology has created new opportunities for digital financial services to accelerate and enhance financial inclusion, amid social distancing and containment measures. That said, the study highlighted that the pandemic could also aggravate preexisting risks of financial exclusion and give rise to new risks to the fintech sector itself. Looking ahead, deepening the financial access of low-income households and small businesses could also support a more inclusive postpandemic recovery.

CONCLUSIONS

To support an agenda for sustainable and inclusive growth which is critical to create the jobs for the large and growing number of youth, South Asia needs to further increase the dynamism in its financial system as countries in the region undergo middle-income transitions. As a largely bank-based system, upgrading the efficiency of financial intermediation through the banking system remains imperative. As the analysis in this chapter shows, even before the pandemic, the efficiency of the PSBs, a large share of the financial system, declined in relation to their peers. For a sustained postpandemic recovery, the urgency of implementing long-standing reforms in the PSBs to improve the efficiency and volume of credit allocation, including by strengthening their risk management, governance, and capitalization has increased further. This also highlights the need for the PVBs to play a larger role in credit intermediation. It should also be noted that improved governance is critical for the efficiency of both public and private commercial banks. Going beyond the volume of credit intermediation, the financial inclusion agenda prioritized by the South Asian countries can improve the quality of growth. In this respect, digitization can help democratize financial access.

REFERENCES

Acharya, V. V., A. Agarwal, and N. Kulkarni. 2010. "State Ownership and Systemic Risk: Evidence from the Indian Financial Sector during 2007–09," (manuscript).

Barajas, A., R. Chami, C. H. Ebeke, A. Oeking. 2016. "What's Different about Monetary Policy Transmission in Remittance-Dependent Countries?" International Monetary Fund Working Paper 16/44.

Barth, J. R., G. Caprio, and R. Levine. 2001. "Banking Systems around the Globe: Do Regulation and Ownership Affect Performance and Stability?" in *Prudential Supervision: What Works and What Doesn't* (pp. 31–96). University of Chicago Press.

Barth, J. R., G. Caprio, and R. Levine. 2004. "Bank Regulation and Supervision: What Works Best?" *Journal of Financial intermediation* 13 (2): 205–248.

Berger, A. N., R. DeYoung, H. Genay, and G. F. Udell. 2009. "Globalization of Financial Institutions: Evidence from Cross-Border Banking Performance," *Brookings-Wharton Papers on Financial Services: 2000* (1): 23–120.

Bian, B., R. Haselmann, V. Vig, and B. Weder di Mauro. 2017. "Government Ownership of Banks and Corporate Innovation." https://repository.graduateinstitute.ch/record/296562?ln=en

Boston Consulting Group and Indian Banks' Association, 2019. "EASE Reforms for Public Sector Banks." https://media-publications.bcg.com/EASE-reforms-for-public-sector-banks.pdf

Brei, M., and A. Schclarek. 2013. "Public Bank Lending in Times of Crisis," *Journal of Financial Stability* 9 (4): 820–830.

Caprio, G., and M. S. Martinez Peria. 2002. "Avoiding Disaster: Policies to Reduce the Risk of Banking Crises," in *Monetary Policy and Exchange Rate Regimes: Options for the Middle East*, edited by E. Cardoso and A. Galal. American University in Cairo Press.

Carvalho, D. 2014. "The Real Effects of Government-Owned Banks: Evidence from an Emerging Market." *The Journal of Finance* 69 (2): 577–609.

Chen, S. and J. S. Kang. 2018. "Credit Booms—Is China Different?" International Monetary Fund Working Paper WP/18/2.

Claessens, S. and N. van Horen. 2012. "Being a foreigner among domestic banks: Asset or liability?" *Journal of Banking & Finance*, 36 (5): 1276–1290.

Cull, R., M. S. Martinez Peria, and J. Verrier. 2017. "Bank Ownership: Trends and Implications." International Monetary Fund Working Paper 17/60.

Das, S. and V. Tulin. 2017. "Financial Frictions, Underinvestment, and Investment Composition: Evidence from Indian Corporates." International Monetary Fund Working Paper 17/134.

Demirguc-Kunt, A., L. Klapper, D. Singer, S. Ansar, and J. Hess. 2018. Global Findex Database 2017: Measuring Financial Inclusion and the Fintech Revolution. Washington, DC: World Bank.

Farazi, S., E. Feyen, and R. Rocha. 2013. "Bank Ownership and Performance in the Middle East and North Africa Region." *Review of Middle East Economics and Finance* 9 (2): 159–196.

Fernández, A., M. W. Klein, A. Rebucci, M. Schindler, and M. Uribe. 2016. "Capital Control Measures: A New Dataset." *IMF Economic Review*, 64 (3): 548–574.

Gonzalez-Garcia, J. R. and F. Grigoli. 2013. "State Owned Banks and Fiscal Discipline." International Monetary Fund Working Paper 13/206.

Gupta, P., K. Kochhar, and S. Panth. 2011. "Bank Ownership and the Effects of Financial Liberalization: Evidence from India," International Monetary Fund Working Paper 11/50.

Hodge, A, and R. Moussa. 2021. "Financial Sector Polices in South Asia during the COVID-19 Pandemic," in *Policy Advice to Asia in the COVID-19 Era*, edited by Chang Yong Rhee and Katsiaryna Svirydzenka. IMF Departmental Paper, 21/04.

Herwadkar, S, K. M. Neelima, R. Verma, and P. Asthana. 2019. "Labour Cost Efficiency of Indian Banks: A Non-Parametric Analysis." *RBI Bulletin*, April.

Iannotta, G., G. Nocera, and A. Sironi. 2007. "Ownership Structure, Risk and Performance in the European Banking Industry." *Journal of Banking & Finance* 31 (7): 2127–2149.

Inter-American Development Bank (IADB). 2005. "Unlocking Credit: The Quest for Deep and Stable Bank Lending." Economic and Social Progress Report 2005.

International Monetary Fund (IMF). 2017. "India—Financial System Stability Assessment." IMF Country Report No. 17/390.

International Monetary Fund (IMF). 2018. "Financial Inclusion in Asia-Pacific." IMF Departmental Paper 18/17.

International Monetary Fund (IMF). 2019. "Fintech: The Experience So Far." IMF Policy Paper 19/024. https://www.imf.org/~/media/Files/Publications/PP/2019/PPEA2019024.ashx

Khwaja, A. I., and A. Mian. 2005. "Do Lenders Favor Politically Connected Firms? Rent Provision in an Emerging Financial Market." *The Quarterly Journal of Economics* 120 (4): 1371–1411.

Lane, P.R., and G.M. Milesi-Ferretti. 2006. "The External Wealth of Nations Mark II: Revised and Extended Estimates of Foreign Assets and Liabilities, 1970–2004," International Monetary Fund Working Paper 06/69.

La Porta, R., F. Lopez-de-Silanes, and A. Shleifer. 2002. "Government Ownership of Banks," *The Journal of Finance* 57 (1): 265–301.

Micco, A., and U. Panizza. 2006. "Bank Ownership and Lending Behavior." *Economics Letters* 93 (2): 248–254.

Micco, A., U. Panizza, and M. Yanez. 2007. "Bank Ownership and Performance. Does Politics Matter?" *Journal of Banking & Finance* 31 (1): 219–241.

Önder, Z., and S. Özyıldırım. 2013. "Role of Bank Credit on Local Growth: Do Politics and Crisis Matter?" *Journal of Financial Stability* 9 (1): 13–25.

Ozaki, M. 2014. "Finance Sector Reform in Nepal—What Works, What Doesn't." ADB South Asia Working Paper Series, No. 28. https://www.adb.org/sites/default/files/publica tion/42959/south-asia-wp-028_1.pdf

Reserve Bank of India (RBI). 2019. Financial Stability Report, Issue 19, June.

Reserve Bank of India (RBI). 2020. Discussion Paper on Governance in Commercial Banks in India, June.

Sahay, R., M. Čihák, P. N'Diaye, A. Barajas, S. Mitra, A. Kyobe, Y. N. Mooi, and S. R. Yousefi. 2015. "Financial Inclusion: Can It Meet Multiple Macroeconomic Goals?" IMF Staff Discussion Note 15/17. September.

Sahay, R., U. Eriksson von Allmen, A. Lahreche, P. Khera, S. Ogawa, M. Bazarbash, and K. Beaton. 2020. "The Promise of Fintech: Financial Inclusion in the Post COVID-19 Era." IMF Departmental Paper 20/09, July.

Sanyal, P., and R. Shankar. 2011. "Ownership, Competition and Bank Productivity: An Analysis of Indian Banking in the Post-Reform Period." *International Review of Economics & Finance* 20 (2): 225–247.

Sapienza, P. 2004. "The Effects of Government Ownership on Bank Lending." *Journal of Financial Economics* 67 (3): 717–735.

Sensarma, Rudra. 2006. "Are Foreign Banks Always the Best? Comparison of State-Owned, Private and Foreign Banks in India," *Economic Modeling* 23: 717–735.

Svirydzenka, K. 2016. "Introducing a New Broad-Based Index of Financial Development." International Monetary Fund Working Paper 16/5.

World Bank. 2013. Global Financial Development Report 2013, Rethinking the Role of the State in Finance.

Xiao, S., and S. Zhao. 2012. "Financial Development, Government Ownership of Banks and Firm Innovation." *Journal of International Money & Finance* 31 (4): 880–906.

Index

economic complexity
  by country, 175–176*f*, 175–178
  defined, 174*n*1
  drivers of, 181–187, 181–182*t*, 183–186*f*
  policies to foster, 178–179
economic reforms. *See* postpandemic era
    policy directions
education
  COVID-19 pandemic and, 6, 7*f*, 51
  digitalization and efficiency of spending
    on, 139–143, 140*t*, 141*f*, 142*t*
  export diversity and, 181, 185
  gender and, 44–45, 115–116
  improvements in, 33–34, 33–34*f*
  in India, 30, 43–45, 44*t*
  literacy rates, 6, 20, 20*f*, 33
  methodology and data on, 55, 55–56*t*
  teleworking opportunities and, 189
  youth unemployment, 66
Ehrmann, M., 288
e-id and e-signature systems, 24, 109,
    129–130, 130*t*, 131*f*
elderly people
  adult care services for, 110
  old-age pension schemes, 72–74
  social assistance spending on, 110
electricity
  from coal-fired power plants, 153
  COVID-19 pandemic and, 51
  improvements in, 9–10, 9*f*, 36–39,
    37–38*f*
  India, additional spending results,
    45–46, 45*n*14, 46*t*
  infrastructure needs in, 265, 266*f*
employment. *See* labor market
employment protection legislation (ELP)
  automation and, 82–83*b*
  effect on employment and informality,
    77–80, 78*t*, 79*f*, 86, 89*f*
  overview, 71–72, 72*f*, 75–76, 76*t*
  resource misallocation in India, 80–82*b*
energy
  oil and gas industry, 7–8, 7*f*
  renewable energy, 46, 153–154, 154*f*
  subsidies for production of, 154–155
  taxation on production of, 154–156,
    155*n*6
The Energy and Resources Institute,
    152*n*3

e-procurement systems, 133, 133*t*, 134*f*
European Union (EU)
  carbon emissions from, 151, 151*f*
  trade liberalization in, 12
exchange rate targeting, 285–286,
    292*n*17, 295–297, 301
export diversification strategy, 171–193
  conceptual framework, 178–181, 179*f*
  COVID-19 and, 187–189, 188*f*
  defined, 174*n*1
  drivers of, 181–187, 181–182*t*,
    183–186*f*
  India, structural change in, 190–191*b*
  progress on, 172–178, 172–177*f*
export processing zones, 241–244,
    243*n*11, 243*t*
extreme weather-related events, 147,
    156–157, 157*f*

F
Fay, Marianne, 157
FDI. *See* foreign direct investment
fertility rates, 65, 70
Financial Access Survey of IMF, 24
financial depth, 307, 308*f*
financial development and inclusion,
    303–327
  bank efficiency, assessment of,
    317–321, 319–320*f*
  banking sector overview, 306–316,
    306–310*f*, 312*f*, 313–314*t*, 315*f*
  COVID-19 pandemic and, 52
  financial inclusion, 321–325,
    322–323*f*, 324*b*
  literature review, 316–317
  overview, 304–306, 305–306*f*
Financial Development Index of IMF,
    304–305, 305*f*
financial inclusion, 117, 305, 321–325,
    321*n*13, 322–323*f*, 322*n*14, 324*b*
financial openness, 311, 312*f*
Financial Sector Assessment Program of
    IMF, 320
fintech, 323–324
fiscal actions for climate change,
    162–163, 162*t*
fiscal stimulus during COVID-19
    pandemic, 4–5, 64*b*
Fitch Connect, 318*n*8

flexible inflation targeting (FIT)
  defined, 286*n*2
  in India, 286–292, 289–290*f,* 289*n*9,
    299–300
  in Sri Lanka, 297, 297*n*19
Flexible System of Global Models
  (FSGM), 264, 270–272
Fontagné, Lionel, 219*n*16
food prices, 6–7, 95–96
foreign direct investment (FDI)
  economic convergence and growth,
    207–208, 208*n*11, 209*t*
  financial openness and, 311
  GVC participation and, 208, 218
  special economic zones and, 242
foreign-owned banks, 311, 313*t,* 316
Francois, J. F., 256
fraud
  digitalization to reduce, 25
  social protection mechanisms and,
    109–110
free trade agreements (FTAs)
  challenges of, 255–256, 257*f*
  GVC expansion and, 212
  regional trade integration and, 236–
    237, 237*f*
  reinvesting in, 23
  South Asian Free Trade Area, 227
Frey, C. B., 82*b*
FSGM (Flexible System of Global
  Models), 264, 270–272

G
Garcia-Escribano, Mercedes, 29, 139*n*11
Garg, Amit, 152*n*3
Gaspar, Vitor, 40–41, 48, 51, 53*n*15
gender, 113–125
  COVID-19 pandemic and, 5, 66,
    117–118
  cultural norms, 115, 117
  current gender inequality, 113–117,
    114–116*f,* 116*t*
  digitalization as labor market
    opportunity, 119–123, 120–121*t,*
    121–122*f*
  education enrollment and, 44–45,
    115–116
  employment barriers for women,
    115–117, 116*f*

financial inclusion and, 321–322,
  322*n*14
inclusive economies and, 118–119, 118*f*
labor market institutions and, 74–75,
  78–80, 79*f*
labor market participation, reforms
  to increase, 21–22, 22*n*12, 83–85,
  84*f,* 110
labor market participation rates, 16,
  16*f,* 66, 68*f,* 113
maternity leave, 74–75
microfinance and, 323
patriarchy and, 115, 117
policy discussions, 123–124
women-owned enterprises, 115, 117,
  122–123
Gennaioli, Nicola, 208
Ghate, Chetan, 285, 290
Gini index of inequality, 95, 100, 101*f*
Giri, Rahul, 179
glacier retreat, 147
Gleb, Alan, 109
Global Climate Fund, 165
Global Competitiveness Index of WEF,
  244, 244*n*14
global financial crisis (2008–09), 230,
  238, 290
Global Financial Inclusion (Findex)
  database of World Bank, 305
Global Gender Gap Report 2017 of WEF,
  113–114
globalization
  history of trade integration, 228–229
  trade in services and, 188
global value chain (GVC) participation
  benefits of, 210*t*
  benefits of greater trade integration
    and, 218–222, 220–222*f*
  COVID-19 pandemic and, 197
  FDI volumes and, 208, 218
  of India, 197
  integration, policies to boost, 214–218,
    215–216*f,* 216–217*t,* 219*t*
  intermediate goods and, 207,
    207*nn*8–9
  regional trade integration and, 230
  special economic zones and, 242
  trade openness and, 206–207, 206*n*7,
    206*t*